WHEN YAMAMOTO RAN WILD
THE PACIFIC WAR: PEARL HARBOR TO MIDWAY

MARK CARLSON, CL, ACS

Mechanicsburg, PA USA

Published by Sunbury Press, Inc.
Mechanicsburg, PA USA

www.sunburypress.com

Copyright © 2024 by Mark Carlson, CL, ACS.
Cover Copyright © 2024 by Sunbury Press, Inc.

Sunbury Press supports copyright. Copyright fuels creativity, encourages diverse voices, promotes free speech, and creates a vibrant culture. Thank you for buying an authorized edition of this book and for complying with copyright laws. Except for the quotation of short passages for the purpose of criticism and review, no part of this publication may be reproduced, scanned, or distributed in any form without permission. You are supporting writers and allowing Sunbury Press to continue to publish books for every reader. For information contact Sunbury Press, Inc., Subsidiary Rights Dept., PO Box 548, Boiling Springs, PA 17007 USA or legal@sunburypress.com.

For information about special discounts for bulk purchases, please contact Sunbury Press Orders Dept. at (855) 338-8359 or orders@sunburypress.com.

To request one of our authors for speaking engagements or book signings, please contact Sunbury Press Publicity Dept. at publicity@sunburypress.com.

FIRST SUNBURY PRESS EDITION: June 2024

Set in Adobe Garamond Pro | Interior design by Crystal Devine | Cover by Lawrence Knorr | Edited by Sarah Peachey.

Publisher's Cataloging-in-Publication Data
Names: Carlson, Mark, author.
Title: When Yamamoto ran wild : the Pacific War : Pearl Harbor to Midway / Mark Carlson.
Description: First trade paperback edition. | Mechanicsburg, PA : Sunbury Press, 2024.
Summary: *When Yamamoto Ran Wild* is the full and detailed account of how the United States, battered and beaten after Pearl Harbor, rose like a phoenix from the ashes and stopped Yamamoto's wild run. It reveals why the attack on Pearl Harbor was the worst mistake the Japanese ever made.
Identifiers: ISBN: 979-8-88819-150-7 (paperback).
Subjects: HISTORY / Military / Naval | HISTORY / Wars & Conflicts / World War II / Pacific Theater | HISTORY / Military / Strategy.

Designed in the USA
0 1 1 2 3 5 8 13 21 34 55

For the Love of Books!

This book is gratefully dedicated to a dear friend, Linda Stull, who for the past decade has been my most staunch cheerleader, advocate, and tireless editor. Linda has not only encouraged me in my long and slow quest for self-respect and a place in the literary pantheon, she has often saved me from myself when I was about to do something stupid or ill-advised. Every book and most of the articles I have written have her sweat and tears in its pages, and she is the person who made me the writer I am today. While she did not actually help me on this book, her fingerprints are between its covers, because I heard her voice in my mind as I wrote, keeping to the suggestions and advice she willingly gave me over the years.

I say this without reservation: If I had never known Linda, none of my books or articles would exist today. She is the most loyal and honest friend I have ever had.

Thank you, Linda

CONTENTS

Introduction ... 1

CHAPTERS

1. The Land of the Rising Sun ... 5
2. Yamamoto the Visionary ... 17
3. Prelude to Infamy—1939 to 1941 ... 33
4. Climb Mount Niitaka ... 59
5. The Stage is Set ... 91
6. Visions of Ruin ... 110
7. Running Wild ... 173
8. Nimitz Takes Command ... 199
9. Victory Disease ... 221
10. The Navies ... 242
11. Striking Back—The Doolittle Raid and the Coral Sea ... 258
12. The Principle of Calculated Risk ... 282
13. The Terrible Resolve ... 303

Photo Gallery ... 140
Glossary ... 309
Appendix: What Did Roosevelt Know Before Pearl Harbor? ... 311
Acknowledgments ... 317
Selected Bibliography ... 319
Index ... 322
About the Author ... 335

INTRODUCTION

In his 1909 book *Valor of Ignorance*, author Homer Lea predicted that Japan would attack the United States. He stated that the U.S. had no idea of the grandiose and fanatical ambitions of the Japanese militarists, and that we would be taken completely by surprise by an invasion in the Pacific. This was thirty-two years before Pearl Harbor.

> "Historically, despite Washington's, and other cogent advice, to make due preparations for war, it is traditional and habitual for us to be inadequately prepared." —Captain Ernest J. King, 1932

During the Second World War, Fleet Admiral Chester W. Nimitz, commander in chief of the United States Pacific Fleet, led the largest and most powerful military armada in world history. Under his command were thousands of ships, tens of thousands of aircraft, and millions of men and women between the West Coast of the United States and Australia. His fleet and aircraft would dominate over 53,800,000 square miles of ocean. By September 1945 his navy and Marines had fought and defeated the powerful and unconquerable Japanese Empire. When it was over, the Imperial Navy was a tiny fragment of its former glory, a handful of small, battered ships huddling from the eyes of the world.

But that was all in the future as the nation absorbed the crushing blow dealt at Pearl Harbor on December 7, 1941. The island of Oahu, Territory of Hawaii, long known as an idyllic tropical paradise far out in the peaceful blue Pacific, had become a place of disaster and defeat.

The Second World War has generated more than its share of books, but here I am adding to the literary and historical record. I read more than a hundred books per year, and in the past five decades I'm certain I've only scratched the surface. Hundreds of authors and historians have covered virtually every aspect of the war, from the prelude to the last horrible moments over Nagasaki.

No matter how much I think about the most intense and largest war in human history, I can't help but return to those first six months of the Pacific War. When the fires still raged over the Pacific Fleet's mighty battleships, and bodies were still being pulled from the oily waters of Pearl Harbor, the United States Navy, Army, Marines, and Air Corps' admirals and generals were desperately searching for a way to fight back against the nation that had so wounded America.

In the years between the world wars, Japan was often harshly perceived as a small, backward copycat nation of strange little, yellow, bucktoothed people. They would never become a world power despite having defeated the Russians at Port Arthur and Tsushima. After all, the Russians under Czar Nicholas II were hardly a force to be respected. But the pragmatic Japanese, with their national culture for secrecy and politeness, had learned well from their naval and air attachés in London, Berlin, Paris, and Washington. By the mid-1930s, they had not only built one of the world's most powerful and largest navies, they were leaders in cooperative tactics.

This book is an account of the first months of the Pacific War. While my original intent was to focus on the period from the morning of December 7, 1941, to the afternoon of June 4, 1942, I realized early on that some foundation had to be laid down before taking such a bold step into history. In order for the reader to understand how the United States and Japan came to wage war in the Pacific, I chose to begin with a short history of Japan, the career of Admiral Isoroku Yamamoto, and the events in the year prior to the attack on Pearl Harbor. There is certainly no shortage of books on those subjects, but I will provide a background for the following six months of the war.

In other words, to quote Sun Tzu in *The Art of War*, written in the sixth century BC, "You must know your enemy in order to defeat him."

I freely admit I'm hardly the first author to specifically cover this period and subject. John Toland, one of the giants of military history, wrote *But Not in Shame: The Six Months After Pearl Harbor* in 1961. This is an excellent book, but it focuses primarily on the invasion and conquest of the Philippines, with only short accounts of Guam, Malaya, Wake, and the Java Sea campaigns. Toland wrote it sixty years ago, and much new information has come to the surface, primarily through the work of Gordon W. Prange, Edwin Palmer Hoyt, and Samuel Eliot Morison, to name a few. Toland and his contemporaries had the enviable advantage of interviewing living veterans and witnesses, but today's researchers have more information at their fingertips than Toland could ever have dreamed.

I have often said that "history is never chiseled in stone." It is an ever-shifting sea of sand and dust that reveals its lost secrets while others disappear forever. So here I am, standing on the shoulders of giants to add to their work with what has been revealed in the past seven decades.

In late 1940, when Prime Minister Konoye told the commander in chief of the Combined Fleet, Admiral Isoroku Yamamoto, that Japan and the United States would be at war in the next year, the admiral said, "I will run wild for the first six months or a year, but I have no confidence in the second or third year." The chief instigator of the Pearl Harbor attack was eerily prescient in his words. Almost exactly six months after his bombers and fighters left Oahu with columns of black smoke rising into the blue Hawaiian skies, four of the Imperial Navy's front-line carriers were on the bottom of the sea north of Midway. It was, as Walter Lord said, an incredible victory. Midway was the most obvious turning point. The dates between the Pearl Harbor attack and the Battle of Midway encompass the falls of Guam and Wake Island, the conquest of the Philippines and Singapore, the battles of the Java Sea and Coral Sea, the Doolittle Raid, and a dozen other fights and campaigns.

After Midway, with half its hulking carriers gone, and Australia out of reach, Japan was on the defensive. The next major campaign was in the Solomon Islands and Guadalcanal. After that, the Gilberts, Marshalls, Carolines, Marianas, Iwo Jima, and Okinawa pointed like a steel arrow at Japan's very heart. The total victory over Japan took four months less than three years, an astoundingly short time considering how badly the nation had been hurt at Pearl Harbor, Wake Island, and the Philippines. But those first six months set the stage for the rest of the war.

Here the reader will meet and hopefully understand and respect men like Chester Nimitz, William Halsey, Frank Fletcher, James Doolittle, Raymond Spruance, Joseph Rochefort, and a dozen other officers and sailors who determinedly struggled during those first six months to fight for their nation on the seas, land, and in the air over the Pacific. To that list I will include Isoroku Yamamoto, Minoru Genda, Chuichi Nagumo, Mitsuo Fuchida, and other officers of the Imperial Japanese Navy. While it would be easy to label them a gang of evil warmongers, I'll let the reader decide.

Many of my readers will be too young, and I include myself in that category, to have lived during the Second World War, so it may be difficult to imagine what it was like in the days, weeks, and months after hearing of the attack on Pearl Harbor. The closest I can come is the terrible day of September 11, 2001, coincidentally almost exactly sixty years after the first bombs fell on Battleship

Row. It will help to recall the empty feeling of horror, the confusion, and the loss of confidence in our way of life to comprehend what went through the minds of Americans on the night of December 7, 1941. Would we be invaded by the Japanese? Did Hitler help Hirohito to destroy our proud battle fleet? How would we fight back? Could we fight back? What would war be like for our families, friends, and neighbors? No one knew, not even President Franklin Roosevelt and the War and Navy Departments.

If you want to understand an artist, you look at his work. To understand how Japan planned and fought the war, we should examine the nation, its navy, and its commanders. I hope this will help the reader understand how and why the Pacific War evolved. Pearl Harbor serves as an example of how meticulously the Japanese planned their naval campaign. But it also illustrates the Imperial Navy's intense belief in their racial and military superiority. This was a mistake the American commanders also made, at least in the first six months of the Pacific War. A mouse never underestimates the cat.

I use the military twenty-four hour clock except in a civilian context. So 3:55 p.m. will be 1555. Also, certain military terms and unit designations, such as Task Force 17, will be repeated as TF 17 for brevity.

A note on the books' chronology: I tried to maintain a timeline that followed the events, but in some cases, such as the invasion and fall of the Philippines, I strived to keep the entire campaign and defense in one chapter, even though other events, such as the Doolittle Raid and Coral Sea, happened before the surrender of Corregidor in May 1942. Those events are related in later chapters.

Remember Pearl Harbor!

Mark Carlson
San Marcos, California
July 2023

CHAPTER 1

THE LAND OF THE RISING SUN

"Supreme excellence consists in breaking the enemy's resistance without fighting." —Sun Tzu

Japan. A land of snow-capped volcanoes and cherry blossoms, of small fishing villages and sprawling cities, of old ways and advanced technology, of beautiful poetry and violent death, of ancient traditions and constant change, of respectful manners and brutal savagery. The island nation is an archipelago made up of four major islands—Hokkaido, Honshu, Shikoku, and Kyushu—along with about 3,000 smaller islands, protectively surrounding an inland sea.

Directly west is Korea, beyond which lay China, both traditional enemies of Japan. The total land area of Japan is about 146,000 square miles, smaller than California. Three hundred miles south of Kyushu is Okinawa, beyond which are the Philippines. The vast Pacific was the barrier between Japan and the rest of the world.

The cities of Kyoto, Tokyo, Hiroshima, Nagoya, Kobe, Nagasaki, Yokohama, and a dozen others grew to be among the world's great cities. Japan was and still is a nation dependent on the sea. Nearly the entire country was a garden with virtually every acre, even on slopes, planted and harvested. Rich in growing land and surrounded by fertile fishing grounds, Japan's only abundant natural resource was coal. This presented no problem for the growing population until 1853, when Japan lost its centuries-old isolation.

The culture and history of Japan were born more than a thousand years ago. Japan evolved into a militaristic society in which death was little more than passing from the earth into heaven. But unlike Western religions, in which heaven is a reward for a life well spent in peace and love, the Japanese have long believed that the way to heaven was to die gloriously and honorably in battle against the enemy. The warrior class, known as the Samurai, were fiercely loyal and were not only willing to die, but desired the ultimate honor of death for their lord. The Samurai, a word that literally means "to serve," were the core of Japanese pride and military spirit. The Code of Bushido, the way of the warrior, defined Japan's cultural identity from medieval times. By the twelfth century, feudal warlords ruled the land. They provided the Samurai with the divine sanction of the ruling class. This infusion of Samurai and their blood code soon spread to nearly every part of the culture.

Little had changed in Japan for hundreds of years, leaving the nation in a state no more advanced than medieval Europe. The Shoguns never allowed any ships to enter the ports. Foreign sailors were either killed or sent into slavery.

The isolation insulated Japan from the virus of foreign ways, but it also prevented Japan from developing an industrial economy. For the next few centuries, Japan was still in the Middle Ages while Europe and America began the Industrial Revolution. Soldiers still carried the sword and bow, even as the rest of the world used rifles and cannon.

In 1852, President Millard Fillmore, frustrated by Japan's refusal to open its ports to trade with the West, ordered Commodore Matthew Perry and a United States Navy squadron to Tokyo. Perry, who had studied Japanese history and culture and learned the language, took two steam warships into Tokyo Bay. It was culture shock of the highest order when the simple Japanese fishermen and farmers beheld tall-masted steamships for the first time. Sailors armed with rifles and pistols lined the decks, and dozens of black cannon poked their deadly muzzles at the sampans and fishing craft. Perry took a longboat ashore and told the locals that he wished to meet with the highest officials in the land.

The arrival of the Americans was a complete and disheartening shock to the Japanese. It would be on par with an alien invasion in the modern world. The ruling Shoguns tried to make a show of force, but to no avail. The superiority of the Americans was far above what the Samurai could even dream of.

The July 1853 visit to Japan tore down the wall of isolation. Trade and diplomatic relations were established with the United States, Great Britain, Spain, France, Germany, and the Netherlands. Japan was changed forever, but its deeply rooted militaristic culture remained. Being forced to leave behind their millennia-old culture and adopt new ways was akin to what the native Americans had to endure from the white man. It was humiliating to a proud and ancient land.

From that point on, Japan was a nation, not a group of cities, villages, and islands. The individual took second place to the state. In 1868 a civil war tore through the land and placed Emperor Meiji on the throne. The capital city, Edo, was renamed Tokyo that same year. Under his reign, Shinto became the state religion, and the emperor was deemed a descendant of the sun goddess Amaterasu.

Still the Samurai Bushido code was the underlying moral and cultural code of the land. In what became known as the Meiji Restoration, a parliamentary government was established with a prime minister as the head.

The Meiji Restoration presented a means to protect Japan from foreign colonization. The nation was to accept modern industrializing while still embracing traditional values. Emperor Meiji was eager for Japan to learn and grow by sending hundreds of young men and military officers to London, Washington, Paris, and Berlin to absorb every aspect of a modern industrialized society. The best students were sent to Western universities to learn science and technology. They learned other languages and the secrets of manufacturing, then brought that knowledge home. It was from this point on that Japan, a resource-poor nation, had to import raw materials it had never needed before. Oil, rubber, and iron ore were imported to support and feed the growing industries. A new conscript army, based on German and French models, was formed in 1872, not of Samurai but of draftees, whose devotion was to their duty, their officers, and ultimately, the emperor. The officers who had studied at foreign war colleges and served as military envoys returned with valuable information on the organization, structure, tactics, and strategy of the Western armies and navies. While they were impressed with and emulated the Royal Navy, they most admired the German Army, particularly the well-organized general staff.

By the 1870s, Japan had reached the point where it was ready to attempt colonial expansion. Korea, directly west across the Sea of Japan, was a longtime enemy. Meiji sent two gunboats and three transports to force a commerce agreement with the Korean government. It was reminiscent of what Perry had forced on Japan twenty years earlier.

But it was not only Japan who had designs on Korea. Mainland China considered Korea one of its own protectorates. Within a decade, China had to deal with a series of Japanese-incited riots in Korea. This led to the first Sino-Japanese War. In 1894, Japan captured the Korean capital of Pyongyang and headed into Manchuria. With virtually no chance of stopping the well-equipped and motivated Japanese troops, China was forced to accept humiliating peace terms.

In April 1895, China signed the Treaty of Shimonoseka, in which Japan was paid twenty million taels, equivalent to about seventeen million pounds sterling, in war reparations. China also had to cede the Island of Formosa, now Taiwan, the Pescadores, and part of Manchuria.

At first, Japan controlled the Liaodong Peninsula at the northern shore of the Yellow Sea between China and Korea, which included Port Arthur, but the triple alliance of Germany, France, and Russia forced Japan to cede Port Arthur to Russia. The newly established Imperial General Staff considered it another case of the West interfering with Japan's rightful claim to Asian land.

Over the next six years, Japan doubled the size of its military. Seeking greater naval power, Japan's naval minister contracted for several modern warships to be built and launched in Great Britain. In 1904, these were the most modern warships in the world, but the launch of the all-big-gun battleship *Dreadnought* in 1906 drastically altered the equation of what constituted a modern surface fleet. Japan was to put her new fleet to use almost immediately.

Japan made an astonishing leap forward in industry and technology. This prompted the next revolution among military officers. Japan was ready to expand and seize its own colonies. In fact, any internal opposition to this growing policy was considered traitorous. Few officers dared voice their opinion. One highly regarded university professor stated, "Japan was destined to dominate other nations."

Port Arthur, on the Yellow Sea, was still in Japan's crosshairs. In 1904 the Imperial Navy sent its new ships to bombard Port Arthur, damaging the Russian fleet and driving the army from Manchuria. This defeat prompted Czar Nicholas II to send the larger Russian Baltic Fleet on an 8,000-mile voyage around Europe, through the Suez Canal, to the Indian Ocean, through the Java Sea, and on the north Pacific. It required six months for the fleet to reach the Sea of Japan to confront Admiral Heihachiro Togo's new fleet in the Strait of Tsushima between Japan and Korea. After a brilliant naval fight by Togo, fourteen Russian ships were sunk, with the loss of nearly 5,000 lives. Among the officers serving on Togo's ships was a young midshipman, Isoroku Yamamoto. The battle clearly indicated how far the Imperial Navy had advanced. They were the first to use wireless telegraphy in battle, modern cordite propellants, and super quick fuses on their shells. Togo's battleships had better fire control and greater range than even the most modern Russian ships.

Eager to end what might have become a protracted war, President Theodore Roosevelt intervened by sending Chief Justice William Howard Taft to meet with Japanese Prime Minister Katsura Taro to mediate a treaty between Japan and Russia.

One of the terms of the treaty was that Japan agree not to invade the Philippines, a protectorate of the United States after the cessation of the Spanish-American War, and that the United States would not protest the colonization of

Korea. Japan came off the better in the Treaty of Portsmouth. Port Arthur and the lower half of the Sakhalin Island were under Japanese control, and Japan had gained commercial supremacy in Manchuria.

But another treaty term denied Japan a large cash indemnity from Russia. Japan had almost bankrupted itself to pay for the war. The reactionaries in the government resented Roosevelt's "interference" in their affairs. This became a major catalyst in the growing antipathy between the two nations. Japan's ministers and military officers began to consider the United States their primary obstacle to expanding the empire into the Pacific and Asia.

There was a purely racial reason for the smoldering resentment. During the 1860s, when a transcontinental railroad was being constructed across the United States, thousands of Chinese laborers were recruited to work. With the job completed, many jingoistic American businessmen and robber barons were eager to send the Chinese back home. But alongside the Chinese were the immigrant Japanese. They did not work on the railroad or other civil engineering projects but started small businesses and raised families. They sent their sons to school and became prosperous citizens. This was resented by the same racist men who wanted the Chinese out, and in the wake of Teddy Roosevelt's appeasement policies after the Treaty of Portsmouth, it led to the 1908 "Gentlemen's Agreement" to limit Japanese immigration quotas. This was one of the most insulting blows to Japanese pride and left an open wound in the hearts of men who had favored open commerce and relations with the United States.

At this same time, the Panama Canal was being laboriously dug across the fifty-mile jungle-infested isthmus. Strongly supported by Roosevelt, the canal was intended to provide a fast means for the United States Navy to travel between the Atlantic and Pacific. During the Spanish-American War of 1898, the new battleship *Oregon* had sailed 13,000 miles from San Francisco to the Caribbean to join the fleet for the Battle of Santiago de Cuba.

The canal was still years from completion, and Roosevelt wanted to display American naval power. In 1905 he publicly stated, "In a dozen years, the English, Germans, and Americans who now dread one another as rivals in the Pacific, will have reason to dread the Japanese more than they do any other nation."

During his first term, Roosevelt pushed Congress to pass a $100 million bill to construct ten new battleships, four armored cruisers, and seventeen other vessels. This gave the U.S. Navy more battleships than any other nation, save Great Britain.

In December 1907, Roosevelt sent his "Great White Fleet" of sixteen battleships and a dozen auxiliary ships on a so-called Goodwill Cruise around the world. It was a way, as the president said to Navy Secretary Victor Metcalf, "to learn the problems and mistakes involved in a long cruise in peacetime, rather than in war." After leaving Norfolk and turning south, the seven-mile parade of white and buff painted warships doubled Cape Horn and made several ports of call in the Pacific, including Yokohama, where Isoroku Yamamoto saw the impressive spectacle. The entire voyage took nearly a year and covered 43,000 miles. It was as much a show of force as of diplomacy, the "Big Stick."

One of the great ironies in history began in 1902, when Japan and Great Britain, each seeking to protect their Pacific possessions, entered into a mutual defense treaty. The terms of the Anglo-Japanese Treaty were that if either party were attacked by an outside power, the other would join the conflict. When the Great War began in August 1914 between Britain and Germany, Japan took full advantage of its treaty obligations. This was a blank check for Japan to realize some of its colonial ambitions and seize German colonies in China and the Pacific. Tokyo sent a message to Berlin, demanding that the island groups of the German-held Marianas, Marshalls, Carolines, and the port region of Tsingtao be surrendered to Japan. No reply was received, and the Japanese Empire formally declared war on the German Empire.

After Admiral Maximillian von Spee took his East Asia Squadron out to fight the Royal Navy, Tsingtao was largely undefended. By October 1914, Japan had captured the port city and taken possession of the three island groups, including Palau. With one sweeping campaign, Japan expanded its territory to encompass virtually the entire western Pacific.

The 1919 Treaty of Versailles mandated all former German possessions north of the equator to Japan. The League of Nations and Mandate Commissions believed the island nations, comprising the region known today as Micronesia, were politically, culturally, and economically underdeveloped. While they were instructed not to place military bases on the islands, that was exactly what the Imperial General Staff intended to do.

Japan was also told not to attempt to expand its territory beyond the mandate. By 1920, the government in Tokyo was refusing any inspection of the region. Japan formally withdrew from the League of Nations in 1932, further isolating itself from the eyes of the rest of the world.

With one stroke of a pen, Japan found itself the sole ruler of a vast area of inhabited islands across the northern and western Pacific. While the total land area was little more than 800 square miles, consisting of about 1,300 islands and atolls with a population of about 60,000, the total area encompassed nearly three million square miles, roughly the size of the entire United States west of the Rocky Mountains. The 1902 Anglo-Japanese Treaty had served Japan well. Furthermore, the Imperial General Staff drew up plans to send troops to the islands in case of war. They became the outer defense of the Home Islands. The Marshalls, Marianas, Palau, and Carolines would play a critical role in the war to come.

One major aspect of the mandate soon became apparent to the United States. The three island groups lay directly astride the main shipping route between Hawaii and the Philippines. Navy and army planners feared that in a war between the United States and Japan, the Philippines were doomed. There was no way to defend a nation more than 7,000 miles from the West Coast.

As far back as 1905, a dispute arose between General Leonard Wood—Army Chief of Staff, hero of the war in Cuba—and Admiral of the Navy George Dewey, victor of the Battle of Manila Bay. The two most senior uniformed officers in the country waged a seven-year war of opinion concerning the defense of the Philippines. Wood, citing the army view that a naval base at Olongapo on Subic Bay on the coast of Luzon northwest of Manila, would be difficult to defend, was in favor of a larger naval facility in Manila Bay, where it could be covered by large coastal guns. Dewey, who had sailed his fleet into Manila on the morning of May 1, 1898, and destroyed the Spanish fleet, favored Olongapo. By 1913, it was decided, as a cost-saving measure, that the base would be at Cavite in Manila, which Dewey considered a trap. Even so, Cavite was hardly what any officer would call a complete base for naval operations. Pearl Harbor, 5,000 miles from Manila, was given that role. Congress refused to devote further funds to construct a full base there and a large one on Guam in the Marianas. The shortsighted refusal would come to haunt the United States.

ı

The robber barons and industrialists of the Gilded Age had enthusiastically supported Japan's own expanding economy since it meant more profits. But by the 1920s, it became apparent the Japanese were a hardy, clever, scheming people. They were also becoming increasingly dangerous. Like any person who plays with fire, the Americans who dealt with the Japanese were likely to get burned.

The 1920s were a time of economic depression in Japan. The moderates in the government were blamed, primarily by the right-wing conservative reactionaries, for the fall in employment and years of crop failures. This was a decade before the stock market crash in the United States. With a growing population, Japan faced nationwide famine. It was commonly believed that the moderates were leading the nation to ruin. Joining the rest of the world was not the answer.

The only real source of pride was the great military victories against the Russians and Chinese. Japan's military was one of the few growing enterprises. With the power of the anti-Western reactionaries increasing, a subtle but unmistakable change began to appear in the most innocent of places: bookstores.

Several books turned up in the stores of Tokyo and other major cities. The most popular dealt with war between the United States and Japan. There were popular titles like *The Alaska Air Attack*, *The Assault on Hawaii*, and *The California Attack*. These and others, along with a flurry of magazine articles, lectures, and radio broadcasts, were another indicator of Japan's growing militarism and disenchantment with the West.

But there was a hidden aspect to that militarism. Of all the major combatant powers in the Great War, Japan was the only nation that had not seen the kind of total war experienced on the Western Front from 1914 to 1918. The Japanese Army, for all its organization, size, training, and power, was ill-prepared for total war on the modern battlefield. None of the officers and troops, even those who had seen fighting in the First Sino-Japanese War and the Russo-Japanese War, had ever faced the kind of carnage wrought by massed artillery and machine guns. The officer corps was indoctrinated in the code of Bushido, that spirit, determination, and cultural and racial superiority would always win out over a numerically superior enemy. They believed that loyalty and aggressiveness would overcome any advantage in weaponry. Offense was the key to victory, no matter what. This was evidenced by their victories over the Koreans, Chinese, and Russians. To attack an enemy and drive home a victory was worth any cost in lives.

Even though Great Britain and the United States were considered the prime enemies of Japan, English was not even taught in their advanced officer colleges. Nor was there any attempt to study the cultures and ideologies of the potential enemies. Japanese officers, particularly those in the army, failed to heed Sun Tzu's well-known maxim, "To know your enemy is to win half the battle."

In 1922 the major naval powers—Great Britain, the United States, France, Italy, and Japan—were invited to participate in a Naval Arms Limitation Treaty. Intended as a way to avoid the same kind of arms race that nearly bankrupted Great Britain and provoked the Great War with Germany, the conference would set down a comprehensive formula for the five nations to agree on the number and tonnage of surface ships each could launch. Since the conference took place in the years before the aircraft carrier was considered a practical vessel in naval warfare, it only dealt with cruisers and battleships.

While the treaty was intended to limit naval construction, it had one serious effect on world history. Great Britain had always had the largest navy in the world. The Admiralty was eager to keep its place but had to accept the United States as an equal player in the naval arms race. What was more important was to keep Japan's growing power from reaching alarming levels. In 1921, Japan ranked third in strength behind the two major powers. The British intended to cut the enormous costs of maintaining a worldwide fleet, limiting the size of the Far East Squadron. In order to reduce any chance that Japan might take advantage of this, the treaty laid down a 5/5/3 ratio of capital ships, with the U.S. and Britain being allowed to launch five ships to every three in Japan, France, and Italy.

The Japanese delegation resisted the terms since their naval war planners insisted on maintaining a fleet that was 70 percent of the United States Navy, the minimum needed to assure victory in a war with the West.

Under pressure from Congress, Secretary of State Charles Evans Hughes likewise pressured the Japanese to sign the treaty by promising that the U.S. would not fortify the Philippines, Guam, or Wake Island. Since they were more than 5,000 miles from Hawaii, it would have been difficult to fortify or support them in any case. At that time, major fleet movements were measured in weeks instead of days.

The senior Japanese delegate Tomo Saburo agreed to the terms. This forced some major changes in the Imperial Navy, one of which was to cancel the launch of new battleships and convert them into aircraft carriers. Since the aircraft carrier was not included in the treaty, Japan would be free to build as many as necessary, the first being *Hosho* in 1922.

But the most telling result of the 1922 Washington Naval Treaty was how it affected Japan's political power balance. The right-wing reactionaries were outraged by the terms of the treaty, insisting that the pro-Western moderates in the government had sold out Japan.

As things turned out, neither side planned to honor the treaty terms, but Japan came off better in the long run.

An indicator of the Imperial Army's growing aggressiveness was made clear in 1922 when Colonel Kanji Ishiwara, who had been in Berlin for two years as a military attaché to study logistics and tactics, met with an American military attaché. Ishiwara, who would one day command the Fourth Army in Manchuria, was invited to visit Washington before returning to Tokyo.

With studied self-confidence, Ishiwara said, "The only time I plan to visit the United States is when I arrive as chief of the Japanese Army of Occupation."

In 1927, the right-wing Prime Minister Baron Tanaka Giichi drew up what amounted to a strategic war plan called the "Tanaka Memorial," which laid out the steps to incite and win a war with the West. The first step was to send troops into Manchuria.

Added to this was Japan's increasing need for resources. As an isolated and largely agricultural island nation, Japan imported oil, rubber, iron ore, and a dozen other raw materials from China, the Dutch East Indies, French Indochina, the Soviet Union, and the United States. To the reactionaries, this was intolerable. Japan required raw materials but was not in a position to purchase them, especially with a depressed economy and currency.

The logical place to start was Mainland China. With Manchuria garrisoned by Japanese troops, seizing more land was only a matter of time and logistics.

The first elements of the huge Guangdong Army, about 12,000 men, were poised to invade Manchuria in 1927, but a communiqué from the State Department in Washington warned that Manchuria was the property of the Chinese, and that any military action there would bring the United States into the matter. While the diplomatic move did postpone the invasion, by 1930 the need to move in and take China's limitless resources forced the decision to invade.

At that time, the growing communist movement under Mao Tse-tung was conducting its own campaign against the Republic of China's nationalist forces under General Chiang Kai-shek. Mao's troops were supported by the Soviet Union, which provided materiel and advisors. With his attention and resources used to counter the communists, Chiang needed help from the West. It was the perfect moment for the Guangdong Army to move south into Manchuria and China in 1931. This sparked the Second Sino-Japanese War, which would last for a decade. Japanese diplomats worked to convince the United States and Great Britain that the invasion was the only means of safeguarding Japanese interests and that the Republic of China had consistently reneged on trade agreements. These entreaties had their effect because most Americans were focused on their own problems during the Great Depression. Less than 20 percent of U.S. citizens cared about what was happening between Asian races halfway around the world. The growing power of Nazism and Adolf Hitler in Germany was also taking the attention of U.S. government and military officials.

Throughout the mid-1930s, it became apparent that even the Guangdong Army had a tiger by the tail. As the Japanese drove deeper into northern China, General Chiang Kai-shek's Nationalist Army, on the move and fighting a guerilla campaign against the invaders, was proving to be a serious impediment to General Iwane Matsui's forces. By 1937, as more troops and weapons were sent into China, the Japanese press lamented the "China Problem," in which millions of yen, thousands of men, and shiploads of supplies were being consumed. For Japan, the invasion and conquest of eastern China was akin to what the Soviet Union would later face in Afghanistan in the 1980s.

But it did not deter the Imperial General Staff and prime minister from supporting the increasing war in China.

Japan also began looking with greedy eyes to the south. There were still great advantages to moving into French Indochina, the Philippines, Malaya, Borneo, the Dutch East Indies, and Australia. Even with the Guangdong Army tied down in China, there were still plenty of troops for the task. Japan had never stopped increasing the size of its army, conscripting men from ages seventeen to forty, either for active service or as reserves.

The Imperial Navy was also on the rise, with new ships being launched from the sizeable yards at Yokohama, Kure, and Nagasaki. Huge new battleships were being designed, and the fleet of aircraft carriers was already larger than those of the United States and Great Britain. But there could be no doubt that any Japanese advance to the south would provoke a strong diplomatic and possibly military response from the West.

When the Japanese ambassador to Germany, Saburo Kurusu, signed the Tripartite Pact with Nazi Germany and Fascist Italy in September 1940, it was a clear indicator that the lines were being drawn in the seas. As the third member of the Axis, Japan had aligned itself with two fascist governments actively waging war with England and the rest of Europe. The pact stipulated that if any of the three signatories were to be attacked by any nation not engaged in the war, the other two members of the Axis Alliance would declare war on the attacker. Since the only two countries not yet involved were the United States and the Soviet Union, which had a nonaggression agreement with Germany, this left little doubt about which nation the pact meant.

The American ambassador to Japan, Joseph Grew, who liked and respected the Japanese people, was convinced that a "showdown" with Japan was inevitable. In a December 1940 letter to President Franklin Roosevelt, he wondered whether it was "to our advantage to have that showdown sooner rather than later."

Enter the pivotal figure in the growing conflict. The commander in chief of the Imperial Navy's Combined Fleet, Admiral Isoroku Yamamoto. Of all the men who played important roles between 1930 and 1940, Yamamoto was the one man in the Imperial Navy who saw only disaster in a war between Japan and the United States. He was also the most opposed to that war. Yamamoto knew and understood the American people and, most of all, their industrial capacity. No one in Japan in the early 1940s worked harder to avoid a war with the U.S., but in the end, he was chosen to fire the first shot.

CHAPTER 2

YAMAMOTO THE VISIONARY

"A good commander is benevolent and unconcerned with fame."
—Sun Tzu

The year 1938 was a pivotal one. On January 28, Roosevelt went before Congress to request the Vinson Naval Act to create a two-ocean navy. Congress passed it, appropriating a billion dollars to build the nucleus of a larger navy. Then he sent Harry Hopkins, his advisor and sometimes chief of staff, to the Midwest and Pacific to find out how quickly the aircraft manufacturers could convert to a wartime footing. Hopkins later said, "The President was certain that war was coming to America. He believed that airpower would win it."

In this, Roosevelt was uncannily prescient. Chief of the Air Corp General Henry Arnold had met with the president to discuss the air power gap between the United States and Germany, still considered the main adversary. Germany had three times more available aircraft than the U.S. This was a serious concern, and neither man wanted a repeat of the debacle at the start of the Great War, when the United States had to depend on foreign aircraft to fill out its squadrons.

With Roosevelt's approval to tool up for the expansion of the Air Corps, the ball began rolling which would eventually make the United States the most powerful air force in the world. But it had to be done fast.

In August a new admiral was appointed commander in chief of the Japanese Combined Fleet. His name was Isoroku Yamamoto, a man who came to represent the power and identity of the Imperial Navy. Standing only five feet, three inches tall, with broad shoulders and a closely shaven head, Yamamoto had the face of a benign Buddha. But his dark, wide-set eyes and full lips under a straight nose hid a sharp and determined mind. Yamamoto was the perfect naval officer, loyal to Emperor Hirohito, and Japanese to the core. A skilled card player, he was a gambler, not afraid to take chances, but he also had a highly developed ability to see the truth. He had a sharp wit but could cut with barbed sarcasm when confronting stupidity.

Born in Nagaoka in 1884 as Isoroku Takano, he was adopted at the age of sixteen by the old Yamamoto Samurai clan, which had no male heirs. His given name was unusual, the ideograph for the numbers five, ten, and six, a source of pride for his fifty-six-year-old father having a son at that advanced age. From boyhood Yamamoto had been fascinated by the navy, watching the hulking warships moving along the coastlines. In 1901, having secured an appointment to the Eta Jima Naval Academy, Yamamoto traveled to Hiroshima and took the ferry to the small island where he would begin his education as an officer in the Imperial Navy.

His natural charisma and quality of leadership were immediately apparent—gifts that would never leave him. He was popular and even-tempered among the often hotheaded cadets. In 1904 he graduated as a midshipman, eleventh in his class, and was assigned to the armored cruiser *Nisshin*, part of Admiral Togo's fleet at the Battle of Tsushima on May 27, 1905. He was wounded when a deck gun exploded, tearing a chunk of flesh from his left thigh and peppering his body with fragments. He also lost the first two fingers of his left hand. But the young midshipman simply wrapped his bleeding hand in a scarf and stayed at his post.

Yamamoto was interested in studying foreign lands, the United States being a favorite subject. Carl Sandburg's biography of Abraham Lincoln was one of the first books he read about Americans. He was aware of the antipathy between his own nation and the United States, but he fervently hoped a war could be avoided.

Yamamoto was in Yokohama when Teddy Roosevelt's Great White Fleet dropped anchor. Taking advantage of the goodwill between the American and Japanese officers, the future admiral toured and inspected the big warships, absorbing as much as he could.

He served on ships in Sasebo, Korea, and patrolled the Manchurian coast. In 1909 he served on a cruiser as part of a squadron paying a return goodwill visit to the American West Coast. Stopping in Seattle and San Pedro, Yamamoto became acquainted with American Navy officers, mostly ensigns or lieutenants. A few would one day be commanding fleets in the war to come.

He rose in rank and responsibility, learning every aspect of command and handling ships. By the 1910s he was not only one of the most popular officers in the Imperial Navy but also recognized as a rising star. When Japan gained possession of the Pacific Mandate of the Carolines, Marshalls, and Marianas after the Great War, Yamamoto had reached the watershed point of a naval career—the rank of lieutenant commander. This was the "make or break" point for officers. There was no doubt he planned to continue in his chosen profession.

In 1919 he was a member of a naval contingent sent to America to study English at Harvard. It was there he learned the skill of playing bridge and poker. One American officer, Lieutenant Arthur McCollum, who worked in the Far East section of Naval Intelligence, made a point of studying Yamamoto, seeing him as a likely future flag officer.

While in the U.S., Yamamoto was promoted to full commander. He traveled to Chicago and Detroit, studying American production lines at the Ford and Oldsmobile factories. Greatly impressed with the American ability to produce huge numbers of automobiles, trains, planes, and machines, he made careful note of what he saw. It was apparent to Yamamoto that Japan could never compete in an arms race, let alone a war with the United States.

The new commander was fascinated by aviation, which was already growing rapidly in Europe and America. Although he had faithfully followed the traditional doctrine of battles between fleets of surface ships, Yamamoto saw great potential in the airplane. Most naval officers considered the airplane useful only for long-range observation and reconnaissance, but Yamamoto was, using his newfound grasp of English, reading the books and editorials of General William "Billy" Mitchell. After returning from Europe at the end of the Great War, Mitchell strongly promoted air power as America's first line of defense. He believed airplanes could sink battleships, the powerful warships that had defined a nation's sea power.

When Mitchell proved this in a series of tests in the Chesapeake Bay in 1921, sinking the German dreadnought *Ostfriesland* with air-dropped bombs, it made a huge impression on Yamamoto. The United States Navy, however, continued to fight Mitchell's growing claims that battleships were obsolete, and refused to stop launching them. Several ships that would be at Pearl Harbor in December 1941 were commissioned between 1921 and 1929, including *Arizona*, *Nevada*, *Tennessee*, *West Virginia*, and *Maryland*.

While Yamamoto would later fly his flag onboard the battleships *Nagato* and *Yamato*, he was convinced the airplane was the Imperial Navy's future.

When the 1922 Washington Naval Treaty was signed, Commander Yamamoto was back in Japan. The Japanese delegation was of two minds, the Fleet Faction and the Treaty Faction, with the former totally opposed to Japan being forced to limit the size of its navy. Japan was already planning to build and launch eight new battleships and eight cruisers. The Treaty Faction favored the limitations as a means of keeping the peace and avoiding a drain on the already weakened economy. In the end, the Treaty Faction won out, at least for a tie. The United States was to scrap 800,000 tons of its own ships, either in commission or under construction. Japan was to scrap 400,000 tons. But this reduction was largely illusory. Scrapping old ships would allow for new ships with bigger guns and more efficient oil-fired boilers. The Imperial General Staff had no intention of following the strict terms of the treaty.

Meanwhile, Commander Yamamoto continued to rise in the navy. He favored the treaty, seeing long-term benefits to a reduction in warships. But another officer, Commander Chuichi Nagumo, was opposed to any reduction. Even as Yamamoto and Nagumo served in their respective duties, they were intense rivals from that point on, which would become a problem in 1941 and 1942.

In 1923, at the age of thirty-nine, Yamamoto was promoted to captain and given command of the fast cruiser HIJMS (His Imperial Japanese Majesty's Ship) *Fuki*. But the ever-restless officer did not want to serve in surface ships. He had his eye on naval aviation. At that time, the only planes in the navy were reconnaissance floatplanes, intended to launch from cruisers and battleships.

At last Yamamoto was assigned to the staff of the Kasumigaura Aviation Corps. Here the cadets learned to fly floatplanes off the lakes. To reach this point, they first had to be graduates of Eta Jima. Even though Yamamoto was too old to be trained as a pilot, he did learn to fly, and put his efforts into considering the growing importance of naval aviation. In this he was in total agreement with an American officer, Captain William F. Halsey, who earned his wings in 1935 at the age of fifty-two. Yamamoto and Halsey would become well acquainted in the years to come.

In 1924 Yamamoto was appointed the head of the Kasumigaura Air Academy, and began making changes in the training and application of airplanes in the navy. It took some time for him to gain the respect of the cadets, but he was soon liked for his even discipline and fair leadership. He intended to make the Kasumigaura officers into the core of a new branch of the Imperial Navy.

But later that year, he was suddenly ordered to Washington to serve as the Japanese naval attaché. Having no choice, Yamamoto turned over the reins of the academy to his replacement, hoping his initial goals would be honored. He need not have worried. As the *Tanyo Maru* sailed out of Yokohama, several Kasumigaura cadets flew over and made simulated dive bombing runs at the ship. Yamamoto stood on the bridge, a silent smile on his round face.

While stationed at the Japanese Embassy on Massachusetts Avenue in Washington, Yamamoto often met with and even played bridge with many American Navy officers. The Americans considered the Japanese naval officer and concluded that if war ever came, it would be Yamamoto who would lead an attack on the West Coast. At the same time, Yamamoto was learning all he could about the American Navy, watching as some ships were built, others scrapped, and two converted into aircraft carriers.

The 1922 Washington Treaty stipulated that any ship under 33,000 tons could be converted into aircraft carriers. In 1925 the United States converted the collier *Jupiter* into the *Langley*. The Imperial Navy had launched *Hosho* in 1922, the first ship ever built from the keel up as a carrier. Larger carriers were soon constructed: the Japanese *Akagi*, converted from a battleship, and the American *Lexington* and *Saratoga* from two 29,000-ton battle cruisers.

Yet the American carrier force was shackled, not with mooring lines but with antiquated policy. They were considered, by the traditional "big-gun" fleet, as only the "eyes of the fleet." Even as late as 1939, cadets at Annapolis were discouraged from joining the naval air arm because of its limited potential.

But Yamamoto watched the growing importance of naval aviation with interest and pride.

In December 1926, upon the death of Emperor Taisho, Hirohito became Emperor of Japan. He gave his reign the title of "Enlightened Peace." Yamamoto, always loyal to the sovereign, was impressed by the new emperor, and had every intention of doing his best for Nippon. Yamamoto gave several lectures at various war colleges, including Eta Jima, where he talked to the cadets and faculty about America, not in military matters but its morals and culture. He said it was important to understand and know the Americans, something the army and navy was failing to do.

Yamamoto took command of the new carrier *Akagi* on December 10, 1928. *Akagi* was the pride of the Imperial Navy carrier fleet. Yamamoto was eager to test and develop his ideas about carrier warfare, and he had his chance during war games in the Sea of Japan. A simulated strike against opposing forces was to prove the concept of offensive carrier warfare. But it was a disaster. The strike force got lost in a storm and crashed at sea. Every plane and pilot was gone. From that point on Yamamoto wanted his pilots and aircrew to learn the skill of aerial navigation and radio direction finding.

He would not lose good men and expensive planes to bad weather.

Ever since *Hosho* and *Akagi* had entered service, the Imperial General Staff considered carriers only useful for defending the main battle fleet. Yamamoto was determined to show that planes armed with bombs and torpedoes could be a formidable striking force. But the change would take time. He advocated the development of new and better weapons, more rigorous training, and improved communications. At the end of 1929 he was assigned to the Naval Affairs Bureau in the Navy Ministry. Here he could make a real difference, pushing through new ideas to improve the naval aviation branch.

But again, he was pulled away, this time to be a special assistant to the Japanese delegation to the 1930 London Naval Conference. With his superb English, Yamamoto was well suited to advise the delegates. The conference was intended to adjust the already shaky terms of the 1922 treaty. It was obvious that the signatories, with the exception of Italy and France, were taking advantage of the large loopholes in the original treaty.

The Japanese delegates, primarily in favor of fleet expansion, demanded that Japan have parity with the United States and Great Britain or they would refuse to participate. In fact, it was generally known among the delegation that the Fleet Faction would prefer dismissing the treaty terms. Yamamoto was still with the Treaty Faction, content with the existing 5/5/3 ratio. But to maintain some unity, he and the other Treaty Faction adherents worked to increase to a 5/5/4 ratio. He tried to explain this to his fellow delegates.

There were two reasons for Yamamoto to support the original 1922 terms. First of all, he had traveled all over the United States and was very aware of its immense industrial capacity. The thought of Japan going to war with the U.S. was unthinkable. Japan could not, under any circumstances, win a protracted war with the mighty nation across the Pacific.

The other reason was the growing number of carriers in the Imperial Navy. By 1930 Japan would have more carriers than any other nation, and Yamamoto believed the naval aviation branch would ultimately supersede the vaunted battle fleet. Japan did not need more battleships.

But his arguments fell on deaf ears. Added to this was the worsening economic depression.

Ever since the end of the Great War, Japan's economy was faltering, and the huge expense of maintaining a navy and army was bankrupting an economy that could only survive through high-interest loans from foreign banks. Prices rose while employment dropped. The worldwide price of silk, one of Japan's most lucrative exports, fell by half. Other exports were reduced by 30 percent. Protests and increased pressure from the moderates finally forced the Japanese Army to withdraw some of its troops from Siberia, where they had been stationed for over a decade. The American stock market crash in October 1929 spread its red ink to the Pacific and hit Japanese markets. Stocks fell as banks and businesses failed. Widespread famine and starvation followed. The only answer seemed to be for Japan to increase its market to Manchuria, China, and Southeast Asia.

At the London conference, Yamamoto used his poker face to read the faces of the American and British delegates. His command of English gave him a great advantage. Some of the matters discussed led only to stalemates. The United States wanted a moratorium on all battleship construction; the Japanese and British did not. The British wanted all submarines to be outlawed, an obvious outcome of the nearly disastrous U-boat campaign of the Great War. But Japan and the U.S. did not want to give up submarines.

Japan pressed for a 5/5/4 ratio for capital ships, but Britain and the U.S. stood firm on the old 5/5/3 number.

When asked, Yamamoto tried to explain why the Fleet Faction insisted on a 70 percent ratio. It was based on the advances in ship design, oil fuel, navigation, aircraft carriers, and aviation. The old 1922 terms were no longer relevant.

The conference seemed to be at a deadlock.

Yamamoto openly derided the Fleet Faction by saying, "What difference does it make if Japan has sixty or even seventy percent of the United States Navy's ships? Japan would still not be able to win a war with America or Great Britain."

Then-Emperor Hirohito intervened by telegram. He told his delegation that if the treaty failed, it would reflect badly on Japan. It would appear that Japan was more interested in building a larger navy than in promoting peace. That ended the matter for the moment, and the treaty was signed with the terms preferred by the Treaty Faction and the West. Yamamoto, somewhat relieved that there would be no war between Japan and the Western navies, could relax. But upon returning to Japan, he saw widespread depression and increasing militarism. The 1930 London Naval Treaty did not solve the problem. In fact, it played right into the hands of the right-wing reactionaries, who used it to stage a military revolt in the government. The world was one step closer to war in the Pacific.

Japan had begun enlarging its army in Manchuria after 1931, when a bomb exploded aboard a Japanese-owned railroad train. While the incident was minor, it was the excuse the Imperial General Staff used to send the Guangdong Army south into China. Given Japan's record of provoking international events, the bomb was almost certainly planted by the Japanese. The region of northern China occupied and claimed by the Guangdong Army was renamed Manchukuo and occupied for the next ten years.

In 1935, the naval air arm was at last moving toward the goal set by Yamamoto. The naval affairs department put in an order with the Link Company in Binghamton, New York, for thirty Link Pilot Trainers. The trainer, which looked like a child's airplane ride at an amusement park, proved to be an excellent and safe means of training cadets to fly with precision. With supreme irony, the largest customer of Link Trainers until 1940 was the Imperial Japanese Navy.

Yamamoto, still deeply involved in improving the naval air arm, was pressured in 1936 to take the post of the navy's vice minister, analogous to the American assistant secretary of the navy. In Japan the post was held by a uniformed officer. Yamamoto, who loathed politics, at first refused but soon gave in. He was to carry out the orders of navy minister Osami Nagano. This put him in an odd position. Being vice minister made him a potential target for the violent right-wing reactionaries who were trying to gain military control of the government, but his well-known record of working hard to increase the size of the navy and the air arm made him relatively immune to assassination. He was not happy in the post, knowing that the navy minister, although a moderate, was a supporter of a treaty with Nazi Germany. Yamamoto did not trust the Germans, and did his best to distance himself from any connection with the pro-German group.

Yamamoto's involvement with the naval treaties and his views about a war with the Western Powers were well known. He boldly stated, "Japan would be committing suicide to go to war with the United States."

While the Fleet Faction continued to fight against the army's maneuvers to control the government, other factors reared their heads. Japan's lack of raw materials and resources grew more critical. For instance, the mining of copper yielded about 75,000 tons per year, less than half of what the army and navy needed. Iron ore mining yielded even less, at 12 percent of requirements, and oil was less than 10 percent. As for rubber, Japan produced none at all. The nation's industrial manpower was also far below what it should have been. In 1936, about three million workers were employed in shops and factories with five or more workers. But the same number were in "cottage industries" with fewer than five people in each shop.

This was a tiny fraction of what most U.S. factories were employing.

The solution was nearby. Manchuria had mountains of iron ore, and the Philippines possessed a rich source of copper. The Dutch East Indies supplied oil, while rubber was plentiful in British Malaya.

As for how Japan would obtain these valuable resources, that was easily done. Japan would invade and seize them. Japan would take her rightful, God-given place at the head of the Asian nations.

General Hideki Tojo was appointed head of the Kempeitai, which served as the intelligence and administrative arm of the army in China. The government was forced to accede to the army's relentless push to gain full power. Then-Prime Minister Koki Hirota was unable to form a new cabinet and resigned. The next cabinet was formed with a moderate at the head, who was actually on good terms with the reactionaries. He appointed a new navy minister, Admiral Mitsumasa Yonai, who had been a good friend of Yamamoto's since the Russo-Japanese War.

Not surprisingly, Yonai chose to name Yamamoto as his vice minister. Yonai was well respected in both the army and navy, and worked well with Yamamoto.

Meanwhile, Hirohito admired and was on good terms with King George V. The emperor wanted no part of war with the West. But by May 1937, he had to accept that the current cabinet would not hold together. The emperor was in a quandary. If he appointed an army general as prime minister, he would be giving the army control of the government. The army had already declared that it wanted no politician to be prime minister. The only man who might hold off disaster was Prince Fumimaro Konoye, a member of the royal family. While born to a life of ease and luxury, Konoye had a strong influence on both government officials and military officers. He was persuaded to keep Yonai and Yamamoto in their current posts to counterbalance the army's continued efforts to control the government. One of his appointments was General Sadao Araki as minister of education in May 1937. This proved to have a strong impact on the future of Japanese youth. Araki took every advantage of his new post, making the Code of Bushido part of every boy's education and upbringing. From that point on, every boy was taught to revere the emperor, that to die for Japan was glorious, and that their very existence was tied to that of Japan. The man who dictated the education of Japan's children was a fierce proponent of expansions and supported the secret biological warfare research institution, Unit 731, in Manchuria. He was later convicted of war crimes and sentenced to life imprisonment.

The prime minister was trying to prevent the army from taking over the government, and the only way to do this was to give the army what it wanted in China. As far back as 1932, Japan maintained troops in Manchuria, supposedly to protect Japanese-owned railroads and businesses.

On the humid night of July 7, 1937, an incident occurred that sparked a war between Japan and the nationalist forces of General Chiang Kai-shek. The historic Marco Polo, or Lugou Bridge over the Yongding River in Peking, now Beijing, was the site of an incident between the Japanese Guangdong Army and the Chinese Army. Units of each were crossing the bridge in opposite directions, whereupon they stopped and began to argue about who had the right to use the bridge. With little provocation, the Japanese fired on the Chinese, who returned fire. This is generally considered the beginning of the bloody Second Sino-Japanese War. Hideki Tojo had masterminded the incident on the Marco Polo Bridge.

On the other side of the Pacific, the growing Imperial Fleet was a subject of both concern and scorn among American Navy officers. While the Japanese were building new ships, they would not be worthy of anything but contempt from the large and powerful United States and Royal Navies. However, one disturbing element of the Japanese fleet was their aircraft carrier.

Since the launching of *Hosho* and *Akagi* in the mid-1920s, the Imperial Navy had built and launched the largest and most advanced carrier force in the world. Of greater concern were the highly secret super battleships *Yamato* and *Musashi*, due to be launched in 1941. With nine 18.1-inch main guns and more of smaller calibers, the two 70,000-ton warships would be the largest and most powerful battleships in the world. Moreover, the Imperial Navy trained its gunners to exacting standards for day and night combat.

Yamamoto was largely responsible for the new breed of naval aircraft. Rather than derivative copies of American and British designs, the latest fighters, dive, and torpedo bombers were original and superior to any ever put into service. Yamamoto had overseen the development of the Mitsubishi A5M Claude, more advanced A6M Zero fighter, the Aichi D3A Dive Bomber, and the Nakajima B5N torpedo and high-level bomber. He also signed off on the new Mitsubishi G3M and proposed G4M twin-engine bombers for both army and navy use. Ironically, it would be in one of the latter in which he was killed in April 1943.

Yamamoto was proud of the superiority of his carrier fleet and aircraft over those of the Western Powers. Admiral Chuichi Nagumo, whose experience had been in destroyers, agreed that the IJN's most important fleet units were the carriers. It was one of the few instances where Yamamoto and Nagumo agreed.

In September 1937, as the Manchuria situation came closer to the boiling point, Yonai and Yamamoto were pleased with the appointment of Admiral Shigeyoshi Inoue as head of the Naval Affairs Bureau, where Yamamoto had worked several years earlier. Inoue was opposed to any treaty with Germany and Italy. The so-called Triumvirate of the three admirals had the army factions watching and waiting. A two-billion-yen appropriation was granted to build more ships and planes.

By now three new divisions of troops had been sent to China while army bombers daily dropped explosives on Shanghai. When a Japanese cruiser was bombed by Chinese planes, it sparked a nationwide call for the navy to move up the Yangtze River and shell the city. To ministers Yonai and Yamamoto, the use of navy warships and carriers to bomb Shanghai was unthinkable. But they had no power to prevent it. The Navy Ministry did not plan operations—that was the job of the Naval General Staff and Combined Fleet. Several warships, from carriers to destroyers, were employed in blockading the Chinese coast and bombing Chiang Kai-shek's positions.

After two more divisions landed in China, Admiral Rokuzo Sugiyama, chief of staff of the navy's Third Fleet in the China Sea, assured Hirohito that he could solve the China problem in a month. The daily papers and radio broadcasts, heard by the United States Embassies in both Shanghai and Tokyo, continued to report on the China Problem. Most urban Japanese supported more action in China, but the greater part of the population, who lived on farms and in small fishing villages, were ignorant of the worsening situation.

In Washington, determined to show Japan the folly of its ways, President Franklin D. Roosevelt signed a bill that cut off all exports of scrap iron. This was only the first of many embargoes of vital war materiel to Japan. President Roosevelt told the press, "Japan is an aggressor nation." He was determined to use whatever means at his disposal to show Japan that the United States would not stand for any military force in China.

But Roosevelt was well aware that the United States military was hardly in a position to be a threat to Japan. After the Great War, Congress began cutting the budgets of both the army and navy until they were a shadow of their former strength. The fleet was down to a third of what it had been in 1920. Even the Marines, once an elite branch of the Navy Department, numbered little more than 16,000 officers and men, smaller than the New York City Police Department. As for the army and navy air forces, they ranked sixteenth in the world, far behind even France and Italy. To call the situation a disgrace was hardly enough.

Meanwhile, General Tojo in China sent a message to Tokyo that Chiang Kai-shek's Nationalist Army was growing stronger due to support from the United States. Hirohito was under great pressure from the reactionaries to capture Shanghai and Nanking. Prime Minister Konoye advised the emperor to approve the campaign. In his private writings, Hirohito revealed that his main reason for approving the campaign was the fear that the Soviet Army would invade northern Manchuria and sweep south before the Japanese Army could consolidate its forces. The government-controlled press spread propaganda that China was being supported and manipulated by the United States and Great Britain. A clash between the United States and Japan was inevitable, and it finally happened in December 1937.

The Yangtze River, flowing for 3,100 miles through China and past the old cities of Shanghai and Nanking, was one of China's most important navigable waterways. Much of the world's history was carried on the ever-flowing river, known to the Chinese as "Long River."

In 1935, the United States, in order to protect its citizens, property, shipping, and economic interests in China, had contracted for river gunboats to be built and manned by U.S. naval crews. They were to patrol the river against the ever-present threat of pirates.

One of those gunboats was the *Panay*, assigned to the Asiatic Fleet, based in Hong Kong. At 435 tons and less than 200 feet in length, *Panay* had a shallow draft, enabling her to patrol along the river's marshes and reeds. Lieutenant Commander James Hughes, an Annapolis graduate, was assigned to *Panay* in 1936. His boat patrolled up and down the river, which flowed into the Yellow Sea. With an armament of two 3-inch guns and a brace of .50- and .30-caliber machine guns, *Panay* was more than able to protect itself and American interests against any waterborne adversary. To declare her identity, *Panay* flew large American flags at bow and stern.

On the late morning of December 12, 1937, *Panay* was moving downriver from Nanking, where her fifty-five-man crew had rescued four U.S. Embassy officials, five American refugees, and several correspondents who were in danger from the Japanese attacks on the city.

At noon, seeing no threat, Hughes stopped the boat so the crew could have lunch. At about 1330 hours, they heard the drone of approaching aircraft. That was nothing new, and the crew continued to enjoy its lunch. Then a quartermaster yelled, "The Japs are letting bombs go!"

Overhead, a flight of ten new Imperial Japanese Navy Aichi D3A dive bombers, led by Lieutenant Masaki Okiyama, screamed down from the sky. The *Panay* was anchored, an easy target. Okiyama released his 150-kg bomb, which hit the pilothouse just as Hughes was attempting to radio his squadron commander. With his legs broken and bleeding, Hughes yelled for his crew to cut the anchor line and return fire. One of the correspondents, Universal News Service's Norman Alley, grabbed his movie camera and filmed the attack. He later said, "the Japs flew so close I could see the grinning pilots."

The crew manned the machine guns and began firing at the swooping planes displaying bright red "meatballs" on the wings.

Jim Marshall of *Collier's Magazine* said it was impossible for the Japanese, who were flying so low, not to know they were bombing Westerners instead of Chinese. Marshall was hit by fragments in his upper body.

Panay's executive officer, Lieutenant Arthur Anders, took command but was struck by shrapnel in the throat. A native of Vallejo, California, Anders had moved his family to Hong Kong, where his wife gave birth to their first son, William, in 1933. William Anders would later join the air force and become a member of the Apollo 8 mission to circumnavigate the moon in 1968.

Panay was riddled with holes, and sinking. Anders used a piece of chalk on a bulkhead to tell the crew to "Take to lifeboats! Stay as close to shore as possible. Return the boats." The lifeboats were lowered and filled with civilians and crew, who began rowing for shore. Others dived in and swam.

Okiyama's planes began strafing the boats and swimmers with machine guns. As the stranded crew reached the thick mass of reeds along the riverbank, an armed Japanese launch roared downriver and began shooting into the men on shore. Then it veered off and came alongside the nearly sunken *Panay*. A few men scrambled aboard and began searching for classified papers and code books.

Thirty minutes after the first bomb fell, *Panay* sank, the first United States craft to be sunk by the Imperial Japanese Navy.

The shipwrecked sailors and civilians walked to Shanghai, carrying seventeen wounded. Two sailors were dead. While they trudged south, they were hunted by Japanese soldiers. There was no doubt the attack was deliberate, and the Japanese knew exactly whose ship it was.

Panay was not the only victim of Japanese bombs that day. Three American tankers and three Royal Navy gunboats were also sunk.

Yamamoto, while forewarned of the attack but unable to stop it, made a personal visit to Ambassador Joseph Grew at the American Embassy in Tokyo. He sincerely apologized for the attack. The apology was so convincing that Grew, who liked and respected the admiral, was persuaded to accept that the *Panay* sinking was an unfortunate mistake. Then Yamamoto convinced Navy Minister Yonai to fire the task force admiral who had launched the strike. This was a clear indication that he and Yonai had no part in the incident.

The day after *Panay* sank, General Iwane Matsui, commander of the Japanese Expeditionary Army, marched into Nanking. General Chiang Kai-shek's defeated forces headed south, but the reprieve was temporary. Matsui, an expert on China, was prepared to follow and destroy the Chinese troops to the last man.

Matsui, hoping to avoid provoking the United States, ordered his troops to avoid damaging the property of non-Chinese businesses. But his troops, most of whom were ill-trained and little more than armed thugs, entered the city with every intention of raping, looting, burning, and killing. This became known as the "Rape of Nanking," which resulted in the murder of nearly a quarter of a million men, women, and children. It was a dark harbinger of how Japanese troops treated conquered peoples. Such wanton and widespread barbarity had not been known since the times of Attila the Hun and Genghis Khan. Even German Army officers who followed and advised Matsui were appalled at what they saw in Nanking.

In the United States, news reports, including those from the correspondents on the *Panay*, prompted hundreds of editorials and letters. Secretary of State Cordell Hull, the veteran statesman from Tennessee, condemned the sinking of *Panay* as "the actions of wild, insane Japanese admirals and generals."

But in the White House, Roosevelt made the decision to have the newsreel footage altered so the faces of the Japanese pilots could not be seen. This was an attempt to keep anti-Japanese sentiments from spreading and leading to a war America was not ready to fight.

In a protest to the Japanese ambassador, the State Department said the Japanese pilots were guilty of "reckless flying," an obvious attempt to give the Japanese a chance to back off without further bloodshed. In reply, Japan sent a check in the amount of $2,214,007.36 to pay for damages and loss of life.

The furor over the *Panay* incident soon blew over, largely due to Yamamoto's sincere entreaties to Ambassador Grew. But the glowing red ember of Japanese imperialism and American outrage was not being quenched.

The dominant opinion among U.S. military officers was that the attack on *Panay* was deliberate despite Japanese claims of mistaken identity. It was meant to test how Americans reacted and fought against attack. The pacifist American reaction was more than enough proof for the Japanese high command that the United States was a paper tiger.

Further proof was provided by the Republican-led isolationists, which had been a powerful lobby in Washington. The Depression was beginning to ease off, with higher employment from large defense contracts. War was on the European horizon, no matter what might be happening in the Pacific, and the America First movement had less influence on the public, who was more concerned with matters at home. So in May, Roosevelt pushed through the Naval Expansion Act, authorizing another 200,000 tons of ships and 3,000 aircraft for the fleet. Admiral Arthur Hepburn led a panel of five engineers and planners who decided how to strengthen the Pacific bases. The December 1938 Hepburn Report recommended additional fortification to the existing bases at Pearl Harbor, Midway, Johnson, and Palmyra Islands, as well as the Philippines.

At the top of the list was Wake Island. Being closer to Tokyo than Honolulu, Wake was the most remote Pacific possession and would be a strong link in the distant chain that protected Hawaii and the West Coast. Hawaii was the key base, with Midway and Wake next in order of importance, and Guam far down the list. A budget of $7.5 million was proposed, but the isolationists were not ready to fold, and they protested what they considered a provocation to Japan. A compromise took Guam off the list and the budget was cut so Wake, Palmyra, and Midway would be lightly reinforced. Then Georgia Congressman Carl Vinson, head of the Naval Appropriations Board, agreed to leave Wake as it was. As for Guam, it was sacrificed, being considered indefensible.

In Tokyo, the rabid Fleet Faction was at last growing in power and influence. The United States was now deemed the prime enemy of Japan.

But the Japanese Army was not ready to face the kind of war that would result in a sustained conflict with Great Britain and the United States, both of which had officers who had fought on the bloody Western Front in the Great War. In August 1939, Japanese troops fought a fierce battle with a Soviet Army in southeastern Manchuria. For the first time, Japanese soldiers faced sustained artillery, armored cavalry, and mechanized warfare. The Soviets drove the Japanese back with heavy losses. It was a shock to the Guangdong veterans, and a harbinger of what was to come. But it had little impact on the immediate policies and operations of the Imperial General Staff.

Things moved fast in 1939. Germany's bloodless conquests of Austria and Czechoslovakia influenced the new prime minister, General Nobuyuki Abe, to force the removal of Admiral Yonai. General Abe wanted a navy minister who would not be so opposed to army expansion. Yonai was dismissed, along with Yamamoto. But the last act Admiral Yonai performed was to appoint Admiral Isoroku Yamamoto as commander in chief of the Combined Fleet. He was now the most senior and highest-ranking line officer in the Imperial Navy. This was not only because Yonai believed his protégé was the best man for the job, but it would save Yamamoto from assassination. From that point on, Yamamoto lived at sea.

At Osaka, he saw his fleet in its entirety. Over seventy battleships, carriers, cruisers, destroyers, and support ships. The third largest navy in the world was all his.

Yet in his mind's eye, Yamamoto saw that same great fleet in desperate battles against a growing number of powerful American ships. Taking a launch out to the battleship *Nagato*, he and his predecessor performed the ceremonial change of command. When Yamamoto's flag was hoisted up the mainmast, he was in full command.

The new issue at hand was the inevitable Tripartite Pact between Berlin, Rome, and Tokyo. Many in the government were unsure of Japan's risk and exposure from the treaty. There were more than seventy meetings to puzzle out the possibilities and details. Japan was hardly ready to fight a one-ocean war without having to engage in another one halfway around the world. Yet there was no other option but to move on.

For Japan, the man who would have to carry out the navy and war ministry plans was Isoroku Yamamoto.

In Washington, Roosevelt was doing his best to make the United States ready for a war he hoped could still be avoided. He was done with sending conciliatory messages to Berlin. "America has been a slumbering giant," he said. "Now it is awakening. The agressors had better watch out." This was vintage Roosevelt. It is curious that the "slumbering giant" quote would be attributed to Yamamoto rather than the president of the United States.

CHAPTER 3

PRELUDE TO INFAMY—1939 TO 1941

"In politics stupidity is not a handicap." —Napoleon Bonaparte

From the moment Yamamoto raised his flag on *Nagato*, he went right to work. Most of the early days were concerned with getting to know his staff and commanders. They all knew of him and a few had worked with the admiral in the past. Despite the normality of the duty, the tension in the air was palpable. The war talk among the officers was so thick it could be cut with a knife.

September 1939 brought two major changes to the world and Japan. On September 1, Adolf Hitler's legions invaded Poland, initiating the Second World War. This led to a declaration of war from France and Great Britain. Josef Stalin, general secretary of the Communist Party of the Soviet Union, wanting no part of a European war, was placated by the nonaggression pact with Hitler. The Nazis ran virtually unchecked across Eastern and Western Europe, taking Belgium, Denmark, and Norway, virtually cutting Great Britain off from mainland Europe.

At 0250 hours in Washington, the phone rang next to Roosevelt's bed. He picked it up and said, "Yes?"

It was his ambassador in Paris. "It's started, Mr. President. The Germans are moving divisions across the Polish border and there is heavy fighting."

Roosevelt sighed. "Well it's come at last. God help us all."

Another historic, little-known event happened the same day Hitler's troops moved into Poland. General George C. Marshall was appointed chief of staff of the army, a post he would hold until the end of the war. This was a perfect example of FDR's skill in choosing the right man for a hard job. His next would be that of Admiral Chester W. Nimitz in December 1941.

Roosevelt sent one of his last messages of appeasement to Berlin, asking Hitler not to invade weaker nations. With the wit he was fond of displaying before his lackeys, a smiling Hitler promised not to invade the United States. This was aimed at America's low ranking in international military strength, which, in 1938, put it behind Poland.

The victorious sweep across Europe by the Third Reich's army and air force further reinforced the Japanese Imperial General Staff's certainty that their own method of amphibious attack and conquest would win the day in southern operations. They truly believed that their officers and men, trained for aggressive land war, would conquer the Americans, British, and Dutch just as they had in Russia and China. But what the General Staff failed to grasp was that Hitler's legions were masters of combined arms warfare. Superb airborne troops, the trained *Fallschirmjäger*, had no parallel in Japan, except for a single division formed in the late 1930s that only saw action during the invasion of Sumatra in the Dutch East Indies in 1942. The same went for Panzers, the fast-moving tanks that overwhelmed their enemies. It must also have escaped the Imperial Army General Staff that the Polish Army, shackled by antiquated equipment and a government unable to act, was an easy victory. With massed armor, artillery, mechanized and airborne troops, and tactical bombers, the Wehrmacht ran over Poland within weeks. Japan's armies were far behind the Germans, but with little understanding of how to fight a modern war, they joined Germany and Italy.

On September 27, 1940, Japanese envoy Saburo Kurusu signed the ten-year Tripartite Pact at the Chancellery in Berlin, making Japan the third member of the Axis Alliance. Yamamoto, who did not trust or even respect the Nazis and Hitler, knew the new alliance was of no value to Japan.

On that same day, Emperor Hirohito, in an attempt to put a good face on the matter, released a statement. "We certainly hope to bring about a cessation of hostilities, and the restoration of peace. Hence the government's decision to ally itself with Nazi Germany and Italy, nations that share the same good intentions as ourselves." Even allowing for the Japanese sovereign's insulation from the mainstream of political intrigue, it is incredible that Hirohito could have been so deluded.

In the meantime, things were moving fast in Europe. In May 1940, Germany began its drive into France. When France fell in June, a surrender was signed and a new fascist government formed. The Vichy French, under Marshal Philippe Pétain, negotiated with Japanese Foreign Minister Yasuke Matsuoka to work out the planned occupation of French Indochina by the Japanese Army.

Near the end of September 1940, just after the Battle of Britain had ended and the Blitz begun, Yamamoto was called to meet with Prime Minister Konoye. They discussed the worsening situation. The admiral updated Konoye on the current and future state of the navy and naval air arm. This was the one ray of light on the darkening horizon. Konoye, in his characteristically quiet and moderate voice, told his Combined Fleet commander that war with the United States was inevitable and would probably begin within a year.

There was a long pause in which Yamamoto considered his reply. Then he said, in clear and deliberate words, "If I am told to fight regardless of the consequences, I will run wild for the first six months or a year, but I have utterly no confidence in the second or third year."

Then he added, with his voice low and somber, "The Tripartite Pact has been concluded and we cannot help it. Now that the situation has come to this, I hope you will endeavor to avoid a Japanese-American war."

He had made his position clear, but Yamamoto had no confidence in Japan's political leaders. He well knew that Konoye did not want war with the U.S. but the prime minister did want his military forces to invade the Philippines and the Dutch East Indies.

In a letter to a fellow naval officer and friend, Yamamoto wrote that the way the ministries protested and wailed at the American economic pressure was like a spoiled boy who wanted instant gratification of his needs. He further stated that if Japan invaded Singapore and the Dutch East Indies, as the Imperial General Staff planned, it would lead directly to war with Great Britain, the Netherlands, and their ally, the United States, before those operations were half over.

He concluded that Japan "should not launch unless we are prepared." His last sentence was a harbinger of the future. "If war cannot be avoided, it would be best to decide on war with America from the beginning. This will lead to a war in which the nation's very fate will be at stake." Yamamoto was a patriot and devoted to his emperor. But above all, he was a pragmatist. He saw only destruction for Japan if the war began before he was ready.

On September 22, 1940, General Aketo Nakamura, not wanting to lose the element of surprise, ordered the Japanese 22nd Army to enter Indochina and cut the last remaining Chinese-controlled railroad to the coast.

In Washington, Secretary of State Cordell Hull reported the invasion to Roosevelt. The lines had been drawn. Germany was taking control of mainland Europe. Great Britain was standing alone. There seemed to be no stopping the Third Reich. Now Japan was moving south into China and preparing to invade French Indochina. In August, Roosevelt asked Congress to approve a $5 billion naval expansion bill. It would allow construction of new battleships, carriers, cruisers, destroyers, and a huge fleet of transports and tankers. He also began the nation's first peacetime draft and a call-up of all reservists.

To the Japanese prime minister, Roosevelt's move toward a larger navy and mandatory enlistment were aimed directly at Japan. Although Roosevelt was wary of Japanese military expansion in Asia, he was most concerned with supporting isolated Great Britain.

At this time Tokyo appointed a new ambassador to the United States, the sixty-four-year-old retired admiral Kichisaburo Nomura. Standing six feet tall with a soft, warm face behind round glasses, Nomura had a good reputation in Washington. As a naval attaché during the Great War, he became friendly with the then-Assistant Secretary of the Navy Franklin D. Roosevelt.

Before leaving for America, Nomura met with the newly reappointed Prime Minister Konoye and war minister Hideki Tojo. He asked them not to "expect miracles of him." He was well aware the right-wing expansionists and even the German ambassador in Tokyo had tried to block his appointment. Yet Konoye was willing to try anything to hold off a war with the United States. Tojo, with his fingers in the expansionist pie, wanted Nomura to buy time for Japan to increase its military strength before committing to a war.

American Ambassador Joseph Grew was also trying to defuse the worsening situation. He tried to convince Konoye not to commit to any future moves that could not be recalled. Grew, due to a hearing impairment, had never learned Japanese, a serious handicap. But he had good translators, and even his wife, Alice, sometimes served in that post. Alice Grew spoke perfect Japanese and had a personal connection to Japan. Her grandfather was Commodore Matthew Perry, who had forced Japan to open its borders in 1853.

Grew, a prolific diarist, wrote of his feelings at the time. "If any Americans who counsel appeasement were to read any of the current articles in leading Japanese magazines, wherein their real desires and intentions were given expression, they would realize the utter hopelessness of a policy of appeasement. We had better keep our powder dry and be ready for anything."

The next diplomatic move was a partial embargo of goods and materiel to Japan, including petroleum. Feeling backed into a corner, the prime minister wired Nomura to take the hard line and demand that all embargoes be lifted and that the United States recognize the newly conquered region in French Indochina and Manchuria and stop supporting Chiang Kai-shek.

But Cordell Hull was under equally rigid orders. Japan had to leave China and Indochina and pay restitution to the two nations, and cease preparations for aggressive moves in the Pacific.

The year 1941 began with Emperor Hirohito making his annual invocation for peace. But his hopes were already in vain. Forces both within and beyond the Japanese sovereign's control were moving forward, pulling the world closer to war in the Pacific. This was the year that Hitler would order his armies to invade the Soviet Union, when the Royal Air Force fould fight the Luftwaffe during the Blitz, and when the North Atlantic would become a rapidly growing graveyard for merchant ships and U-boats.

While half of the world was at war, the Pacific had yet to smell the smoke of battle. All of Micronesia, Manchuria, northern China, and Northern Indochina were occupied by the Japanese. But the warlords in the Imperial General Staff were not satisfied. They had their eyes on the Philippines, Malaya, the Dutch East Indies, and Singapore, all within the so-called "Greater East Asia Co-prosperity Sphere." The term denoted Japan's ultimate aim to control all of eastern Asia and the western Pacific from Alaska to Australia. The simple reason: raw materials and resources Japan did not naturally possess.

While the powerful Japanese army and navy were well up to the job of attacking, invading, and conquering each of those lands, there was no escaping the consequences. The Americans, British, Chinese, and Dutch would not fail to mount a vigorous response. Known as the "ABCD" nations, their own governments would decide what to do about Japan. Diplomacy would be the first step, followed by sanctions and embargoes, but sooner or later, the Japanese would have to deal with a military force.

With Great Britain and the Netherlands already under siege by Germany, China and the United States were left to deal with the increasing Japanese threat. Prime Minister Konoye had no reservations about expanding the empire's boundaries into China, French Indochina, and beyond. But he was anxious to avoid war with the United States. Nomura's job was to try and use diplomacy to defuse the growing enmity in the Pacific.

Ambassador Nomura and Secretary of State Cordell Hull were both veteran statesmen and dedicated to the subtle art of diplomacy. Both wanted to avoid war, but each had to carry out their orders. There was really no chance of a peaceful settlement. Neither side would or could give in, and even a compromise was unlikely. Nomura and Hull were the first warriors in a war not yet declared.

As it stood, the largest Allied naval fleet on the Pacific was the United States Navy, based in Bremerton, Washington; Alameda, Hunter's Point, San Pedro, and San Diego in California; and Pearl Harbor in Hawaii. The smaller Asiatic Fleet was based at Cavite near Manila in the Philippines. Great Britain had a naval and army presence in Singapore and Hong Kong, but the bulk of the Royal Navy was occupied with protecting the Home Islands and the Atlantic convoys from German U-boats. Along with the small Australian and Dutch Navies in the South Pacific and Java Sea, the United States would have to bear the greatest part of the load.

With every intent of carrying out their ambitious plans against the ABCD nations, Japan had to find a way to neutralize, damage, or destroy the U.S. Pacific Fleet. Only then could the invasions of the Philippines, Malaya, Singapore, and the Dutch East Indies be carried out without hinderance. This was the task Isoroku Yamamoto was facing as 1941 began. Ironically, the man most insistent on avoiding war with the United States was largely responsible for igniting that very war.

The idea of attacking Pearl Harbor was not new; he had considered it as far back as early 1940, but the prospect was far from solid. Many factors had to be taken into account. True, Pearl Harbor was 2,000 miles closer to Japan than the American naval bases on the West Coast, eliminating the need to cross the entire Pacific for the attack.

On January 26, Yamamoto, disgusted with the pro-war aims of the right-wing element in the government and army, wrote to a friend, "Should hostilities break out between Japan and the United States, it would not be enough that we take Guam and the Philippines, nor even Hawaii and San Francisco. To make victory certain, we would have to march into Washington and dictate terms in the White House."

To this he added, with a touch of his characteristically acerbic sarcasm, "I wonder if our politicians have confidence in the final outcome and are prepared to make the necessary sacrifices." This statement baldly showed his opinion that the United States was not a fragile house of cards that would be toppled with one push.

The right-wing jingoists published his statement but left out the final sentence. As published, Yamamoto was promising to dictate peace terms in the White House.

While it appeared to the uninformed that Japan, with its powerful army and navy, might invade California and march unopposed across the continental United States, no one in Washington took such a threat seriously. According to military historian and author Gordon Prange, Japan would have to land troops on the Pacific coast, march inland, push across mountains, deserts, and vast plains, fighting for every mile, and occupy Washington itself.

Such bombastic posturing aside, in early 1941, the key issue facing Yamamoto was throwing away the old fleet doctrine. The Imperial Navy had traditionally been a battleship navy, with cruisers and destroyers screening the larger ships while submarines scouted ahead to find and pick off enemy vessels. The warships would wait for an enemy force to come to them, somewhere near the Home Islands, where there were good lines of communication and support.

The enemy force, steaming farther and farther from its own bases and lines of supply, would be more vulnerable. It was the simple idea of setting a trap and luring the enemy into it to be destroyed. The two fleets would deploy into battle lines, the big guns trained out at the ships on the horizon. The same situation as at Trafalgar, Tsushima, and Jutland. The few surviving American ships would be hunted down and sunk by submarines.

There was little doubt among the senior officers that with the huge new battleships coming down the ways, a major victory at sea was certain.

But Yamamoto knew better. He was not, at heart, a defensive tactician. The old plan was a defensive one. He had to find a way to support two objectives. First, to have forces available to move south to the Philippines and Dutch East Indies, and secondly, to protect the navy's left flank from an American attack. Even now, Japan did not have enough surface warships to do both jobs. The only solution was air power. Having been deeply involved in expanding and improving the naval air arm, Yamamoto was keenly intent on using the new fast carriers.

He would move the axis of attack from the Home Island to the Hawaiian Islands. This would force the United States Navy to come out and defend their base. This was the only way the Japanese fleet could overwhelm the enemy. If war had to come, Yamamoto was determined to force the issue and fight the Americans on his own terms.

The man who originally proposed the idea of an air attack on Pearl Harbor to Yamamoto in 1940 was Rear Admiral Jisaburo Ozawa, considered to be the best air fleet commander in Japan's navy. He supported the concept of massing the carriers into one large task force. But in 1940, it was still too radical and disruptive to the Imperial Navy's organization.

As to when Yamamoto first proposed the idea of striking Pearl Harbor, the best sources are the writings of Vice Admiral Shigeru Fukudome, who served as Yamamoto's chief of staff between November 1939 and April 1941. Fukudome, a true asset to the commander in chief, was respected at all levels. He later said Yamamoto first suggested the idea of attacking Pearl Harbor around April 1940. By that summer it was apparent that the naval air force had reached a level of efficiency that made such an audacious move feasible. Dropping aerial torpedoes on ships in a harbor seemed a likely way to sink and damage a fleet in a protected anchorage. Fukudome once heard Yamamoto murmuring to himself about whether aerial torpedoes could be used in Pearl Harbor.

While Fukudome did not put much stock in his superior's musings, he was aware that the Naval General Staff had often used an attack on Hawaii as part of its annual war games. But nothing came of it as the idea was considered preposterous.

By December 1940, almost exactly a year before the Day of Infamy, Yamamoto decided an aerial attack on the American naval base on Oahu was the only key to success.

Yamamoto continued to press a higher level of attack training on his carrier crews and pilots. The seed of the idea took root. He envisioned a task force made up of several ships around a core of carriers. For the past decade, carriers had been singly assigned to each fleet, providing aerial defense against enemy planes and ships. Yamamoto wanted to use the carriers in an offensive role, to attack far ahead of the task force. Pearl Harbor would be the perfect target for just such a pioneering task force. It would have to be a surprise attack, a problem for which Yamamoto had no immediate solution.

But he did have a precedent to consider. The Italian Regia Marina had based its First Battle Squadron in Taranto, a deep-water harbor in the sole of the Italian boot. In November 1940, the Royal Navy, wary of dictator Benito Mussolini's alliance with Germany, planned an aerial attack on the harbor. Generally there were five battleships, seven heavy cruisers, two light cruisers, and at least eight destroyers moored in the deep water.

A single carrier, *Illustrious*, launched twenty-four Fairey Swordfish biplane torpedo planes at the Italian fleet. It was a small force, but it inflicted severe damage to three battleships, one heavy cruiser, and two destroyers. Two of the British planes were shot down. The surviving ships were pulled out of Taranto and moved to a safe location, where they remained for the rest of the war.

The attack on Taranto gave Yamamoto plenty to think about. This was solid proof that an aerial strike could succeed. But he also knew that unlike Taranto, Pearl Harbor was only about forty feet deep. Any air-dropped torpedo would plunge to nearly seventy feet before rising to its preset striking depth.

In need of an informed opinion, Yamamoto had Fukudome present the idea to Admiral Takijiro Onishi, who had a skill for finding the important factors in any operation. Onishi was something of an intellectual, having published *The Ethics of the Imperial Navy* in 1938. History would mark Onishi as the father of the kamikaze in 1944.

Onishi read over Yamamoto's proposal and gave it serious thought. But neither he nor Yamamoto had the authority to initiate operational plans. That was the purview of the Naval General Staff, whose officers were, on the whole, in favor of a debilitating strike on Hawaii.

But Yamamoto's status in the navy was such that no one challenged his operational concept. He wrote to the new navy minister, Admiral Koshiro

Oikawa, that the Imperial Navy should "fiercely attack and destroy the American main fleet at the outset of the war, so the morale of the U.S. Navy and her people would sink to the extent that it could not be recovered."

He went on to say an attack should be made on the American air forces and navy in the Philippines at the same time. "The enemy's untrained forces' morale would sink to such an extent that they could scarcely be of any use."

It is amazing that the man who knew and respected the United States so well should be so completely wrong about the spirit of the American public.

With Onishi and Fukudome in his inner circle, Yamamoto left it in their hands. In February, Onishi sent a message to the staff officer for air aboard the carrier *Kaga*, Commander Minoru Genda, who was undoubtedly the best air officer in the navy. He would soon become the most crucial link in the chain that led to Pearl Harbor.

Upon reaching the headquarters of the Eleventh Air Fleet, Genda met with Onishi. He both liked and admired the admiral and needed no encouragement to look over the proposal.

After reading the operational concept, Genda nodded, and said, "It is difficult, but not impossible."

From that point on, Genda was the key figure in planning the attack.

Commander Minoru Genda, born in 1904 near Hiroshima, possessed dark, piercing eyes and a superb analytical mind. The man who would help plan the most critical naval operation in Japan's history seemed destined for the role. He earned his pilot's wings in 1929, graduating at the top of his class. After six years of posts in several air assignments, Genda was, by 1935, considered Japan's top fighter pilot, and soon became the most respected fighter instructor in the navy. He formed an aerobatic unit known across the country as "Genda's Flying Circus."

He was known for being daring and even reckless in the air, the kind of gambler who would put everything on one roll of the dice. In this he was kin to Yamamoto. They had become acquainted aboard the carrier *Riyjo* in 1933, when Yamamoto was a division commander. They found they shared an equally progressive view of naval air power.

Genda had much in common with General Billy Mitchell and General Julio Douhet, the most outspoken advocates of strategic air power in the 1920s. The American and Italian believed that large, long-range, multi-engine bombers were the ultimate projectors of national policy. Back in 1924, not long after proving that aircraft could sink capital ships, Mitchell had stated, "It is the nation that has vision enough to see new weapons before war has shown its need that will win." That was Genda's aim.

Ever since the Imperial Navy began adding carriers to the fleet, the role of fighters had been only for defense. In common with the United States Navy, the Japanese considered the aircraft carrier the "eyes of the fleet." They were to fly patrol over the task force, never venturing beyond the horizon. The dive and torpedo bombers—the striking power—would leave the fleet behind and fly unescorted to attack land targets or enemy ships. Genda, who never hid his light beneath a bushel, scorned this practice. "What good is a bomber that does not reach its target?" He advocated that only a few fighters remain with the fleet, while the others escorted and protected the bombers. This would also have the advantage of securing the air over the target, in what today is called air superiority.

He was not alone in this view. Yamamoto was in full agreement. "The idea of using fighters in a purely defensive role is wrong," he said to some of Genda's detractors.

When Genda was appointed to the Yokosuka Air Corps in 1934, he found fertile ground for his theories, which soon became known as "Gendaisms."

He strongly supported Yamamoto's plans to introduce new fighters and bombers to the navy. Five years before designer Jiro Horikoshi designed the vaunted Mitsubishi A6M Zero, Genda said that fighters must be fast and maneuverable.

But Genda was not through. He further suggested the Imperial Navy should be reduced to four classes of ships: carriers, submarines, cruisers, and destroyers. All the battleships then under construction should be converted to carriers, and the rest scrapped. He openly said the new super battleships *Yamato* and *Musashi*, still on the way and slated for commissioning in late 1941, were "the China Wall of the Imperial Navy."

In 1921 General Billy Mitchell had proven that even the old Martin MB-2 biplane bombers could sink battleships. And like the petulant Mitchell, Genda did not suffer fools gladly. He was short with those who disagreed with him, especially the supporters and members of the "Big-Gun Club," the battleship faction. Some even thought him insane.

But Genda had the ear and support of the commander in chief.

After graduating with honors from the Naval Staff College, Genda was posted to the Second Combined Air Corps in China. This was a cooperative unit made up of army and navy flyers. There he gained valuable combat experience flying the Mitsubishi A5M Type 96 fighter, the predecessor of the Zero. From there he was assigned as naval attaché in London, where he saw the opening moves of the Second World War. He was in London during the first days of the Battle of Britain and made note of how the German Luftwaffe and Royal Air Force fought the air war.

In November 1940, he returned to Japan and, upon being promoted to full commander, was assigned to the First Air Fleet. This was to be his post for the next three years.

Even while working in the post of First Air Fleet air officer, Genda was constantly studying the tactics of carrier operations. The Imperial Navy's standard practice of assigning a single carrier to each task force for defense wasted the potential of a great striking force. He advocated having six carriers for every operational sortie, giving the task force a considerable offensive punch. Six carriers could launch as many as a hundred bombers with about thirty fighters for escort and ground suppression.

With his mentors Yamamoto and Onishi behind him, Genda slowly changed the way the Japanese used their carriers. When Onishi told him that Yamamoto was eager to sink as many American battleships as possible, Genda had other opinions.

The key target of the attack should be the United States Pacific Fleet's aircraft carriers. He strongly pushed the idea that the Japanese task force should get as close to Oahu as possible in order to launch more than one attack wave. This was Genda's mantra: "strike, strike again, and keep striking until the enemy is totally destroyed."

In Hawaii, even as Yamamoto and Onishi laid out the early concept of an attack on Pearl Harbor, a new commander in chief of the U.S. Pacific Fleet was taking command. Vice Admiral Husband E. Kimmel stood on the quarterdeck of the battleship *Pennsylvania* on the warm and clear Saturday morning of February 1. With sixteen other flag officers, division and ship commanders, Kimmel read the orders to take over from Vice Admiral James O. Richardson.

Then, with his large blue eyes glowing under the peak of his white cap, he said in a Kentucky drawl, "I can say only this. That it shall be my personal motto to guide the fleet at the highest level of efficiency and preparedness. And I will attempt to carry this to the best of my ability."

Anyone who knew and worked with Kimmel had no doubt he would keep his word. He was known and respected for his absolute devotion to his duty. He did not care for "yes men," and took pains to see that every department aboard the ships he commanded performed beyond the standards of the navy. With Kimmel, the term "shipshape and Bristol fashion" was the only way to go, from the lowliest steward to the commanders of battleship divisions.

The U.S. Pacific Fleet had long been based in San Diego, but in May 1940, at the same time France was falling to Blitzkrieg, the fleet was moved, lock, stock, and barrel, more than 2,000 miles southwest to the green and lush island of Oahu.

Pearl Harbor was an excellent sheltered harbor on the south coast of the island. It had been under more or less constant construction and upgrade since the early years of the century. Admiral Richardson, who had commanded the U.S. Fleet since early 1940, had made the mistake of questioning and resisting the orders from the White House regarding the disposition of the fleet. He firmly believed Pearl Harbor was at risk and the fleet should return to California.

Secretary of the Navy Frank Knox, who was in Roosevelt's inner circle, relieved Richardson of command and personally told him, "You hurt the president's feelings."

Knox reached down the list of flag officers to find Vice Admiral Husband Kimmel, one of the most experienced officers in the navy. He was considered an excellent leader and an expert in naval gunnery. Even though he had never served on carriers, he trusted their value and striking power.

Admiral Kimmel was the commander in chief of the United States Fleet, or, in one of the most unfortunate acronyms, CINCUS, pronounced "sink us." He was the senior uniformed officer in command of over a million tons of ships in three oceans. Later, the Pacific, Atlantic, and Asiatic fleets would be divided into separate commands, whereupon Kimmel would be made commander in chief of the Pacific Fleet, or CINCPAC.

That sunny Saturday morning, dressed in spotless tropical whites with gleaming gold braid on his epaulets, Kimmel surveyed his new command. The United States Pacific Fleet had nearly a hundred ships of all types at Pearl. Four battleship divisions, more of heavy and light cruisers, four carriers, flotillas of destroyers and destroyer escorts, minelayers and minesweepers, submarine squadrons, tenders, oilers, and a dozen other types crowded the lochs and anchorages. While the numbers changed with ships returning to Bremerton and San Diego for refitting, Kimmel commanded the most powerful Pacific fleet and naval base.

Three days later, another new officer came to Hawaii, aboard the Matson liner SS *Matsonia*. Major General Walter C. Short, the new commander of the Hawaiian Department, walked down the gangway to meet the officers of his new command. While Kimmel looked the part of a navy admiral, Short looked more like an accountant—slim, bookish, and hard-eyed. But his ability, experience, and dedication were unquestioned. Having served in the United States Army since 1902, the Illinois-born Short had served in posts all over the United States, from Fort Sill, Oklahoma, to the Presidio in San Francisco. He was sent to Mexico with Pershing and fought with First Corps in France, specializing in crew-served weapons like machine guns and anti-aircraft artillery (AAA). A line officer throughout his career, Short was efficient but not known for being a hard worker. He did his job and expected his subordinates to do theirs.

At a ceremony at the Hawaiian Department Headquarters at Fort Shafter, Short took command and was promoted to lieutenant general. From the start, Short knew his primary duty was the protection of the Pacific Fleet at Pearl Harbor and the defense of the Hawaiian Islands. He would also oversee the shuttling of multi-engine bombers from the mainland to the Philippines.

But when he began to discuss those three requirements with his staff, Short found that his department was undermanned and under-equipped. The army in Hawaii had been infused with newly trained draftees from the States. To add to his concerns, Short was told by Secretary of War Henry Stimson that while there were plans to send fighter planes and AAA batteries to Hawaii, there was no mention of when they would arrive.

Among the defenses Stimson promised were mobile radar units. These would arrive in June. It would be up to Short and his air officers to make use of this new technology and train the men to work them.

Shortly after assuming command, Short received a letter from Army Chief of Staff George C. Marshall, one of the most respected officers in the country. Marshall, keeping his finger on the pulse of the diplomatic negotiations and the current state of the nation's preparedness, wrote, "Our first concern is to protect the fleet. My impression of the Hawaiian problem has been that no serious harm is done us during the first six hours of known hostilities, thereafter the existing defenses would discourage an enemy against the hazards of an attack."

These words would come back to haunt Marshall. In the first six minutes of war with Japan, Yamamoto's bombs would virtually cripple the Pacific Fleet.

Marshall felt that sabotage and submarine attack were more to be feared and guarded against than an air strike. He believed there was no real chance of a carrier task force being sent to Hawaii. His view was that Short's air forces would discourage any air attack or landing.

Short agreed. Sabotage would become the most serious threat. Hawaii was home to more than 160,000 Japanese, about a third of whom were born in Japan.

Marshall further told Short to do his utmost to work on a cordial basis with Kimmel and the navy. The long-standing rivalry between the United States Army and Navy went far beyond the annual academy football game. Competing for budgets and equipment, there were deeply rooted resentments between the services, particularly in peacetime. But Short had already met with Kimmel, and they found a mutually friendly working and personal relationship. This would continue for the rest of the year.

Regarding his concerns about protecting his planes at Wheeler and Hickam Army Air Bases, Short inquired with the army engineers about bunker protection for the fighters and bombers. Concrete or sandbag revetments would prevent enemy planes from destroying the entire air force. The cost would be about $1.6 million, which was minimal considering the cost of the planes.

Kimmel and Short had their work cut out for them. But they would soon find the situation in Hawaii was not static.

In Japan, Admiral Onishi met with Yamamoto to discuss Genda's suggestions. They read over the pages, which enumerated the most important points:

- The attack must be a total surprise.
- The U.S. aircraft carriers must be the primary targets.
- The airfields and land-based aircraft must be destroyed on the ground.
- Every available carrier should be included in the task force.
- The attack should make use of level bombers, torpedo bombers, and dive bombers.
- Fighters should provide cover for the task force and with the strike force.
- The attack should be made at dawn to ensure accurate bombing.
- Refueling at sea will be necessary.
- Battleships will be of no help and only increase the fuel expenditure.
- All planning must be done in the strictest secrecy.

Genda pulled no punches, his views on the battleships being a good example. Yamamoto had the nucleus of the Pearl Harbor attack plan by March. For the next five months, he and his growing team worked out the route, timetable, communications, at-sea refueling, and which ships would be used. Working with the intelligence assets in Hawaii, they determined when the battleships and cruisers left port, how long they remained at sea, and where they moored. Photographic reconnaissance established the various areas in Pearl Harbor where the navy yard, repair facilities, and submarine base were located. More intelligence told them where the major airfields were located and what defenses were in place. Oahu had many targets for consideration, and nearly all had to be destroyed or at least neutralized.

The first problem that had to be addressed was what Yamamoto had known since November 1940. After a dredging operation to accommodate deep-draft battleships in the 1920s, Pearl Harbor's waters averaged about forty feet deep. But dropping a 2,000-pound torpedo from an altitude of 300 feet caused the torpedo to dive to at least 70 feet before leveling out. They'd have to try something new.

There was no doubt that an aerial torpedo attack on the moored battle fleet would cause the most destruction. Torpedoes had one major advantage over bombs. As military historian John Keegan put it, "water transmits shock far better than air. The incompressibility of liquid creates a 'water hammer' effect that drives the full force of the detonation to the target's hull."

The Type 91 aerial torpedo had been in service since 1931, one of a family of excellent weapons for submarines, midget subs, and aircraft. During the summer of 1941, the Type 91 would undergo serious revisions.

As for the high-level bombers, they would be armed with armor-piercing bombs modified from battleship shells. Dropped from an altitude of 12,000 feet, they would reach nearly the speed of sound in the fall, which ensured that the heavy bomb would penetrate deck armor and explode deep within the bowels of a ship.

The only point Genda did not succeed in promoting was his post-attack plan. He advocated following up the attack with an amphibious landing to take Oahu. He believed that taking Hawaii would drive the Americans back to the mainland, and Japan would have an excellently equipped forward base to anchor the empire's eastern flank.

But this plan fell on deaf ears, even those of Yamamoto. He knew an amphibious operation entailed many more ships, most of which were earmarked for southern operations. It would also require a very long supply line from Japan, which would need surface ship escorts sailing under the constant threat of submarine attack.

During the first week in April, Yamamoto shifted his flag to the battleship *Mutsu* while *Nagato* was undergoing refit. April would be a full month for the Japanese and Americans. On *Mutsu*, Yamamoto met with two officers: Captain Tomiko Kuroshima and Commander Yasuki Watanabe. He presented the Onishi-Genda plan to the officers and waited for their response. Kuroshima, whose quiet and introspective manner earned him the nickname "Gandhi," was Yamamoto's senior operations staff officer.

One of the issues under discussion was the torpedoes. So far, no means had been devised to make them work in the shallow Pearl Harbor waters. And the torpedoes were the most important weapons in the planned attack scheme. This was a serious obstacle, but he was not about to abandon it without every effort being made to find solutions. That was where Kuroshima and Watanabe, a member of his staff, came in.

The commander of the Combined Fleet was empowered to draw up plans for an operation handed down from the Naval General Staff, the opposite of how an operation was normally handled. To explain, the Imperial Navy was divided into three main elements: Navy Ministry, Naval General Staff, and Combined Fleet. Their responsibilities, according to Gordon Prange in *Miracle at Midway*, were totally separate. The ministry oversaw the budget, ship construction, weapons procurement, and personnel, and acted as liaison with the cabinet, while the Naval General Staff concerned itself with operation of the fleet, logistics, and preparation of war plans. The Combined Fleet's job was to devise, plan, and carry out operations approved by the General Staff. In the case of the Pearl Harbor attack, Yamamoto first conceived the idea and intended to have a fully developed plan in place before presenting it to the Navy Ministry and General Staff.

Kuroshima and Watanabe were tasked with studying the operation and finding solutions before drawing up the actual details to be presented to the Navy Ministry. The Naval General Staff's role would be to oversee the operation once it was approved.

Kuroshima divided Yamamoto's staff into four groups: operations and supply, communications and information, navigation and meteorology, and lastly, air and submarine attack.

On April 10, the Imperial Navy formed the First Air Fleet that included two carrier divisions, an unprecedented change in its standard organization. The First Carrier Division included the *Akagi* and *Kaga*, while the Second Carrier Divison included the newer *Soryu* and *Hiryu*, the latter under Admiral Tamon Yamaguchi from the Second Fleet. The First Air Fleet initially consisted of *Akagi* and *Kaga*, each of 26,500 tons, which carried about a hundred planes and a crew of two thousand. *Soryu* and *Hiryu*, both launched in 1937, displaced about 20,000 tons.

This was a major step toward Genda's dream of forming an all-carrier task force. But there was opposition, primarily from Admiral Mineichi Koga, commander of Second Fleet. He was a battleship commander and said that removing *Soryu* and *Hiryu* from the fleet would deprive his big-gun ships of air cover. He was of course adhering to the old doctrine that carriers should defend the fleet.

On the same day the First Air Fleet was formed, Admiral Osami Nagano was appointed chief of the Naval General Staff. He was the senior uniformed officer in the Imperial Navy. Like Yamamoto, he had once been navy minister and commander of the Combined Fleet. Nagano inherited the navy at the very point where war with the United States was all but imminent. Also, like Yamamoto, he spoke English and had enjoyed his five years in America. Nagano wielded the power of approving or killing any operational plan.

Also on that fateful day of April 10, Admiral Shigeru Fukudome was reassigned to the Naval General Staff. In his role, he had the power to influence the General Staff. And being right from Yamamoto's inner circle, he was in a position to see the Pearl Harbor attack plan moved ahead.

In his place was Rear Admiral Seiichi Ito. A tall, handsome officer who would die in the fatal suicide charge of the battleship *Yamato* in April 1945, Ito was let in on the Pearl Harbor plan almost immediately. Conservative by nature, Ito had reservations but followed his orders to coordinate the Combined Fleet staff in their duties.

Now that the new First Air Fleet had been formed, it needed a commander.

It was a given among the officers of the new unit that the man who would command it had to be someone who knew how to command aircraft carriers and airmen. But the navy's seniority policy meant only one man could be assigned to command the new air fleet.

Enter Vice Admiral Chuichi Nagumo, a name that would become second only to Yamamoto in the minds of the United States Navy in the coming years. In contemporary photos he appears in full bemedaled and braided uniform, his face under a bullet-shaped dome showing an intense look of concentration. He could easily be mistaken for a Japanese Bull Halsey, but Nagumo was a quiet and gentle man. He treated his subordinates with kindness and gave them his full support.

It is interesting to note that although Nagumo had no prior connection with naval aviation, he would be the most effective and longest-serving Japanese carrier admiral during the Second World War.

Nagumo and Yamamoto were far from friends, although they maintained a civil working relationship. To offset Nagumo's lack of carrier experience, Rear Admiral Ryanosuke Kusaka was assigned as his chief of staff. One of the most pragmatic officers in the IJN, Kusaka was the perfect man to guide Nagumo through his new command.

It was Kusaka who was first informed about the planned attack on Pearl Harbor, and he briefed the new First Air Fleet commander. When Nagumo heard this, his reaction was negative. He was astounded that the commander in chief, whom he had always admired for his sagacity and calm command, would even consider such a preposterous idea. He pondered the absurdity and impossibility of sailing a large task force more than 2,500 miles across the open Pacific under radio silence, coordinating at-sea refueling, avoiding enemy air patrols, and arriving in the right place near Hawaii at the exact moment specified by the plan. Nagumo would resist the operation right up to the last moment.

Kusaka believed the operational planning would break down during refueling, which had never been done on such a scale, and early trials were plagued with problems. The entire round-trip voyage between Japan and Hawaii was nearly 6,000 miles long. Every ship, whether destroyer or carrier, had differing characteristics in handling and speed. The slow oilers would have to accompany the task force to within a few hundred miles of Hawaii and wait for the warships to return. Anything could go wrong—accidental ramming in poor weather could end the entire venture.

On April 10, the very day the IJN formed the First Air Fleet and Yamamoto met with his new chief of staff, Roosevelt met with four members of his cabinet: Secretaries Frank Knox of the Navy Department, Henry Stimson of the War Department, Cordell Hull of the State Department, and Henry Morgenthau of the Treasury Department.

Roosevelt was under considerable pressure from two sides. On the one hand was the solid block of the America First isolationists, with its popular spokesman Charles Lindbergh. The group believed Great Britain was doomed to fall to the Nazis, and to assist them in any way was a waste of money and materiel. Roosevelt also had to appease the Senate and Congress, who were eager to keep the nation from moving closer to war. He was being vilified by the Republicans in the House and Senate, along with papers like the isolationist *Chicago Tribune*, run by "Colonel" Robert McCormick, who were looking for any excuse to accuse Roosevelt of driving the nation into war. Lindbergh, along with most of the isolationists, believed that the two vast oceans were more than enough of a buffer to keep the warring world at bay.

"What more could we ask than to have the Atlantic on the east and the Pacific on the west," Lindbergh said in one speech. "An ocean is a formidable barrier, even to modern aircraft."

This was one of the aviator's most shortsighted predictions, especially in light of his own achievement in spanning the Atlantic by air a decade earlier. He should have known better.

The topic under discussion was how to support Great Britain's desperate attempts to protect the vital Atlantic convoys. The Royal Navy was stretched to its breaking point to keep the sea lanes open between North America and Europe. Using everything from destroyers to battleships, they fought Hitler's deadly U-boats all the way across the vast sea. Roosevelt wanted to find a way to assist without breaking the neutrality laws. The idea was to draw a line running north and south from a point exactly halfway between Brazil and Africa. The line cut the Atlantic in nearly equal halves. The United States Atlantic Fleet, under the command of Vice Admiral Ernest J. King, would patrol the western Atlantic, find the U-boats, and report their location to the Royal Navy. While simple in concept, it would require many more ships than the Atlantic Fleet had. Essentially, the United States had to cover two oceans with a one-ocean navy. Roosevelt had gotten Congress to approve a $5 billion bill to expand the navy, but there would be no substantial result for at least another year.

Roosevelt had also gotten Congress to approve a half billion dollars to increase the army and air corps, but it was a drop in the bucket compared to what would be needed. The $50 million of that amount allocated to the Air Corps would increase its air strength in fighters and bombers, from 5,500 to 6,000 aircraft, and none, not even the new Curtiss P-40B Tomahawk, were equal to those already fighting in the skies over Europe.

During that historic meeting between Roosevelt and select cabinet secretaries, four points were agreed upon:

- Germany is the primary and most dangerous enemy.
- The focus of the U.S. Navy should be on helping Great Britain defeat Germany.
- If Japan opens a war in the Pacific, it will be on the defensive.
- The existing U.S. Pacific Fleet should operate offensively and destroy Japan's economic infrastructure.

The second and third points are indicative of the still-prevalent view that the Japanese Navy was not strong enough or capable of being a serious threat to the United States. Japan would only attack weaker and unprotected Pacific nations.

But the main point, that the Atlantic needed ships, meant Admiral Kimmel's fleet was the only source.

Admiral Harold Stark, chief of naval operations, wrote to Kimmel that he believed the situation in the Atlantic was dire, but in the Pacific, the Japanese "looks a trifle easier to manage." Then he added, "I have had several long talks with Admiral Nomura, and unless I am completely fooled, he earnestly desires to avert a crisis with us."

Stark believed Ambassador Nomura was sincere in his attempts to soothe the rising tensions between the two nations. But he had no way of knowing that

Nomura's real job, which even Nomura himself did not know, was to buy time while his nation prepared for war.

Stark went on to tell Kimmel the current situation in the Atlantic would "not even see the British through to the end of the year, if that." He directed Kimmel to prepare a force to be sent to the Atlantic, consisting of, in part, the battleships *New Mexico*, *Idaho*, and *Mississippi*. A carrier, preferably *Lexington*, was also to be detached. Along with a flotilla of destroyers and auxiliary ships, the force was to be sent in small groups to avoid attracting undue attention. Of course, any capital ships passing through the Panama Canal would be noted in both Berlin and Tokyo.

Stark realized the effect this would have on CINCPAC's strength, but the German U-boat threat took precedence. Roosevelt wanted to prevent any suggestion that the Pacific Fleet was being weakened, so he pared down the initial detachment to the carrier *Yorktown* and five destroyers. But that was only the beginning. Kimmel keenly felt the loss of every ship, but he followed his orders. The Pacific Fleet was insufficient to protect the Philippines, more than 5,000 miles away and on the far side of the Japanese-held Mandate Islands.

Fortunately the protection of Hawaii was the job of the U.S. Army under General Walter Short. His bombers were considered to be the best long-range force to find and sink any Japanese force approaching Hawaii. Army Chief of Staff General George C. Marshall believed the growing force of Boeing B-17 Flying Fortresses was more than a match for any enemy naval task force. Marshall undoubtedly took this view from Billy Mitchell. But as time would reveal, the use of high-level bombers to sink fast-moving ships only resulted in wasted fuel and bombs.

A message from Prime Minister Winston Churchill's cabinet on or about May 8, stated, "the removal of capital ships from the Pacific would actually be a deterrence to any Japanese intent to go to war." This astonishing opinion was based on the idea that coordination and cooperation in the Tokyo-Berlin Alliance was much stronger than it really was. Supposedly, sending ships to the Atlantic would prompt Germany to tell Japan to avoid provoking the United States into war. Unlike the close cooperation between Great Britain and America, Japan had no intention of being led by Pied Piper Hitler. The Naval General Staff was not about to tailor its fleet deployments to support Germany, no matter the terms of the Tripartite Pact.

Meanwhile the Japanese were bombing Rangoon in Burma, at the end of the vital Burma Road from India. The route brought supplies, weapons, and materiel to the Nationalist Army and the British colonies at Malaya. The bombing of a helpless city and the disruption of the route led Chiang Kai-shek to petition the United States for aid in the form of pilots and aircraft to defend the city. This led President Roosevelt to sign the approval for forming the American Volunteer Group, or AVG, which became famous as the Flying Tigers. Roosevelt called the unorthodox measure a "guard duty to keep the Japanese from swallowing up all of Asia." The more than 300 pilots and mechanics who joined the AVG were Navy, Marine, and Air Corps personnel who gave up their commissions to join under the authority of the Chinese Air Force. They were to defend Rangoon and the Burma Road from Japanese bombing raids. By the time the three AVG squadrons were formed in China, Pearl Harbor had been attacked, changing their mission to one of attack as well as defense.

During the summer of 1941, Kimmel oversaw the detachment of three transports, three oilers, and ten auxiliary ships. The battleships *New Mexico*, *Idaho*, and *Mississippi*, the carrier *Yorktown*, four light cruisers, and seventeen destroyers went to the Atlantic. This was about a quarter of his entire fleet—ironically more ships than would be lost on December 7.

This did not go unnoticed in Tokyo. Lieutenant Takeo Yoshikawa, an IJN intelligence officer, had been in Hawaii since March, having arrived with the new Consul General Nagao Kita on board the liner *Nitta Maru*. Masquerading as a Japanese consulate clerk named Tadashi Morimura, he had been traveling around Oahu in taxis and chartered planes and watching from the hills around the navy and army bases. He wrote detailed messages transmitted via the consulate to the Naval General Staff. His reports detailed the number and types of ships in the harbor along with their disposition, deployment schedules, and other important facts. He noted the departure of *Yorktown* and the three battleships, and saw there were fewer cruisers than during the previous week. His messages, transmitted in the diplomatic Purple Code, were read by Naval Intelligence in Washington. They were soon being called the "Bomb Plot" messages.

To anyone reading these reports, the IJN was anxious to know as much about the U.S. Fleet disposition and strength as possible. More reports listed the number of planes on the Army air bases of Hickam, Bellows, and Wheeler, as well as the patrol schedule.

But nothing was done. Yoshikawa continued to send his reports right up to the first few days in December.

In mid-June, Kimmel was called to Washington to confer with Stark. Feeling this was his opportunity to lay out his concerns, Kimmel went with the evidence of how vulnerable to attack Pearl Harbor was. Kimmel explained that the single channel meant it would take at least three hours for his battleships and cruisers to clear the harbor in case of an air attack. These points were well founded, and showed that Kimmel was aware of the risks and his ability to deal with them.

To Stark, this may have sounded like the ghosts of admirals past, as Richardson had voiced these same concerns in January. But Kimmel did not suggest sending the fleet back to California. He accepted the need to keep the fleet in Hawaii.

He was "prepared to consider a war in offensive terms." If there was a war with Japan, Kimmel was ready, even eager to sortie from Pearl and meet Yamamoto in battle. The closer to Japan the Pacific Fleet met the enemy, the better.

Kimmel met Roosevelt on June 9 at the White House. While their discussion was amicable, he was put off by the president's effusive reaction. As mentioned, Kimmel did not like "yes men," and Roosevelt was far too mollifying for such a serious subject.

Roosevelt told his Pacific Fleet commander that Cordell Hull was meeting with Japanese diplomats, but the president did not provide any information on the ongoing negotiations. This was odd, since FDR was not holding back with King or even MacArthur.

Then the president asked Kimmel if he thought he could manage with only three battleships, as Stark had apparently suggested.

Kimmel lost his temper. "That's crazy! That would be a perfect invitation for Japan to attack." Kimmel was under the delusion that the number of battleships was what was keeping Yamamoto in his home waters.

Kimmel asked Roosevelt if the Pacific Fleet might have the new battleships *Washington* and *North Carolina*, which had just been commissioned into the navy. Their nine 16-inch main guns and modern radar suites were state of the art. Roosevelt did not commit to the new ships, but he did affirm that he had no intention of detaching any more capital ships from Hawaii to the Atlantic.

This was a great relief to CINCPAC. The loss of *Yorktown* alone had cut his carrier force by a third. The detachments of three oilers forced him to keep the fleet close to Pearl. With full tanks, the old battleships had a radius of 2,000 miles from base, which fell far short of the Philippines. As Kimmel left, he felt that FDR was doing a lot of wishful thinking.

Then another watershed event occurred in Europe. Hitler threw away the Molotov-Ribbentrop Pact of nonaggression and invaded the Soviet Union on June 22. This was another reason, according to the Atlantic Fleet commanders, to pull more ships from Hawaii. It was just as well Kimmel was not present in Washington when this happened.

That day marked the moment when the United States became the sole major neutral nation.

As for Japan, the attack on Soviet Russia had a deteriorating effect on its relations with Germany. In view of the obvious racist attitude of Nazi Germany, the Axis Alliance between Japan and Germany had always been an abnormal one. The Japanese and Germans had only one thing in common: They both believed they were the chosen people and racially superior to all other peoples.

On July 26 the U.S. State Department received a revealing message from the prime minister of Thailand. He had been talking with the German military attaché in Bangkok, who had warned him against any serious alliance with Japan. "You cannot trust Japan. Germany would settle with Japan after they had won the war in Europe." This was an indicator that there was no honor among fascists. But like so many other diplomatic events, it remained under wraps.

In Japan, the First Air Fleet was reaching its expected level of readiness. Since June, Genda had been working with the torpedo plane crews. This was his first priority, since the torpedo strike was most critical to success and required the most extensive training. He chose Kagoshima Bay on the southern coast of Kyushu for this purpose. The bay was roughly the same size and shape as Pearl Harbor, even though most of the features were volcanic and reached higher elevations. He wanted to give the pilots a chance to fly over confined waters, just as they would have to do at Oahu. The city of Kagoshima, with its buildings and tall smokestacks, would provide the pilots the kind of tight confines they would experience coming over the navy yard on the eastern side of Pearl.

From June and into the late summer, the Nakajima bombers swooped low over the city, rattling windows all through the daylight hours. They dropped dummy torpedoes and evaluated the result. The IJN had yet to find a way to slow their fall into the water.

Back in 1939, the designers at the Yokosuka Naval Base had experimented with variants of wooden fins on the torpedoes, which slowed the weapon's entry into the water to where it only fell to about fifty feet. But it retarded the torpedo's impact. Further tests, combined with a lower release altitude, reduced the depth to roughly forty feet, the maximum depth to allow using them in Pearl Harbor.

Genda wanted no more than ten meters, about thirty feet. He was the only officer who knew the reason. Testing a release at forty feet showed mixed results. While dropping so low prevented the torpedo from driving itself into the mud of the harbor bottom, it required the pilots, in less than twenty seconds, to maneuver the heavily loaded planes around land installations and line up at a dangerously low altitude before pulling the torpedo release.

But the torpedo bombers were only a part of Genda's complications. His high-level bombers also used the Nakajima B5N and would be dropping bombs on the armored decks of battleships. Dive bombers were inadequate for the task. During testing at Kasumigaura, it had been established that an armor-piercing bomb had to weigh at least 800 kilograms, nearly a ton, in order to penetrate thick deck armor. The navy would provide 16-inch shells from the *Nagato*-class battleships. These were cylindrical with an angle to the warhead. Now fitted with fins and having the body ground down to make it more streamlined, and then dropped from about ten to twelve thousand feet, the explosives would penetrate thick armor plate. They were designated Type 99 No. 80-3 aerial bomb, and carried about forty pounds of high explosive. They were the first specialized weapons to be created specifically for the Pearl Harbor attack.

As for accuracy, the early results were poor, with only about 10 percent of bombs hitting their targets. This had to be improved to at least 70 percent. Genda collected the best bomber pilots from Yokosuka to train the First Air Fleet's level bomber pilots.

The standard formation was of nine planes in three three-plane elements, a triangle arrangement, where the lead bomber would drop, followed immediately by the rest. This almost certainly ensured, assuming the lead plane was on target, that most of the Type 99 bombs would hit the ships.

Part of the problem was the lack of a precision bombsight like the American Norden. All Japan's high-level bombers used a modified German Boyko bombsight, the same as used in the Heinkel He-111 and Junkers Ju-88 medium bombers. Like most bombsights, it depended on skilled pilots and experienced bombardiers.

For three grueling weeks, the pilots flew again and again, tightening their formation and timing. The best results were achieved when, instead of the common practice of the pilot merely flying the plane while a bombardier released the bomb, the pilot did it. Although it went against the grain to have the pilot burdened with both jobs, this method achieved far better results. Within three weeks, the nine-plane formations managed about 30-40 percent hits, which was at least four times better than previous attempts. Genda accepted this and moved on.

Even if the torpedo problem was not worked out, the level bombers could theoretically do enough damage to the U.S. Pacific Fleet to keep them out of action for six months as Yamamoto hoped.

To Roosevelt and his advisors, the Philippines seemed to offer something of a bastion against Japanese aggression. Even though the U.S. had agreed not to fortify the archipelago in 1922, it was obvious Japan had already broken its own promises. The problem, as it had been since 1898, was how to defend the Philippines, so far from Hawaii and the West Coast. On July 26, the same day the State Department received that intriguing message from Thailand, Roosevelt put out an order that brought the Philippine Army under American command. This became known as U.S. Armed Forces, Far East, or USAFFE.

General Douglas MacArthur, who had been in Manila to advise the commonwealth government, was brought back into service as a major general and began working to use whatever troops and aircraft he had to build up the defense of the archipelago.

Eight thousand miles away, Roosevelt, who was receiving daily reports from the Far East through Commander Arthur McCollum at OP-20G, the Naval Intelligence unit in the Navy Department, and from Cordell Hull, finally decided to make Japan listen to reason. On August 1, he ordered that all Japanese assets in America be frozen and a total embargo placed on petroleum and high-octane aviation fuel to Japan. It would be impossible for Japan to import enough oil and fuel from the Soviet Union, Iran, and Peru. The distance to the latter nations made it difficult to keep the petroleum lifeline open.

Japan had about eighty million barrels of oil, enough for about three years of peacetime use, but only two years under wartime conditions. The nation needed about 500,000 tons annually in reserve. The peacetime navy required about 300,000 tons per month.

While Roosevelt did not intend to strangle Japan, he was adamant that U.S. oil and fuel would not be used to support Japan's aggressive moves in the Far East. But Japan had provoked Roosevelt with its continued expansion into China and Indochina. Instead of doing the prudent thing, the Japanese Army General Staff only looked at its distant goals of limitless resources.

If Japan had withdrawn from Indochina, Roosevelt would likely have ended the embargo. But the leaders in Tokyo demanded that the United States not only lift the embargoes, but recognize Japan's possession of Manchukuo, Korea, China, and Indochina.

Even the Japanese newspapers, read by Joseph Grew, continued to spout the mantra that the five-year-old China problem would be resolved. They also seemed to present the unshakable optimism that the southern expansion was not only inevitable, but preordained by Divine Right. Japan was destined to occupy and control those lands.

Diplomatic protest, which had been issued to Germany and Japan in ever-increasing numbers, failed. No one in Tokyo was interested.

The United States Army and Navy high command took advantage of every month, every day that diplomacy could deliver. They needed time to build ships, planes, tanks, and guns, and train the draftees brought into uniform by the peacetime draft of November 1940. In Hawaii, Kimmel and Short worked to find the best defense with what they had.

According to Gordon Prange, whose frank appraisal of the events leading up to the December 7 attack is among the most absorbing accounts ever written, "the embargoes were not a malicious attempt to bait Japan into war, but designed to make it stop, look, and think twice."

But the Japanese people, from the lowliest fisherman to the emperor himself, were not the most pragmatic of races. Instead of stopping to consider the consequences of their actions, they saw only their God-given destiny.

Easily offended, they reacted hotly to the slap of Roosevelt's embargoes as a personal insult to their rights as rulers and leaders of Asia. The Japanese retorted not with reason, but with increased bellicosity.

This was the last point at which any compromise was possible, and it ended with war in the future.

CHAPTER 4

CLIMB MOUNT NIITAKA

"There is no instance of a nation benefitting from prolonged warfare." —Sun Tzu

During my research for this book, I read through several online issues of *Time* magazine from October to December 1941. While there was no shortage of articles and editorials concerning Japan and the Pacific, I found no mention of a danger to Pearl Harbor. One would expect the media to be more alert to the international situation than the government or military.

But one editorial in the national affairs pages was entitled "Advice to Japan." It is worth reading.

> You are on Hitler's list before us. That was what Saburo Kurusu was hearing in Washington last week. The Japanese envoy saw Secretary Hull and then remained in seclusion, less like a diplomat awaiting new orders than like a casualty in the war of nerves. The U.S. suggestion was enough to give any diplomat an attack of nerves: long before Hitler is prepared to take on North America, he must have Japan completely subservient to his will. No complete list of Japanese proposals reached the public. But it was reported that to most of them—Japanese pledges not to invade Siberia, to get out of French Indochina, to make many minor concessions—the U.S. continued, to quote *Mein Kampf*. Aside from the moral issues involved, the U.S. cannot let Japan—and Hitler—get control of China's huge man power. Four points were given as summing up Secretary Hull's counter demands on the Japanese:
>
> 1. that Japan withdraw from the Axis.
> 2. get out of China and French Indochina.

3. renounce aggression.
4. observe the principle of equal trade opportunity in the Pacific.

Can any Japanese Government withdraw from China? Japan has spent a million lives there. But is the U.S., in demanding that Japan get out of China, denying her a place to live?

Said Raymond Clapper [news service journalist and commentator], "In a peaceful Pacific, with opportunity open to all nations, with vastly increased trade upon which Japan is so dependent, her chances are much better."

It was rumored that, if Japan would play ball, the U.S. would put up $100,000,000 to help Japan switch from a war to a peace economy; that Japanese war supplies to Russia would keep Japan's factories going. Saburo Kurusu made only one statement: He asked for silence. Japanese newspapers headlined doubts of the success of his mission. There were no signs that Japan could still think of a peaceful Pacific. Tension was increased when the U.S. Consulate at Saigon, in Japan-dominated Indochina, was bombed. As U.S.-Japanese talks made no progress, Secretary Hull held two conferences with the representatives of Australia, Britain, China, and the Netherlands. The U.S. occupation of Dutch Guiana was a powerful demonstration of U.S.-Dutch collaboration, a warning that there would be more collaboration if Japan should move against the Dutch East Indies. At last Saburo Kurusu called on Secretary Hull again, this time at night at his hotel, and stayed for three hours. There was still no statement. Around the brownstone Japanese Embassy, biggest and loneliest in Washington, the atmosphere was like a hospital street where the signs read "Quiet, Please."

This week a Japanese business expert on the U.S. gave eight U.S. "weaknesses" showing that it is no match for Japan:

1. the national debt.
2. a "spoiled child mentality."
3. low national morale (at the first defeat Lindbergh will lead a revolt).
4. Roosevelt, "a buffoon."
5. hesitance.

6. "Americans excite easily and cool easily."
7. disunity—with 20,000,000 Negroes, 10,000,000 unemployed, 5,000,000 trade unionists.
8. inflation.

This is very interesting not only for the revelation that there was some interest in the U.S. government to "buy" peace with Japan, even though the figure mentioned was woefully inadequate, but that a so-called business expert in the U.S. listed some of the more pressing issues that made America a pushover for Japan. Whoever this man was, he did point out what he considered weaknesses. But they were not to play a role in the upcoming war. The other interesting point is the author's opinion that Charles Lindbergh, spokesperson for the America First isolationists, would lead a revolt. That might be possible in Japan, but not in a democracy. In fact, right after Pearl Harbor, Lindbergh tried to reactivate his commission and return to active duty.

All in all, the author's points were nothing more than racist blustering.

The above editorial was in the December 1, 1941, issue of *Time* magazine, less than a week before the Pearl Harbor attack.

Even with the advantage of 20/20 historical hindsight, it is hard to imagine what President Franklin Roosevelt might have done differently in the months leading up to Pearl Harbor. He was in a three-sided box: one wall consisting of the Axis powers, the second of the isolationsts, and the third of Congress.

Ambassador Nomura was in a four-sided box, seeing the winds of war blowing ever harder. Nomura was perceptive enough to realize he was fighting a losing battle, primarily because his own government was not giving him the weapons and ammunition he needed to win or even reach a draw. He was a modest and humble man, qualities that were less than useful in August 1941. On August 4, he wired Tokyo and requested another man be sent to assist him in furthering the negotiations. This was a shrewd move on his part—if diplomacy failed, he would not be the sole scapegoat.

The choice of the former ambassador to Germany, Saburo Kurusu, would add another layer to the negotiations. Kurusu had signed the Tripartite Pact with Germany. He spoke idiomatic English, had even married an American woman, and was unlikely to misinterpret any comments in the heat of tension. But he was also sent to ensure that the only means of saving the situation was that America give in to Japanese demands. He was not the gentle giant Nomura was, but a clever and sharp diplomat. He had met his wife, Alice Little, in

Chicago in 1914, and they had three daughters. Each later married American men, including an army officer.

In Tokyo, Navy Minister Nagano and the Naval General Staff, seeing that there was no turning back, at last seriously looked at Yamamoto's Pearl Harbor plan. With the embargo in place, Japan was eating away at its limited stock of oil and fuel. Time was running out.

The Pearl Harbor attack was all but inevitable, at least from Yamamoto's standpoint. Japan's civilian leaders might have been looking through rose-colored glasses, believing there was still a chance of a negotiated peace. But at that moment the Combined Fleet and Yamamoto were planning an attack "guaranteed to rouse the United States to such cataclysmic fury that nothing short of unconditional surrender would satisfy the national temper," according to Gordon Prange.

When word reached Tokyo that the German Wehrmacht was meeting fierce resistance from the Red Army, the Japanese Army General Staff was elated. The Soviets were fighting back and Hitler's vaunted legions were on the defensive. This meant there was little chance the Russians would invade Manchuria in 1941, as previously feared. The army commanders in Korea agreed to keep sixteen divisions in Korea in the event a move into Siberia was ordered.

At present there was a neutrality agreement between Japan and the Soviet Union, but with Josef Stalin busy with Germany, it would be a golden—that is to say, Heaven-sent—opportunity to invade Siberia.

But at that point, the focus of the Imperial Army was to continue moving south. The inevitable war with Great Britain and the United States would probably begin around the end of November.

On August 10, a new figure entered the scene—Rear Admiral Matome Ugaki, a firm and fervent supporter of what was by now known as Operation Hawaii. Ugaki became Yamamoto's fourth and last chief of staff, filling the post left by Seiichi Ito, who was to be the next vice chief of the Naval General Staff. Ugaki was one of Japan's best naval officers and a respected expert on naval strategy.

In Hawaii, Kimmel and Short were still trying to bring order from the chaos created by the evolving situation in Europe. Short would not get the planes he requested.

He read a March 1941 report prepared by the commander of the Fifth Bombardment Group on Oahu, Colonel William Farthing, and presented by Admiral Patrick Bellinger of Patrol Wing 2 and Major General Fred Martin, commander of the Hawaiian air force. It outlined what was considered a likely move by the Japanese on Hawaii. The report stated, among other points, that "the Pacific Fleet must have freedom of action without regard to the defense of the Hawaiian Islands." In this, Martin and Bellinger confirmed that the ultimate defender of Oahu was the United States Army. "An enemy will not venture an attack against the Hawaii Islands until establishing control of the sea. Raids by surface vessels, submarines, and carrier-based aircraft may be expected."

In addition, the report noted that the enemy would likely employ a maximum of six carriers. This was at a time when the entire United States Navy had only six carriers. At that same time, the IJN was fighting with the Naval General Staff to be given that number of carriers for Operation Hawaii.

Furthermore, the report stated that the enemy task force would approach the islands under cover of darkness and attack at dawn.

While the Martin-Bellinger Report was detailed and remarkably prescient, it assumed an attack would not come until *after* a formal declaration of war. In other words, the Pacific Fleet would already have left Pearl when the enemy arrived. This was wishful thinking, to say the least.

In Part Four of the report, which concerned air assets for Hawaii, the report said that in order to prevent an enemy carrier force from reaching Hawaii, there should be enough long-range patrol planes to provide 360 degrees of coverage during daylight hours. But with the American war industry slowly bestirring itself and most of those planes being allocated to Atlantic patrol, where would these planes come from?

The report ended with a strong suggestion: "In order that the Air Corps be able to find and destroy the enemy carrier force, a minimum of 180 four-engine long-range heavy bombers and 36 long-range torpedo planes be sent to Hawaii as soon as possible." This incredible point was driven home with the ironic comment that "such a force would cost less than a single battleship." This might be considered a jab at the navy, but it was true.

Unfortunately, according to Air Corps Chief of Staff General Henry "Hap" Arnold, there were only 108 Boeing B-17 Flying Fortresses in the entire country, and they were committed to mainland defense and the training of new bomb groups. The only B-17s slated to leave the states were earmarked for the Philippines and Britain.

Even while doing his level best to protect the islands and their bases, Short had one serious lapse of judgment. On August 6, Wheeler Army Air Base, located north of Pearl, held a "Gala Day," inviting the public to tour the field. This was intended to show the large population of indigenous Japanese on Oahu that the Air Corps was powerful and prepared. The only restriction was that no cameras were allowed.

This was not an obstacle to Takeo Yoshikawa, who toured the base, making detailed mental notes as to the number and types of planes, and even how they took off on patrol. This report immediately went to Tokyo.

Yoshikawa had been busy. His most important messages, termed by OP-20G, Naval Intelligence, as the "Bomb Plot" messages, broke Pearl Harbor into five areas, labeled A through E. He listed the number and types of ships in each area, regularly updating the information so the IJN had an up-to-date picture of what lay in Pearl Harbor on any given week.

On August 25, the man who would personally lead the Pearl Harbor strike, Lieutenant Commander Mitsuo Fuchida, arrived on *Akagi* to the cheers of the assembled pilots. "The Boss is back!" they shouted. After being promoted to full commander, Fuchida accepted the post of senior flight commander, not only overseeing all of First Air Fleet's airmen but leading them in battle.

Fuchida was not yet privy to Operation Hawaii. Genda, a good friend, had been watching from the wings as Fuchida reached the pinnacle of his profession. He was the best man for the job. Pragmatic but emotional, hard-headed but discreet, dedicated to his duty and intelligent, Fuchida would soon be, along with Genda himself, pivotal to the training of the First Air Fleet's pilots.

At thirty-nine, Fuchida was slim with an almost aesthetic face. He had a ready wit and smiled easily. But he could be taciturn when duty demanded. Fuchida took on the difficult job of training and organizing the level, torpedo, dive bomber, and fighter pilots. This would not be easy, since every carrier's air group and squadron flew as a unit from bases in Shikoku and Kyushu. Fuchida would have to make the carrier air groups work as a team.

His first job was to improve the accuracy of the dive bombers. Since 1935, an average of only 45 percent of bombs hit their targets. As the weeks of intense training passed, the dive bombers scored as high as 60 percent, far better than the level bombers were scoring. Then there were the fighters. Lieutenant Shigeru Itaya was assigned to *Akagi* back in April when the First Air Fleet was formed. A brilliant and intuitive fighter pilot, Itaya graduated at the top of his Eta Jima class. He was personally chosen by Genda to train the fighter squadrons of the First and Second Carrier Divisions.

Their new mounts, the Mitsubishi A6M Type 00 fighter, were state of the art for 1941. Not even the vaunted Supermarine Spitfire of Battle of Britain fame could outfight and duel with the Zero.

Fast and incredibly nimble at low altitudes, the Zero carried both machine guns and cannon. Itaya's pilots learned to dogfight singly and in groups, always with a greater number of opponents. No other navy's fighter pilots were subjected to such demanding training. They were trained to take off and land on carriers, strafe enemy guns and parked aircraft, and, above all, attain air superiority over their target. It was the job of the fighters to protect the slow, heavily laden bombers.

But there was a serious problem, one that would plague Japan throughout the war. The Mitsubishi plant in Nagoya could not produce the planes fast enough to satisfy the army in China and Indochina, and the navy at Kagoshima. Even in late August there was no guarantee the First Air Fleet would have the Zeros it needed for Operation Hawaii. At least two waves were planned for the strike, and Genda needed enough fighters to escort the two strikes to Oahu, and leave enough behind to protect the carriers.

This was one of the reasons the Naval General Staff was not ready to commit to the Pearl Harbor attack. To make matters worse, the A6M's twin 20mm wing-mounted Type 99-II cannon, each carrying 100 rounds, were also in short supply. During training, most of Itaya's planes carried only one cannon.

Fuchida worked his crews hard, evaluating every bomb and torpedo drop to get the best results. He did not want to waste a single weapon.

Then in September, the First Air Fleet received a shot in the arm. The newer, faster sister aircraft carriers, *Shokaku* and *Zuikaku*, were commissioned. They became the Fifth Carrier Division under Rear Admiral Chuichi Hara. The new ships were faster than the other four carriers and carried more planes. Their air groups had been training in Kyushu. Now they joined the new flattops.

Interestingly, neither Nagumo, Yamaguchi, nor Hara had worked in naval aviation. But Hara was a torpedo specialist.

While this important event was being worked out in the First Air Fleet, Yamamoto was talking with the commander of the Sixth Submarine Fleet, Admiral Mitsumi Shimizu. The commander in chief had decided, like any good gambler, to double down his bets. He wanted a submarine element in Operation Hawaii. This was in fact a regression to the old naval plan of having subs patrol ahead of a fleet to find enemy ships for the surface force. Yamamoto planned to have a flotilla of subs leave a week ahead of the First Air Fleet. Once in Hawaiian waters, they would take station around the islands. At least two subs were to patrol around Lahaina Roads at Maui, another anchorage for the Pacific Fleet. The submarines would act as scouts and prevent any movement of U.S. ships and be in place to rescue downed aviators.

There was a second element to the submarine force. Five more long-range subs under Captain Hanku Sasaki would carry five two-man midget submarines on their first combat deployment. Each sub carried two Type 93 torpedoes. Their mother subs would carry them to a position just outside the harbor entrance. The 78-foot midget submarines, known as *Ko Hyoteki*, or "Scaly Dragon," were a new weapon in the IJN. Under the command of Lieutenant Naoji Iwasa, the midget subs were to be released and enter the harbor by whatever means available. There they would take up position around Ford Island and await the air attack. Ten torpedoes would add a healthy percentage to those carried by the planes.

This was Yamamoto's insurance in case the air attack failed or did not inflict crippling damage on the American ships. It was an unusual move, as Yamamoto had never worked with submarines before. But it is a good example of his gambler's penchant for stacking the deck in his favor.

The few air officers in the fleet who knew of the submarine involvement in Operation Hawaii felt it was a waste of time. Genda did not like having to coordinate with undersea forces in such a complex operation. But in truth, there would be little interchange other than in timing.

On September 5, Prime Minister Konoye met with Emperor Hirohito to present the current status of diplomatic and military matters. The report angered the Emperor. He pointed out to his prime minister that preparations for war were being put ahead of negotiations with the United States. He told Konoye he wanted to meet with the chiefs of the General Staffs. This was unheard of, but the emperor wanted to hear his senior military officers state their opinions.

Konoye was in a tight spot. The emperor had never inserted himself into such matters, but he had the right to do so. The prime minister's post was dependent on the armed forces, particularly the army.

Ministry Admirals Nagano and Sugiyama met privately with their sovereign, who made it clear he wanted the negotiations to be the primary means of settling the dispute with the United States. He further reminded Sugiyama that back in 1937, he had assured Hirohito he would have the China problem resolved in a month. "That was four years ago. Are you trying to tell me the same thing again?" The emperor's voice was laced with royal sarcasm. "Has it been resolved?"

Sugiyama was contrite, saying it was difficult to handle a campaign over a large area with an army of guerillas operating with American support.

The meeting ended with the two officers and Konoye having their marching orders to ensure diplomacy had priority.

In early September, the First Air Fleet operations officers were told of Operation Hawaii. Some were shocked, others simply nodded. Since they had been kept out of the inner loop, they had only a basic understanding of the overall objectives of the Pearl Harbor attack. It was explained that in order for the army and navy to complete the southern operations against the Philippines, Singapore, and the Dutch East Indies, Pearl Harbor and the U.S. Pacific Fleet had to be neutralized. It was incumbent upon the Japanese force to do all they could to ensure success. Only a few officers knew that the Naval General Staff and Admiral Nagano had yet to approve Operation Hawaii.

Air crew training intensified through September, now with the squadrons of the Fifth Carrier Division catching up to the others. During the last week in September, Genda visited Commander Fuchida in his quarters aboard *Akagi*. "Yamamoto plans to attack Pearl Harbor," Genda told him.

With wide eyes, the First Air Fleet's chief pilot suddenly realized what all the specialized training had been about.

But Genda wasn't finished. "You are to be flight leader of the strike force."

Recognizing the supreme honor and responsibility given to him, Fuchida nodded and said he would accept.

Now that Fuchida was part of the inner circle, he and Genda worked on finalizing the actual attack plan. This meant compiling the list of land and ship targets, the types of bombs to be used for each, and the approach to those targets. With twenty-six operational squadrons to work with, Fuchida decided which pilots would serve as flight leaders.

There were still problems with the torpedoes, but he put his faith in Japanese engineers to solve them while he made certain the bombers could hit the U.S. ships moored around Ford Island. A further problem concerned where the battleships were moored. Instead of a single line from quays F1 to F8 on the island's eastern shore, many of the big ships were "double parked." This meant that no torpedo could reach the inner ships.

Fuchida himself favored the high-level horizontal bombing with the new 800-kg armor-piercing bombs. Further training would increase their accuracy so they could hit both columns of ships. Bombing from 12,000 feet ensured a bomb penetrated the heavy deck armor, but it also meant a deterioration in accuracy. Bombing from 9,000 feet, as Fuchida advocated, resulted in more hits but was only reasonably certain of doing maximum damage. AAA had to be taken into account.

On October 2, Yamamoto met with Onishi to discuss the timetable for Operation Hawaii. It had to be launched before winter so there would be a chance of good weather over the mid-Pacific. Also, the Eleventh Air Fleet, consisting of Carrier Divisions Three and Four, had to move south to attack the Philippines before winter. The commander in chief wanted to hit Hawaii in late November or the first week in December. Onishi, while still dreading the prospect of launching two major campaigns at once, agreed.

Admiral Nagumo called a staff meeting on *Kaga* on or about October 2. In attendance were his chief of staff Admiral Kusaka, carrier division commanders Yamaguchi and Hara, the captains of all six carriers and their air group officers, and, of course, Genda and Fuchida.

"I asked you here because we are going to attack Pearl Harbor in case Japan and the United States go to war," Nagumo said in a somber voice. "We must make every effort to be successful. We must maintain secrecy, but we cannot devote ourselves to training under a total veil of secrecy." From his somber tone, it was apparent to his listeners that Nagumo had serious reservations about the attack.

Genda used a map and model of Pearl Harbor to illustrate the locations of moorings, the navy yard, and other key targets. He outlined how the two torpedo attacks on the eastern and western shores of Ford Island would proceed and the progress of adapting the Type 91 torpedoes for the job. He also stressed specialization for the bombers. For instance, dive bombers tasked with hitting ships should concentrate only on that type of training, while the bombers slated to hit airfields would practice with that type of target in mind.

Fuchida wanted to inform his squadron and flight leaders about the objective, believing this would increase their zeal and dedication to the operation. Kusaka, after considering it for a long moment, agreed.

Yamamoto knew that Nagumo and Kusaka were not enthusiastic about the attack. But they continued to do their duty as the weeks passed.

At prominent locations around the Pacific rim, Allied listening stations, using Radio Direction Finding, or RDF, had operators on twenty-four-hour duty to pick up any and all Japanese wireless military and merchant radio traffic. These posts, located in San Francisco, Seattle, the Aleutians, Hawaii, San Diego, Panama, and Corregidor in the Philippines, coordinated with British and Australian stations to intercept and locate Japanese transmissions. Any messages were relayed to Station HYPO at Pearl Harbor, to a room located in the basement of the Navy Yard Administration Building. This will be discussed in more detail in Chapters 10 and 11. The Combat Intelligence Unit, or CIU, run by an eccentric and brilliant naval officer named Commander Joseph J. Rochefort, collected and examined the Japanese Navy's code, known as JN-25. But other messages were sent via the underwater telephone and telegraph cable running between Hawaii and Tokyo.

At the end of September, HYPO picked up some disturbing radio intercepts and relayed them to OP-20G in the Office of Naval Intelligence in Washington. From as far back as 1940, OP-20G had employed the machine codenamed "Magic" to decrypt the Japanese diplomatic "Purple" code. Purple was used for confidential communications between Tokyo and all its consulates and embassies. In the case of Hawaii, a tap was placed on the undersea cable running to Tokyo via Wake Island and Guam. The army's Signal Corps routinely monitored all transmissions from and to the consulate in Honolulu. While most messages were innocuous, some important messages sent in the Purple code caught the army's attention.

One was particularly ominous. An order went out to all Japanese merchant ships at sea. This meant the Marus, the ships and liners plying the seas to Europe, Africa, and the Americas. Thousands of these ships were told to return to Japan by the second week in November. This was a clear indication that Japan, an island nation dependent on sea trade, did not want its merchant vessels at risk if and when war began. They would be easy targets for Allied submarines. It was another one of those behind-the-scenes maneuvers that made diplomats and admirals in Washington wary.

All over the world, Japanese merchantmen discharged their cargoes or loaded up and set course to the Home Islands.

In early October, a serious shake-up came for the First Air Fleet. On board *Akagi*, Admiral Yamaguchi burst into Nagumo's office and raged that his carrier division of *Soryu* and *Hiryu* was to be detached and included in the southern operation with the Eleventh Air Fleet. This was intolerable to the firebrand Yamaguchi, who had favored the Pearl Harbor attack from the beginning. Nagumo told his fellow flag officer that *Akagi* was also to be detached. It had been this way before *Shokaku* and *Zuikaku* joined the fleet.

The idea of attacking Pearl with so few carriers was absurd, and Yamaguchi fumed. He threatened to resign.

Nagumo said placidly, "The order came from the Naval General Staff, so there is nothing we can do about it."

Yamaguchi stormed out of the office. From that point on, a blizzard of memos and messages flew through the fleet and the offices of the Naval General Staff. Even Yamamoto was upset but far calmer. Yamamoto was offered more battleships to offset the loss of the carriers, but he said that would be of no help and could hinder the operation.

A few days later, infuriated by Nagumo's willingness to accept the loss of three carriers, Yamaguchi again stormed into Nagumo's office. He began railing so loudly that the fleet commander ordered him to leave. At the door, Yamaguchi turned to look at Nagumo and barked, "If you are wrong, I will kill you!" He meant every word.

On October 16, after heated and sustained meetings with the ministers of the navy and army and War Minister Hideki Tojo, Konoye resigned as prime minister. This was a crushing blow to the men still hoping to avoid war with America. Konoye had met repeatedly with Tojo. Two days earlier Konoye told Tojo that Japan must stand down its preparations for war and accept the United States' demands for a withdrawal from China and Indochina. The following day, Tojo met with the cabinet and said that unless the negotiations bore fruit by early October, which had already passed, war with the United States would be declared on December 8 (December 7 Hawaii time).

Hirohito, having few options, named Hideki Tojo as the new prime minister, a move that all but guaranteed a war.

Yamamoto held a special meeting of Combined Fleet admirals and their staffs on board *Nagato* on October 13. He said he intended to have the First Air Fleet ready the moment it appeared that negotiations were breaking down. Then he invited the flag officers to speak their minds. No official minutes were taken. It was totally off the record. However, he made personal notes afterward.

Admiral Ugaki began by stating his view that once a decision was issued by the commander in chief, "every officer must set aside his own views and follow orders to the best of his ability."

Yamamoto then said, "Since the operational order is still being finalized, now is the last time for each of us to express his opinion or suggestions." He finished by saying it was time to have complete unity.

The fleet navigational officer said that the Pearl Harbor attack would be virtually impossible if carried out any later than the first week in December. This would apply to the southern operation fleets as well as the First Air Fleet. Onishi, still convinced that Operation Hawaii was not feasible, expressed that the Philippines, Singapore, and Malaya operations would need more carriers to provide air support. Admiral Nobutake Kondo, commander of the Eleventh Air Fleet, made the astounding and courageous suggestion that the United States be left alone and that Japan focus its efforts on fighting the British in Singapore and Malaya.

Then Nagumo spoke up. He sounded like a volcano close to eruption as he expressed his strong reservations against the Pearl Harbor attack. Kusaka seconded him.

Not surprisingly, Yamaguchi was one of the few who openly supported Operation Hawaii. Having been cut from this campaign by the removal of the Second Carrier Division, he was in favor of the Pearl Harbor attack even if his ships were not involved. "Hawaii must be attacked at the outbreak of war," he said, probably glaring at Nagumo as he said it. He also cautioned against extending the Imperial Navy's assets and capabilities too far. Seizing the important harbor at Rabaul on the northern tip of New Britain in the Bismarck Sea was going too far, too soon.

The general opinion of the assembled admirals was that preparations had gone on for too long. The United States was likely already preparing to sortie the Pacific Fleet to meet the Imperial Navy at sea.

Then Admiral Yamamoto stood and addressed the officers. "I have listened to the comments and suggestions of all the officers here, and they will be considered carefully and any constructive suggestions incorporated into the forthcoming fleet orders." Then he paused. "I realize some do not think well of my plan, but the operation against Hawaii is a vital part of Japan's grand strategy." Then he said in a tone that brooked no argument, "As long as I am commander in chief, Pearl Harbor will be attacked."

His word was the final say.

In Washington, Roosevelt met with Knox and Stark to discuss the new Japanese government. They were all of the opinion that the Far East was at risk of attack. Stark wired Kimmel to send patrol planes to Midway and Wake for daylight patrol in a 100-mile radius. Kimmel did this and added more patrols around Oahu. Thus, by mid-October, CINCPAC had patrols searching for any Japanese subs, planes, or ships in the central Pacific. But they were under one restriction. Even if they spotted Japanese forces anywhere near Wake, Midway, or Hawaii, they could not make any aggressive moves. That was a direct order from CNO Stark.

The United States Joint Army and Navy Board had formulated a series of war plans in 1903, long before the Great War. It hypothesized how to win a war with several possible enemies, including Japan, Germany, Mexico, Italy, Russia, France, and even Great Britain. The plans depended on the battleship for success. In the era before long-range heavy bombers, or even reliable fighters, the big warships and submarines were the key to winning any war with a seagoing foreign power. Each nation was assigned a color, such as red for Great Britain, black for Germany, and green for Mexico. The plan concerning Japan was called Orange.

The aircraft carrier was still two decades in the future. Over the next thirty years, the war plans, eventually called Rainbow, were upgraded and modified to include new weapons, including carriers and long-range bombers. But a lot of Rainbow depended on up-to-date intelligence on the capabilities of a potential enemy. The plans were kept in a locked safe at the Navy Department in Washington.

War Plan Orange was on the minds of senior army and navy officers as the war clouds grew to the West. The War Plans Division had to find a way to utilize Plan Orange in accordance with the current strength of both the United States and Japan. But with the removal of battleships and a carrier from Pearl Harbor earlier that year, Orange had to be upgraded.

One of the key bases for Orange was the Philippines. But since the islands had not been fully fortified and supported, there was no doubt Japan could and would conquer the Philippines in short order. They lay 5,000 miles away on the far side of the Japanese-owned Mandate Islands, far from any hope of saving. Japan could transport more than 50,000 troops to the Philippines in the first week of a war, and 300,000 would be in place within a month. The only friendly forces available to fight back were about 11,000 American and Filipino troops, the latter poorly equipped. The total number of aircraft, including bombers and fighters, was under 200. Some of the fighters were obsolete older models.

General Douglas MacArthur, revered by the Filipinos, was confident in his ability to protect and hold the islands, but he needed a great infusion of men, planes, equipment, ammunition, food, and other war materiel.

War Plan Orange, even the most updated version, still presumed that the U.S. Pacific Fleet would deploy four battleship divisions, three or four carriers, and scores of cruisers, destroyers, and submarines to find and destroy the Japanese fleet. But there were two flies in the ointment. First, the fleet would not sail until after a declaration of war by Japan, and would have to be accompanied by oilers to refuel the fuel-hungry battleships. Even the newest, the *Colorado* class, which included *Maryland*, had about a 4,000-mile radius of action. In fact, there was barely enough fuel in the enormous tanks at Pearl Harbor to support a major fleet operation to the western Pacific.

The destroyers, having limited fuel capacity, needed periodic replenishing. Submarines, having diesel-electric propulsion, were the only warships that could make it to the Philippines and back without refueling.

As for a battle to the death, Orange was little different from what Genda had worked so hard to overcome in the Imperial Navy back in 1935. There was as yet no real experience of carrier warfare in the United States Navy in 1941. The learning curve would be very steep.

In Japan, Admiral Kusaka met with Yamamoto after speaking with the Navy General Staff. He told the commander in chief that support for Operation Hawaii was still uncertain among the high command. For Yamamoto, this was the moment for him to force the issue. He sent senior staff officer Kuroshima to Tokyo to do just that. Kuroshima was to secure the consent of the Navy General Staff and navy minister for Operation Hawaii. He was also to demand the return of the Second Carrier Division. The Pearl Harbor attack could not possibly succeed with only three carriers. Kuroshima carried a bomb that would at last force a solid decision.

On October 18, he met with the Naval General Staff and presented the proposal. Kuroshima wanted to know why the staff was still vacillating. He was told that the Pearl Harbor attack was too risky. There were still large technical difficulties with refueling, torpedoes, weather, and communications. Committing six carriers would also jeopardize the southern operation.

After hearing this, Kuroshima detonated the bomb handed to him by Yamamoto.

"Admiral Yamamoto insists that his plan be adopted at once. I am authorized to state that if it is not, then the commander in chief of the Combined Fleet can no longer be held responsible for the security of the empire. In that case he will have no alternative but to resign, along with his entire staff."

The explosion of this verbal bomb sent shockwaves through the Navy Ministry. There was no doubt Yamamoto was deadly serious.

This went up the chain to the chief of the Naval General Staff, Osami Nagano. Although he had little faith in the attack, Nagano finally agreed. Japan could not do without Yamamoto. He did not see the ultimatum as a treasonous act—it was accepted in Japan as a means of forcing a decision on a difficult matter.

Nagano had only two conditions: that the Pearl Harbor attack not interfere with the southern operation nor weaken its forces. He also approved returning the Second Carrier Division to the First Air Fleet. When Kuroshima returned to *Nagato*, he told Yamamoto that the Naval General Staff and Navy Ministry had approved Operation Hawaii.

The approval of Combined Fleet Order No. 1 in the first week of November removed all official obstacles to the plan. The Imperial Japanese Navy was, if negotiations failed, ready to go to war.

For the first time the Naval General Staff officers and the combined fleet had a common goal and would work together with more efficiency and motivation. This in itself was a big leap forward, and some of the more perplexing technical problems were close to being solved.

An interesting historical question is whether Yamamoto was serious about resigning. The answer is probably not, but he had the Imperial Navy by the throat, and they knew he was too valuable to lose. Nagano might well have called the bluff, and if Yamamoto and his staff resigned, the navy would have been finished with the bothersome Pearl Harbor attack once and for all. In that case, Yamamoto would probably have been proven right and Japan defeated in less than two years. But we will never know.

Down in Kagoshima Bay, Fuchida's pilots were making progress in reducing the depth of torpedoes. But try as they might, they could not keep them from dropping to less than twenty meters, nearly sixty feet, which was at least twenty feet too deep. Since Fuchida and the torpedo squadron commander, Shigeharu Murata, could not tell them, the pilots grumbled about the unreasonable restrictions.

But the technical miracle was about to happen. At Yokosuka Navy Base, the engineers who had designed and modified the Type 91 torpedo were at last finding a solution by using a box-like fin fitted over the after end of the torpedo. Originally conceived as a way to stabilize the weapons during their fall to the water, the new design stayed attached as the torpedo hit the surface. The wooden case broke off just late enough to slow the fish to retard its plunge. The boxes were painted silver, according to a source at Pearl Harbor after the war. The torpedoes only sank to about ten to twelve meters, about thirty to thirty-six feet, just right for Pearl Harbor.

But Fuchida and Murata were not out of the woods just yet. The Yokosuka shop could only deliver thirty modified torpedoes by the middle of October and fifty more by the end of the month. The last batch of a hundred would not reach the fleet until November 30. The First Air Fleet was scheduled to depart Japan on November 26.

But there was a ray of hope for the level bombers. By the end of October, the pilots were achieving scores of about 70 percent, far higher than expected. The less experienced pilots of the Fifth Carrier Division, *Shokaku* and *Zuikaku*, had been unable to train in night and low-light conditions. For this reason, Fuchida suggested to Genda that the first wave not launch until dawn around 0600 hours, so the pilots would reach Pearl Harbor around 0800. This was incorporated into the general plan.

The persistent issue of refueling still remained. Japan's tradition of fighting naval battles in or near home waters led to the navy having few long-range capital ships until well into the 1920s. Of the First Air Fleet's thirty ships, only seven had the range to make it from the Kurils to Hawaii without refueling. Kusaka took on this last serious obstacle. The navy managed to successfully refuel destroyers and light cruisers underway, but pumping thousands of tons of fuel oil into the big carriers was both difficult and dangerous. Kusaka secured a waiver from the Naval Affairs Ministry to allow *Akagi*, *Hiryu*, and *Soryu*, as well as one of the battleships, to carry extra fuel in auxiliary tanks. Prior to this, such tanks were too dangerous to carry and only used in emergencies. But Kusaka obtained the means to allow those ships to carry enough fuel to get them all the way to Hawaii and part of the way back before being forced to refuel. Kusaka had solved one of the most troublesome problems facing the First Air Fleet.

As October turned to November, Fuchida began advanced tactical training. He broke them up into two groups: Itaya's fighters, and the bombers under Murata. They conducted mock dive, level, and torpedo attacks on the task force while the fighters took the role of American planes. This would give the bomber crews a taste of what a real strike would be like.

At last Genda had managed to expedite the delivery of the last batch of modified torpedoes. With the First Air Fleet scheduled to leave on or about November 25, the last of the new fish would be loaded aboard *Akagi* and *Kaga* with a week to spare.

The six carriers and their escorts sailed from Kyushu to Hitokapu Bay in the Kuril Islands in the north. The bay was deep and sheltered from prying eyes. By early November the entire strike force had assembled in the bay.

On or about November 5, Nagumo decided it was time to inform the First Air Fleet's squadron commanders and flight leaders of the upcoming mission. As recollected by surviving Japanese officers, Nagumo said, "Since diplomatic negotiations with the United States seem to be breaking down, and that war may be unavoidable, this task force will leave Japan and head east to attack the American naval and army bases in Hawaii."

At that point Genda outlined the operational and attack plans. Then Fuchida explained how the two waves would be organized and their course. He pointed out how they were to approach and overfly Oahu and head for their specific targets. The two waves would approach from the north and split into several groups, enveloping Oahu in a deadly web, north, east, and west. He used a pointer to tell each squadron commander which ships, air bases, and facilities they were to attack.

Genda added that there might be a third wave, depending on what Fuchida reported on the success of the first two waves. The decision would be up to Nagumo, but Genda was very much in favor of a third and even a fourth wave.

In that room on *Akagi*, there was a palpable electric tension. The airmen were astonished at hearing of their target, even though they had been speculating for months. Now they at last knew where those specialized bombs and torpedoes were to be used. Smiles and handshakes were exchanged.

In the Imperial Palace in Tokyo that same day, high-level Naval General Staff and Combined Fleet officers briefed Emperor Hirohito on the first phase of the upcoming war. He listened impassively to the plans for the projected attacks and conquest of the Philippines, Guam, Wake Island, Singapore, and later, the Dutch East Indies and Java. While not a serving officer, Hirohito did hold admiral's rank in the IJN and was well versed in naval operations.

American Ambassador to Japan Joseph Grew was sending regular diplomatic messages to Cordell Hull in Washington. Grew was becoming nervous, believing Japan was actively preparing to attack the United States and Great Britain. His primary sources were the increasingly bellicose local newspapers and radio broadcasts, but he had no way to know what the fleet was actually doing.

On November 3, Grew sent a message to Hull: "Japanese sanity cannot be measured by American logic." He was trying to impart how dangerous the situation was becoming.

At the Yokosuka naval base, the advance ships of Operation Hawaii slipped out of port and headed east. The Sixth Submarine Fleet's Second Squadron was on its way to play its part in the attack on Hawaii. They took a northerly course to stay well clear of Midway, then turned south to approach the Hawaiian Islands, where they would deploy between Oahu and Kauai. Their orders were to watch for any movement of the American fleet and to torpedo any ships that left the harbor after the air attack.

One day later, five more *I*-class submarines left the naval base at Kure, south of Hiroshima, and threaded the Bungo Strait between Kyushu and Shikoku. Turning east, they too headed for Hawaii. Aboard each sub was a single Ko Hyoteki Type A midget submarine. Seventy-eight feet long and painted dark green, they carried two Type 97 torpedoes and a crew of two.

Aboard *Nagato*, Yamamoto spoke to the Air Fleet commanders. He hoped that the attack would be a complete surprise, but he understood the Americans too well to expect they would be completely unprepared. The U.S. Navy would fight back, he said. "Japan has fought many worthy enemies in the past, the Mongols, Chinese, Koreans, and Russians, but in this operation, we will meet the strongest and most resourceful enemy of all. Admiral Kimmel is no ordinary adversary. He is able, gallant, and brave. We can expect him to put up a courageous fight. He has probably taken steps to defend his command." Yamamoto suggested they should be ready for any opposition. He concluded, "You may have to fight your way into the target."

Admiral Suzuki, Yamamoto's intelligence chief, met with Nagumo. He outlined what Yoshikawa had sent regarding the air defenses on Oahu. He explained that the navy PBY Catalina flying boats usually took off around 0800 hours and remained on patrol until 1200. "After having lunch, they take off again and do not land until sunset. The patrol planes do not fly before dawn nor after sunset."

By mid-November the Imperial Navy had sent out so many false radio messages in the JN-25 code that the cryptanalysts in Hawaii were unsure of the location of several Japanese carriers. Commander Joseph Rochefort, the head of Kimmel's Combat Intelligence Unit under Captain Edwin Layton, deduced the deployment of the submarines but had no clear idea where Nagumo's carriers were, or where they might be headed. He had correctly worked out the specific ships and organization of the IJN's southern operation, but of the First Air Fleet, he could only speculate. As one of the most skilled and clever codebreakers in the navy, Rochefort was worried.

Meanwhile, Kimmel urged the Navy Department in Washington to send him and Short everything they had on possible Japanese intentions and capabilities. But Stark only sent CINCPAC what the CNO felt he needed to know. Stark was more worried about the Philippines and Singapore than Hawaii. Pearl Harbor was a strong, well-fortified base and not in danger of being attacked from 4,000 miles away.

But still Kimmel tried to find out. He often asked Layton for any idea where the IJN might be headed other than to the south. Surprisingly, the IJN was not making much effort to conceal the location and composition of the task force assembled for the southern operation. This may have been because Yamamoto wanted to give the United States intelligence community something to chew on while the First Air Fleet prepared to depart for Hawaii. But Japan's intent to move south and take the Philippines and Singapore was hardly a secret.

The mass of false messages seemed to indicate that Japan was playing a game of musical ships. The carriers *Akagi*, *Kaga*, *Soryu*, *Hiryu*, *Shokaku*, and *Zuikaku* were apparently scattered from Hokkaido in the north of Japan to as far south as Formosa. The carriers near Formosa, slated for the attack on the Philippines, were from Carrier Divisions Three and Four.

Rochefort and his superb team of codebreakers were slowly assembling information. They managed to put together a picture of what was being done in Japan for the southern operation. But they had missed the all-important movement of all three of Nagumo's carrier divisions to Hitokapu Bay.

As for the Japanese diplomatic Purple code used by the foreign office, Kimmel and Short had to depend on the Navy Department to learn what was happening between Tokyo and Washington. The codebreaking machine, "Magic," a marvel of communications technology, had only been provided to Manila, Singapore, Panama, and Bletchley Park in England.

In the absence of solid information, Kimmel was operating in a partial vacuum. He would have been shocked if Stark had provided the many Magic intercepts concerning Yoshikawa's September Bomb Plot message. But he never saw them.

On November 23, Yamamoto met with his staff to review last-minute instructions. "If negotiations with the United States are successful, I will send a message to the First Air Fleet to break off and return to Japan. I will send the recall no later than one o'clock on the afternoon of December 7." By this he meant 1300 hours on December 6, Hawaii time.

On board *Akagi*, moored in Hitokapu Bay, Nagumo called all the First Air Fleet admirals and captains to the last meeting before leaving. There were only three days before the mighty armada left to cross the Pacific.

"Our mission is to attack Pearl Harbor," he said somberly. Then he explained that if negotiations with the United States should succeed, the task force would turn and head back to Japan. If the First Air Fleet was sighted by the enemy prior to the day of the attack, they were to turn back. But if the Americans spotted the force during the launch, they were to fight it out. He looked at his battleship, cruiser, and destroyer captains. "I urge you to give this your maximum effort," he said.

Their course would roughly follow the Great Circle route at 35 degrees North Latitude, well north of the Pacific shipping lanes between North America and the Far East.

Then Minoru Genda stood. There would be two attack waves, Genda began. The first, led by Fuchida, would consist of fighters and all types of bombers. They would launch at 0600 hours, about 230 miles north of Oahu. Reaching Pearl at about 0800, they would strike all the air bases and the capital ships in the harbor. The second wave, launched at 200 miles at 0700, would be led by Commander Shigekazu Shimazaki off *Shokaku*, with fighters, dive, and level bombers. Fuchida was to remain over the target and direct the bombers to specific ships and targets that needed to be hit again.

Fuchida made a point of telling the dive bomber pilots to be on the lookout for any ships in or near the channel, or for any ships trying to escape. If they could sink or disable a large ship in the channel, it would block the harbor for months, in effect achieving Yamamoto's prime goal.

Fuchida, in the lead level bomber, would be first to pass over Oahu's northern coast, about twenty minutes before reaching Pearl. He would decide if the enemy air defenses were on alert. If he saw AAA bursts in the sky and fighters taking off from Wheeler, he would have to evaluate the chances of success. If, however, he saw no activity over the air bases and Pearl, he would radio the now-famous code, "Tora! Tora! Tora!" (Tiger! Tiger! Tiger!) that surprise had been achieved.

So far, this book has only used the official Japanese designation of the Japanese aircraft. For the rest of this book the code names used by the United States military will be used. All bombers were given female names, such as Kate, Val, Betty, Nell, and Sonja. Fighters had male names, like Zeke, Hamp, Tony, Claude, and Oscar.

The Nakajima B5N Type K torpedo and level bomber was known to the U.S. as the Kate. At 33 feet long with a 50-foot wingspan, the Kate had retractable landing gear and a crew of three: a pilot, observer/bombardier, and gunner.

It had a 14-cylinder Nakajima Sakae air-cooled radial engine to generate 1,000 horsepower. It cruised at about 235 knots and had a maximum ferry range of 1,200 miles. The single flexible gun mount was a Type 92 7.7mm machine gun with a drum magazine holding 97 rounds.

The Aichi D3A Type 99 dive bomber was the Val. The IJN's primary early war dive bomber, it had fixed landing gear, giving it stability in a dive. The Val was 33 feet long with a 49-foot wingspan.

The crew consisting of a pilot and gunner were expected to cruise at 12,000 feet and nose over in a steep dive of nearly 80 degrees, then use a Type 99 telescopic gunsight during a dive on a target. The engine was a Mitsubishi Kinsei 54 14-cylinder air-cooled radial piston engine, generating close to 1,200 horsepower, almost the same as one of the early Boeing B-17 Wright Cyclones. It cruised at 250 knots with a range of 840 miles. It was armed with one flexible Type 92 7.7mm machine gun and twin 7.7mm guns in the cowling. The Val could carry a single 250-kg bomb under the fuselage and two 60-kg bombs under the wings.

With a length of 29 feet and a large wingspan of 39 feet, the Mitsubishi A6M Type 00, Zeke or Zero had low wing-loading, giving it superb maneuverability at low altitudes. The single pilot had excellent visibility from the large canopy to aim and fire his twin cowling 7.7mm machine guns, each with 500 rounds. The A6M's killing power was in the two 20mm wing-mounted Type 99 cannon. Each held sixty rounds. The Zero cruised at about 335 knots and had a phenomenal ferry range of over 1,900 miles, better than U.S. fighters. Its maximum ceiling was close to 33,000 feet. Like the Kate, the Zero had a 14-cylinder Nakajima Sakae air-cooled radial engine at 950 horsepower, giving it a superb power-to-weight ratio.

The plan for the air attack was as follows:

Air Attack Pearl Harbor, Organization
From an original document prepared by Commander Fuchida

First Wave: Commander Mitsuo Fuchida

Level Bombers: Commander Mitsuo Fuchida
First Flight: 49 B5N armed with 800-kg armor-piercing bomb
15 from *Akagi*
14 from *Kaga*
10 each from *Soryu* and *Hiryu*
Target: Battleships

Torpedo planes: Lieutenant Shigeharu Murata
Second Flight: 40 B5N armed with 800-kg torpedo
12 each from *Akagi* and *Kaga*
8 each from *Soryu* and *Hiryu*
Target: Battleships and cruisers

Dive bombers: Lieutenant Commander Kakuichi Takahashi
Third Flight: 51 D3A armed with 125-kg or 250-kg general-purpose land
  bomb
26 from *Shokaku*
25 from *Zuikaku*
Target: Air bases Wheeler, Hickam, Ford

Fighters: Lieutenant Commander Shigeru Itaya
Fourth Flight: 45 A6M armed with twin 7.7mm and twin 20mm guns
10 each from *Akagi* and *Kaga*
8 from *Soryu*
6 from *Hiryu*
5 from *Shokaku*
6 from *Zuikaku*
Targets: Air bases Wheeler, Ford, Hickam, Barbers Point, Kaneohe
Two A6M aborted on takeoff

Total: 189 aircraft (6 aborted, mechanical trouble)

Second Wave: Lieutenant Commander Shigekazu Shimazaki

Level bombers: Commander Shigekazu Shimazaki
First Flight: 54 B5N armed with 25-kg general-purpose land bombs
27 each from *Shokaku* and *Zuikaku*
Target: Air bases Ford, Hickam, and Kaneohe

Dive bombers: Lieutenant Commander Takeshige Egusa
Second Flight: 80 D3A and A6M armed with 250-kg or 60-kg general-purpose bombs
18 each from *Soryu* and *Hiryu*
18 from *Akagi*
26 from *Kaga*
Targets: Air bases and ships

Fighters: Lieutenant Commander Saburo Shindo
Third Flight: 36 A6M armed with twin 7.7mm and twin 20mm guns
9 each from *Akagi*, *Kaga*, *Soryu*, and *Hiryu*
Targets: Air bases Ford, Hickam, Wheeler, and Kaneohe

Total: 170 aircraft

After completing their strikes, the two waves would rendezvous north of Oahu's western coast and turn north to find the carriers.

Genda explained that depending on what happened, they would either launch a third wave or be ready for an American counterattack. He personally wished that the task force would remain near Hawaii and continue to strike until every target and facility of use to the enemy was destroyed. But he knew that was unlikely, primarily due to Nagumo's caution.

In the last week before departure, each ship underwent final preparations. Fuel tanks were topped off. The officers and crew checked the communications, engines, guns, electrical systems, and navigations. The destroyers conducted test firings.

On the afternoon of November 25, Yamamoto sent his final message to Nagumo, telling him that the First Air Fleet was to depart Hitokapu Bay on November 26 and proceed east to the final rendezvous on December 3.

At 0600 hours in the predawn of November 26, blinker lights flashed from the flagship. "Prepare to depart."

At once the officers and crews of the First Air Fleet's ships raced to their stations. Engines rumbled to life, having been lovingly maintained for weeks.

Anchor chains rattled through the hawseholes as crewmembers pulled in the weed-laden anchors. Captains surveyed their commands while keeping an eye on the black bulk of *Akagi*. Signalmen called out that *Akagi* had sent the final signal. Propellors churned the black waters as the leading destroyers and cruisers headed out of the dark bay. Finally, the huge battleships and carriers moved out, leaving the silent, black coastline behind. Under the cold predawn sky, the choppy waters off the coast were the color of gunmetal. When all ships were clear, they assumed their positions.

The First Air Fleet was on the way to Hawaii and war.

They cruised at a speed of less than 15 knots so the slow oilers could keep up. This was a risk, but no less so than any others facing Nagumo's fleet.

Akagi was the oldest ship in the task force, followed by *Kaga*. *Soryu* and *Hiryu* were only six years old. *Shokaku* and *Zuikaku* had only been commissioned in August and September, respectively. Operation Hawaii was, in fact, their shakedown cruise.

On six hangar decks more than 350 planes were being checked over and given extra care and maintenance. Their deck crews cleaned and polished every plane to look its best for the historic event.

At that same time in Pearl, Kimmel had only two carriers in port. *Saratoga* was in Puget Sound Navy Yard for repairs. Her older sister, *Lexington*, was just entering the channel after an eight-day patrol. *Enterprise* was in port, being refueled and provisioned for her trip to Wake Island to deliver a squadron of Marine fighters.

In battleships, Kimmel had four times more than Nagumo. If it came to an old-fashioned duel between battleships, Kimmel had a numerical advantage. But this was illusory, as his were older, slower, and most important, shackled in port. He could not deploy his fleet unless either nation declared war.

Nearly all Americans, from ordinary citizens up to the president, felt sure that Japan would not attack any American base without first declaring war. It was an unwritten but usually followed rule among the world's nations to declare war first. Even Adolf Hitler followed this protocol in most cases.

But Japan had attacked and invaded Manchuria, Korea, China, and Russia without first declaring war.

In Washington the meetings between Hull and the Japanese envoys were getting nowhere. They could not—and, in Japan's case, would not—come to a compromise. Japan demanded that the United States recognize their mainland conquests and cut off support for Chiang Kai-shek. Hull was equally adamant that Japan leave Manchuria and French Indochina.

Nomura did his best, but he believed his government did not really want a peaceful resolution. It nearly broke the old statesman's heart.

On November 30, Nomura acknowledged a message from Tokyo that on December 6, Washington time, he would receive a long message. It would be in fourteen parts. The final part would be transmitted early on the morning of December 7.

Three days after the First Air Fleet departed Japan, Army Chief of Staff General George C. Marshall and Chief of Naval Operations Admiral Harold Stark, both convinced that Japan was about to launch an attack somewhere in the Pacific, sent a message to the Pacific commanders:

> Negotiations with Japan appear to be terminated to all practical purposes. Japanese future actions unpredictable but hostile action possible at any moment. If hostilities cannot, repeat, cannot be avoided, the United States desires that Japan commit the first overt act. Prior to Japanese hostile action, you are directed to undertake such reconnaissance or other measures you deem necessary, but these measures should not, repeat, not alarm the civil population or disclose intent. Should hostilities occur you are to carry out the task assigned in Rainbow 5, so far as they pertain to Japan.

The message, received by both Short and Kimmel, concluded with, "Japan is expected to make an aggressive move within the next few days, an amphibious expedition against either the Philippines, Thai, or Kra Peninsula or Borneo. This dispatch is to be considered a War Warning."

It requires little imagination to guess what the two Hawaiian commanders thought upon receipt of this message. While it first told them to be on alert and take precautions, it did not mention Pearl Harbor or even Hawaii. Short later admitted he thought it was directed at General MacArthur in Manila. It told them nothing they could not have guessed, even with the lack of solid intelligence from the War or Navy Departments.

Short and Kimmel put their forces on standby for an alert.

On the morning of November 28, the carrier *Enterprise* left Pearl Harbor, accompanied by three heavy cruisers and six destroyers. After clearing the channel, the three-year-old ship, known to her crew as the "Big E," headed west. An hour later she and her escorts turned into the wind while the 18 F4F Wildcat fighters, 36 SBD Dauntless dive bombers, and 18 TBD Devastator torpedo bombers of Air Wing 6 landed. Also coming in for a landing were twelve more

F4F Wildcats with Marine Corps markings. They were with VMF-211 under the command of Major Paul Putnam, bound for Wake Island.

In *Enterprise*'s flag quarters, Vice Admiral William F. Halsey, a man who would soon become famous and feared across the Pacific, read over the orders he had written for Captain George Murray.

Halsey spoke into the microphone that broadcast his words over the ship's speakers:

> *Enterprise* is now on a war footing. At any time, we must be ready for instant action. Hostile submarines may be encountered. Steady nerves and stout hearts are needed now.
> 28 November 1941
> W. F. Halsey, Vice Admiral U.S. Navy
> Commander Air, Battle Force

Kimmel had ordered Halsey to take the carrier and escort to Wake Island far to the west, where the Wildcats of VMF-211 would strengthen the Marines garrisoning the remote island.

Halsey, already well-known for his aggressive and audacious actions, favored reinforcing Wake. When Kimmel asked Halsey if he wanted to take any of the battleships along, the admiral, with jutting jaw and bushy eyebrows, snorted. "Hell no. Too slow. I want to be able to move fast."

Kimmel agreed. He explained that *Enterprise* would be on a war footing and might be in danger of attack by Japanese ships and planes. This delighted Halsey, who was ready for anything, even if it might precipitate a war. In his opinion, the only reason any Japanese ships would be so far east was for war.

Halsey, who was known for colorful statements, had said earlier in the year, "We will be happy to share the Pacific with the Japs. We'll take the top half, and they can have the bottom half."

In Tokyo, Prime Minister Hideki Tojo met with Navy Minister Nagano. Tojo was monitoring the messages coming in from Nomura in Washington. Nomura was well aware of the First Air Fleet's departure. Tojo told Nagano, "I need to know when Zero Hour is. Otherwise, I will not know when to cut off diplomatic relations with the United States."

Nagano, understanding this, said, "Zero Hour is December 8." This was December 7 in Washington.

Tojo nodded curtly. Then he asked, "We cannot keep our diplomats in the dark, can we?"

Someone in the room said, "Our diplomats will have to be sacrificed. What we want is to carry on the image of diplomatic negotiations to the very last minute to keep the United States thinking about the problem."

And thinking they were. Captain Edwin Layton had been diligently trying to determine where three of Japan's carrier divisions were. On December 2, he met the admiral to explain that he had no idea where six of the big carriers were.

A perplexed look appeared on Kimmel's face as he read over Layton's report. The phrase "homeland waters?" stood out.

"What? You don't know where the carriers are?"

"No, sir," Layton said.

"You haven't any idea where they are?"

"No, sir. That's why I added a question mark. I don't know."

Kimmel tried to grasp this unbelievable statement. "You mean to say that you, the intelligence officer, don't know where the carriers are?"

Layton shook his head. "No, sir, I don't."

"You mean they could be coming around Diamond Head and you wouldn't know it?"

"Yes, sir, but I hope they'd have been sighted before now."

Kimmel smiled. "I understand." He seemed almost amused at his best intelligence source losing the six biggest carriers in the Japanese fleet.

CINCPAC nodded and let the matter go. Kimmel needed solid information and facts; in short, anything that would indicate whether the Japanese fleet, known to be at sea, was heading south or east.

That is where matters stood five days before the attack.

In his agitation, Layton had forgotten to remind CINCPAC of a translation of a Japanese book entitled *When We Fight*, published in 1933. It predicted that if war between the United States and Japan came, Pearl Harbor would be the first target.

Still, Layton, like most of the men struggling with the magnitude of the crisis, could not believe that the Imperial Japanese Navy, for all its size and modernity, could possibly consider launching two major moves at the same time.

Yamamoto's chief of staff, Admiral Ugaki, waiting aboard the flagship *Nagato*, was told by his superior that the time had come to transmit the "go" signal to Nagumo.

Ugaki went to the battleship's radio room and, handing the coded message to the senior radioman, watched as the words "*Niitaka Yama Nobore*" went out over the Combined Fleet frequency. The now-famous phrase "Climb Mount

Niitaka" informed the First Air Fleet they were to proceed with the attack. There was no turning back.

Takeo Yoshikawa, still on the job, made one more reconnaissance of Pearl Harbor. His final transmission, relayed from Tokyo to Nagumo, reported no unusual activity in the harbor. He had seen no extra air patrols, no barrage balloon, and an absolute absence of an alert.

To Nagumo, this was a relief. The fleet had refueled from the oilers, which remained well north of Midway, guarded by destroyers. A special force consisting of an oiler and two destroyers broke away from the fleet and turned southwest. This was the Midway Neutralization Force. The First Air Fleet turned south, directly toward Oahu.

On December 5, another carrier, the old, beloved "Lady Lex," *Lexington*, left Pearl and followed the same routine as her younger sister *Enterprise* a week earlier. Once her air wing was on board, her escort of three heavy cruisers and five destroyers headed west and then northwest toward Midway. This small force was designated Task Force (TF) 12 under Rear Admiral John Newton.

On board *Lexington* were eighteen Vought SB2U Vindicator dive bombers of VMSB-231. They were being carried to Midway Island, 1,200 miles northwest of Oahu.

Through careful planning and not a little luck, Kimmel had managed to remove his last two aircraft carriers from Pearl Harbor only two days before Nagumo arrived. This was one of the most important breaks for the United States in the coming months.

In the headquarters of the Security Intelligence Communications Office in Washington, one of the many cryptanalysts had been working overtime on a message transmitted via cable from the Japanese Consulate in Honolulu to Tokyo.

Yoshikawa's original Bomb Plot messages had been intercepted and decoded with the Magic machine. Even though the Bomb Plot communications showed a disturbing interest in the movement and location of Pearl Harbor's warships, nothing was done. It was decided that they were merely a way for the Japanese to study U.S. Navy operations.

On the morning of Saturday, December 6, Eastern Standard Time, Dorothy Edgers, a skilled translator, found a December 3 message in the Consular code that listed the capital ships in Pearl Harbor.

Edgers took the message to Commander Alwin Kramer, the department head. He read it over carefully and thanked Edgers. While he may have thought it important, Kramer had more pressing matters on his mind. He was decoding a long fourteen-part Japanese diplomatic message. So far, thirteen parts had been received between 2100 and 2200 hours via Station SAIL at Bainbridge Island, Washington. When decoded by the staff, it painted an alarming picture. After making four copies, Kramer personally took the text of the thirteen parts to Admiral Stark, but he was at the theater, watching *The Student Prince*.

When Stark finally saw the text, he told Kramer to wait until the full message had been translated. A frustrated Kramer left the other copies with the War and State Departments and the White House. President Roosevelt read over the text, which ran to fifteen typed pages. He looked at his friend Harry Hopkins, and said with grim finality, "This means war."

Cordell Hull, who received the text, shook his head. "I wash my hands of this affair."

Even though he was now certain that negotiations would not end the crisis and that Japan would attack, Roosevelt's hands were tied. First, the United States could not declare war on Japan and attack, especially on short notice. It was not the way he wanted to begin a world war. Also, doing so would alert the Japanese that the United States was reading Japanese messages, an ace in the hole no one wanted to turn over.

Then there was the America First Committee, the isolationists who fought to keep America out of a European war. Their spokesman, Charles Lindbergh, vocally opposed to aiding Britain, had many allies in the House and Senate. Going against many of Roosevelt's policies and intentions, the pilot, once the most famous and admired man in the world in 1927, had made an enemy of the White House. It was a wound that would never heal.

Japan would send the fourteenth part to its embassy on Massachusetts Avenue the following morning. Kramer and his staff would be ready to decode it for Hull, Marshall, Stark, and the White House before Nomura and Kurusu could deliver it.

Kramer had no trouble imagining what that final part would contain.

On Friday, December 5, three battleship divisions, along with their light cruiser and destroyer escorts, steamed one by one up the narrow channel leading into Pearl Harbor. Every ship went to its assigned berth, the battleships along Ford Island. Only *Pennsylvania*, in drydock, and *Colorado*, on the west coast, were not berthed.

The battleships had spent a long week of gunnery and fleet exercises south of Oahu. By noon, *Arizona* shut down her engines and boilers for the last time. Aboard her were 1,512 officers and men, along with the division commander, Rear Admiral Isaac Kidd.

It was good to be back in port. Hawaii was one of the most sought-after duty ports in the navy. *Arizona* was a lucky ship. She had won her share of gunnery contests and had the best band and the best boxing team in the navy. Several sets of brothers served on *Arizona*. She had been featured in the 1933 Jimmy Cagney and Pat O'Brien film, *Here Comes the Navy*, and some of the movie's most memorable scenes were filmed on the battleship. Many sailors seen in the background were still serving on *Arizona* in December 1941.

That Saturday night, December 6, was typical for the military on Oahu. Although it was the second week of the low-level alert triggered by the message Kimmel and Short received from Washington, most soldiers, sailors, airmen, and Marines were off duty, ready for a fun evening of bar-hopping, dances, poker, and any of the many other recreations offered in the Polynesian paradise. While men walked guard duty around sensitive buildings and ammunition dumps, and every ship in the harbor had its duty watch on deck, there was no real sense of urgency or concern. The years of peace since the Great War had embedded a sense of confident security in their minds. America was powerful and untouchable. If and when war came, they would be ready.

On *Enterprise*, heading back from Wake, the off-duty crew gathered on the spacious hangar deck, crowded with aircraft. The vast metal cave had the characteristic smell of oil, hot metal, and rubber as they sat on rows of folding chairs to watch Gary Cooper in *Sergeant York* projected on a large panel.

Far west across the Pacific, the Imperial Navy and Army were preparing for southern operations. In Formosa and Indochina, bombers, fighters, transports, and submarines were being readied for the attack on the Philippines. Convoys of troop transports were heading for Thailand to be used as a springboard for the invasion of Burma and Malaya. A small task force was ready to move on Guam in the Marianas, while an even larger force was waiting at the huge base at Kwajalein in the Marshalls to attack Wake Island. In short, every U.S. and British Pacific possession was about to be attacked by Japan.

On the eve of war, no one mentioned the threat to Pearl Harbor. While in retrospect, it seems unbelievable that the men in Washington apparently did not consider the Pacific Fleet to be at risk, in all fairness, they were operating in a partial vacuum. There were several indicators that Japan had set its crosshairs on Pearl Harbor, but the fact remained that no one in Washington, the navy, or the army truly believed that the small nation of strange and inscrutable people was capable of simultaneously launching two major fleet operations.

At Hamilton Army Air Field in central California, General Henry "Hap" Arnold, chief of the Army Air Corps, was briefing the crews of twelve Boeing

B-17s of the 38th and 88th Reconnaissance Squadrons. The twelve heavy bombers were to fly from California that night to Hawaii, arriving at Hickam Field around 0800 hours. After rest and refueling, the planes were to fly to Wake Island and on to Clark Field in the Philippines to beef up General Lewis Brereton's Far Eastern Air Force under MacArthur.

South of the Pearl Harbor channel, five *I*-class submarines waited for their cue to act. Mounted on the deck of each sub was a midget submarine. Between 2359 and 0300 hours the five subs would surface and launch their deadly brood. The five midgets would then move into the patrolled security zone around the harbor entrance and make their way in, hopefully undetected.

The torpedo officer aboard *I-24* was Lieutenant Mochitsura Hashimoto, who, three years and seven months later, would achieve an infamy of his own when, as commander of the submarine *I-58*, would sink the heavy cruiser *Indianapolis* between Tinian and Leyte, resulting in the deaths of over 900 Americans.

Shortly before midnight at Fort Shafter, a phone call was made to the program manager of Honolulu radio station KGMB. He was asked to keep the station broadcasting music all night. Normally the station went off the air at midnight. But the Army Air Corps had a standing agreement with KGMB to remain on the air when they were expecting a flight from the mainland. The Air Corps paid for the extra broadcast time. This would help the twelve B-17s to home in and find Oahu. But they would not be the only ones listening.

Admiral Kimmel, during a final meeting with his staff that evening, mentioned that he had been invited to the Japanese consulate by Consul General Nagao Kita for champagne the following morning. His aides urged him not to go, and Kimmel said he had no intention of going. As things turned out, it was one small bit of good fortune for Kimmel that he would not be sipping champagne with the Japanese on the morning of December 7. Instead, he had a golf date with General Short.

He went to his official residence overlooking Pearl and retired at 2130 hours.

One of the few strokes of luck for the U.S. Navy occurred on the afternoon of December 6. A destroyer in Halsey's Task Force 8 had a wire rope over the side, which caught up in one of the cruiser *Northampton*'s propeller shafts, causing the ship to halt. The task force halted and waited until divers could go down and cut the wire free. It was several hours before the cruiser, Rear Admiral Raymond Spruance's flagship, could proceed. TF 8 had been scheduled to arrive back in Pearl early on the morning of Sunday, December 7. It would be late.

At the plush Royal Hawaiian Hotel, often called the "Pink Palace," in Waikiki, a normal Saturday night dance party came to an end. The band played the traditional "Star Spangled Banner" at midnight, signaling the end of the party.

As he stood at attention with his wife, Captain Edwin Layton, CINCPAC's intelligence chief, waited as the civilians and military personnel did the same. When the music ended, he watched with unease as the crowd, hugging, kissing, and waving goodbyes, left the ballroom. He wanted to scream, "Wake up, America!" while grabbing his complacent nation by the scruff of its neck. But he and his wife went home.

CHAPTER 5

THE STAGE IS SET

In the 1942 classic film *Casablanca*, café owner Rick Blaine, played by Humphrey Bogart, is speaking with his piano player, Sam, portrayed by Dooley Wilson.

> **Rick:** Sam, if it is December 1941 in Casablanca, what time is it in New York?
> **Sam:** Ah, my watch has stopped.
> **Rick:** I bet they're asleep in New York. I'll bet they're asleep all over America.

Pearl Harbor is a natural inlet on the southern coast of Oahu in the Territory of Hawaii. To the east lies the city of Honolulu. Roughly shaped like a tree with four large branches from a central trunk, it has about eight square miles of water, with a mean depth of forty to fifty feet. There are four main lochs off the center, dominated by a flat island. The lochs are named for the direction from the center—West, Middle, East, and Southeast Lochs—which provided excellent safe anchorage and about twelve miles of docking for ships.

Ford Island, encompassing about 440 acres, was located at the mouth of East Loch. The channel, about 600 feet wide and four miles long, was dredged in the early years of the century. In 1941, the Pearl Harbor Navy Yard, which included the two drydocks, repair facilities, administration, and submarine base, were in Southeast Loch, whose mouth faced the east shore of Ford Island. Along the east and western shores of the island were the heavy mooring quays for capital ships. The hulking concrete mooring piers were numbered F1 to F14, which circled Ford Island counter-clockwise to the southwest tip. The opposite shore had more mooring for cruisers.

The lochs served as anchorages for auxiliary ships, while seaplane and submarine tenders moored north of Ford Island. The navy hospital was on the eastern shore of the channel, with Hickam Army Air Base behind it. Hickam was home to the army's Fifth Bombardment Group.

Naval Air Station Ford Island hosted the fighter, dive bomber, and torpedo squadrons while their carriers were in port. Its huge hangars were among the most prominent structures on Oahu. West of the channel were the aboveground tanks for ship and aviation fuel.

West of the harbor was Pearl City, home to navy personnel, civilian workers, and their families.

On any given day, at least until the summer of 1941, about 130 ships and craft of all types were based at Pearl. The battleship divisions, each numbering three ships, under a rear admiral, had the choice moorings along Ford Island facing the navy base. Ships entered through the channel and angled to port and up along the west shore of Ford, then turned starboard and came south. In this manner, all the capital ships faced the channel.

At the Navy Yard, a long concrete pier, called the "ten-ten" dock for its length of 1,010 feet, usually held a half-dozen ships awaiting repair or time in the immense concrete drydocks. Constructed in 1919, Dry Dock No. 1 was 1,000 feet long, 138 feet wide, and 35 feet deep, capable of holding the largest ships, often more than one at a time. A second, larger drydock was completed by the fall of 1941.

A huge red and white movable crane, one of the most distinctive features of the navy yard, hovered over the docks like a protective mother over her gray-painted brood. The yard never slept, maintaining and refitting Pearl's ships. Far into Southeast Loch was the submarine base and piers, with four boats lying low in the water. Pearl was home to Submarine Squadron 2.

On the morning of December 7, 1941, Pearl had about 103 ships of all types. Two destroyers and two minesweepers were on patrol outside the channel, covering the security zone. The most important ships in port that morning were moored at or near Ford Island. Below is a list of ships that played a prominent role in the hours to come.

Starting at the southeastern end of Ford Island were the battleships of three divisions, an oiler, and one repair ship.

F3: *California* (BB-44)
F4: *Neosho*, fleet oiler
F5: *Maryland* (BB-46), with *Oklahoma* (BB-37) outboard
F6: *Tennessee* (BB-43) with *West Virginia* (BB-48) outboard
F7: *Arizona* (BB-39) with repair ship *Vestal* (AR-4) outboard
F8: *Nevada* (BB-36)
F10: seaplane tender *Tangier* next to seaplane ramp

F11: *Utah* (BB-31/AG-16) AAA training ship
F12: *Raleigh* (CL-7)
F13: *Detroit* (CL-8)

In Middle Loch, the seaplane tender *Curtiss* (AV-4) was moored at X22.

Also in Middle Loch were destroyers, tied up in groups of four or five. At X4 were *Aylwin* (DD-355), *Farragut* (DD-348), and *Dale* (DD-353), with *Monaghan* (DD-354) outermost.

In Dry Dock No. 1 was *Pennsylvania* (BB-38), her hulking shape dwarfing destroyers *Cassin* (DD-372) and *Downes* (DD-375).

In floating drydock YFD2 was the *Shaw* (DD-373), one of the old "four piper" cans.

Deep in Southeast Loch, past the Navy Yard, was the submarine base, home of Submarine Squadron 2. In the slips were four submarines: *Narwhal* (SS-167), *Dolphin* (SS-0169), *Tautog* (SS-199), and *Cachalot* (SS-170). They were the only subs in Pearl that morning.

Tied up opposite the concrete 1010 dock at B2 were the light cruiser *Helena* (CL-50) and the old cruiser/minelayer *Oglala* (CM-4).

In West and East Lochs were more ships, but few of these figured in the attack.

Northeast of Pearl in the broad valley between the two blue-green craggy mountain ranges, Wheeler Army Air Base was the home of the 15th Army Pursuit Group, with three runways of over 6,000 feet. Wheeler's Curtiss P-36 and P-40 fighters were General Short's main fighter defense. He had ordered all his planes to be parked in long lines, wingtip to wingtip along the tarmac and guarded against sabotage.

North of Wheeler was the sprawling expanse of Schofield Barracks, home of the army's 24th and 25th Infantry Divisions. Nearby Fort Shafter was the headquarters of the Hawaiian Department and the office of General Short.

About seven miles west of Pearl City was Marine Corps Air Station Ewa Mooring Mast Field, where the Marines based their fighters and bombers. Ewa was formerly a base for the navy's airships, and the rusting stub of the mooring mast still jutted up from the windward end of the field.

On Oahu's eastern shore was Kaneohe Bay. An inlet eight miles by two, it covered seventeen square miles to shelter Naval Air Station Kaneohe, the navy's Catalina PBY patrol plane squadrons. Patrol Squadron VP-14 was based there, where long concrete ramps led from the water's edge to the tarmac alongside twin hangars.

Bellows Army Air Base was on the southeastern cape east of Diamond Head and Honolulu. There were several army and navy satellite fields around the island for emergency use and for basing more aircraft. In all, there were close to 400 army, navy, and Marine aircraft on Oahu.

Shortly after 0015 hours on the morning of December 7, Lieutenant Commander Hiroshi Hanabusa, commander of the Japanese submarine *I-24*, looked through his periscope over the black waters south of Oahu. As one of the submarines in the Special Attack Unit, *I-24* and four other *I*-class boats carried a single midget submarine. The subs were ten miles off the southern coast of Oahu, within sight of the lights of Waikiki.

Between 1215 and 0333, the five submarines came close to the surface and launched their midget submarines.

The Security Zone was patrolled by the destroyer *Ward* (DD-139), already a remarkable ship before she arrived at Pearl Harbor in January 1941. As one of the 111 *Wickes*-class fast destroyers, she was built and launched in the chaotic last year of the Great War. A desperate need for fast escorts for Atlantic convoys and anti-submarine patrols led to the construction of the class at ten shipyards around the country. Mare Island Naval Shipyard in Vallejo, California, laid down the keel on May 15, 1918, and launched her two weeks later on June 1. She was commissioned as *Ward* on July 24. Even for a crash wartime shipbuilding program, no other ship of the class was put into commission in less time. Named for Commander James Harmon Ward, the first officer in the U.S. Navy to be killed in action in the American Civil War, *Ward* was sent to the Atlantic to serve as one of the picket ships to support the Navy's Curtiss NC flying boats during their 1919 transatlantic flight from Newfoundland to the Azores. Piloting the NC-1 was the future admiral Marc Mitscher.

Returning to the Pacific, *Ward* was decommissioned in 1921. Twenty years later, as war raged in Europe again, *Ward* was recommissioned and sent west to Pearl Harbor.

On December 5, 1941, Lieutenant Commander William W. Outerbridge took command of the old destroyer, then attached to Division 80. Raised in Ohio, the thirty-five-year-old Outerbridge was considered an excellent officer, having graduated from Annapolis in 1927. *Ward* was his first sea command, and he was eager to prove himself.

Even though she was already twenty-three years old, *Ward* was still a fast, agile, sturdily built warship. At 314 feet long with a beam of 30 feet, *Ward* was almost the same size and displacement as a *Balao*-class submarine. But with her twin turbines pumping out 26,000 shaft horsepower, she could move at an impressive 30 knots. Her main gun armament consisted of four Mk IX 4-inch rapid-fire guns.

In the cool predawn of December 7, 1941, the last night of peace, a waning moon broke through the clouds over the calm waters off southern Oahu. Red buoys marked the restricted sea area. At 0340, minesweepers *Crossbill* (AMc-9) and *Condor* (AMc-14) finished their sweep of the restricted area. *Condor*'s 17-man crew was tired and waiting for dawn and breakfast. Ensign R. C. McCloy, *Condor*'s officer of the deck, or OOD, spotted a small dark object in the water about 50 yards off the port bow. It was moving at 9 knots. He called it to the attention of the veteran quartermaster, who identified it as a periscope. There were not supposed to be any subs in the Security Zone. At 0357 hours, using halyard blinkers, *Condor* alerted *Ward*, then on its inshore patrol.

Outerbridge ordered the ship to battle stations. All eyes strained in the dark as *Ward* approached the location of the sighting, but by 0435, they had seen nothing and secured from General Quarters.

Condor, whose crew had lost sight of the object at about 0400, resumed moving toward the red and black markers that denoted the entrance to the channel. Seaman First Class Ray Chavez, who died in 2019 at the age of 106, told me that he and the rest of the crew had been "working all night sweeping the eastern area. We were ready to head back to Pearl for chow. But the sighting of a possible sub sent everyone up on deck. It was too dark and the moon kept disappearing behind clouds. I never saw a thing. But when we heard later that a Jap midget sub had made it into Pearl and was sunk by the *Monaghan*, we were sure it was the one following us."

The heavy anti-submarine nets were opened at 0458 hours for the minesweepers. Since another ship was due in shortly, the net was not closed until 0840 hours, far too late to do any good.

Condor's sighting was not reported to the Fourteenth Naval District. Submarine sightings were far from uncommon in the months as tensions between Japan and the U.S. increased. But none of the "sightings" were found to be real. This was the first piece of bad luck for Pearl Harbor.

Three hundred miles north-northwest of Oahu's Kahuku Point, thirty-one gray-painted ships plowed at 24 knots through the choppy predawn seas. In the lead was Rear Admiral Sentaro Omori's flagship, the light cruiser *Abukuma*, followed by four destroyers of the First Destroyer Squadron, on alert for any sign of American ships. Three miles farther aft were the battleships *Ie* and *Kirishima*, with heavy cruisers *Tone* and *Chikuma* on the flanks.

Then came Nagumo, Yamaguchi, and Hara with their carrier divisions. They were in two long columns, each ship about 1,500 yards ahead of the next.

In the starboard column was the old and beloved *Akagi*, followed by *Kaga*. To port were *Soryu* and *Hiryu*. Behind them, as befitting the newest ships in the fleet, steamed *Shokaku* and *Zuikaku*. They were flanked by more destroyers, with two more watching the rear. Every carrier bore a huge rising sun painted on its foredeck. Farther behind were three submarines under Captain Kijiro Imaizumi.

Japanese warships, prefaced with HIJMS for His Imperial Japanese Majesty's Ship, were named according to their types. Carriers, the newest class of ships in the IJN, were given spiritual or symbolic names. The six carriers of the First Air Fleet were:

HIJMS *Akagi* "Red Castle"
HIJMS *Kaga* "Increased Joy"
HIJMS *Soryu* "Green Dragon"
HIJMS *Hiryu* "Flying Dragon"
HIJMS *Shokaku* "Lucky Crane"
HIJMS *Zuikaku* "Happy Crane"

The night sky was cloudy, partially hiding the waning moon. The First Air Fleet was drawing nearer to an island whose inhabitants were enjoying the last sleep of peace.

Six thousand miles to the east, Lieutenant Commander Alwin Kramer was awakened by a call from his office that they had just received the fourteenth and final part of the Japanese communiqué via Station S on Bainbridge Island. Kramer dressed and kissed his sleeping wife goodbye. It was just after 0720 when he arrived and read over the message.

The contents were not, as Kramer had believed, a declaration of war, but an accusation that the United States had failed to compromise while solving the issues between the two nations. In essence, Japan blamed the U.S. for failing to reach an agreement, so Japan broke off the discussion.

Kramer took copies to Stark and the War and Navy Departments. It was said that the acrimonious tone of the fourteenth part made it plain that the United States could expect war at any moment. Surprisingly, this message failed to incite any action by Roosevelt or the navy. They did not even send a warning to Kimmel. This may be due to the lack of a formal declaration of war in the message.

Then another short message from the new Foreign Minister Shigenori Togo in Tokyo to Nomura was intercepted and translated. It said, after the embassy had decoded the fourteenth and last part, Nomura and Kurusu were to deliver it personally to Cordell Hull at precisely 1300 Eastern Standard Time, 0730 in Hawaii. They were also ordered to have all the embassy's code books, cipher machines, and secret papers burned.

The last line of the message was cold and abrupt. "After that, things are automatically going to happen."

Nomura did not need the abilities of a sage to guess what the full message would likely be. An ultimatum and declaration of war.

At 0950, Navy Secretary Frank Knox and Secretary of State Cordell Hull read over their copies. Hull knew Nomura was to personally deliver the full text to him at 1300, but he already had the full text. What truly worried the statesman was that Sunday was an unusual day for any diplomatic exchange. Something serious was up.

But there was one small ray of hope. As far as anyone at the War Department knew, the United States Pacific Fleet was ready to move out of Pearl Harbor. The November 29 war warning would have been enough to give Kimmel and Short reason to put their forces on alert. According to War Plan Orange, Kimmel would have deployed his capital ships and was looking for the missing carrier task force believed to be at sea. In other words, the U.S. Navy was ready to fight the Japanese on nearly equal terms.

Colonel Rufus Bratton, chief of Army Intelligence, wanted to make sure Hawaii was alerted. He began a frustrating series of phone calls and visits to find General Marshall or any senior officer authorized to send a definite war warning to Short, and then on to Kimmel.

At last, Bratton located Marshall, who read over the newest message from Togo. The chief of staff agreed that Hawaii, as well as the Philippines and Panama, should be told to go on full alert.

As seen in Twentieth Century Fox's epic *Tora! Tora! Tora!*, Marshal wrote it in longhand for Bratton, who took it to the Army Signal Office and Lieutenant Colonel Edward French. But they had difficulty reading Marshall's writing. After doing this at about 1130, French tried to send it over the air. The warning was received in Panama, Presidio and San Francisco, the Caribbean, and the Philippines. But due to unusual atmospheric conditions, the transmission was not received in Hawaii. Unwilling to use the navy's system, French told his subordinate to send it as a telegram. Thus, another important indicator that might have given Pearl Harbor ample warning was lost until it was too late.

At 0530 hours, as the planes of the first wave were spotted on the carrier flight decks, heavy cruisers *Tone* and *Chikuma* launched two Zero floatplanes from their catapults. The aircraft circled the task force once, then turned south, disappearing in the gloom. They were to fly at high altitude over the waters between Oahu and Maui, to determine if any U.S. ships were anchored in the deep waters of Lahaina Roads. Genda hoped this was true, since it would make hitting those ships easier, and sinking them in the deep water would make them impossible to salvage.

He was reading over a recent dispatch from Tokyo, sent by Yoshikawa thirty-six hours earlier. It listed the most important ships in Pearl as of that time. Nine battleships, three light cruisers, and seventeen destroyers. Middle Loch also had four more light cruisers and two more destroyers. The list did not mention submarines, support and auxiliary vessels, oilers, or mine ships. But to Genda's disappointment, there were no carriers or heavy cruisers in port. The "nine battleships" were the eight ships of Battleship Divisions 1, 2, and 3, and the old battleship *Utah*, long since converted to an anti-aircraft training ship. In many accounts, *Utah* is referred to as a "target ship."

Yoshikawa's report also said no barrage balloons or torpedo nets were evident. This was good news for Murata's torpedo planes.

Most accounts have between 91 and 103 ships of all types in the harbor that morning. The variation is caused by whether the count includes yard boats or other small craft. Neither Yamamoto nor Genda ever expected to hit or damage more than a quarter of the ships present. The ships moored at or near Ford Island, the Navy Yard, and in Southeast Loch were the most important targets.

Up on the still-dark flight decks, the wind off the bows swept through the men and first wave of planes. It was bitterly cold and wet with salty spray. Up on the masts, signal flags snapped in the strong wind. Every ship bore the soon-to-be infamous *Kyokujitsu* naval ensign, with the red rising sun and sixteen red rays.

First in line were the gray-painted Zero fighters. The black cowlings and bright red Hinomaru "meatball" emblems were highly distinctive in the sky over Pearl Harbor. They circled the task force while the bombers lifted their heavy burdens into the dawn sky. The Val dive bombers, with their general-purpose bombs, were ahead of the long, sleek, green-painted Kate level and torpedo planes, the most important aircraft of the strike. They were at the after end of the flight decks as they needed the longest takeoff rolls to get airborne. Slung under their bellies were the triumph of Japanese technology, the long and deadly Type 91 aerial torpedoes. Each was fitted with the silver-painted wooden fins that would allow them to reach America's vaunted battle fleet in the shallow waters of Pearl Harbor.

On the bow of each carrier was a steam vent that spewed a thin stream of vapor that quickly disappeared in the cold air. The vent provided a visual indicator of wind direction. On board *Akagi*, Nagumo ordered the "Z" flag raised to the top of the mast. During the historic battle of Tsushima in 1905, Admiral Heihachiro Togo hoisted the flag, with its intersecting red, yellow, blue, and black triangles, over his flagship *Mikasa* just as the Russian fleet was spotted. The flag had come to represent the same call to duty as Nelson had at Trafalgar. "Do your duty."

Nagumo ordered the fleet to turn east into the wind. With ponderous majesty, the First Air Fleet turned to port, the smaller ships rolling in the steep swells. The big carriers pitched in the steady 40-knot wind over the bows.

Genda glanced at the bridge chronometer. The minute hand crept with agonizing slowness toward the twelve on the face. The hour hand was directly over the six. Looking at the short, black-clad man with the gold insignia on his collar, Genda saw Nagumo nod. It was exactly 0559 on December 7, 1941. Genda stepped onto the narrow catwalk over the flight deck. The icy wind tore at his tight black cap, held on only by the chin strap. He saw Fuchida standing up from his seat in the first Kate in the pack. His friend waved, a grin on his narrow face. Around his helmet was a white hachimaki silk scarf with the rising sun over his forehead. Genda waved back and signaled the officer on the port bow to begin launching the first wave. Genda looked into the brightening dawn to see *Soryu*, Yamaguchi's flagship, silhouetted against the eastern dawn. Her decks were packed with more aircraft. He could see a veritable cape of spray streaming behind the carrier, driven by the power of over eighty planes. He knew the same was coming off *Akagi* and the other four carriers.

With *Akagi*'s plane engines roaring, it was nearly impossible to hear anything else on the open deck. Another flag was hoisted to the signal mast. It was a bright red triangle with a single white disk. The flag remained up for a full minute, then was lowered. It was 0600 hours, time to launch.

The first Zero, piloted by Lieutenant Commander Shigeru Itaya, remained in place as he stood on the brakes. He was waiting for the launch officer to snap his red flag down at the exact moment *Akagi*'s bow began to rise. When he saw the signal, Itaya shoved the Zero's throttle forward to maximum power. Spears of blue flame shot out of the snarling engine's exhaust ports as the small plane shot forward to the end of the wooden deck. It looked like the end of the world as Itaya pulled back on the control stick as the nimble plane flew off the deck and disappeared.

Nagumo felt a chill until the fighter appeared farther ahead, rising into the purple dawn sky. The deck crew shouted "*Banzai!*" as they raised their hands in salute. The glowing eastern horizon glinted off the clean canopies as each fighter and bomber drove hard up the long wooden decks to claw their way into history.

When all 183 planes were assembled over the task force, Fuchida led them south into the brightening morning. On the carriers, the deck crews immediately began bringing the second wave of aircraft up to the flight decks for the 0700 launch.

Just as Itaya lifted off from *Akagi*, the U.S. Navy tug *Keosanqua* (AT-38) was heading out to meet supply ship *Antares* (AG-10), which had passed Barbers Point on the southwestern tip of Oahu. *Antares* was returning from Palmyra Island, towing a 500-ton barge (often misidentified as a target sled), and waiting for the tug to take the barge into the harbor. A pilot was on the tug to guide *Antares* through the channel. As the sun crested the eastern horizon, heralding another perfect Hawaiian Sunday morning, *Antares*'s captain, Commander Lawrence Grannis, subsequently spotted a black object that appeared to be a small submarine conning tower. The ship's log states: "Sighted strange object bearing 226 degrees true, distance about 1,500 yards on starboard quarter." It was on a converging course between the barge and the ship, and according to Grannis, "appeared to be having some difficulty maintaining depth control."

Several officers and crew spotted it, and at 0630, the sighting report was sent to the *Ward*, cruising a mile to the southwest. This time there was plenty of sunlight. With the *Ward* turning to parallel the *Antares*, the small object was clearly defined with the sun behind it.

There was no doubt, even though no one on *Antares* and *Ward* had ever seen anything like it before. It was certainly a submarine, painted a dark green and coated with sea growth. The oval-shaped conning tower was only about two feet high and had tiny glass ports. The sub was moving at 9 knots, clearly headed for the *Antares*.

Overhead, Ensign William Tanner of Patrol Squadron 14, out of Kaneohe, also spotted the sub. But he assumed it was an American sub in distress. Circling low, he ordered one of his crew to drop two smoke markers to assist the *Ward* in finding it.

On *Ward*'s bridge, the helmsman was the first to see the small conning tower. He and the quartermaster of the watch agreed it was some kind of submarine. The quartermaster called Lieutenant (jg) O. W. Gepner, *Ward*'s executive officer. After seeing for himself, he called out, "Captain, come to the bridge!"

Outerbridge, catching some sleep on the chart room cot after the earlier alert, pulled a robe over his undershirt and boxers, and came through the door to the wheelhouse. Gepner pointed to the sub and handed him the binoculars.

The time was 0637. Outerbridge, despite his lack of command experience, knew they were seeing a sub in the restricted area, a clear violation. No subs were to enter the area without escort and without approval from the commandant of the Fourteenth Naval District.

He made his decision quickly. "Call the crew to battle stations and go to full speed." It was now 0640. The first wave of Japanese fighters and bombers were about 140 miles out, and the second wave of pilots and crews were climbing into their planes.

The water around *Ward*'s stern boiled as she changed heading toward the sub. Immediately her crew emerged from hatches and doors to run for the gun mounts and depth charge racks. One man was already on Number 3 mount and had pulled a 4-inch shell from the ready rack. In less than a minute, *Ward* was ready for combat. From his lofty vantage point, Tanner saw the three wakes as they neared their confrontation. *Antares* was turning north to enter the outer buoys that marked the channel entrance. The sub's wake was about to intercept the larger ship's course.

The *Ward* was charging ahead at 25 knots to get between the two ships. As she came abreast of the barge, Outerbridge ordered a turn to port, which pointed the bow into the area between the sub and *Antares*'s wake. All the guns were ready, and he ordered them swung to starboard. Every man on watch on the bridge, in the guns or on deck, saw the small dark object as they moved in.

Outerbridge, still in skivvies and robe, ordered the ship slowed as they approached the sub. It was only about a hundred yards off the starboard bow. At exactly 0645, Outerbridge said, "Commence firing!" The phone talker on the bridge repeated the order.

Number 1 gun on the bow fired first. The gunner could not use his regular sights since the sub was too close. He aimed by peering right down the barrel "like a squirrel gun." The heavy Mk IX gun boomed, clearly heard across the quiet waters off southern Oahu. It was the first American shot of the Second World War.

But it missed, hitting the water twenty yards past the sub and raising a tall waterspout. The sub showed no reaction. Then Number 3 gun atop the galley deckhouse boomed at a range of fifty yards and scored a direct hit, punching a large hole where the conning tower met the hull. The sub rolled to starboard, then wallowed and slowed as *Ward* moved closer.

"Cease fire!" Outerbridge ordered.

When the sub sank and came under *Ward*'s stern, he yelled, "Roll four depth charges!"

With four blasts on the ship's whistle, the crews on the stern rolled four Mark 3 420-pound depth charges into the roiling water behind the ship. The chief torpedoman said he saw the sub directly over the first charge. Four successive rumbles sounded as boiling masses of white seawater erupted in the destroyer's wake.

Then Ensign Tanner, now recognizing this was probably a hostile sub, came in and dropped two Mark 3 depth charges where he had last seen the sub. Then he reported his actions to Kaneohe Bay.

There was no sign of the sub. *Ward* circled the site, but her crew only saw the iridescent slick of oil on the surface. The water was 1,200 feet deep.

At 0651 Outerbridge sent a coded message to the watch officer of the Fourteenth Naval District in Pearl Harbor. "We have dropped depth charges on submarine operating in defensive sea area," but almost immediately he considered this message too ambiguous, as many false sub sightings had been reported in the last few months. Three minutes later he sent: "We have attacked, fired upon, and dropped depth charges upon submarine operating in defensive sea area." This second message was intended to alert the navy that *Ward* had actually seen and fired on a sub, not merely dropped charges on a suspected sonar contact. The message was received by the Bishop Point radio station and relayed to the Fourteenth Naval District.

For the next thirty minutes, nothing else happened.

Commander Mitsuo Fuchida led his fighters and bombers south. Itaya's forty-five Zero fighters were at 14,000 feet in the lead and around the bombers. At 9,800 feet, the forty-nine level bombers were in triangle-shaped formations. To starboard at 11,000 feet were Takahashi's fifty-one dive bombers, while Murata's forty torpedo planes flew at 9,200 feet. As the sun rose and broke through the low clouds to the east, Fuchida felt it resembled the navy battle flag—a good omen.

At about 0700, he tuned the bomber's radio to Honolulu station KGMB, and the pilot of his plane adjusted his course to follow it south.

But they were being watched. There was a new technology on Oahu that morning. The new mobile radar units, as promised by Marshall, had arrived in August. The SCR-270B units could detect aircraft and ships at a distance of nearly a hundred miles under optimum conditions. Under the command of U.S. Air Corps Colonel William Tetley, the radar truck and trailer units were dispersed around the island at Kawailoa, Wainae, Kaawa, Kokohead, Schofield Barracks, and Fort Shafter, the latter two being used for training.

On November 26, coincidentally the same day the First Air Fleet sailed from Hitokapu Bay, the unit from Fort Shafter was moved north to Opana on a knoll in the foothills of the Koʻolau Range near Kahuku Point at the northernmost tip of Oahu.

Radar was a new technology in warfare. Primarily developed by the British in the late 1930s, they achieved a breakthrough with the invention of the Resonant Cavity Magnetron, which generated strong pulses of radio energy that would bounce off solid objects at great distances. The triumph of Royal Air Force Fighter Command over the Luftwaffe was largely due to the ability to detect enemy planes long before they reached England.

Now the new radar was being put to use along the American West Coast and in Hawaii. Tetley, who headed up the Aircraft Warning System, respected the new technology, but also faced a steep learning curve.

The AWS network of mobile radar units were connected by phone to Fort Shafter's information center, about thirty miles south of Opana. This in turn was linked to the headquarters of the pursuit squadrons at Wheeler and other airfields. The AAA batteries around the air bases were being modernized to accept intercept vectors sent from the radar units.

The SCR-270B unit at Opana consisted of four trucks. The first truck held an enclosed van with generator and rectifier unit, with a second truck bearing the transmitter and receiver. A third truck towed the folding antenna, while the last held the monitoring equipment. The men who operated the units were all volunteers, chosen for their skill with electronic equipment. Private Joseph L. Lockard from Harrisburg, Pennsylvania, and Private George Elliott of Chicago were on the unit from its time at Fort Shafter to when it was moved to Kahuku Point.

Lockard, who joined the army in 1940, was shipped via the Panama Canal to Schofield Barracks in November for his basic training. He had heard of the new radar units and applied, hoping it would further his career. In the months before the arrival of the radar units, Lockard and his fellow soldiers learned the physics of radar and how to use radios.

"We were all privates, with a cadre of non-coms from the infantry to form the unit," Lockard said in a later interview. "There were no specific assignments at that point. We were all trained in everything. In August of 1941, our equipment arrived and we started to learn about it. There were six of the 270Bs. It took two men to operate one unit."

Lockard described his introduction to the radar that would become famous. "The first unit I worked with was on Koko Head from September to November.

The Opana site was about 530 feet above sea level. There were no living facilities at all. We were living in pyramidal tents on the beach at Kawailoa, a good five miles away. The truck would drive up the paved road, turn off away from the sea, and drive up a dirt road another two miles until it reached the radar site."

Considering General Short's mania to prevent sabotage, it is amazing that the remote radar units were not only inactive at night, but unguarded. "The units were locked up at night, but I don't think anyone was worried about sabotage."

One of the most intriguing "what if" moments of the Pearl Harbor story concerns Privates Lockard and Elliott and a lieutenant. For the rest of their lives, these men would be identified with that one hour before the attack.

On the night of December 6 or 7, "I was up there with George Elliott. We knew each other and worked well but we were not buddies or anything. We'd gone up there the night before and stayed overnight in a pup tent. This was because our exercise was going to start at 0400 hours. The Opana site was elevated from the sea, providing a great view out to the north, but Pearl Harbor was far away, beyond a ridge."

When their wind-up alarm clock went off, Elliott and Lockard dressed and climbed into the radar van. Lockard explained that their first job was to report in by phone.

"That telephone line went directly to the information center at Fort Shafter. They had a plotting board. The operator relayed the information to a plotter, who put it on the board. Even on a Sunday, men were working in the information center, but not for the entire day.

"The exercise was meant to provide practice on a day with little air traffic. So, we opened up the equipment and turned it on. This is a 270B I'm talking about, that was connected by cable to the operating van. We had a small plotting table with a map, oscilloscope with all the necessary controls, and a water cooler for the transmitting tubes. And that was connected to the antenna truck, which had copper tubing sections that ran from the transmitter out underneath the antenna truck, which had a metal rig that was laid flat. It was cranked up into place, about 45 feet up in the air. We had to point the antenna at the North Star, otherwise, you wouldn't know where the azimuth was, so we had to do it at night."

Elliott and Lockard endured the icy wind blowing off the Pacific as they operated the new system. "It took two men to operate it because one had to do the plotting and the communication, while the other worked the scope with all its knobs. Our operation period was from 0400 to 0700 hours. At 0700, everyone in the operation network was going to close down because it was Sunday and the end of the program. If it had been a weekday, we'd have been there all day."

Again, this serves to show how badly luck played against Pearl Harbor. While the Japanese intended to catch the fleet in port on a Sunday, the weekend also made it unlikely that the incoming force would be detected. Of course, Genda and Fuchida had no knowledge of the radar units, and even Yoshikawa was unaware of them, but the short duration of the Sunday morning exercise gave them an unexpected advantage.

At 0645, at the same moment *Ward* fired on the midget sub, Lockard was checking his watch. They were to shut down at 0700. That was when the personnel at the information center would go to breakfast. But when the time came, Lockard had seen no sign of the truck that was to come and pick them up. He chose to keep the unit on and gain a few more minutes of training.

"At 0702 Elliott looked into the screen and said, 'What's this?' I said, 'Well, let me see.' There was this thing on the screen. It was the largest blip I'd ever seen!"

At that moment, Commander Fuchida and the first wave were just over 100 miles from Oahu.

"At first, we thought something was wrong with the equipment, so we ran through a series of tests. I checked out the receiver and the transmitter to see if there was anything mechanically wrong. There was nothing electronically wrong that we could see, so we started plotting the blip. We did that for a while, then decided to call in to the information center."

At Fort Shafter, the only man taking calls was Private Joe McDonald. Lockard, who had known McDonald since the States, asked if there was an officer on duty. Told that everyone had gone off to breakfast, Lockard asked his friend to try and find someone to take their report.

"By now," Lockard continued, "it was about 0710 hours. When we first picked up the blip it was about 155 miles away, I believe."

McDonald found an Air Corps officer, Lieutenant Kermit Tyler, of the 78th Pursuit Squadron. "He came back and told me, 'It's okay, it's okay.' I later learned they were expecting a flight of B-17s from the States, but if the B-17s were that far off course, they'd never make it. We continued to track it, and called them back again. This time we got Tyler on the phone with us. He said, 'Don't worry about it.'"

This was only Tyler's second day of duty at the information center.

"We tracked it [the incoming force] within 20-some miles of the island." The incoming blip disappeared in the reflection from the mountain range south of Opana. Lockard concluded, "The truck came sometime after 0730 hours and we closed down the equipment. Halfway back to our camp at Kawailoa, another truck passed us with everybody aboard yelling and waving their hands with the horn blowing like hell. We knew something was wrong, but we didn't know what. We began to see smoke to the south, and when we reached the camp, we were told Pearl Harbor, Fort Shafter, Schofield Barracks, and Wheeler Field were being bombed."

Elliott and Lockard immediately returned to Opana and manned the radar around the clock. More soldiers arrived, armed and ready to repel the expected Japanese invasion that never came.

The story of how the Opana Point radar detected the incoming first wave fifty-three minutes before the attack has become part of Pearl Harbor lore.

At the very moment, Elliott called Lockard's attention to the radar blip, Nagumo's carriers were launching the second wave, led by Commander Shigekazu Shimazaki off *Shokaku*. Intended to number 171 planes, mechanical trouble left four planes behind. The remaining 167 turned south and followed in Fuchida's wake.

At berth F7, *Arizona* was being filled with 1,500,000 gallons of fuel oil for her planned trip to Bremerton, Washington, to repair her bow after a collision with one of her escorts. Also in her bunkers were 180,000 gallons of volatile aviation gasoline for her twin Kingfisher floatplanes. In her forward and after magazines below the waterline were over 1,000 tons of cordite powder charges for her twelve 14-inch guns.

The Zero floatplane launched by the cruiser *Tone* reported that no U.S. warships were in Lahaina Roads, which disappointed Genda and Fuchida. The plane then scouted the area south of Oahu, looking for any American warships. It did see the *Ward*, but a single destroyer was not worth reporting. One of the few lucky breaks for the United States was that the plane failed to see *Enterprise* heading for Pearl from 200 miles west.

The RCA station in Honolulu received Marshall's warning at 0733, three minutes after Nomura and Kurusu were to meet with Hull. There was no mention of the dispatch being priority or urgent, so it was given to a young Japanese American boy. The courier, not realizing the import of what he was carrying, climbed onto his bicycle and pedaled for Fort Shafter.

At the Japanese Embassy in Washington, Nomura paced and fretted while the fourteenth part of the ultimatum was laboriously decoded. It is ironic that Roosevelt and his cabinet had already read the full message that morning.

Nomura realized he would be late to his meeting with Hull. It should be noted that Nomura was not privy to the Pearl Harbor attack, but he would have been less of a statesman if he did not suspect what would happen.

THE STAGE IS SET

In the lead Kate, now passing east of Oahu, Fuchida used his powerful binoculars to determine if they were on course. He was delighted to see Kahuku Point pass his bomber's starboard wing. Sliding open the observer's canopy, he held out a flare pistol and fired. The red flare exploded and signaled the formation to turn off for their individual attack plans. The torpedo bombers banked to the southwest and descended to their approach altitude of 2,000 feet. The Zero fighters sped ahead to take position to shoot down any American planes in the sky. The level and dive bombers split up to begin their runs on the air and naval bases.

At 0739, Fuchida saw Pearl Harbor in all its naval majesty, spread out before his plane. There were no barrage balloons, no AAA burst, no American fighters climbing to intercept them, and no sign of an alert. With emotions shaking him, he ordered the signal sent to the First Air Fleet. "*Tora! Tora! Tora!*"

Genda's fervent hope had been realized. Total surprise.

The sky over Oahu looked like an immense azure bell. Between the two mountain ranges, several pure white cumulus clouds drifted over the flat expanse of green and red sugar cane and pineapple fields. It was a beautiful, quiet Sunday morning, only three weeks from Christmas. Over the harbor a few scattered skeins of clouds marked the otherwise clear sky. It was warm for December, and a brisk 10-knot breeze slid over the base from the north.

A few civilian planes were in the air, including a yellow Interstate Cadet flown by a student pilot under the guidance of Cornelia Fort. Her bright yellow biplane was north of Pearl when she suddenly noticed a few, then scores, of gray and green planes passing by, headed south. The bemused Japanese pilots watched as Fort took control, peeled away, and headed for John Rodgers Airport near Hickam. Fort soon returned to the mainland and became the second woman inducted into the Women's Air Force Service Pilots (WASP) to ferry planes from factories to military bases. She was the first WASP fatality when her BT-13 crashed in Mulberry Canyon, Texas.

The first wave of planes flew low over the cane fields as hundreds of workers cut the tall sugar cane stalks for the C&H and Dole companies.

At 0745, the bands of every capital ship in the harbor gathered for morning colors. Most of the battleships had scrubbed white canvas awnings over the bow and stern, offering shade to the deck crews. Spotless white cord wound around the gangway handrails as the morning OOD inspected his departments. The ships were ready for the admiral's inspection on Monday.

Admiral Husband Kimmel, commander in chief of the U.S. Pacific Fleet, was in his home in the hills overlooking the harbor, dressing in his tropical whites. His golf game with Short would have to wait, as he wanted to get more information on the *Ward*'s sighting of a submarine just off the harbor channel. This was serious, and he did not for a moment think it was a false alarm.

At 0750, Fuchida signaled for the attack to begin.

Murata, leading the torpedo planes eastward from the coast, watched as they broke into groups of eight planes each. They descended and headed for the western shore of Ford Island, silhouetted in the bright golden sun reflected off the calm water.

The first target to feel Japanese steel and lead was MCAS Ewa Mooring Mast Field, directly under the advancing bombers. Itaya's nine leading Zeros found forty-seven American planes on the ground that Sunday morning, with nineteen VMSB-232 Vultee SB2U Vindicator dive bombers and VMF-221's remaining Brewster F2A Buffalos. The Zeros strafed the neat ranks of planes, clustered at the center of the tarmac to guard against sabotage, which until that morning was considered the primary threat. The tank containing 10,000 gallons of aviation fuel erupted in a huge orange fireball.

In less than fifteen minutes, the entire line of Marine Aircraft Group 21's planes was in flames. Not a single U.S. Marine fighter managed to get into the air, but several officers and men found machine guns and rifles to shoot back at the attackers. The base commander, Lieutenant Colonel Claude Larkin, was wounded while he directed the defense. One Marine private named Merle Thompson shot at Lieutenant Yoshio Shiga's Zero with his Colt .45 while swearing at the top of his lungs.

Fortunately, forty-four of MAG-21's ninety-two planes had been deployed to other bases prior to December 7.

Murata led the groups of Kates each southeast, banking north, then west over Hickam Field and Southeast Loch. There they dropped to 150 feet and aimed at the formidable line of gray battleships. High overhead, the dive bombers were already beginning their attacks.

The first bomb dropped on Oahu on December 7 was loosed by one of the dive bombers, but it missed the seaplane base and exploded on the muddy shore of Ford Island's southwest end.

On board his flagship, the old minelayer *Oglala*, Admiral William Furlong saw the explosion. At first, he thought it was an accident by a careless American pilot, but when the Val flew past him, Furlong saw the bright red disks painted on the wings and fuselage. "Japanese! Man your stations!" he yelled as he raced to the radio room to alert the other ships in the harbor.

"All ships in harbor sortie!" but it would take irreplaceable minutes for the entire base to realize what was happening.

The first torpedoes loosed on the U.S. Pacific Fleet were carried by Kates from *Hiryu* and *Soryu*, heading in two groups at the western shore of Ford Island. At F11 was the old battleship *Utah*. But even with most of the superstructure replaced with AAA guns, it looked like either a battleship or small carrier. At 0755, two brilliantly modified Type 91 torpedoes slipped into the shallow water and, true to Genda's hopes, did not plow into the harbor bottom. *Utah*, who had once counted a man named John Dillinger among its crew, rocked from the blast and leaned hard over. Directly astern, the light cruiser *Raleigh* was hit by a second torpedo, flooding her forward engine room and two fire rooms. A third torpedo screamed between *Raleigh* and the cruiser *Detroit* at F13. The Type 91 did not explode, instead burying itself in the shoreline mud.

One Japanese pilot chose to go over Ford Island and aim for the *Pennsylvania* but, seeing she was in the concrete drydock, loosed one torpedo at the old *Oglala*. The weapon slid under the minelayer and hit the inboard ship, the cruiser *Helena*. The blast caused great damage. *Oglala* was literally raised out of the water from the detonation of 700 pounds of high explosive. The ship, which had been in service since the Great War, rolled over. One of her crew said, "She died of fright."

Kimmel was on the phone with one of his staff, listening to the report of *Ward*'s attack. Just then a yeoman burst into the aide's office and yelled, "Signal from the tower! The Japs are attacking Pearl Harbor! This is no drill!"

Kimmel slammed the phone down and ran outside, calling for his car and driver. Then he stopped on the grassy slope of his lawn and saw his entire world going up in flames.

All over the harbor and airfields, he saw explosions and towering spouts of white water from torpedo hits on his proud battle line. The quiet Sunday morning had become an orgy of destruction punctuated with the thud of AAA fire and the snarl of aircraft engines. As his car screeched to a stop under the long porte cochere, he watched as his beautiful fleet and hundreds of his men died.

He knew it was his fault.

CHAPTER 6

VISIONS OF RUIN

"Invincibility lies in the defense; the possibility of victory in the attack." —Sun Tzu

The attack on Pearl Harbor on December 7, 1941, was a watershed moment that tore away every preconceived notion of how a modern naval war was fought. In a way, the fires alongside Ford Island were a crucible in which the impurities of prewar doctrine were cooked out even as the new navy was made strong and flexible.

This chapter is not merely another account of the events of December 7, 1941, but is meant to relate the personal memories of a few of the men who were there. No matter how meticulously researched, no history of December 7 can relate every human story. There would have been tens of thousands, and more than three thousand can never be known.

Some of the most intriguing events are well worth describing. I chose to provide accounts of the men who witnessed the attack on Battleship Row, the untimely arrival of the B-17s from California, and the brave actions of two men at Kaneohe Bay. While several fighters managed to get into the sky over Oahu that morning, the exploits of Ken Taylor and George Welch are worth relating. I chose these portions of the attack because I was fortunate to know some of the men involved: John Murphy of *Vestal*, Jack Evans of *Tennessee*, Stuart Hedley of *West Virginia*, Woody Derby of *Nevada*, Ray Richmond of *Oklahoma*, and Ray Chavez of *Condor*. Along with Earl Williams of the 38th Reconnaissance Squadron and John Finn of VP-14, I learned much about the attack and its effect on the people who lived through it. The best personal account is from *Arizona* survivor Donald Stratton in his book, *All the Gallant Young Men*.

I will link these with concurrent events around the harbor and the airfields.

To better understand the first minutes of the attack, remember that no American sailor, Marine, soldier, or airman knew they were about to go to war. The quiet peace they enjoyed in Hawaii was shattered in less than two hours.

Exactly 102 minutes after Lieutenant Commander Outerbridge radioed sighting and depth charging the Japanese submarine to the Fourteenth Naval District, Commander Fuchida ordered the torpedo planes and level bombers to attack the battleships moored at Ford Island.

The battleship *Oklahoma* was outboard of *Maryland* at berth F5. *Oklahoma* is as good an example of the ships alongside Ford Island as any for relating what the Japanese intended to sink.

USS *Oklahoma* was laid down at the New York Shipbuilding Company in Camden, New Jersey, in 1912 and commissioned into the U.S. Navy in 1916, just a year before the nation entered the Great War. She displaced 29,000 tons and was 575 feet long. Her draft of 28 feet enabled the battleship to navigate the shallow waters of Pearl Harbor. Her twelve Yarrow boilers provided 80,000 shaft horsepower. While she was the first battleship in the U.S. Navy to be fueled by oil, she still had older triple-expansion reciprocating engines. These drove her at 20 knots for 8,000 miles. Those numbers were respectable for the 1920s but woefully inadequate by 1941. Her officers and crew of 1,350 were typical of the men who served on the Pacific Fleet battleships. *Oklahoma* had four main turrets: two with twin 14-inch and two with three 14-inch guns. There had been several modifications since 1916, including additional armor and better secondary and AAA armament.

Her armor reflected the times in which she served. Battleships, before the advent of aircraft, carried heavy armor on their sides, since this is where enemy shells from another battleship were expected to strike. For *Oklahoma*, the side armor was 13 inches thick, thinning to 8 inches below the waterline. Her deck armor was 3 inches thick. The second deck was also plated in 1.5 inches of steel armor. While this sounds impressive, it was typical of capital ships of the time. Armor was heavy deadweight. It protected the engines, boilers, magazines, and hull at the cost of speed. Her turrets had 18 inches on the front, presumably facing the enemy, with 5 inches on the roof.

Oklahoma's armor was said to "protect where it matters." As one of her officers said, "If she were hit where it matters, it would not matter. If she were struck by a shell where it did not matter, than that would not matter either."

As for AAA defenses, *Oklahoma* had been upgraded in February 1941. She carried eight 5-inch .25-caliber guns, four 3-inch .50-caliber guns, and eight

.50-caliber water-cooled machine guns. These would protect the battleships from air attack.

But on the morning of December 7, none of these had their firing locks in place and no ready ammunition. Division Commander Rear Admiral Isaac Kidd was to inspect *Oklahoma* on Monday.

One of the defining images of the twentieth century was the horrifying moment when the battleship *Arizona* exploded in a cataclysmic fireball at 0810.

Repair ship *Vestal* was tied up on *Arizona*'s port side. "We were there to do some work on her," said Radioman John Murphy of Oxnard, California. "I was coming off my watch, but wanted something to do. The OOD suggested I go 'next door' to the *Arizona* and make a mail run. I had to wait for the OOD to sign the weather report before I could go over. The sky was clear and quiet. Nothing was happening."

Gunner's Mate Donald Stratton of Nebraska awoke at about 0500 in his cot in the Sixth Division aboard *Arizona*. "I stretched, rubbed sleep from my eyes, and folded my cot. After a shower, dressed in the normal Sunday uniform of clean white shorts and a T-shirt, along with my sailor's cap."

By 0630, Stratton was eating breakfast with the other men in his division. "Typical Sunday chow," he wrote in his book *All the Gallant Men*. "Coffee, powdered eggs, fried Spam, pancakes, and some local fruit."

He was belowdecks at 0755 when the Pearl Harbor signal tower raised the blue and white banner that signaled morning colors. On the fantails of *Arizona* and the other battleships, the bands were ready to play when the national colors were raised on the stern flagstaff.

"After breakfast I saw a box of oranges and took three to bring to a friend who was in sickbay with jaundice. As I passed through the Number 2 casement and out to the forecastle deck and into the sunlight, I heard the drone of aircraft engines and bombs exploding on Ford Island." Watching in disbelief from *Arizona*'s foredeck, Stratton said, "What in hell is happening?" That question was being spoken by a thousand mouths at almost the same moment.

Akagi's twelve Kate torpedo bombers, led by Commander Murata, flew over Hickam Field, avoiding Takahashi's twenty-seven dive bombers. Dropping to 150 feet at 150 knots, he flew past Hickam and banked over the submarine base in Southeast Loch. His twelve planes would be the first to launch torpedoes at Battleship Row. Breaking into elements of three planes each, the bombers spread out for the final approach. Murata was farthest to the right, while Lieutenant Binichi Goto led the left column. Each three-plane element would go in together and drop at the same time. The spacing of each element was intended to ensure that no warship was missed. With all three planes releasing their torpedoes at the same time, the Kates could be past the ships before the torpedoes hit and raised towering waterspouts that could bring them down.

Now at an altitude of 55 feet, Murata aimed at the gray bulk of *West Virginia*. Two hundred yards to Murata's left were Goto's three planes, headed for *Oklahoma*. Within ten seconds, six Type 91 torpedoes slid neatly into the water, the silver-painted wooden fins stripped away by the impact. With a third of a mile to travel at 40 knots, the time to impact was 28 seconds.

"I was going to go ashore on liberty and was in the shower," said one of *Oklahoma*'s yeomen, Ray Richmond. "Suddenly it felt as if someone had picked up the ship, shook it, and dropped it. I hit the overhead." Thinking of the army's habit of dropping sandbags on ships for practice, "I thought, 'Oh, those army planes are dropping really big sandbags on us.' But then the ship shuddered again and I heard the general alarm and bolted for the door. I was naked as a jaybird but I went to my battle station on Number 5 Port 5-inch .51-caliber gun." Richmond felt the huge battleship start to heel over to port from three torpedo hits. "Then the lights went out."

Oklahoma was struck by the first three torpedoes launched by Goto's flight. As the Kates climbed to clear the ship's superstructure, the first two Type 91s slammed into the thinner armor twenty feet below the waterline amidships between the mainmast and funnel. While they tore apart the armor, they did not penetrate the hull itself. Water poured into the fuel tanks in the void between the armor belt and hull. The third torpedo struck in almost exactly the same place, ripping into the hull and allowing water to flood the boiler rooms. The detonation also tore open the longitudinal bulkhead over the keel. Tons of water poured in and the 29,000-ton battleship, once the pride of the navy, began to capsize to port. Two more torpedoes hit the ship, but due to her steepening tilt, they exploded against the thick belt of hull armor.

In twelve minutes, *Oklahoma* rolled over, only stopping when her superstructure hit the muddy bottom. Dozens of her crew, the ones topside when the ship was hit, scrambled over the red-painted hull and dived into the water between her and *Maryland*. There they clambered up the rope ladders, then helped fire the AAA guns. A great red whale, the battleship's screws gleamed like bronze flukes in the morning sunlight.

More of Murata's planes from *Kaga* headed for *California*, *Arizona*, and *Nevada*. The timing of each attack assured a hit every six seconds.

Sixteen more Kates from *Hiryu* and *Soryu* came in from the southwest toward the west side of Ford Island.

Takahashi's twenty-seven Vals from *Shokaku* attacked Ford Island and Hickam Army Air Field with 250-kg Type 98 general-purpose bombs. Another twenty-seven dive bombers from *Zuikaku* went after Wheeler Air Field and Schofield Barracks. Forty-five Zeros provided an air umbrella for the attacking bombers.

Light cruisers *St. Louis*, *Raleigh*, *Honolulu*, and *Detroit*, as well as the anti-aircraft training ship *Utah*, were firing into the sky only four minutes after the first bomb fell. Tracers of 20mm rounds streaked into the blue morning sky, while the 1.1-inch mounts and .50-caliber machine guns chased the bombers. As good and determined as the gunners were, they could not fire for long. Most of the ammunition was locked up belowdecks. Only the OOD or the chief quartermaster held the key. On some ships, those important men could not be found. There are stories of gunners using crowbars and even pistols to break open the ammunition stores.

California was tied up at F3, forward of the oiler *Neosho* (AO-23). Two of the battleship's 5-inch AAA guns and two .50-caliber machine guns were ready for use, with fifty-five rounds for the bigger guns and 400 rounds in belts for the machine guns. At 0803, eight minutes after the attack began, *California*'s gunners were already firing back. The sky began to fill with black AAA bursts, but several were the white bursts of practice shells, an indicator of the confusion during the defense.

Two Kates came in at 0805 and released their torpedoes. One struck *California* under the armor belt between Number 2 turret and the bridge. The torpedo tore a hole ten feet high and twenty-four feet wide, letting tons of water pour into the hull. With her AAA guns still firing, *California* began to sink with a five-degree list to port. Two Val dive bombers scored hits on her deck. Damage control continued to slow the rate of sinking until one of the level bombers put an armor-piercing bomb into the forward deck, causing severe damage and a fire that spread. When electrical power died, there was no choice but to let the ship sink. She could be salvaged later. *California* took three days to settle on the harbor bottom. The heroic actions of her crew resulted in four Medals of Honor for valor, the most ever for a single ship in a battle. Three of those were posthumous.

At Ford Island, Takahashi's dive bombers destroyed over half of the air station's planes. The two large hangars burned from the inside as aircraft fuel tanks exploded.

At berth F6 astern of *Oklahoma* at the center of Battleship Row was *West Virginia*, known with affection as "Wee Vee" by her crew. Her distinctive cage masts and those of *Tennessee* stood out clearly against the blue early morning sky.

In *West Virginia*'s quartermaster berth was Seaman Stuart Hedley of West Palm Beach, Florida. He related what happened. "I was in my dress blues and looking forward to going ashore to a church picnic. Then the PA called out, 'Away all fire and rescue crews!' Then the bugler—that would have been Marine Corporal Richard Fisk—blew the general alarm. I ran up five decks to my quarters to grab my hat, and a Bos'n's Mate kicked me in the seat of the pants and yelled, 'Get to your battle stations on the double! This is the real thing!'"

Upon reaching the main deck, Hedley saw planes coming in from all directions. "I saw a torpedo plane going over us and the pilot was laughing like anything."

The 33,500-ton battleship was hit by seven torpedoes in all, causing the ship to heave as Hedley climbed up the ladder into the bottom of Number 3 turret, just aft of the superstructure. On top of the twin 16-inch turret was a catapult and a Vought Kingfisher floatplane. "I climbed into the turret," recalled Hedley. "I was at the pointer station of the port 16-inch gun while my friend Crosslin was at the gun trainer's seat. There was a bulkhead between us and the starboard gun compartment. A small hatch down near the deck was dogged down tight."

On *Arizona*, Stratton tried to absorb what was happening. "Craning my head up, I recognized the red meatballs on the planes doing the bombing."

As the General Quarters sounded, he ran for his battle station, the port AAA director near the bridge. He felt a shudder he believed to be a torpedo, but no Type 91 fish hit the battleships. Instead, nine of the level bombers from *Kaga* and *Hiryu* hit *Arizona* four times, while three more bombs fell in the water, raising tall foaming columns of dirty water. This may be why many thought the ship had been hit by a torpedo.

"One Zero flew so low, the pilot in his leather helmet smirked and waved at me," Stratton said. "Like a grinning devil."

Far overhead, thirty Kate level bombers from *Akagi* and *Kaga* put their crosshairs on the scrubbed teak decks of America's vaunted battle fleet. Under the fuselage of each Kate was a Type 99 armor-piercing bomb modified from 16-inch naval shells.

The AAA gunners began loading and firing the 3-inch guns, but since the Vals and Zeros were flying so low, they had to avoid hitting *Vestal* and men on Ford Island. "We turned our sights straight upward to hit the high flying bombers. No matter how we set the altitude of the shells, the Japanese planes were too high."

Watching from his elevated post on the port side, Stratton saw the utter chaos of planes bombing and strafing Pearl Harbor. *Oklahoma* was leaning far over, and *West Virginia*, just forward, had taken several torpedo hits. Flames from burning planes and hangars on Ford Island and Hickam Field sent black columns of smoke into the blue sky.

Stratton was working the AAA fire control. "One bomb hit Number 3 turret aft, but did not explode, falling into the sea. Lucky for us," he said with an ironic shake of the head.

Vestal took two hits from dive bombers. "One bomb hit the crew's mess and the other scored a hit where we stored the steel plate. If that steel hadn't been there, the armor-piercing bomb would have gone right through the bottom of the ship."

The bombs started raging fires that threatened to overcome the damage control parties.

Forward of *Oklahoma* and *Maryland*, the fleet oiler *Neosho*'s gunners were firing their AAA guns. Just five minutes before the attack, *Neosho* had finished offloading several tons of volatile aviation fuel into the Ford Island distribution system. If she had been hit when full, the blast would have turned the nearest battleships into crematoriums. It was a rare bit of luck that day.

Aboard *Tennessee*, seventeen-year-old Seaman Jack Evans of Corcoran, California, was on duty. "On Friday we had been told we would be getting an inspection by Rear Admiral Isaac Kidd on Monday. So we polished all the brightwork and locked the ammunition for the deck guns away in the magazines. I had just finished my cleaning station and was in the uniform of the day: white shorts, black socks and shoes, white pullover and cap. I was standing in our living space in the forward battle dressing station when General Quarters sounded. One of my mates said 'This is a helluva time for the ship to hold a drill in port on Sunday morning.' Then a Bos'n's Mate said, 'This is no drill!' When I reached the main deck, I saw Ford Island totally wrecked. Zeros were strafing the planes and a hangar had its door hanging off. I could see we were in trouble."

Nevada was tied up aft of *Arizona*. Her band was just finishing Morning Colors when the Kates bored in and released their torpedoes. Her crew scattered to their battle stations when the bombs and torpedoes came in.

Down in her crew's quarters was Woodrow "Woody" Derby of South Dakota. "I was in my bunk, reading. A few minutes before 0800, the alarm sounded. I went to my battle station in the magazines for the 5-inch guns. We were all down there and on alert. I couldn't see a damn thing."

Two of the battleship's boilers were still on line. At just after 0805, a Kate dropped a torpedo that struck her port side, causing some flooding. "I felt the ship shuddering from the guns up on deck," said Derby. "There was one big lurch and we looked around, but none of us knew we'd been hit by a torpedo."

Jack Evans scrambled up the ladder on the outside of *Tennessee*'s foremast. Looking like a cylindrical lattice, the cage masts were strong and light. "There were about eight of us in the foretop," he said. "The foretop was like a metal bucket with a roof and a waist-high metal shield. We were about 122 feet off the water and could see everything. My job was to report aircraft to the fire-control center phone talker. I saw plenty." Evans chuckled. "I looked north towards the center of the island and watched the smoke rising from Wheeler Field and Schofield Barracks. To the east past *West Virginia* and *Oklahoma*, a really big column of smoke was rising over Hickam. I saw this one plane with fixed landing gear fly right over. The man in the rear seat looked at me. If I'd had a potato, I could have hit him."

Nevada's captain ordered the engine room to prepare to get underway. He wanted to clear the harbor. This was what Genda was hoping for, and Fuchida was on alert for a ship moving up the channel.

In *Vestal*'s radio room, John Murphy was busy intercepting and passing on the scores of frantic radio messages filling the airways. "Another man came in and slammed the hatch and dogged it tight. It was on the side facing *Arizona*."

Arizona had been lucky so far. At least three dud bombs had hit the ship. Stratton said, "The Zeroes shredded any man on deck. With each pass, the Japanese pilots smiled or waved or made some other mocking gesture. The smug bastards—the whole lot of them were cowards and murderers."

Stratton and his mates were furious at not being able to bring down any Japanese planes. "We were sitting ducks. Then our portside guns ran out of ammo. Ensign Lomax ran below to get more." Stratton paused. "That was the last time I ever saw him."

At 0810, Lieutenant Commander Tadashi Kusumi, leading five Kates from *Hiryu* at 12,000 feet, released an armor-piercing bomb on *Arizona*'s starboard foredeck. The other four pilots did the same. What happened next was seen by virtually everybody in the area. The bomb impacted just forward of the second turret and plunged through four decks down to the space between Number 1 and Number 2 Handling Rooms, igniting propellant for the forward guns in an incandescent detonation that tore the heavy armored steel of the proud ship like tissue paper as it blew out her side and bottom. The entire forward portion of the ship was destroyed.

Stratton said, "It seemed as if the middle part kind of half buckled and settled back down. The explosion gutted the forward decks and the turrets and conning tower fell into the flaming crater."

The blast swept over Ford Island and the nearby ships, knocking men down and into the burning water.

Jack Evans was in his lofty perch 120 feet over the water. "I was looking forward when the *Arizona* blew up. I hung on because the explosion made the mast whip back and forth in the hot blast and I thought it would snap. When I looked back, the *Arizona* had been lifted about 20 feet out of the water. Then her keel broke in two and she sank."

A wave of water lifted *Tennessee* several feet as an inferno of burning fuel oil enveloped her stern.

Vestal's John Murphy said, "Suddenly there was a huge roar outside and our ship rolled way over. It sounded like the whole world had gone up. If that hatch hadn't been dogged down, everybody in the radio room would have been killed." Yet the immense blast did some good. Like a hard wind, it extinguished the blaze on the repair ship.

On Ford Island, the firefighters were heroically assaulting the flames from the burning planes and hangars. At 0812, the water pressure died to a trickle. No one then knew it, but the shattered *Arizona* had settled on the 12-inch water main from the navy base.

In *West Virginia*'s Number 3 turret, Stu Hedley and Crosslin were listening to the sounds of battle. "Crosslin said, 'Stu, let's see what's happening out there,' and pulled the sight cap off the periscope. We both looked out and—*bam!*—there went the *Arizona*. Over thirty bodies flew through the air. It was terrible to watch."

Arizona had turned into a twisted, blazing funeral pyre for 1,177 officers and men. Also killed were Rear Admiral Isaac Kidd, commander of Battleship Division 1, and Captain Franklin Van Valkenburgh.

Having just reached his office in the submarine base administration building, Admiral Kimmel watched with mounting horror and grief as he saw hundreds, even thousands of his men—sailors and officers—die on burning ships and in the flaming water. He stood by the window while his staff came and went with reports and questions. The phones rang constantly while the building shook from nearby bomb explosions. A few moments after *Arizona* exploded, a spent .50-caliber bullet, probably from a gunner on one of the ships, shattered the window and struck Kimmel in the chest. It was spent, leaving only a smear of grease on his white tunic. In an uncharacteristically quiet voice, Kimmel said somberly, "It would have been merciful had it killed me."

Another bomb fell toward Hedley's turret. "It hit the wing of the OS2U floatplane on the catapult over the starboard gun. The admiral's plane next to it was blasted off the turret. The bomb came right through the five inches of steel into the starboard gun compartment. It didn't explode but it hit the recoil cylinder on top of the gun. The burning fuel from the plane ignited the glycerin in the cylinder in a flash fire and killed eleven men."

The hatch between the two 16-inch guns was torn loose and flew past Hedley and Crosslin, slamming into the port turret wall. "The blast threw us back eight feet into the elevating screw. Crosslin said, 'Stu, let's get the hell out of here!'"

By this time, *West Virginia* was listing at least 15 degrees to port. "We were on the port quarterdeck and the water was up to my knees. We saw *Oklahoma* capsize, and I was sure we were going to roll over."

Lieutenant C.V. Ricketts, one of the ship's damage control officers, ordered the voids between the battleship's starboard armor belt and hull flooded. This saved *West Virginia* from the fate of *Oklahoma*. She settled into the mud of the harbor bottom.

Jack Evans watched as a bomb struck the corner of *Tennessee*'s Number 2 turret. Splinters from the blast mortally wounded Captain Mervyn Bennion of *West Virginia* as he directed the battle from his ship's flying bridge. Bennion died in the arms of Captain's Orderly Doris Miller, who would later be awarded the Navy Cross for heroism in defending the ship. Bennion's last words were "Abandon ship!" He posthumously received the Medal of Honor.

Tennessee was hit again. "Another bomb hit Number 3 turret just at the hole where the gun comes through and killed about four men."

Meanwhile, Ray Richmond and his crewmates were struggling to climb out of the black prison of *Oklahoma*, slowly turning over to port. "I was feeling my way along in the dark and finally reached a room with a deck hatch," he said. "Sailors were being pulled up by hands reaching through the hatch. I looked and realized they were of Commander Kenworthy, the captain, and the executive officer, Commander Hubbard. But I was too short to reach them and they suggested I go out through the casemate of the nearest 5-inch gun." Richmond found himself looking down at the water, twenty feet below. "The water between us and the *Maryland* was burning, filled with bodies and swimming men. *Oklahoma* was almost upside-down."

Richmond realized he would have to jump far out to clear the armor blister at the waterline. He jumped as far as he could but hit hard on his lower back against the riveted steel. "I felt a shock of intense pain. I couldn't feel my legs and I had to use my arms to scoot down the hull. It was like thick metal shingles," he recalled. "Then I slid into the oily water and ducked under." *Maryland* was about fifty feet from *Oklahoma*. "As I swam, I pushed bodies away from me and when I came up for air, I had to use my hands to clear a space of oil so I could get my head out and breathe." More than 400 men were trapped in *Oklahoma*'s hull.

Richmond finally reached a rope ladder on the side of the battleship. "There were a bunch of men trying to get up that ladder, and they kept using my head for a step."

Near exhaustion, the sailor almost didn't make it up to *Maryland*'s deck. "Then a man reached down and pulled me up by my hair."

Vestal's commander, Captain Cassin Young, had been blown over the side into the water when *Arizona* exploded. Her executive officer, suddenly in nominal command, assessed the situation. The ship had taken two bomb hits and was right up against the burning battleship. The water was on fire, and hundreds of men were dead or dying. He ordered the crew to abandon ship. John Murphy said, "Captain Young managed to climb back up a ladder to the deck. He countermanded the abandon ship order and got us underway and beached us on Area Landing."

On *West Virginia*, Hedley and Crosslin reached the starboard rail and looked at the spreading film of burning oil in the water between them and *Tennessee*. "We were going to shinny over on one of the hawsers like the other boys were doing," he said. "But then a Zero flew right between the Wee Vee and *Tennessee*, machine-gunning the boys out on the hawsers."

Hedley spotted the extended barrel of one of the 5-inch guns. "I asked Crosslin, 'Have you ever run down a railroad rail? You see those 5-inch guns? We're going to run across those barrels and jump down on *Tennessee*'s deck.' So, we did. When we got there, we were told to get to the beach. 'How?' I asked a chief petty officer. 'Swim, you idiot!' We stripped down and jumped into the water and swam underwater to the beach of Ford Island. Every time I came up to breathe, I inhaled hot, burning air."

To the surprise of both Americans and Japanese, the air was no longer the sole domain of Japanese bombers and fighters. Two blue and gray Douglas

SBD Dauntless dive bombers approached Barbers Point and MCAS Ewa. They were from *Enterprise*'s Scouting 6, having launched from the carrier at 0630 to personally deliver the information on the Wake Island reinforcement operation. The pilots were the air wing leader, a Mormon named Lieutenant Commander Howard "Brigham" Young, and his wingman. *Enterprise* was still eight hours out, near Kauai. Behind Young's SBD were the other seventeen SBDs of Scouting 6. Young and his wingman saw the burst over Ewa and Pearl and first assumed it was a drill. But when Japanese fighters saw them and turned to attack, Young's radio message was picked up in *Enterprise*'s radio room. It was quickly run up to Halsey's quarters, where he had just showered and dressed. He took the message and read it. "Air raid Pearl Harbor. This is no drill."

At first, he feared that the arrival of his SBDs had spooked some gunners, but a second message was handed to him. "Japanese planes are attacking Pearl Harbor."

He ordered General Quarters and ran to the radio room for more updates.

More Dauntlesses arrived over Oahu, the pilots not recognizing the danger. Not only were Japanese fighters turning to fire at them, AAA gunners on ships and land shot at everything that flew. One SBD pilot was shot down, screaming into his radio, "Don't shoot! I am American!"

Halsey sent fighters aloft to patrol ahead of the task force, while he waited for more information.

A riot of confusing reports came in over the next few hours.

"Two enemy carriers thirty miles, bearing 085 from Barbers Point!"

"Enemy landing party headed for the ammunition depot."

"Japanese paratroopers and landing craft at Kaneohe."

"Eight enemy transports rounding Barbers Point."

Halsey, never one to wait and see, ordered the signalmen to hoist the flags for "Prepare for battle." This was followed by the biggest American flag on board.

On the flight deck, every available dive and torpedo bomber was armed. They would launch once the enemy carriers were found. The drone of Wildcats filled the air as they provided Carrier Air Patrol (CAP) over the task force.

At 0845, the second wave, led by Commander Shigekazu Shimazaki from *Shokaku*, fanned out over Oahu and headed to their assigned targets. Unlike Fuchida, Shimazaki would not have the element of surprise. Approximately fifty minutes after the first bombs fell, Shimazaki's attack ensured that his planes would face alert and angry American gunners. The sky over Pearl was a forest of columns of black smoke intermingled with drifting skeins of AAA bursts.

Seventy Val dive bombers from *Akagi*, *Kaga*, *Hiryu*, and *Soryu* had been ordered to hit the American carriers, but with none in port, they concentrated their bombs on the ships around Ford Island and the navy base.

The aviation fuel tanks on Ford Island had not been hit, since the second wave bombers were hunting ships and planes. A perceptive ensign turned on the water sprinklers, covering the tanks in a protective haze of water.

"Dive bombers came in and put fourteen bombs in the water on *Tennessee*'s starboard side," Jack Evans said. "The Japs didn't hit the ship at all, but the bombs killed a lot of swimming men and destroyed all the ship's boats."

Nevada was underway and steering past the burning hulk of *Arizona*, the sunken *West Virginia*, and the capsized *Oklahoma*.

Evans watched *Nevada* go by from *Tennessee*'s foretop. "The only big ship moving was the *Nevada*. She was low in the water and the bombers went after her."

Woody Derby said, "We were hit by three more bombs as we moved down towards the harbor mouth. I went on deck shortly after we got moving and just thought 'Oh my God!' I was stunned about all those burning ships. The water was on fire, and the *Arizona* was just a big tower of fire and smoke. We were going to beach her at Hospital Point, but I guess it was not a good place to be, so the harbor tugs pulled us over to the opposite bank and we settled into the shallow water with our bow buried in a grove of trees."

Ray Richmond, after his escape from the capsized *Oklahoma*, was able to get some clothing and worked at a AAA gun for two hours. "When it was all over, I collapsed in pain," he said. "I didn't learn until later that my back was broken."

Jack Evans also didn't escape the attack unharmed. "I didn't realize some fragments from that first bomb on turret Number 2 had hit my legs until after the attack was over," he said. "One of my buddies said 'Hey Jack, you're hit.' I looked down and saw four tracks of dried blood running down both legs. I didn't want the Purple Heart but I got it."

Stu Hedley went to the infirmary on Ford Island and, after receiving clean clothes, began helping to care for wounded men. Among them was Donald Stratton, who was one of only six men on *Arizona*'s forward superstructure to survive the blast that destroyed their ship.

In Dry Dock No. 1, *Pennsylvania* finally came under attack. At 0907, a high level bomber put one of the 800-kg armor-piercing bombs on the battleship's boat deck on the starboard side. Even though she was essentially trapped, the battleship received little real damage. But her crew and officers suffered high casualties. Destroyers *Cassin* and *Downes*, forward of *Pennsylvania* in the same drydock, were caught in a raging fire from one of the bombs hitting flammable materials. They were abandoned and ripped open by explosions.

Of all Kimmel's battleships, *Maryland* was the least damaged, sheltered by the whalelike hull of *Oklahoma*. As with *Tennessee*, the bomber pilots seemed to have trouble hitting her.

Nine Zeroes of the second wave went for Bellows Field. Lieutenant Aeda led his nine planes to strafe the planes on the runway. Three P-40s were taking off but were shot down immediately.

Aeda flew to Kaneohe to the north and joined the dive bombers working over the airfield. He attracted the attention of an aviation ordnanceman named Sands, who carried a .30-caliber Browning Automatic Rifle. The heavy gun had a magazine with twenty rounds and was hard to aim at full automatic. Yet Sands stood and aimed right at the round Sakae radial engine and emptied the full clip at it. Bullets pockmarked the concrete on either side of Sands. But he never flinched. The Zero seemed to shudder and zipped over the navy man, then crashed off the airfield perimeter. There is no way to know if Sands shot it down, or if Aeda deliberately dived his damaged fighter into the ground, but the result was the same.

One of the most fascinating moments of the Pearl Harbor attack was, in fact, a one-man defense of a navy air base.

John William Finn was born on July 23, 1909, in the farmland surrounding Los Angeles. He joined the navy in 1926 in an age of gangsters, biplanes, speakeasies, flappers, and jazz.

"I wanted to work on airplanes," he told me in an interview in his home in 2007. He worked his way up the ranks to become an aviation chief ordnanceman in 1936. He married Alice, a lovely woman with blue eyes and golden hair, and joined VP-14 at NAS Kaneohe Bay. Finn was popular and respected at Kaneohe. His unrivaled skill at working on guns and ordnance was almost legendary.

As the senior ordnance chief at the base, Finn was off duty that Sunday morning. "I was in bed with my wife," he said, "when I heard planes going over. Alice went to look out the window." The Finns lived in navy housing out of sight of the base. Alice said some planes were flying toward the base. Then Finn heard the unmistakable sound of machine gun fire.

Donning his white chief's cap, shirt, pants, and shoes, Finn kissed his wife and ran out to his 1938 Ford. "I didn't even button up my shirt. Charlie Clark ran out of his house and together we roared off. I heard more machine gun fire. 'No one's supposed to be firing today,' I thought. 'It's Sunday.'"

Finn turned a curve in the road leading to Kaneohe Bay just after 0800 hours. The air was alive with the chatter of machine gun fire and the snarl of radial engines. "I saw a whole bunch of fighters flying low over the PBY Catalinas and hangars. I saw that red circle on the wings."

Base Commander Hal Martin had little chance of stopping the attack. He had 300 enlisted men and 30 officers, plus about 95 Marines. His patrol squadrons consisted of 36 Consolidated PBY Catalina flying boats, four of which were tied to buoys in the bay. The rest were on the tarmac and in the two huge hangars. While in flight, the PBYs were able and fast, but on the ground, they were fat sitting ducks.

Kaneohe's planes and facilities were the target of two groups of bombers and Zero fighters from *Shokaku* and *Zuikaku*. Smoke and flame were rising from the helpless Catalinas on the tarmac and moorings in the harbor.

Finn stopped near Hangar Number 3 and ran inside, shouting orders to his men to grab anything that would shoot. He grabbed a .50-caliber machine gun he'd almost finished repairing. "I knew what was wrong with it," he said, his brow furrowing at the memory. "I dragged that thing outside."

The only available mount was a light instruction tripod, used only for training. "It wasn't made to take the gun at full automatic, but I used it anyway." Finn's men brought him ammunition belts and he got the gun working.

"The bombers were much too high and dropping bombs on the base, but the Zeros were low and I figured I could hit them. I looked and saw one coming out of the notch in the ridge to the south. He was just a dot at first but I saw him. I had real good eyesight in those days." He chuckled. "Anyway, he got closer and that big radial engine was just like a bull's-eye. I got him in my sights and started banging away. He never wavered but then he was past, with smoke trailing off his engine. I couldn't traverse that gun fast enough to keep him in sight. It's not like the movies. Those guns are heavy. But I saw that one hit the ground. One Jap down."

He shot at every plane that flew close to him. Although Finn wasn't the only one shooting back by that time, he was the most exposed. "I felt things plucking at my pants and unbuttoned shirt," he said. "I knew the Japs were shooting but didn't worry about it. Hell, I was so mad! I didn't have the sense to be scared." Splinters from 20mm shells and machine gun bullets inflicted more than twenty wounds, including a serious one to his knee.

When the attackers finally withdrew at 0930, they were fewer in number.

John Finn was responsible for at least two Zeros shot down by his determined fire. "I wasn't the only one shooting back," he said firmly.

Finn, along with other chiefs and officers, organized the firefighting, recovering what weapons could be used and seeing to the wounded. "We thought they'd be back. And I was mad as hell. Everywhere I looked I saw burning planes and smoke."

Finn stayed on duty all day, ignoring the blood from his wounds. "I was ordered to the base hospital at 0200 the next morning but the doctors were too busy with other wounded." Nearly twenty-four hours after the first bombs had fallen, he was hospitalized for three weeks.

"I didn't know anything about a medal," he said. "But word got around. I heard I was going to get one of the Medals of Honor. There were fifteen of them awarded for that day," he pointed out. "And ten of them were posthumous."

On September 14, 1942, Finn, dressed in his spotless duty whites and accompanied by Alice, stood to attention aboard the carrier *Enterprise* as Admiral Chester W. Nimitz, commander in chief of the U.S. Pacific Fleet, draped the silken blue ribbon around Finn's neck, from which hung the bronze Medal of Honor.

"Alice said it looked nice on me. I still didn't think I'd earned it. After all, I was alive."

John William Finn was later promoted to lieutenant, serving in the States since his wounds prevented him from active service. He retired from the United States Navy in 1956. Until his death at age one hundred in 2010, he was the oldest and last living Medal of Honor recipient for the Pearl Harbor attack. As a personal note, I was honored to know John Finn as a good friend.

While the first wave was busy destroying the air bases and ships, the twelve B-17s from California arrived over Oahu. In what has to be the world's worst case of "being in the wrong place at the wrong time," the big bombers, out of fuel and unarmed, flew into the maelstrom of the attack.

At 2100 hours on December 6, two new B-17Es and four older B-17Cs of the 38th Reconnaissance Squadron of the 19th Bombardment Group, commanded by Major Truman "Ted" Landon, began taking off from Hamilton Field near San Francisco Bay. The big bombers had each been loaded with extra bomb bay fuel tanks and supplies to get them all the way to Clark Field in the Philippines, where they would reinforce General Lewis Brereton's Far Eastern Air Force.

They passed over the lighted expanse of the Golden Gate Bridge, then turned southwest for the 2,400-mile flight to Hickam Field in Hawaii. Major General Henry "Hap" Arnold, chief of the Air Corps, personally briefed them on their destination. He had warned them that war was imminent and that they might encounter enemy action when they reached the Philippines. At this, Major Landon questioned the wisdom of having the guns and Norden bombsight sent separately by ship to save weight. After considering this, Arnold agreed the planes should carry their .30-caliber and .50-caliber Browning machine guns but no ammunition. Staff Sergeant Joe Angelini, who was in Lieutenant Robert Richard's plane, later told author Gene Salicker, "We had guns aboard but no ammunition. We asked for 200 rounds for each gun at Hamilton but they said you'll get all your ammunition in Hawaii. The ground crews were worried about excess weight, and heavy wood gun crates would have only added to the problem."

As for the top-secret Norden bombsights, they were mounted in the nose of each plane. They were considered so classified that bombardiers were ordered to detach and destroy them in case of capture.

At 2210, the next seven B-17s of the 88th Reconnaissance Squadron, led by Captain Richard Carmichael, left California behind. Two hours later, the plane flown by Richard Ezzard reported engine trouble and turned back. The twelve remaining B-17s flew on through the night. Each plane was on its own, the navigator plotting the course. Only rarely did any crew see another of the flight.

Lieutenant Kermit Tyler, who had told Privates Lockard and Elliott not to worry about the large radar blip coming in from the sea, did not know the B-17s were flying singly. If he had understood this, he might have wondered about a large blip of more than a few planes coming from the north. Lockard later said that if the blip he and Elliott had seen were the B-17s from the coast, they were about a hundred miles off course to the north.

While the attack raged over Hickam Army Air Base just east of Pearl Harbor, officers ran out from their quarters, some nearly naked. One man, with his robe open, shook his fist at the Japanese in impotent rage. "I knew the little sons of bitches would attack us on a Sunday! I knew it!"

In the tall control tower, Major Gordon Blake, the operations officer, stood with mouth agape as he watched dive bombers dropping bombs on NAS Ford Island and his own field. Great eruptions of orange fire rose from fuel tanks and shredded planes. Neat lines of fighters were ripped apart as Itaya's Zeroes strafed them. Blake had been in the control tower since 0730 hours, waiting for Landon, an old West Point friend, to land.

The first Fortress to make landfall was piloted by Lieutenants Robert Richards and Leonard Humiston in a B-17C named "Skipper." The plane was named for a dog Angelini had adopted, a purebred Scottish terrier puppy. "He was pretty small. He started flying when he was a few weeks old on the tests that we made to determine whether the airplane could make it to Hawaii. We made some flights out of Albuquerque and he flew with me on those missions and I'd have to feed him with a bottle. He was about six weeks old when we flew to Hawaii."

Richards's crew was tired after the long over-water flight but excited to be arriving at the island paradise, but just as Richards was lining up for landing at Hickam, he saw another plane angling in from the left. Suddenly there was the sound of something hitting his big bomber. His bombardier, Sergeant Melvin Zajic, called over the intercom that it had to be U.S. Navy planes conducting a realistic attack simulation with wax bullets. But then Sergeant Joe Angelini yelled from behind Richards, "There are damned holes in the wing!"

Richards, totally taken by surprise, shoved the throttles forward and headed for a low cloud north of the field. But when Skipper emerged, he was again set on by the Zeroes. Thinking the smaller Bellows Field might be safer, Richards banked around to land there.

The second B-17 to approach Hickam was piloted by Lieutenants Bruce Allen and Charles McArthur, Jr. They too were taken by surprise. The bombers were in a dire state. Nearly out of fuel, they were also unarmed. Their machine guns were in boxes filled with rust-preventative cosmoline.

Now, as Allen lined up for landing, the voice of Major Blake came on the Hickam frequency. "The base is under attack! You have a Jap fighter on your tail!" Allen chose to land as fast as he could, wrenching the big plane off the runway and toward a grassy parking ramp. Even as the four propellers on the Wright Cyclone engines slowed, Allen and his crew dived out of the nose and rear hatches to run for cover in the nearby patch of trees. Miraculously none were hurt. The Boeing was strafed but did not burn.

Then the third Flying Fortress approached Hickam. Itaya and his two wingmen dived to attack. With their Sakai engines snarling, the fighters dived with all guns blazing. This B-17C carried one of the most experienced crews in the Army Air Corps. Captain Raymond Swensen and Homer Taylor had ferried an earlier group of B-17s to Hawaii in May. At forty-one, flight engineer Master Sergeant Leroy Pouncey, was the oldest man in the squadron. He could fix anything and was respected by the crew. His assistant engineer was twenty-year-old Sergeant Earl Williams, who would be the last surviving member of the flight when I interviewed him in 2016. A superb mechanic, Williams had joined the Air Corps in 1939, right out of his Ohio high school. Now Williams was standing on the flight deck behind Swensen. In the jump seat beside him and behind co-pilot Ernest Reid was William Schick, the squadron flight surgeon. Schick had joined Swensen's crew at Hamilton Field and intended to take pictures of his odyssey across the Pacific. He was holding the camera given to him by his wife.

Williams decided to head back to the radio compartment past the bomb bay. After negotiating the narrow catwalk and entering the small insulated compartment, he found Sergeants Joe Bruce and Lee Burke. The three men watched the green shores of the island come closer over the broad wings and thrumming engines of the B-17.

"Then all hell broke loose," recalled Williams. Six of Itaya's Zeroes banked around and began firing their machine guns on the helpless B-17 as it came in for final approach. "Suddenly there were a lot of loud bangs and popping noises," he said. "Then the Plexiglas cover over the radio compartment shattered and I saw a fighter flying toward us. I first thought it was an exercise where they had mistakenly put real bullets in the machine guns."

Williams, Bruce, and Burke cowered as a hail of 7.7 mm bullets shredded the cotton insulation on the fuselage, making the air look as if it were snowing. "Then the bullets hit the flare locker and the entire compartment was full of fire." Burke and Bruce ran aft into the waist compartment while Williams went through the forward door into the bomb bay. He closed it, "but the heat came right through. My hair was burned."

Reaching the flight deck, he saw Hickam and Pearl Harbor on fire. Swensen and Reid were trying to land with black smoke filling the plane.

Flight Surgeon Schick kept his head down, unable to take any pictures. He called out that gunfire was coming up from below. American AAA gunners and servicemen were firing whatever they could find at the aircraft, not recognizing the big bombers as their own.

Just then, Schick yelled, "Goddamnit those are real bullets! I'm hit!" Two others of Swensen's crew were wounded as he tried to bring his burning bomber in for landing.

Back in the radio compartment, the magnesium flares burned fiercely, eating into the ribs and spars in the floor. The fire ate big holes in the fuselage. Opening the left window to let the smoke clear, Swensen ordered the gear down. He had to land before the bomber exploded with volatile fuel fumes in the tanks.

Moments later the crippled B-17 hit hard, the weakened fuselage buckling and bouncing back up. Reid recalled, "It took both of us to get the wings level after that first bounce."

As the plane hit again, the waist and tail section tore away and skidded, shedding metal and boxes of supplies. Burke and Bruce held on as the burning plane came to a stop, then ran for their lives.

The forward section, with the trailing edge of the 104-foot wings dragging and spewing sparks, came to a stop. Swensen yelled for everyone to get out. Reid and Williams chose to hunker down next to the heavy landing gear struts rather than risk being out in the open where the Japanese were still strafing. Schick ran for the hangars and was hit in the face by shrapnel. He fell and lay unconscious on the tarmac. Two more of Swensen's men were hit by bullets.

Over Bellows Field to the east, Richards attemped to land on the fighter strip. Suddenly a P-40 Tomahawk rolled onto the runway ahead of the big bomber. Richards yanked back on the control wheel and made a steep turn to come at the runway downwind. He had no fuel left. This was their only chance. The wheels touched down on the short runway, and still moving at over 100 knots, the big plane plowed over a drainage ditch and lost its wheels. Finally, it came to a stop. Skipper would never fly again, but the Zeroes strafing Bellows raked the Boeing with bullets. Skipper did not burn. Joe Angelini tried to remove the secret Norden bombsight but could not do so. He grabbed the dog and climbed out the nose hatch.

By 0815, three of the bombers sent from California had come to rest. Two would never fly again. Soon the first attack wave turned north, back to their carriers. In the short lull, two of the 38th Squadron's planes were able to land. First, Major Landon's new B-17E came in and touched down without being hit, followed by Earl Cooper's B-17C. Five of the six planes of Landon's flight had come to ground.

The other new B-17E, piloted by Karl Barthelmess and Larry Sheehan, landed after a harrowing night. A few hours after takeoff, Barthelmess and Sheehan set the Automated Flight Control System, most commonly called an autopilot, and promptly fell asleep. The navigator, Charles Bergdoll, had made his star shot to pinpoint their location and course to Hawaii. As the plane reached the halfway point, Bergdoll realized the B-17E was less than 3,000 feet over the black Pacific. He tried to wake Barthelmess with no luck. Sheehan was roused and corrected the descent. Back at 6,000 feet, Bergdoll knew that his original navigation was invalidated. With the sun up, he could only use dead reckoning, and he had little confidence in the result. If they ran out of fuel before finding the Hawaiian Islands, they would have to ditch.

Shortly before 0730, an island was sighted to the south. It was Oahu. Bergdoll plotted a course to Hickam. Then they realized there were other planes in the air with them. But instead of more B-17s, the crew saw about fifteen gray-painted single-engine planes in a broad "V" formation, also heading south. Incredibly, the bomber had intersected with the Val dive bombers in the first attack wave. But the Americans were totally unaware that the strange planes were Japanese.

The Japanese planes did not attack the American bomber due to their rigid training and discipline. The attack on Pearl Harbor was still half an hour away, and they could not risk a distress call from the bomber.

Sergeant Lee Embry took some pictures with his Speedgraph camera, not knowing he was taking the first photos of the Pacific War.

The Japanese planes eventually passed, leaving the crew wondering what they had seen. As they banked around the eastern end of Oahu, radio operator Sergeant Nicholas Kahlefent, who was tuned into Honolulu's station KGMB, heard a sudden announcement. "This is not a mock battle! This is the real McCoy!"

Suddenly the rising smoke and distant thuds of explosions became real.

Soon the B-17 was on approach to Hickam Field. But as Barthelmess and Sheehan lined up on final, they were waved off by Blake in the tower. Three times the big bomber put on full power and went around again. At last, they had no choice. They were out of fuel. Barthelmess managed to land. The last of Landon's six planes were on the ground. The officers and crew took shelter where they could.

Still in the air were six more B-17s, led by Captain Richard Carmichael. Having left Hamilton an hour after Landon's squadron, Carmichael's bombers did not make landfall until the first wave had withdrawn. The timing was fortuitous. "I called into Hickam and they told me to land west to east, downwind," Carmichael said. "They also told me the field was under attack. Things had gone to hell in a handbasket."

Seeing that one of the B-17s was burning on the runway, Carmichael chose to head for Wheeler Field near Fort Shafter. But the entire flight line of parked P-40s and other planes were aflame. NAS Kaneohe on the east coast was also burning. It was probably at this point that Taylor and Welch engaged the dive bombers, since at least two of Carmichael's crew reported seeing a dogfight between P-40s and Japanese planes.

With fuel running out, Carmichael chose the only option left—the 1,200-foot auxiliary fighter strip at Haleiwa near the northwestern coast of Oahu.

Haleiwa was the strip from which Welch and Taylor had gotten their P-40s off to attack the Japanese bombers.

Carmichael lined up on the strip and was surprised to see another B-17C taxiing to a stop off the runway. It was the plane piloted by his operations officer, Harold Chaffin. Carmichael and his co-pilot, Captain James Twaddell, used up the entire strip before stopping the plane. Even though the bombers had landed without damage, the worst was not over. While the crew unloaded the machine guns and went in search of ammunition, the sound of radial engines grew louder. A Zero came in to strafe the field. Carmichael and Twaddell ran to the cover of rocks along the beach.

"There we were," Carmichael said, grinning, "the two air heroes cowering under rocks while the sergeants fought back with what they had." The two pilots were nearly drowned when the surf crashed over them.

Meanwhile, back at Hickam, the B-17C, flown by West Point graduate Harry Brandon, aborted his first landing. The wreckage of Swensen's shattered bomber was being pulled off the runway. More Japanese fighters had arrived and the AAA gunners were again peppering the sky with shells. Finally, Blake in the tower gave them clearance to come in downwind.

After what was probably the least difficult landing that day, Brandon taxied to the ramp, where, two hours later, the B-17C was fueled and armed.

Lieutenant Bob Thacker's B-17E also reached Hickam as the second wave of enemy planes were raking the air base. Thacker saw billowing clouds of black smoke and orange fires raging in the harbor while his plane received scores of hits from Japanese fighters. He came in fast and downwind, which overheated the brakes. One wheel caught fire as he and Surles tried to stop the bomber. Just before running out of concrete, Thacker brought the big plane around in a tight ground loop. The fire was put out by the crew.

Still the B-17s came in. Alerted by Hickam and Major Landon, the last pilots had some idea of what was happening. David Rawls and John Compton chose to try for Wheeler. Finding it burning even worse, they went back to Hickam. Smoke from the burning ships at Ford Island provided some cover from the fighters as the pilots banked into the chaotic landing pattern. Just as the B-17E cleared the smoke, a Zero dived and began firing. "We were about two hundred feet off the runway," Rawls recalled. "With our wheels and flaps down, we had no chance of escaping him." The Japanese fighter hit the bomber's wings and an engine. "We made it in."

Sergeant Bob Palmer, in the waist compartment, was the only one of the twelve B-17s crews to shoot back at the Japanese that morning, using the only weapon available—a Colt .45 automatic.

At last, the final B-17E, the last to leave peace behind at Hamilton Field, came over the coast of Oahu. Pilot Frank Bostrom and Wilson Cook found Hickam in chaos. "I called the field at Hickam and asked what the hell was happening," Bostrom said. "We were about seven hundred feet up, and headed in for landing. But about five destroyers began firing at us, cutting off our approach."

These were probably *Blue*, *Monaghan*, *Helm*, and *Aylwin* in the channel.

"An anti-aircraft shell exploded right off our starboard wing." The pilots shoved the throttles forward and headed northwest, hoping to stay clear until the attack was over. But then four Zeros moved in to fire at the bomber from behind. Still at full power but with fumes in the tanks, Bostrom looked for a place to land. He saw Kahuku Golf Course at the northern end of the island. Having little choice, Bostrom banked steeply around a tall smokestack like a racer doubling a pylon at Reno, and leveled out over the 7th Fairway, a 552-yard flat expanse of clean green grass.

"We cut up the course pretty badly," one crewman recalled, "but we made it. The owners of a nearby sugar cane field did not even know there was an attack going on. We told them there was a war on. They invited us into their home and made us big Highballs. We were content to stay there for the duration."

It was a miracle all twelve B-17s landed without being shot down by the hordes of Zero fighters and determined navy and army AAA fire. While over two dozen men were wounded, only one man died—Flight Surgeon William Schick.

Sergeant Joe Angelini flew fifty-four missions in the Pacific over the Solomons and later to Midway. The little terrier Skipper was with him on every mission, wearing a little oxygen mask and life vest. "He did pretty well," Angelini said.

It is generally believed that only two American fighter pilots managed to get into the air that morning. This legend, while thrilling, is not completely true. In fact, at least five fighters scrambled to attack the Japanese bombers.

The satellite airfield at Haleiwa was about ten miles from Wheeler Air Base. In the past month, General Short's staff managed to disperse some of the 15th Pursuit Group's planes to the outlying airstrips to avoid them being in one place in case of sabotage or air attack. Haleiwa had eighteen of the Curtiss P-40B fighters. Two pilots, Lieutenants Kenneth Taylor of Enid, Oklahoma, and George Welch of Wilmington, Delaware, who were new to the 47th Pursuit

Squadron, had been at a dance at the Wheeler Officer's Club on Saturday night, then went to an all-night poker game near their assigned post at Haleiwa. It was dawn when the game ended. All the players were tired but feeling good after a night of fun.

According to a 2019 article by Michael Haskew in *Air Force Times*, Taylor and Welch were leaving and discussing going for a swim when they caught the sound of distant gunfire and explosions. Not directly under the path of Fuchida's bombers, they did not know of the air raid.

But that changed after Welch called Haleiwa and insisted that two Curtiss P-40B Tomahawk fighters be fueled and armed. Jumping into Taylor's 1939 Buick convertible, they raced at nearly a hundred miles per hour to the field, located to the northwest. By now the second wave was coming south down the valley. A Zero peeled off and strafed the speeding car, but Taylor managed to avoid the bullets.

Their olive-drab P-40Bs were ready at the downwind end of the 1,200-foot strip at Haleiwa. Pulling on parachutes and flight helmets, they climbed in and started the V-1710 Allison engines.

One of the ground crew suggested they disperse the eighteen fighters instead of going after the Japanese.

"To hell with that," Welch said. With the characteristic snarl of liquid-cooled engines at full power, the fighters fairly leaped into the morning sky. But they were not fully armed. The P-40B carried twin cowling-mounted .50-caliber machine guns and four .30-calibers in the wings, but there was no .50 ammunition at Haleiwa, so only the smaller caliber guns were armed. This did not deter the eager pilot, who headed southwest toward Barbers Point, where the first planes they sighted were a few of Major Truman Landon's B-17s, who were trying to find a place to land while being shot at by Japanese Zeros. At last Taylor and Welch spotted some of the dive bombers strafing MCAS Ewa Field.

There were twelve Japanese planes, making the odds six to one. But the two Americans did not hesitate, tearing into the slow dive bombers with their wing guns. Taylor brought down two and damaged a third, but soon ran out of ammunition.

Having no choice, they turned north to Wheeler, which was a scene of chaos. The entire line of tightly packed fighters was burning after being strafed by the Zeros. The ground crew were trying to put out the fires. The approaching P-40s attracted the attention of the jittery AAA gunners, who began firing at the friendly planes. Both pilots managed to land and taxi to where a group of officers were overseeing the removal of the few undamaged planes. Taylor and

Welch jumped out. Even with superior offices telling them to leave their planes and help on the ground, the two pilots insisted their planes be refueled and armed with full belts of .50- and .30-caliber ammunition.

Just when Welch's plane had been loaded, another flight of dive bombers arrived and strafed the field. Welch jumped into his plane and shot off the runway. The men arming Taylor's plane panicked and left the boxes of ammo on the wings. Taylor took off anyway, the metal boxes sliding off as he sped down the runway. Their takeoffs took them directly at the approaching dive bombers.

The two Americans were firing at the enemy even as they were lifting off and raising their landing gear. Darting around a cloud, Taylor suddenly found himself among at least eight Zeros and more dive bombers. One rear gunner shot at the American fighter, the rounds peppering the fuselage near the canopy. One round missed Taylor's head by inches, fragmenting on the armor plate behind the seat. His arm and leg were hit by shrapnel.

Taylor later said he didn't worry about the wounds, but "I had the hell scared out of me for a moment." Welch, now diving in, shot down that bomber and Taylor damaged another.

The Japanese planes, while defending themselves, were running low on fuel. They turned north and tried to escape the maddened Americans.

Welch brought down the last Japanese plane five miles offshore, then turned back to land at Haleiwa. With the air battle over for them, Taylor and Welch drove back to Wheeler to report to their squadron commander. Major Gordon Austin pointed out that both of his pilots were still wearing the tuxedo pants and shirts from the Saturday night dance. He yelled at them to get back to Haleiwa and get into the air. "Don't you know there's a war on?"

Taylor and Welch explained that they had already been fighting the Japs.

The two pilots were later credited with at least six and possibly seven of the twenty-nine Japanese planes downed that morning.

It is an interesting fact that of all the military airfields on Oahu, only Haleiwa escaped being bombed or strafed. While Genda was unaware of the small field, it is more likely that Taylor and Welch's lone attacks drove the Japanese planes away.

But there were three more American fighters that climbed into the smoking sky that morning. One of them was a 46th Pursuit Squadron pilot, Lieutenant Lewis Sanders, who was based at Wheeler. Sanders managed to scramble his and two other planes into the sky even as Wheeler was coming under attack. Unlike Taylor and Welch, Sanders and his flight all had full loads of ammunition. He led them up to about 6,000 feet and scanned the sky for enemy planes.

Spotting a flight of six dive bombers, Sanders dived into them, shooting down the leader. The others turned north and left at high speed. Noting that none still carried bombs, Sanders let them go.

One of his wingmen, Lieutenant Jim Sterling, was coming behind another plane but was set upon by a Zero. Sanders turned sharply and moved in behind the enemy fighter, shooting it down. Sterling was shot down but he had managed to bring down the plane he had been shooting at.

Lieutenant Ken Taylor was recommended for the Medal of Honor for his actions over Oahu, but his commanding officer literally shot that down by stating that Taylor had deliberately disobeyed orders when he and Welch took off the second time.

Of the roughly 400 planes on the ground that morning, 181 were destroyed and another 159 damaged. Short's ability to defend Oahu had been virtually wiped out.

Destroyers *Monaghan*, *Aylwin*, *Blue*, and *Helm* raised steam and aimed for the channel, trying to escape the harbor. *Aylwin* and *Helm* endured sporadic strafing and a few bombs, but finally managed to escape. Their captains knew *Enterprise* and *Lexington* were not far away and intended to join the carriers.

For years there was an ongoing dispute whether any midget subs had made it into the harbor. While none of the two-man subs managed to sink any ships in port, it is well documented that one did enter early that morning, most likely under the unknowing escort of minesweepers *Condor* and *Crossbill*. But due to the valiant crews of two U.S. Navy warships, the midget sub never made it out of the harbor.

At 0839, the crew of seaplane tender *Curtiss* sighted a periscope. It was the midget submarine *I-22A*, piloted by Lieutenant Naoji Iwasa. The sub had been launched from the *I-16* and managed to enter the harbor and reach the anchorages north of Ford Island before being spotted.

The sighting was relayed to *Monaghan*, which was moving south toward the harbor mouth. Her captain saw the tiny object in the water. "I don't know what the hell that is, but it shouldn't be here," he said, alerting his gunnery officer.

Monaghan turned to attack the sub. The submarine fired both of its torpedoes. The torpedo meant for the *Curtiss* missed, instead striking the shore of Ford Island. *Curtiss* fired on the partially surfaced sub with her 5-inch guns.

Monaghan drove right at the submarine and managed to graze it. The sub sank. When later raised, it was determined that one of the 5-inch shells from *Curtiss* had decapitated Iwasa in the conning tower.

The *I-24*'s midget, Number 19, was piloted by Ensign Kazuo Sakamaki and Petty Officer Kiyoshi Inagaki. All of *I-24*'s crew waited out the long morning as the air attack continued to hit Pearl Harbor. But nothing was ever heard from their midget sub. Due to a faulty gyrocompass, Sakamaki's sub became hopelessly lost and grounded on the island's eastern shore. Inagaki drowned. Sakamaki became the first Japanese prisoner of war.

At 0925, destroyer *Shaw*, a sister to *Ward*, was burning fiercely in the floating dry dock from two bomb hits on her foredeck. When water pressure was lost, the crew abandoned ship. A few minutes later the fire reached *Shaw*'s forward magazines, which detonated in an immense fireball that rivaled the *Arizona* explosion. A towering mushroom of orange flame seemed brighter than the sun as debris was thrown nearly a quarter of a mile.

By 0945, it was all over. The attackers headed back to their carriers. In their wake, they left three battleships on the bottom, two capsized, five more damaged, and several damaged cruisers, destroyers, and support ships. Hundreds of army, navy and Marine aircraft were burning on the runways across Oahu. And 3,690 American military and civilians were dead and wounded. Over the next several days, holes were cut into the hull of the capsized *Oklahoma* to free 32 trapped sailors. Of her 1,398 officers and crew, 429 died. The hospitals were choked with wounded and dying.

Japanese losses were surprisingly light. The first wave lost five Kate bombers, one Val dive bomber, and three Zeroes. The second wave, which faced an alerted air defense, lost fourteen Val dive bombers and six Zeroes. Although 78 bombers and fighters had been damaged, this was far below what Nagumo and the doomsayers in the Combined Fleet had predicted. Even more wondrous, there had been no attack on the First Air Fleet.

Nagumo, according to Gordon Prange, was in the position of a man who had run full tilt at a locked door only to have it opened just as he reached it. Instead of losing a third of his force, as predicted, they had not suffered a scratch.

In Washington, Cordell Hull read the last words of the Japanese ultimatum as Nomura and Kurusu watched in silence.

Then Hull spoke in a voice as cold as ice. "In all my fifty years of public service, I have never seen a document so crowded with infamous falsehoods and distortions, on a scale so huge, that I never imagined until today that any government on this planet was capable of uttering them."

The old statesman told the Japanese ambassador to leave his office. There is no doubt Nomura felt deep shame and sorrow for what he had unknowingly triggered.

While the message delivered to Hull was not a declaration of war, the fact that it had not been presented to the United States representative until an hour after the first bombs fell on Oahu was considered a deliberate act of aggression. It is entirely possible the late delivery was simply a case of bad luck, but the Foreign Ministry in Tokyo never told Nomura the reason for the 1300 deadline. In any case, the Japanese Navy benefited from those fifty-five minutes.

During the attack, Captain Edwin Layton, Kimmel's intelligence officer, was running down the hall to his office when he was stopped by Captain Willard Kitt, Kimmel's senior gunnery officer. Kitt shook his head and said in a loud voice that carried down the hall, "Here is the young man we should have listened to. You were right and we were wrong."

Ward, after scoring one of the day's two kills, remained on station even while the Japanese bombs and torpedoes wreaked havoc, death, panic, and horrendous damage on Oahu. When the Day of Infamy was over, she moved past the beached *Nevada* near Hospital Point and toward her berth west of Ford Island. It was a day none of her crew would ever forget.

As to the submarine they sank, the *I-20* launched the midget submarine piloted by Ensign Ikira Hiroho and Petty Officer Yoshio Kariyama. They were the closest to the restricted area. In 2002 it was found exactly where *Ward* reported the sinking. Underwater surveys found it fully loaded with two Type 97 torpedoes and a large hole in the conning tower.

But *Ward*'s war career was just beginning, On October 17, 1944, *Ward* carried troops to Dinagat Island for the opening phase of the invasion of Leyte in the Philippines. The next assault was at Ormoc Bay in early December, where *Ward* carried army infantry troops to the beach. During her patrols along the coast, a flight of Kamikaze planes approached. *Ward* was already at battle stations and began filling the air with hot shrapnel. But one of the Zero fighters carrying a 250-kg bomb dived in and crashed into *Ward* amidships, tearing open fuel tanks and setting off ready ammunition at the Number 2 and 3 gun mounts. The fire quickly spread out of control. The destroyer division commander ordered assistance for *Ward* from another destroyer. But even with the added manpower and firefighting assistance, *Ward* was clearly beyond salvage. Her crew was ordered to abandon ship. They climbed into rafts and boats as the old ship wallowed and burned. *Ward* was to be sunk by naval gunfire. In the cold equation of war, she was now a hazard to navigation. After recovering her crew, the destroyer's gunners went to their battle stations. The guns were loaded and trained on the helpless derelict. Many of the gunners, officers, and deck crew may have felt a subliminal sadness at being forced to sink one of their own. The guns barked out as 5-inch shells streaked over the water and hammered the stout old ship. Waterspouts erupted at the waterline as foam and spray vomited from the holes torn in the old steel hull.

After a dozen hits, all firing ceased. The destroyer's officers and crew watched with muted sadness as *Ward* rolled on her side and began to sink. Soon only a spreading cape of bubbles and floating debris was left to mark the grave. There were no memorials or monuments, no epitaphs that remembered her role in the first day of the war. Few of the men watching realized what ship they had just sunk. But one man certainly did.

The duty to sink a derelict ship and remove a hazard to navigation was nothing new. It had been done scores of times during the war. But few men were called upon to sink a ship that had particular personal significance. The man who gave the orders to fire on *Ward* had once stood on her bridge, binoculars in hand, looking at the tiny conning tower of a Japanese midget submarine. His order to fire had been the very first American salvo of the Second World War. From the bridge of the *O'Brien*, Commander William W. Outerbridge sank his first command. The date was December 7, 1944, exactly three years to the day after *Ward* entered history.

Aboard *Nagato* in the Inland Sea, Yamamoto said virtually nothing once receiving the confirmation of the launch of the first wave until the first reports of success arrived. He had been on the settee in the operations room, eyes closed, seemingly asleep but hearing every word. It is not hard to imagine what the commander in chief was thinking. For a gambler like Yamamoto, Operation Hawaii was the biggest risk he had ever taken, and he would either lose it all or win big. Total Japanese dead were fifty-five airmen, nine submarine crew, and one POW.

In the closing minutes of the 1970 Twentieth Century Fox epic *Tora! Tora! Tora!*, Soh Yamamura, portraying Admiral Yamamoto, is being congratulated by his staff aboard the *Nagato*. In a somber voice, he says:

> I had intended to deal a fatal blow to the American fleet by attacking Pearl Harbor immediately after Japan's official declaration

of war. But according to the American radio, Pearl Harbor was attacked fifty-five minutes before our ultimatum was delivered in Washington. I can't imagine anything that would infuriate the Americans more. I fear all we have done is to awaken a sleeping giant and fill him with a terrible resolve.

Then he leaves the suddenly silent staff and walks out to *Nagato*'s foredeck. This is a powerful moment in the film. There is no documented proof that Yamamoto ever spoke or wrote those words, and it may only be a figment of the screenwriter's imagination. But it is likely what he was thinking.

As the last bombs fell on Oahu, the young Japanese-American courier from RCA arrived at Fort Shafter. It was an uncomfortable moment as he handed over the telegram. It was taken up to Short's office, now a bedlam of ringing phones, chattering teletypes and muted conversations. Short took the envelope and read it to himself. He handed it to an aide and said, "Get a copy to Admiral Kimmel."

In Kimmel's office the scene was much the same as he read over the message from Short. Then he cleared his throat and said, "The Japanese ambassador is presenting to the United States, at 1:00 p.m. Eastern Standard Time, what amounts to an ultimatum. Just what significance the date may have, we do not know. But be on the alert accordingly." He paused, looking at the silent officers. "This is signed, George C. Marshall, Chief of Staff."

Stu Hedley, of *West Virginia*, remained in the navy, served through the end of the war, and was present at the surrender ceremony in Tokyo Bay on September 2, 1945. He was adamant that the battleships *West Virginia*, *Nevada*, and *California* were not sunk on December 7. "They were just temporarily on the bottom."

He was right. Except for *Arizona*, *Oklahoma*, and *Utah*, all the battleships were raised, repaired, and back in service by 1944.

A frame from the newsreel of Japanese planes attacking the gunboat *Panay* on the Yangtze River in 1937. *Official U.S. Navy Photo*

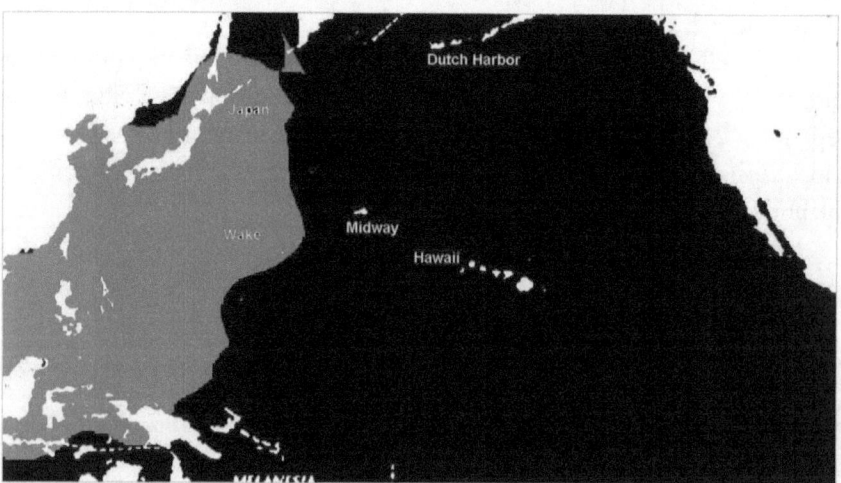
A map of the Pacific Ocean, comprising 53,800,000 square miles between the U.S. and Asia. *Author's Collection*

America's first aircraft carrier, *Langley*, converted from the collier *Jupiter* in 1927. *Official U.S. Navy Photo*

HIJMS *Akagi*, the first large carrier in the Imperial Navy. *Official U.S. Navy Photo*

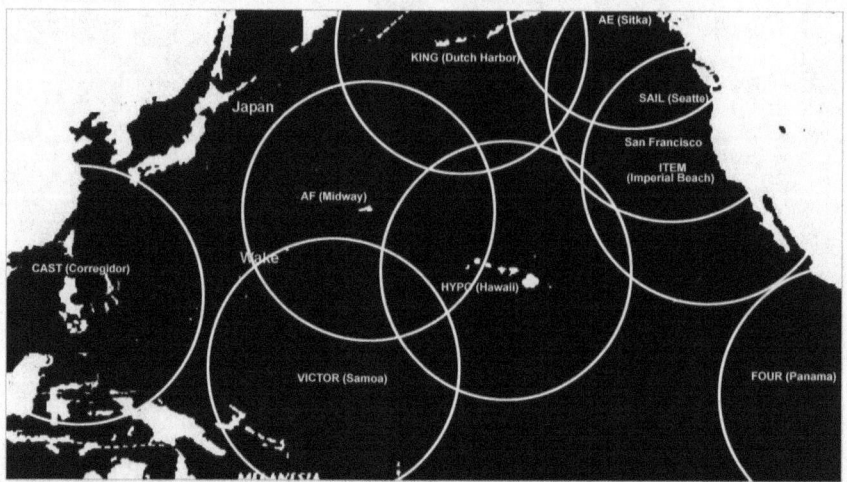

A map of the Pacific Code Stations showing their approximate range. *Author's Collection*

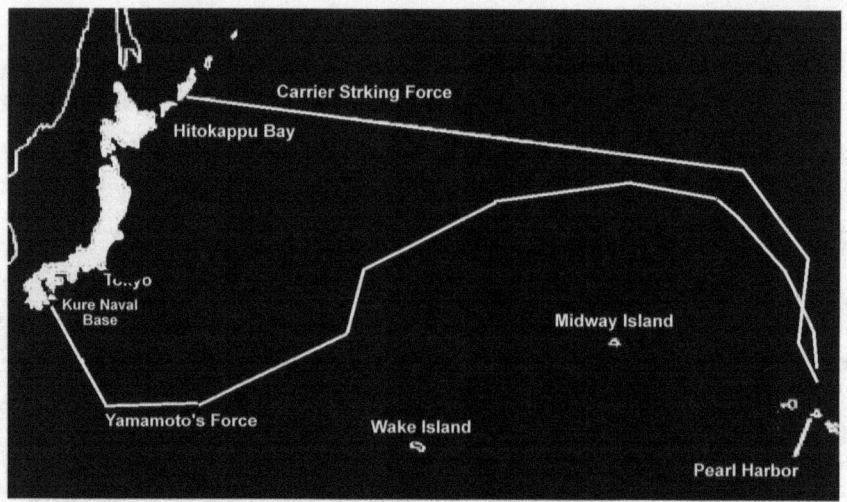

Chart showing route of First Air Fleet from Japan to Hawaii, December 1941. Note route is far north of U.S. islands. *Author's Collection*

IJN Lieutenant Tateo Yoshikawa in his guise as Japanese clerk Tadashi Morimura. *Official U.S. Navy Photo*

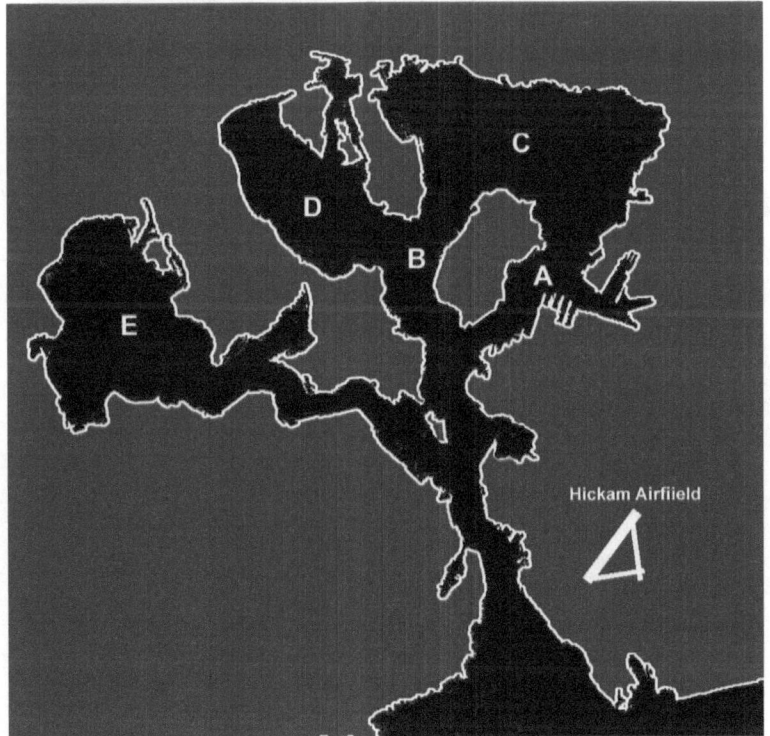

A chart of Pearl Harbor, showing areas designated by Yoshikawa in "Bomb Plot" messages. *Author's Collection*

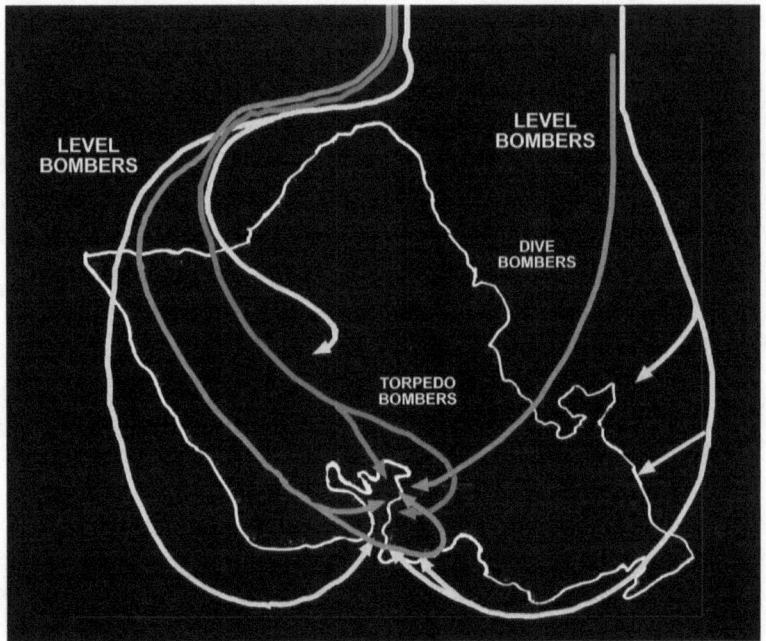

Diagram of routes flown by both first and second attack waves by fighters, dive, torpedo, and level bombers on Oahu. This shows a complex and well-planned strike. *Author's Collection*

Author's artwork showing aerial view of Battleship Row at Ford Island on December 7, 1941. *Author's Collection*

CINCPAC Admiral Husband Kimmel and Admiral Richard "Poco" Smith, 1941.
Official U.S. Navy Photo

Captain Edwin Layton, CINCPAC's intelligence chief under two admirals.
Official U.S. Navy Photo

Lieutenant General Walter Short, Hawaiian Department commander.
Official U.S. Army Photo

Commander Joseph J. Rochefort, the eccentric and brilliant head of Station HYPO at Pearl Harbor.
Official U.S. Navy Photo

Admiral Harold Stark, Chief of Naval Operations prior to Pearl Harbor.
Official U.S. Navy Photo

Commander Minoru Genda, the genius behind the planning for the Pearl Harbor attack. *Official U.S. Navy Photo*

Commander Mitsuo Fuchida, who led the attack on Pearl Harbor. *Official U.S. Navy Photo*

Saburo Kurusu signs the Tripartite Pact with Germany and Italy, forming the Axis Alliance, September 1940. *Imperial War Museum*

The three wise men, Japanese Ambassador Kichisaburo Nomura, Secretary of State Cordell Hull, and Foreign Minister Saburo Kurusu in November 1941. *National Archives*

The most difficult technical achievement of the Pearl Harbor attack, the Type 91 aerial torpedo. *Official U.S. Navy Photo*

The first to detect the incoming raid, the Opana Point SCR-270B Mobile Radar Station. *Official U.S. Army Photo*

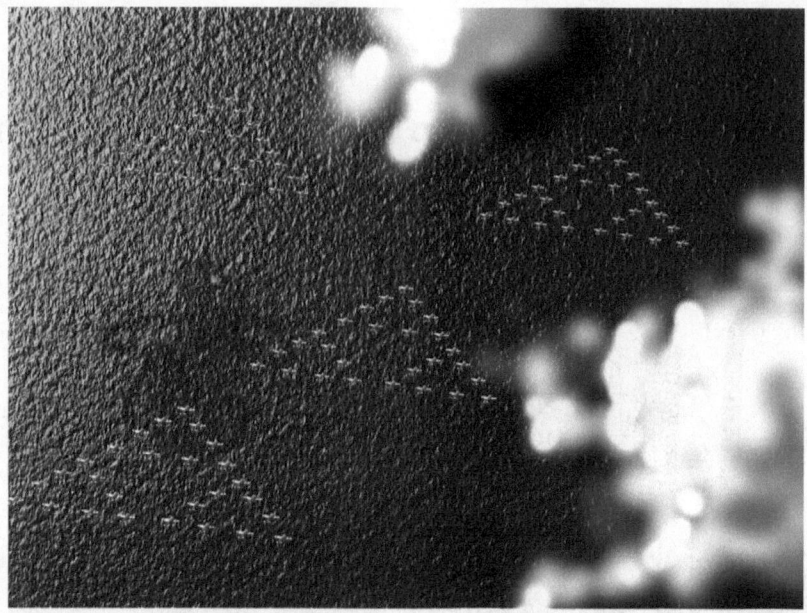

Author's artwork of the Japanese planes in formation approaching Hawaii, December 7, 1941. *Author's collection*

The destroyer USS *Ward*, which fired the first U.S. shot at Japan in the Second World War. *Official U.S. Navy Photo*

Aichi D5A Val dive bomber over Pearl Harbor, December 7, 1941. Note fixed landing gear. *Official U.S. Navy Photo*

The battleship USS *West Virginia* hit by torpedo in first minutes of the attack. Forward of *West Virginia* is USS *Oklahoma*, also hit. *Official U.S. Navy Photo*

One of the B-17s after crash-landing at Hickam Field, in which Earl Williams and most of her crew were able to escape. *Official U.S. Army Photo*

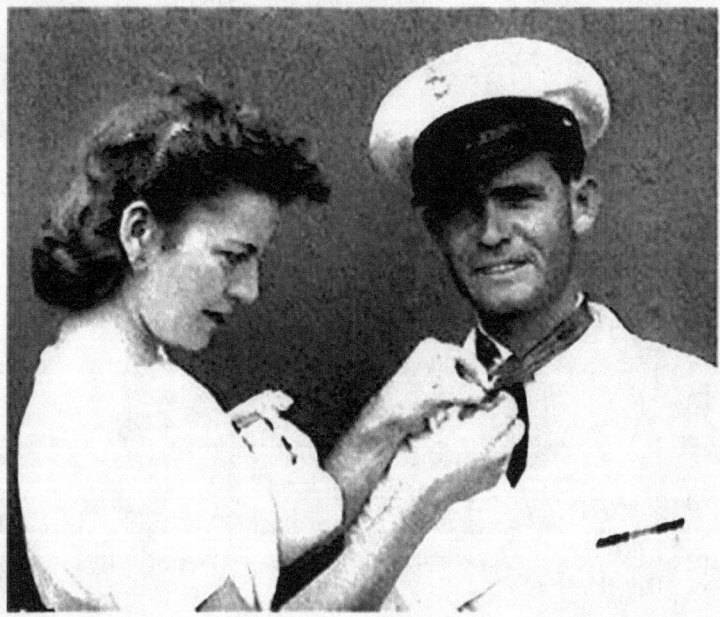

John Wiliam Finn, who fought a determined defense of NAS Kaneohe Bay on the morning of the attack. He was the last surviving Medal of Honor recipient for Pearl Harbor. *Official U.S. Navy Photo*

Pearl Harbor in full swing salvaging the destroyed fleet. All but three ships of the sixteen sunk were put back into service by 1944. *Official U.S. Navy Photo*

The tiny islands of Midway were also hit by Nagumo's First Air Fleet on December 7, 1941. *Official U.S. Navy Photo*

President Franklin D. Roosevelt makes his famous "Day of Infamy" speech before Congress on December 8, 1941. *National Archives*

Wake Island, closer to Japan than Hawaii, was one of the most isolated places on Earth. But it was a threat to Japan, and therefore a target. *U.S. Oceanic and Atmospheric Agency Photo*

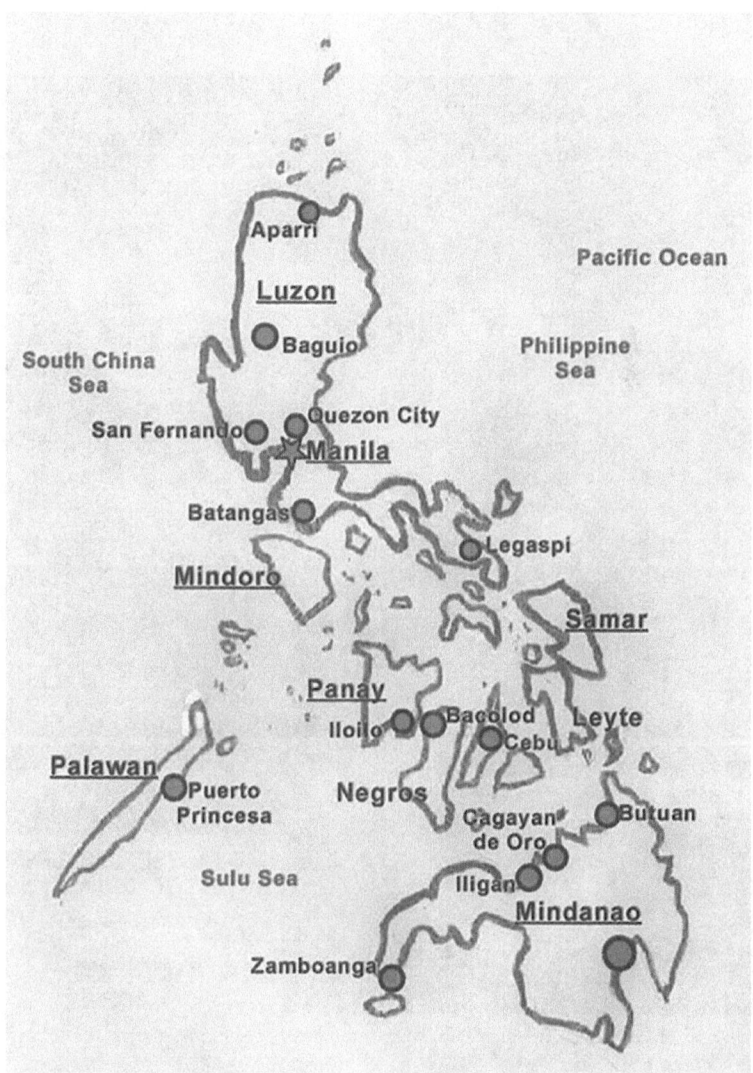

The Philippine Archipelago was under Japanese attack from December 8, 1941 to May 6, 1942. *Official U.S. Navy Photo*

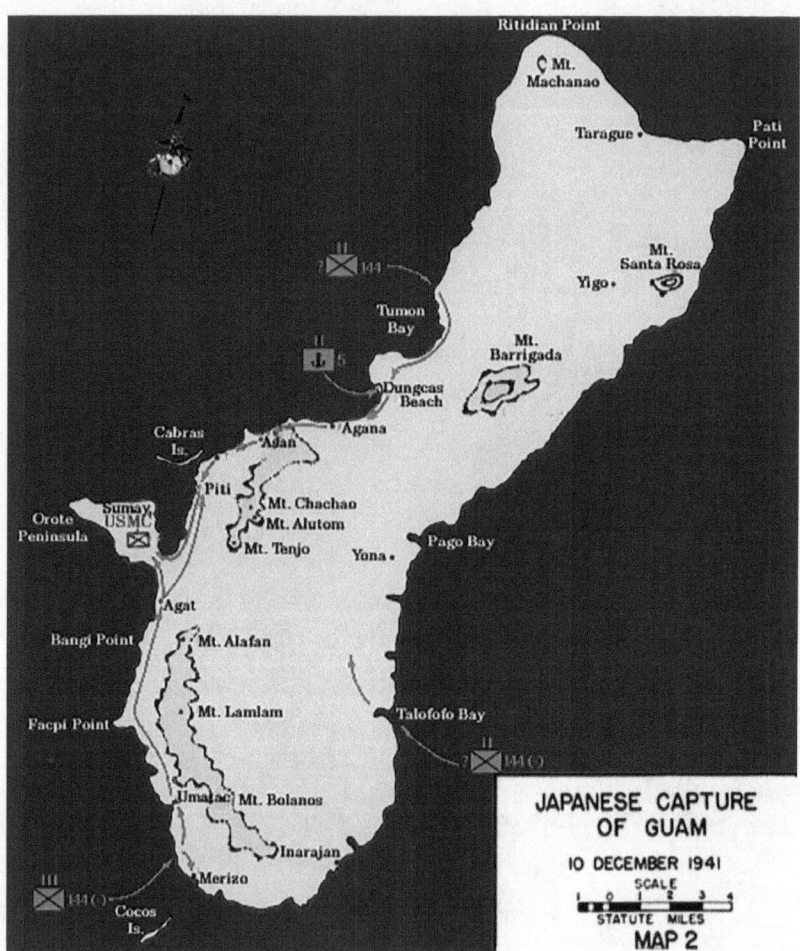

The island of Guam was the only U.S. base in the Japanese-held Marianas. It fell in two days. *Official U.S. Navy Photo*

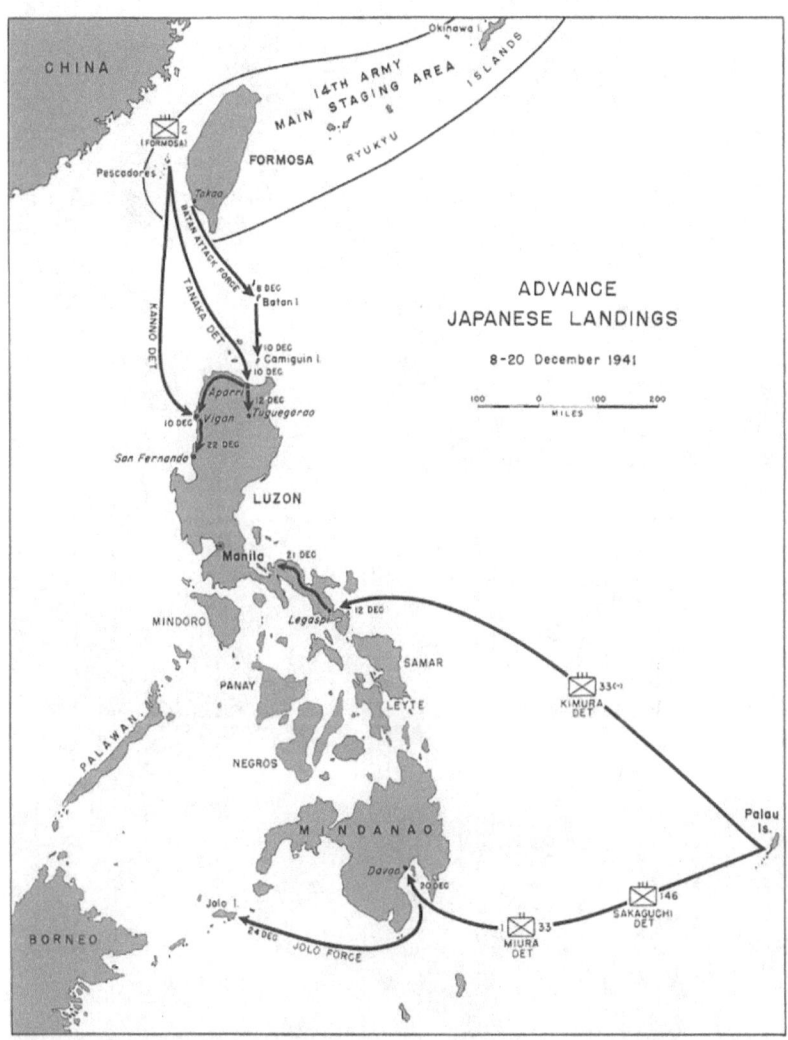

The Japanese invaded the Philippines from their bases in Formosa and French Indochina. *Official U.S. Navy Photo*

Japanese Nell and Betty bombers move in to kill the two Royal Navy capital ships. *Imperial War Museum*

The Battleship *Prince of Wales* and battle cruiser *Repulse* leaving Singapore for their date with destiny. *Imperial War Museum*

General Brereton's B-17s at Iba Field in 1941. *Official U.S. Army Photo*

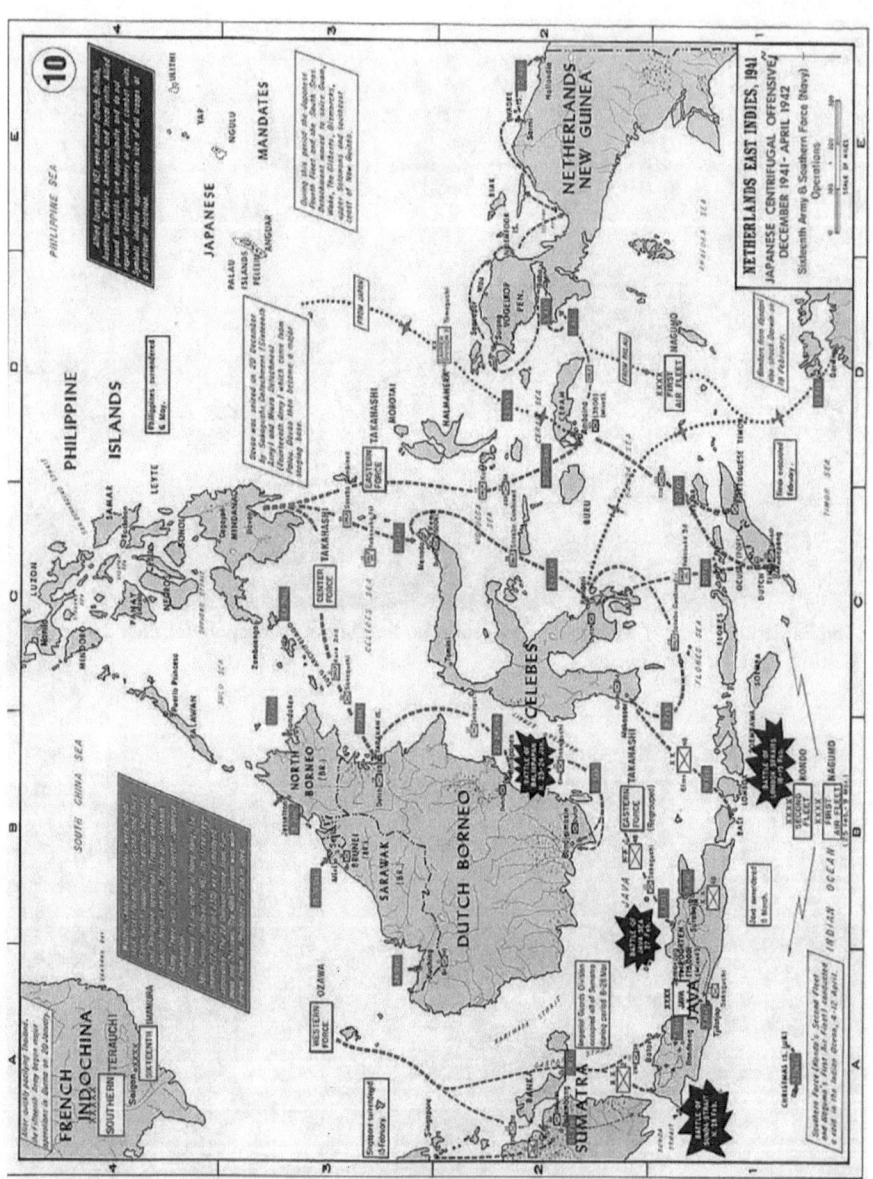

A map showing the Japanese advances in the Dutch East Indies in the winter and spring of 1942. *Naval Heritage and History Command*

Admiral Frank Fletcher.
Official U.S. Navy Photo

Commander Arthur McCollum, whose knowledge of the Japanese Navy was a factor in the prewar days in Washington.
Officiall U.S. Navy Photo

Battleship HIJMS *Nagato*, Yamamoto's flagship in the first months of the war. *Official U.S. Navy Photo*

CINCPAC Admiral Chester W. Nimitz and Admiral William F. Halsey, two old friends. *Official U.S. Navy Photo*

Captain Francis Low, the man who conceived of the Doolittle Raid. *Official U.S. Navy Photo*

A team photo of the Doolittle Raiders with Captain Marc Mitscher, *Hornet*'s commander on the day before the raid. *Official U.S. Navy Photo*

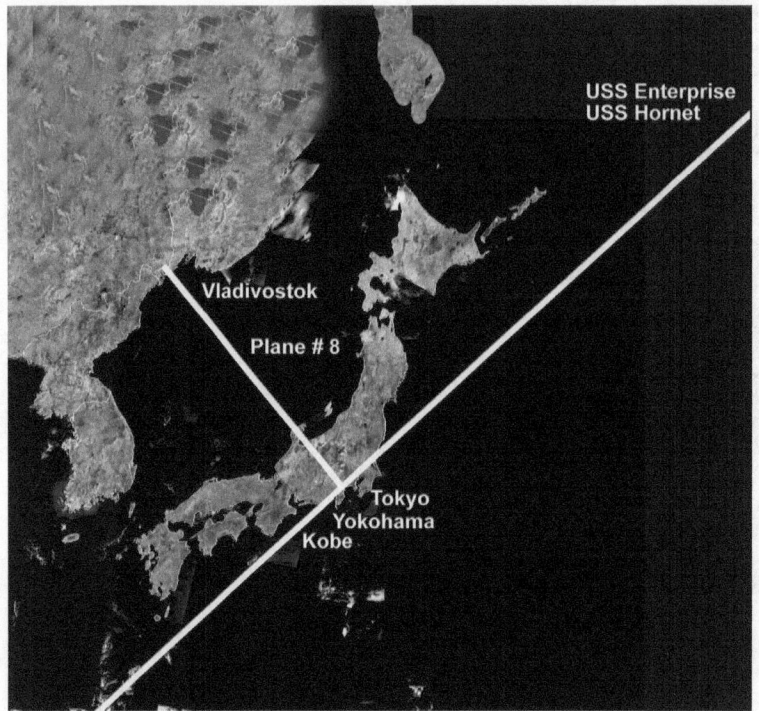

The course taken by Halsey's force and the line of flight for the Doolittle Raiders. *Author's Collection*

The mighty battleship *Yamato* fitting out at Kure Navy Yard prior to entering service in 1942. *Official U.S. Navy Photo*

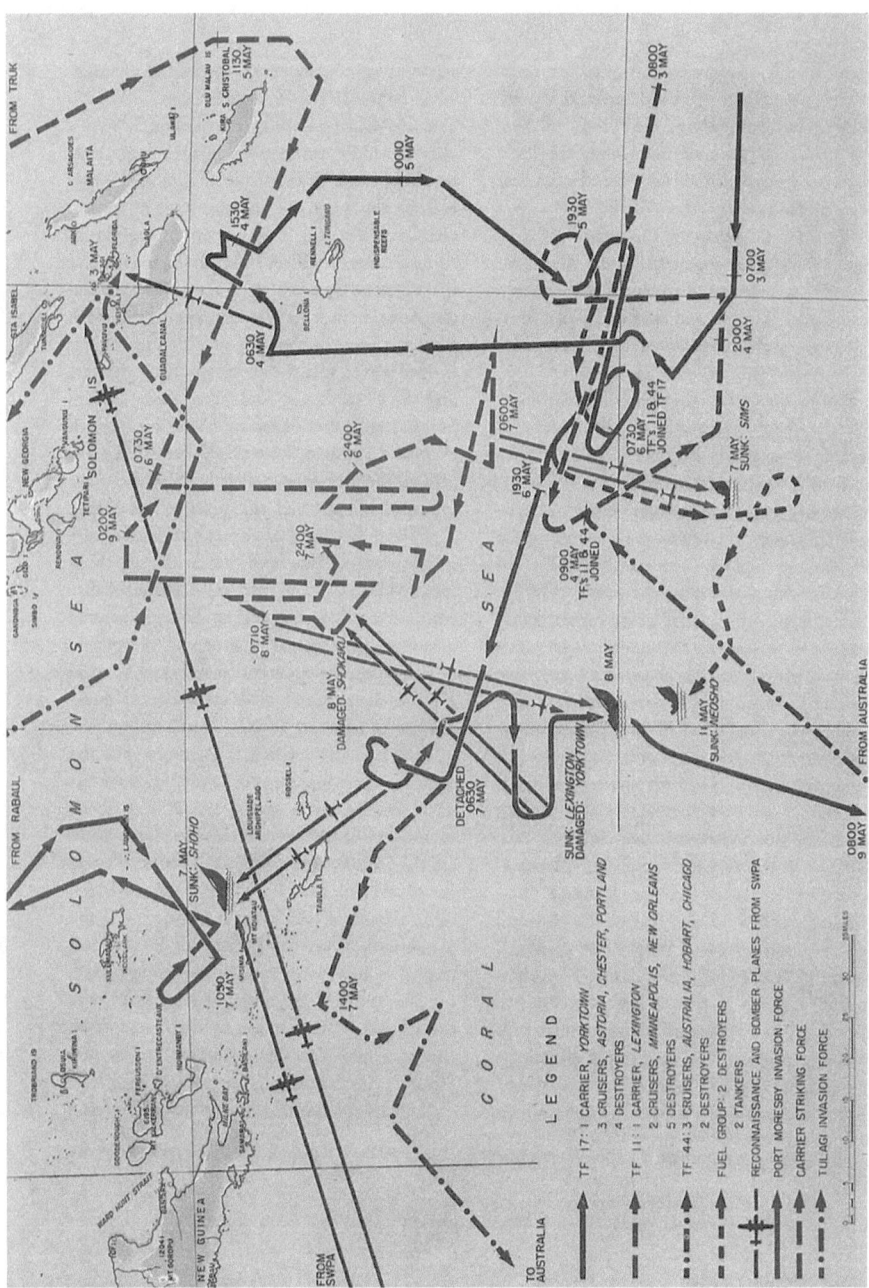

A map showing the courses and movements of the U.S. and Japanese fleets during the Battle of the Coral Sea. *Naval Heritage and History Command*

"Scratch one flattop!" The Japanese light carrier HIJMS *Shoho* under attack by U.S. bombers. *Official U.S. Navy Photo*

The new HIJMS *Shokaku*, one of the Pearl Harbor force bombed by Yorktown's planes. *Official U.S. Navy Photo*

The beloved carrier *Lexington* abandoned at Coral Sea. *Official U.S. Navy Photo*

Dive bombers from *Zuikaku* in formation at Coral Sea, May 7, 1942. *Official U.S. Navy Photo*

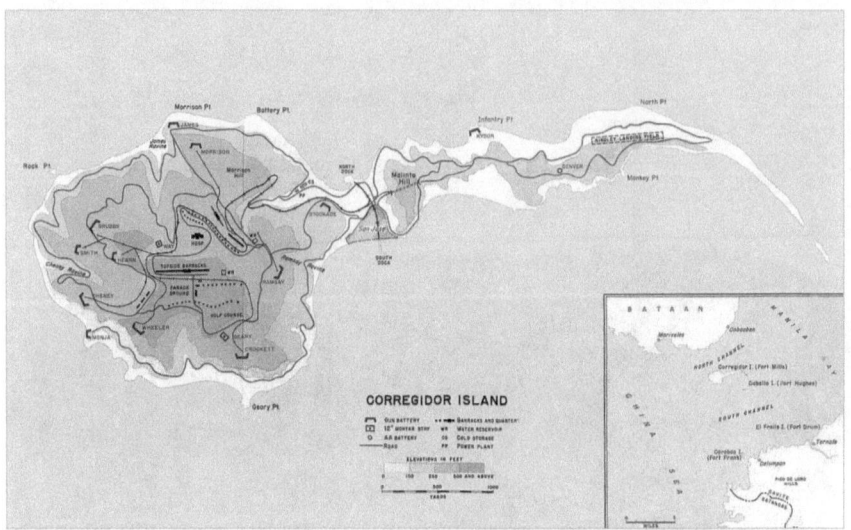

The "Rock," Corregidor Island, at the entrance to Manila Bay, the site of the last American defense of the Philippines. *National Heritage and History Command*

The entrance of Malinta Tunnel where General Wainwright's gallant command held out until May 6, 1942. *Official U.S. Army Photo*

Douglas SBD dive bombers over carriers *Enterprise* and *Saratoga* in 1942. *Official U.S. Navy Photo*

The damaged carrier *Yorktown* being repaired for her surprise return to combat at the end of May 1942. *Official U.S. Navy Photo*

Admiral Raymond Spruance, the man on the spot at Midway. *Official U.S. Navy Photo*

F4F Wildcats of *Hornet*'s VF-8 on deck June 4, 1942. *Official U.S. Navy Photo*

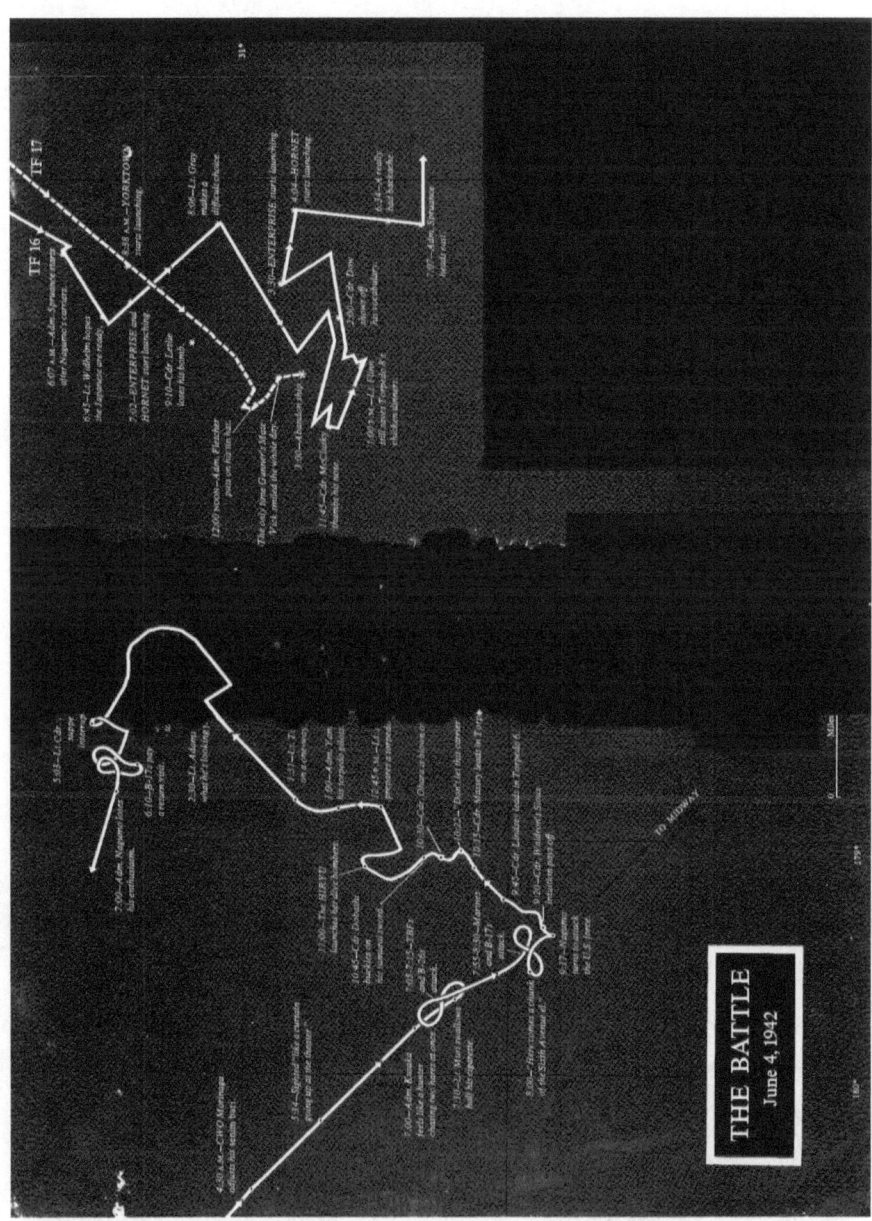

A chart showing the course of the Battle of Midway on June 4, 1942. *Author's Collection*

The ship-killer Douglas SBD Dauntless diving at a target.
Official U.S. Navy Photo

After a long day of fighting, the last of four Japanese carriers, HIJMS *Hiryu* burning, putting Nagumo out of business. This put an end to Yamamoto's wild run. *Official U.S. Navy Photo*

CHAPTER 7

RUNNING WILD

"The quality of decision is like the well-timed swoop of a falcon which enables it to strike and destroy its victim." —Sun Tzu

Pearl Harbor was only the opening move in a game of war that encompassed the entire western Pacific in less than a week. To Commander Koichi Shimada, an Eleventh Air Fleet staff officer, the plans for the multi-layered southern operations resembled a railroad timetable. Thousands of pages long, it had every ship, division, and squadron attacking or landing on enemy-held beaches on a schedule, timed down to the hour. He wondered how anyone could so rigorously plan a major campaign without regard to the reactions and actions of the enemy.

Yamamoto and the Combined Fleet staff planned simultaneous attacks and landings at Guam in the Marianas, Wake Island, Malaya, and the Philippines. This would be more than enough for any navy and army, but it was only the beginning of what Yamamoto had promised Prime Minister Konoye in 1940.

One little-remembered sidebar of the Pearl Harbor attack began after dark, 1,200 miles northwest of Oahu. Midway, a distant part of the Hawaiian archipelago, consisted of little more than 2.5 square miles of land and a lagoon encircled by a reef. A Marine battalion was sent to the island in 1940 and, in the months leading up to December 1941, had been steadily reinforced with shore defense guns, AAA batteries, and shore installations. Eastern Island had three runways, while Sand Island was home to the seaplane base, hangars, and a hotel for the Pan American China Clippers.

Navy Captain Cyril Simard took command of the new NAS Midway in April 1941, later joined by Lieutenant Colonel Harold Shannon of the Marine Corps. Shannon was an old hand at attack and defense, having served since 1914 in Nicaragua and France. Patrol Squadron 21 (VP-21) was assigned to Midway at the beginning of December and began conducting anti-submarine patrols around the island. Midway had one of the SCR-270B mobile radar units sent to the Pacific, the others being on Oahu.

During the planning for the Pearl Harbor attack, Genda was concerned that the PBY Catalinas based on Midway might locate Nagumo's carriers as they withdrew north after the Pearl Harbor strike. To prevent this, the Combined Fleet planners conceived the Midway Neutralization Force, consisting of two destroyers supported by a fleet oiler. They were to detach from the main striking force the day before the attack and wait for orders to shell Midway's airfield at night, hopefully destroying any planes capable of spotting and attacking the northbound carriers.

Destroyers *Ushio* and *Sazanami* and fleet oiler *Shiriya* had to remain south of Midway and out of patrol plane range. The *Fubuki*-class destroyers had been launched in the early 1930s and carried six 5-inch guns. With a top speed of 38 knots, the ships and their crews were veterans of the war with China.

On the morning of December 7, VP-21 had at least four of its PBYs on patrol while the Marines went about their regular duties for a Sunday morning. When the first report, "Air raid Pearl Harbor! This is no drill!" came over the radio, Shannon and Simard ordered a full alert. The Marines ran for the guns and distributed ammunition. The AAA gunners scanned the skies along with the SCR-270B radar unit. More reports came in, and it was soon obvious the Japanese had several carriers near Oahu. The PBYs took off and scoured the waters south of Midway, looking for the enemy fleet. They saw nothing.

The hours passed along with more reports of the attack, sunken battleships, blasted airfields, and hundreds of wrecked planes. Thousands of military and civilians had been killed or wounded.

Dusk fell over Midway by 1830, but still nothing had been seen. Then a lookout on Sand Island saw some blinking lights in the darkness to the south. He called in, but the night remained silent. At 2130, the radar unit picked up ships about twenty miles southwest of Sand Island. The defenders hunkered down while the officers peered through powerful binoculars, trying to pierce the ever-deepening dark. Then they saw two ships steaming directly at the island. It was 2140 hours. The Japanese destroyers were still too far for the 5-inch shore guns to engage, but every gunner was ready for the order to fire.

Aboard *Ushio*, the raid commander, Captain Konishi, watched as the first salvo of 5-inch shells from the two ships screamed toward the low beach, exploding close to one of the shore batteries, putting it out of action. One of Konishi's shells hit the seaplane hangar, while others struck the hospital and power house. A direct hit blew apart a PBY, on the ramp for maintenance, and the spreading flames threatened other nearby planes. Ensign John M. Eaton Jr. of VP-21 directed the removal of the other PBYs while ordering his men to fight the fires. At that point Konishi brought his destroyers closer and resumed the bombardment.

At 2148, Colonel Shannon ordered his batteries to open fire. They had held off, wanting to avoid alerting the Japanese to the position of the remaining guns. The searchlights came on and caught the two destroyers in their blinding white beams. All the 3-inch and remaining 5-inch guns roared in quick succession, sending heavy shells at the enemy ships. At least one hit was observed but most either fell short or missed. But it was a powerful response to what had been a one-sided barrage.

Another Japanese salvo hit Battery H, commanded by Marine Lieutenant George Cannon, Sixth Defense Battalion, mortally wounding him while directing return fire on the enemy ships. Disregarding his wounds, Cannon stayed with his gunners until he was forcibly pulled away for treatment. He posthumously received the Medal of Honor, the first for a Marine in the war.

At Battery H, Corporal Harold Hazelwood maintained the counter-fire.

For several minutes the big-caliber duel continued until Konishi decided his guns could not inflict any serious damage to the island. Laying down dense smokescreens, the ships turned and disappeared into the night. They had fired more than 200 shells at Sand Island, killing four Marines and wounding ten.

The First Battle of Midway was over, having lasted just under an hour. In addition to Cannon's Medal of Honor, Navy Crosses were awarded to Corporal Harold Hazelwood and Ensign John Eaton Jr.

Before dawn on December 8, Nagumo's six carriers and their screening vessels passed Midway without detection. After rejoining the oiler, the destroyers turned to rendezvous with the First Air Fleet.

One interesting note concerns the commander of the tanker *Shiriya*. Captain Minoru Togo was a forty-year-old veteran skipper. He was the son of the famous Admiral Heihachiro Togo, the victor at Tsushima. Even though he did not command a combat vessel, Minoru Togo carried his famous name into the Second World War. *Ushio* was the only ship of the Pearl Harbor attack force still afloat when Japan surrendered in August 1945.

But Midway was still not out of danger. Nagumo, who was elated at the apparent success of the Pearl Harbor strike, had the First Air Fleet moving north past Midway. Later that night, while the task force was 700 miles north of the island, Nagumo received Combined Fleet Order Number 14. "If the situation permits, the task force will launch an air strike on Midway Island on its return trip and destroy it completely so as to make further use of it impossible."

Nagumo was in a quandary. The original Konishi attack had only been intended to keep Midway's airplanes from spotting the First Air Fleet on its way north. Now Order 14 was telling the First Air Fleet to defend itself by turning south and mounting another full-scale air strike against Midway, without careful planning and with all the risks that entailed. Genda was opposed to this operation. It meant great risks for little possible gain.

He proposed an alternative. The First Air Fleet would sail to the anchorage and base at Truk Lagoon in the Carolines, refuel, reprovision, take on board three battalions of army troops, and plan a full attack on Midway. This would secure the Midway Islands, thus providing a base for the eventual invasion of Hawaii.

Genda was convinced that this was the logical next move while the Americans were reeling from the Pearl Harbor attack. It would also bring out the missing American carriers, which the Japanese fleet could then sink. Taking Hawaii would ensure that the remaining ships of the U.S. Pacific Fleet would be destroyed and deny the United States their most important forward Pacific base.

After Genda presented his plan to an open-minded Nagumo, it went up the chain of command to Combined Fleet Headquarters. Yamamoto's chief of staff, Vice Admiral Ugaki, considered it but raised some serious concerns. Japan would have to supply and field its navy and army forces from Japan. The large number of fleet oilers and transports needed for the operation were already committed elsewhere. The rapidly improvised operation required too many assets from the planned Malayan and Philippine landings. It was vetoed at the highest levels—at least for now.

In the end, Midway unknowingly dodged another Japanese bullet. But not for long.

At dawn on December 8 (December 7 Hawaii time), groups of Mitsubishi G3M Nell and G4M Betty medium bombers, accompanied by squadrons of Zeros, lifted off from their bases on Formosa and headed south across the South China Sea. Their targets were the United States Army, Air Force, and Navy bases on Mindanao and Luzon in the Philippines. At the same time more squadrons took off from bases near Saigon in Indochina to bomb British Army, Air, and Navy bases in Malaya, Burma, and Hong Kong. Yet still more flew from Saipan to hit Guam in the Marianas and from the Marshalls to bomb Wake Island.

Yamamoto was now running wild.

THE FIRST TO FALL: PEKING AND GUAM

With the Guangdong Army in full control of Shanghai, the International Settlement and French Concession were the only areas still unoccupied by Japanese forces. The U.S. Marines at Shanghai had been withdrawn to the Philippines in November.

When Pearl Harbor was attacked, the U.S. Embassy detachment consisted of 140 men in Peking, 48 in Tientsin, and 15 in Chinwangtao. Chinwangtao was the port used to bring supplies and men in and out of north China. The men there were on temporary duty to load all the unit's equipment on board the ship that was to arrive on December 9 and transport them to the Philippines. Except for their rifles and pistols, all their crew-served weapons and ammunition had been sent to Chinwangtao.

Early on the morning of December 8 (December 7 in Hawaii), the men on guard duty reported the presence of large numbers of Japanese troops on the walls around the compound, armed with machine guns and mortars. There was no attack on the part of the Japanese, but the Marine officer in command had no choice. He met with the Japanese and eventually surrendered on the reasonable assumption that the entire unit would be considered diplomatic personnel and repatriated. Their surrender was prompted by the 1905 Boxer Rebellion in Peking, when Marines defended the Legation for almost two months before being relieved. The resulting "Boxer Protocol" stipulated that U.S. Embassy Marines would be considered diplomatic personnel and not imprisoned. However, the Japanese did not honor the protocol, and the Marines became the first United States Prisoners of War in Japan.

Rear Admiral William Glassford, the Yangtze River Squadron commander, had ordered the remaining gunboats disarmed by the end of November before turning them over to the Chinese. Not trusting the Japanese to respect U.S. sovereignty, Glassford was ready to evacuate.

On the same day the U.S. Embassy fell, the *Wake* and another gunboat were seized, completing what the Imperial Navy had started exactly four years earlier with the *Panay*.

The river squadron, Peking, and Tientsin detachments were initially held at the Woosung POW camp in Shanghai, then transferred to the Kiangwan POW camp in the same area. In November 1942 and August 1943, about half of the embassy detachment was sent to various POW camps in Japan.

After the war, the embassy Marines were pressured to sign documents that they would not talk about the incident, ostensibly to avoid releasing any information on underground or guerilla units still operating in China. But the more likely reason was that the Navy Department was loathe to admit 200 Marines had surrendered to the Japanese without a fight.

The largest of the Marianas Islands, Guam was south of Tinian and Saipan, which had been ceded to Japan in the Pacific Mandate. But Guam had been a U.S. territory since 1898 and the end of the Spanish-American War. Unlike the coral atolls and reef islands of the Marshalls, Gilberts, and Carolines, the Marianas were true islands, created by tectonic up-thrusting from the sea floor. Guam was the largest island north of the equator between Hawaii and the Philippines.

A small navy base was built in Piti, while the Marines set up barracks at Sumay. A coaling station for navy vessels, protected by a battery of 6-inch coastal defense guns, was in service by 1909. A U.S. Navy captain had the dual role of island governor and base commander, a situation that remained in place until December 1941.

After the 1922 Washington Naval Treaty, Japan and the U.S. agreed not to fortify any of their islands. To the United States, Guam, being virtually surrounded by Japanese-held Tinian and Saipan, was considered indefensible.

While the United States initially honored the treaty by removing Guam's coast guns, Japan continued to fortify Tinian and Saipan, secretly increasing its military presence in the Marianas. For the Japanese, the island had been considered a target for invasion and occupation as early as 1939.

In 1938, the U.S. Navy considered building a larger base, but this was rejected as being too inflammatory under the present diplomatic tensions. Guam had a population of more than 23,000 citizens, and the capital city of Agama and Apra Harbor was one of the best in the area. The only thing Guam lacked was an airfield. The only planes that used the island as a fuel stop were Pan American Airways' China Clippers.

The Imperial Navy had been making photographic reconnaissance flights over Guam since March 1941, and plans for an invasion were complete by September. The 144th Infantry Regiment of the 56th Infantry Division of the newly established South Seas Detachment trained in Korea and Japan. The regiment of 4,800 officers and men shipped out to Chichijima in the Bonin Islands south of Japan in November. Another of the Bonins was an island that would become well known to Americans in 1945—Iwo Jima.

A special naval landing force based in Saipan was to make the initial assault while the main force was carried on nine transports, escorted by a minesweeper, four destroyers, and a division of heavy cruisers. This was far more muscle than was needed to take the island from the U.S. Navy and Marines. The State and Navy Departments did not consider Guam worth reinforcing or defending. But the Japanese penchant for over-thinking every detail and timetable, as at Pearl Harbor, was well in use at Guam and the rest of the Pacific.

Marine Lieutenant Colonel Bill MacNulty was told that, in the event of attack, he and his men were to destroy everything of value to the Japanese and withdraw. How they were to accomplish the latter had not been discussed. Navy Captain George McMillin, the governor, had most of the American civilians evacuated.

At 0445 on December 8 local time, McMillin was informed of the Pearl Harbor attack. He ordered a full alert, but four hours later, Japanese bombers from Saipan began bombing the Marine barracks, port facilities, coaling station, radio station, and the Standard Oil tanks. They also hit the Pan American hotel.

The air strikes resumed the following morning, and that afternoon, four heavy cruisers, four destroyers, and nine transports arrived at Dungcas Beach near Agama. Two more landing forces came ashore at Tumon Bay on the north and Merizo to the southeast.

The island's native Insular Defense Group was quickly overwhelmed. The few Marines still able to fight engaged the much larger landing force, but at 1645 on December 10, Captain McMillin ordered their surrender. Guam was in Japanese hands by 1800. Marine and navy losses were less than fifty killed and wounded.

With the fall of Guam, all of the Marianas was under Japanese control.

During the next thirty-three months, the Japanese inflicted brutal treatment on civilians and captured American personnel, including starvation, beatings, torture, and decapitation.

INTO THE INFERNO: THE PHILIPPINES

At the villa of General Douglas MacArthur, 1 Victoria Street in the exclusive section of Manila, Major General Lewis Brereton, commander of the Far East Air Force (FEAF), was standing before the desk of Brigadier General Richard Sutherland, MacArthur's chief of staff.

"The general is in conference with Admiral Hart," Sutherland replied flatly to Brereton's demand to see MacArthur.

The time was 0450, December 8, just ninety minutes after the radio calls had come in about Pearl Harbor. Brereton needed to see the commander in chief of the U.S. Army Forces in the Far East, or USAFFE. But Sutherland, who jealously guarded MacArthur's time and office, refused.

Brereton persisted, telling Sutherland that he wanted his B-17s to take off at dawn and head north to the Japanese bases on southern Formosa. Seeing that the air force general wouldn't back down, Sutherland said that Brereton could make preparations but not take off. He was concerned doing so would provoke Japan before war was officially declared.

Frustrated, Brereton left and drove back to his headquarters near Manila. He had already told his pilots and ground crews to get the bombers ready. They had no accurate maps or photos of where the enemy air bases were, but he had to act now. He had to hit the Japanese before they came to hit him. The time dragged by and dawn rose over the thickly wooded mountains to the east.

He repeatedly called MacArthur's headquarters, but Sutherland responded with the same caution each time, telling Brereton not to launch a preemptive strike on the Japanese.

Far to the south, Japanese dive bombers hit a seaplane tender and two PBYs on the coast of Mindanao. It was the first overt act by Japan on the Philippines. At the same time, a radio station on the north coast of Luzon, north of Manila, was hit by land-based Zeros.

But Brereton was not told about the small probing attacks. He was most concerned about the thirty-five B-17s on the two largest airfields: Clark on Luzon and the Del Monte Airfield on northern Mindanao. Brereton had over a hundred Curtiss P-40B Tomahawks and Republic P-35 Lancers at Nichols and Eba fields. But they were effectively grounded by Sutherland's hesitation.

Sutherland's intransigence is still hard to believe, but as Flying Tiger ace James Howard said, "Americans all too often booted the incompetent and blunderers upstairs to staff jobs, where they could continue their mistakes." Sutherland was not incompetent, but he was clearly unimaginative or proactive.

At 0715, the FEAF general drove to 1 Victoria Street to confront Sutherland. At last the chief of staff went into MacArthur's inner office and closed the door. A few minutes later, he emerged and faced Brereton. "The general says no. Don't make the first overt act." Brereton countered by telling Sutherland that the attack on Pearl Harbor certainly constituted an overt act.

There was some logic to Sutherland's resistance. Since the Philippines was a U.S. territory and not actually part of the United States, any aggressive moves from the Far East Air Force would be an act of war. The government of the islands in Manila had discussed their status with MacArthur and hoped that by not attacking Formosa, the Japanese might consider the Philippines neutral and not attack. This was extremely naive, but MacArthur had to do the prudent thing.

At 0800, Brereton received a phone call from Major General Henry "Hap" Arnold, chief of the air force, not to let his planes be caught on the ground. Brereton said he was trying to avoid that, but he could not counter MacArthur's orders.

All Brereton could do was order his fighters, based at three airfields on Luzon and Mindanao, to be ready for immediate takeoff in case of an alert. He also had all the fueled Flying Fortresses fly long-range patrols to the west and north, looking for Japanese ships. Three squadrons of fighters began patrolling over Luzon.

At 1015, Sutherland called Brereton and authorized the raid on Formosa. The FEAF recalled the bombers and began fueling them while briefing the pilots and navigators on their targets on Formosa. The fighters, running low on fuel, landed at their field to refuel while others took off to patrol over Clark.

By 1045, the bombers were almost ready. The fighters landed so the pilots could get something to eat. They joked about the sudden alerts and reports that the Japanese had attacked Pearl Harbor. No one seemed to take it seriously.

At 1102, while the aircrews were eating and awaiting reports from a reconnaissance flight to Formosa, all but two of Clark's B-17s were on the ground. The rest of the FEAF's heavy bombers were at Del Monte Field.

Then radar picked up two flights of planes coming in from the west and north. Near chaos erupted and the fighters took off, some heading for Manila, others to Clark, while more went out to sea to intercept the closest formation. The confusion resulted in some fighters flying at top speed to find no sign of the enemy, while others, due to a communications foul-up, never received their orders from FEAF Fighter Headquarters. With fuel running low, they continued to chase reports with no result. This only reinforced the belief that the Japanese were not really coming.

The Formosa-based Japanese Eleventh Air Group was over Clark Field at 1240. Even though three pursuit squadrons were in the air, the Japanese bombers and fighters faced no opposition. They had achieved near-total surprise.

Two B-17 squadrons were on the ground, fueled, armed, and ready for a raid on Formosa that would never happen. The P-40s of the 20th Pursuit Squadron were lining up for takeoff when the first wave of twenty-seven Nells opened their bomb bay doors and released twelve 250-kg bombs on the field. The bombers were in a perfect formation of nine three-plane elements, forming a neat wedge that impressed the Americans. One by one, the fueled B-17s erupted in flame and smoke as the fighters scrambled to take off. Only four made it into the air. By then, the second wave of twenty-six Betty bombers, accompanied by Zeroes, had dropped their bomb loads. The Zeroes strafed the field for half an hour. When they departed, eighteen of Brereton's bombers were in flames and the field hangars and fuel tanks destroyed.

To the north, Eba Field was hit by fifty-four Betty bombers that caught the Tomahawks on the field as they ran out of fuel. All but four were destroyed on the ground.

In less than an hour, the FEAF had lost more than half its planes.

By December 10, all Brereton and MacArthur had left were twelve B-17s, twenty-one P-40s, and eight P-35s. All that remained were a wrecked airfield, cratered runways, burned fuel tanks, and damaged repair facilities.

The Sixteenth Naval District, based in Manila, commanded the U.S. Asiatic Fleet under Admiral Thomas Hart. His force consisted of the heavy cruiser *Houston*, light cruiser *Marblehead*, and thirteen 1,200-ton destroyers from the First World War. Hart also had about twenty-five *Salmon*-, *Porpoise*-, and *Sargo*-class submarines. The big navy base at Cavite and the Olongapo Naval Station were savagely bombed that same day. But Hart, under orders from Washington, had already sent the bulk of his surface ships to Australia. Only the subs, having submerged, survived the attack. Among them were two submarines, which had already gained some notoriety in 1939.

The *Squalus* (SS-192) and her older sister, *Sculpin* (SS-191), had been built and launched from Portsmouth, New Hampshire. In May 1939, *Squalus* went on a test dive out of Portsmouth and suffered a mechanical failure that sank the sub in 243 feet of water when the after compartments flooded. Twenty-six of her crew drowned, and the other thirty-three were rescued in history's first use of a revolutionary diving chamber developed by Commanders Charles "Swede" Momsen and Allan McCann. It was a major triumph for the submarine force since, prior to the rescue chamber's development, nothing could be done to save trapped submariners. It took four months to salvage *Squalus* and several more to put her back into service. In order to keep the sub from carrying the stigma of being jinxed, she was recommissioned as the *Sailfish*. She and her sister sub, *Sculpin*, which played an important role in the rescue, were sent to Cavite. They managed to escape the bombing and served until *Sculpin* was sunk by Japanese depth charges near the Gilbert Islands in November 1943. A sad tragedy occurred when the survivors of her crew were being transported to Japan aboard the auxiliary light carrier *Chuyo*, which was torpedoed by another sub. Only one of the *Sculpin* survivors lived. The sub that sank the carrier was the *Sailfish*, the original *Squalus*.

One of the more famous flights of a single B-17 was that of twenty-six-year-old Captain Colin P. Kelly of Florida. Flying a B-17C of the 14th Bomb Squadron of the 19th Bomb Group out of Clark on December 10, Kelly and his crew went north to the coastal town of Aparri, where a Japanese aircraft carrier had reportedly been sighted. The bomber was only partially fueled and armed because an air raid was approaching Clark. In the bomb bay were three 600-pound general-purpose bombs.

Sighting a large ship north of Aparri, Kelly turned that way, but it was not a carrier. He identified it as a battleship, which he assumed to be the *Haruna*. He made three quartering passes as his bombardier lined up his Norden bombsight from 20,000 feet. On the last pass, the three bombs fell free and straddled what turned out to be the light cruiser *Natori* and a destroyer *Harukaze*, which sustained light damage.

The bomber flew south and was then attacked by Zeroes of the Tainan Group, patrolling over the landing areas. Kelly tried to get clear, but the bomber was too badly damaged by 7.7mm machine gun and 20mm cannon fire. Most of the crew were able to bail out, but the plane exploded and crashed four miles from Clark, killing Kelly and Technical Sergeant Bill Delehanty.

Kelly posthumously received the Distinguished Service Cross and, through most of the war, was credited with sinking the *Haruna*. At that time, the battleship was with Vice Admiral Nobutake Kondo's Eleventh Air Fleet at Malaya, hunting for the battleship *Prince of Wales* and battle cruiser *Repulse*. Curiously, Japan's highest-scoring ace to survive the war, Saburo Sakai, was the flight leader of the unit that shot Kelly down but was never credited with the kill.

Clark Field was abandoned on December 11 as MacArthur ordered his ground forces to the Bataan Peninsula. The few remaining fighters flew sorties to attack Japanese troops moving south from their landing at Lingayen Gulf.

Fourteen B-17s were still flyable, but spare parts, fuel, and ammunition were increasingly scarce. Bombs and fuel were scrounged. By December 23, the same day Wake Island would fall, the Far East Air Force in the Philippines ceased to exist. The survivors flew to Del Monte on Mindanao and on to Australia.

The 31,000 remaining American and Filipino troops were under Major General Jonathan Wainwright. But they were woefully under-equipped. More than a million tons of guns, ammunition, supplies, and equipment were stored in U.S. ports awaiting transport to the Philippines.

The trail that would lead to the long struggle on Bataan and Corregidor had begun. The ordeal would not end until May 1942.

PICKING UP THE PIECES

At Pearl, the frenzied effort to rescue trapped sailors in the capsized *Oklahoma* and extinguish the fires in the oily waters was well underway. Sailors, Marines, soldiers, and airmen worked to bring order out of chaos. One of the first jobs was to lay a new water line to Ford Island. The Fourteenth Naval District public works department began running a new 16-inch water main to replace the one crushed by the sunken *Arizona*.

All over Oahu, men, women, and children, young and old, American and Hawaiian, civilian and military, took stock of the destruction and counted the dead. Thousands of civilians hastily packed their belongings and headed into the hills and mountains, desperate to escape the expected invasion. For weeks, families had no word of the fate of fathers, brothers, sons, and husbands. The hospitals and infirmaries were choked with the wounded. Some had been hit by bullets or shrapnel, choked on oily water, broken limbs from falling from shattered superstructures, or burned. The latter were the worst. Screaming in sheer agony, smelling of roasted flesh, with hair and features burned off their faces, they had gone from a life they understood to one that only meant years of pain and anger.

A call went out from the naval hospital to every civilian hospital and clinic for burn ointments, bandages, morphine, anesthetics, and antibiotics. Civilian and military doctors, nurses, corpsmen, pharmacists' mates, and anyone willing and able to help worked for hours, days, and weeks to heal those among the undeclared war's first casualties. Many died mercifully without ever regaining consciousness. Hastily wrapped in sheets or canvas, they were laid out on the lawn by the naval hospital to await identification and burial in the ever-growing rows of graves in the Punchbowl.

Hawaii's seventy-one-year-old governor, Joseph Poindexter, grieving for the many dead and wounded, was on a direct phone call to Roosevelt in the White House. The president assured the old statesman that every effort was being made to protect Hawaii and its residents. This was hardly likely at the time, since FDR had little information on what had been destroyed and what was left to fight with. Poindexter was persuaded to declare martial law, something not to be taken lightly. A curfew was established to protect innocent civilians as much as to prevent sabotage. Jittery soldiers and Marines would shoot anyone they thought might be an enemy invader and ask questions later. Most at risk were people of Japanese and Asian ethnicity, who quickly learned to stay in their homes for fear of being shot as enemy agents.

Rumors of paratroopers landing in the cane fields and troops arriving on the beaches were rampant. Germans, whom many Americans suspected of being the real culprit behind the attack, were reported to have infiltrated bars, restaurants, stores, hospitals, hotels, and electric companies, and were only waiting for the right moment to emerge and take over the island.

At 2130 hours, *Enterprise*, having recovered the bombers and fighters from the aborted strike, ended its first day of the undeclared war. Except for Scouting 6, which had run right into the Japanese attack, Bombing 6, Torpedo 6, and Fighting 6 were on board.

At 1100 hours on 7 December, *Enterprise* rounded the western tip of Oahu, then turned east for the channel entrance. Considering that the Big E had been scheduled to arrive at 0830, the mishap with *Northampton's* propellor was one of the most fortunate accidents for the navy. Destroyers were on patrol for submarines. Even from twenty miles at sea, the gray pall of smoke hung like a shroud over southern Oahu. All the fighters took off and landed at Wheeler Field to provide more fighter defense.

Just after sunset, the Big E nosed her way into the narrow channel. Her bow cut through water iridescent with oil. Every member of her crew not on duty, and many who were, watched from decks, superstructure, hangar elevators, hatchways, and portholes to see the savage damage done to the fleet they had left only a week earlier. The air reeked of death, of burning oil and bodies. Launches and yard boats skittered across the black harbor like water bugs.

Steaming slowly around Ford Island, the carrier turned east and passed the wreckage of Battleship Row.

This was when Halsey made his famous pronouncement: "Before we're through with them, the Japanese language will only be spoken in Hell." He meant every word.

As night fell, the still-burning *Arizona* illuminated the harbor in a ghastly orange light. The entire harbor was blacked out. Men worked using flashlights or lanterns only when necessary. The pale moon cast a cool blue light on the scene of death and destruction. *Enterprise* tied up at F2, forward of the still-sinking *California*. The Big E was to be refueled and provisioned during the night. As soon as his flagship was secure, Halsey climbed into a launch to see Kimmel at CINCPAC Headquarters. Playing across the black oily waters, the launch was fired upon by nervous machine gunners, but the darkness saved Halsey from being hit. As he entered the darkened building, he saw haggard and unshaven officers and men working by lantern light. Kimmel greeted him with a handshake. His Sunday whites were stained with sweat and a dark smudge on the front. As they sat down, reports came in, one of which concerned a sighting of Japanese troops landing in gliders.

Halsey laughed. Kimmel, annoyed at this reaction, snarled, "What the hell is so funny?"

Halsey, understanding his friend's reaction, explained that gliders would not have the range to reach Oahu, and there was no way Nagumo would have wasted his carrier deck space with such nonsense. He told Kimmel the Japanese were long gone and the danger was over—for now.

Kimmel saw the wisdom of this reasoning and got down to business. They discussed what should be done with *Enterprise* and *Lexington*'s task forces.

Halsey was in favor of chasing down Nagumo, but Kimmel would not risk the only two carriers on what would probably be a suicide mission. He outlined his plans to reinforce Wake Island's small garrison.

Meanwhile, *Enterprise* was being loaded. Since it was impossible to do this in the normal way via Ford Island, she was visited by a small fleet of barges, which began a steady unloading of boxes, crates, barrels, bushels, and bales of food, water, aviation fuel, bombs, torpedoes, medical supplies, spare parts, and the thousand other things needed by a carrier headed into harm's way. Under normal daylight conditions, this usually took a minimum of twelve hours. With every hand working the steady bucket brigade in the long corridors, up and down the ladders, and in cramped storerooms, they accomplished the task in less than eight hours. Halsey intended to have his ship and Task Force 8 out of Pearl before dawn. She was pushed away from mooring F2 by tugs and aimed her gray bow toward the dark channel at 0330. By 0400, she was back at sea and ready to recover her air wing at first light. The Big E was now on the hunt.

When all his pilots were aboard, Halsey gave one of his characteristically blunt and moving speeches to his officers and pilots. He explained the seriousness of the situation and how important it was to fight back as soon as possible. When Halsey was done, one pilot said to a friend, "The Japs had better look out for him!"

He was right. On December 10, *Enterprise*'s scout bombers found three Japanese submarines among the islands, undoubtedly there to pick off any U.S. warships. They were all on the surface, making them easy targets for the SBD's bombs. One sub dived and escaped, but of the other two, one received a direct hit from a Dauntless, while Ensign Dickenson flew through machine gun fire to drop one close to the third sub. The bomb exploded right next to the hull, and the sub went down in a spreading stain of oil. *Enterprise* was the first U.S.

ship credited with sinking Japanese warships in the Second World War. There were more to come.

In Washington, President Franklin D. Roosevelt, wearing the heavy leg braces that helped him walk, accompanied by his son James, stepped up to the Speaker's podium in the House chamber. Every seat on the floor was filled, as were the visitor, VIP, and press galleries. Speaker of the House Sam Rayburn and Vice President Henry Wallace were behind Roosevelt as the president cleared his throat.

"Mister Vice President, and Mister Speaker, and Members of the Senate and House of Representatives," he began in his Hyde Park drawl. "Yesterday, December 7, 1941, a date which will live in infamy, the United States of America was suddenly and deliberately attacked by naval and air forces of the Empire of Japan."

His now famous "Day of Infamy" address ended, "With confidence in our armed forces, with the unbounding determination of our people, we will gain the inevitable triumph, so help us God."

Then his voice became somber. "I ask that the Congress declare that, since the unprovoked and dastardly attack by Japan, on Sunday, December 7, 1941, a state of war has existed between the United States and the Japanese Empire."

Roosevelt's address lasted less than five minutes.

The chamber resounded with cheers and clapping. Roosevelt stepped down, assisted by his son, while Rayburn rapped his gavel for quiet.

The Speaker asked for a vote on the matter. It took only fifteen minutes. The vote was 82 to 1 in the Senate and 388 to 1 in the House. Roosevelt signed the declaration of war at 1610 the same day.

The United States had declared war on Japan. The Sleeping Giant, awakened, now turned its angry red eyes on Japan.

Secretary of War Henry Stimson ordered all reserve army and National Guard units into uniform and to report to their assigned duty stations. With this order, more than 1.6 million American soldiers were called to duty. All over the country, police and security guards were posted on twenty-four-hour duty around defense plants, aircraft factories, dams, reservoirs, refineries, airports, bridges, piers, and power plants to guard against sabotage. Ports all along the eastern and western seaboards were closed to foreign shipping. Airports and railroad stations were shut down to all but military personnel. Radio stations ceased broadcasting weather reports to prevent enemy ships and planes from hearing them.

Even the usually restless situation between labor and management was set aside. A nationwide welders' strike was called off to support the war effort.

DEATH OF THE BATTLESHIP

Several Royal Navy warships under the command of Admiral Sir Thomas Phillips were anchored in Singapore's Keppel Harbor. The fleet arrived at Singapore on December 2 from Cape Town, South Africa. They were centered on the new battleship *Prince of Wales*, the battle cruiser *Repulse*, and four destroyers. They were the most powerful Royal Navy warships in the Far East. *Prince of Wales* had already tasted battle in May 1941, when she and the ill-fated *Hood* dueled the German battleship *Bismarck* and the cruiser *Prinz Eugen* in the Denmark Strait. The 35,000-ton *Prince of Wales* was armed with ten 14-inch guns, while *Repulse*, commissioned during the First World War, displaced 27,000 tons and carried six 15-inch guns. They were to provide heavy naval support to protect Singapore and other British Far East colonies.

Originally the new carrier *Indomitable* was to join Phillips, but she was damaged after running aground in Jamaica while en route to the Panama Canal in November.

The Malaysian Peninsula jutted like a spearpoint into the South China Sea. The most important of Great Britain's Far East colonies, the peninsula was tipped by the island of Singapore and the best harbor in Asia. Malaya, farther up the jutting point of land, was the gateway to China, Thailand (then known as Siam), and Burma. Singapore had a battery of large coastal defense guns capable of doing great damage to an attacking fleet but, with a shortsightedness that boggles the mind, put them in concrete pits that only allowed them to aim out to sea. A land assault from the north had nothing to fear from these big guns.

On the morning of December 8 (December 7 Hawaii time), bombers of the Mihoro Air Group bombed the British air bases at Malaya, Hong Kong, and Singapore to prevent any RAF planes from interfering with the planned amphibious landings at Kota Bharu in Malaya. Lieutenant General Arthur Percival, the commanding officer of the British Far East Command, was confident his Royal Air Force and Royal Australian Air Force (RAAF) fighters and Bristol Blenheim night fighters could handle any Japanese attack. He had been lulled into a false sense of security by the poor performance of Japanese fighters and bombers in the Sino-Japanese War. But those reports concerned older aircraft types, not the highly advanced aircraft being readied to attack his command.

The first Japanese attack by Nell medium bombers of the Saigon-based Genzan Air Group on Malaya resulted in the loss of most of the RAF land-based fighters. The air raid on Hong Kong had put its only airfield out of service. Seventeen Nells hit Singapore's three military airfields. Lieutenant General Tomoyuki Yamashita's 25th Army landed on the eastern shore of the Malay Peninsula, established a strong perimeter, and began to march south toward the island of Singapore, the hub of the British colonial government in the Far East. Percival had expected an amphibious landing directly on Singapore, but his own army of 86,000 British, Australian, New Zealand, and indigenous troops were cut off by the Japanese farther up the peninsula. This meant he could not count on being supplied via the land routes from India and Europe. Even worse, the Royal Navy was on the defensive and vastly outnumbered by the Japanese Eleventh Fleet.

But the officers and men of Phillips's task force felt no reason to fear the Imperial Japanese Navy's ships. In fact, many men were certain that their two splendid capital ships could defeat any enemy fleet within range of their big guns.

The only air cover available was ten American-built F2A Brewster Buffalo fighters of RAAF No. 453 Squadron based at RAF Sembawang at Singapore. The Buffalo had little chance against the swift Zeroes. The pilots were instructed to communicate with the ships, which had by now been named Force Z. Despite the lack of strong land-based and naval air cover for his ships, Phillips was not concerned. His opinion, one shared by many in the Royal Navy, was that the Japanese were not to be taken seriously as a naval and air power.

In a very short time they would learn how wrong they were. Force Z, anchored in the harbor at Singapore, put up a fierce AAA barrage during the first air raid but coud not shoot down any bombers.

Meanwhile, Yamamoto, having heard that Force Z was at Singapore, sent more than thirty new Betty medium bombers to reinforce the Nell bombers at Kanoya and Genzan Air Groups at the new bases built in French Indochina and Siam. Vice Admiral Jisaburo Ozawa, in command of the South Expeditionary Force of the Second Fleet, recognized the threat posed by Force Z and planned the air strike against it using the planes in Indochina. At Takhli and Korat, built by the Japanese in 1940, the word went out that the bombers were to go for Force Z. After the war, these bases would be part of the Royal Thai Air Force and used by the United States Air Force for attacks into North Vietnam.

The powerful and experienced 22nd Air Flotilla underwent specialized training in over-water navigation and low-level torpedo attacks on moving ships. Normally medium bombers attacked land targets or moored ships, but now they were going after ships at sea.

Admiral Phillips had already discussed having American land-based bombers and warships of the Asiatic Fleet support his force to attack the Japanese ships then approaching Malaya. But General Douglas MacArthur and Admiral Thomas Hart would not commit until war was declared and the situation better understood. When Phillips learned of the attacks on Pearl Harbor and the Philippines, it was apparent that the U.S. Pacific and Asiatic Fleets would not be able to help the Royal Navy. The closest American naval base at Cavite on Luzon was literally flattened. Phillips was on his own for the time being. He was unaware of the force being readied against his ships. In any case, he grossly underestimated the skill and ingenuity of the Japanese commanders.

He was encouraged by the fact that no capital ship had ever been sunk at sea by aircraft. Such beliefs hardly constituted solid evidence. *Prince of Wales* had one of the most advanced AAA fire systems in the navy, but the extreme heat and humidity in the area rendered the radar unreliable.

Having learned of a Japanese troop convoy headed for Malaya, Force Z left Singapore at 1700 on December 8 and headed northwest into the Gulf of Siam, looking for the Eleventh Fleet. From there, they turned toward Malaya, where the British Army was still being hammered by Japanese bombers. The plan had been for at least six fighters to be overhead during the day.

The Japanese submarine *I-65* reported the British ships at 1400 on December 9, and Ozawa issued his orders. He had the Second Fleet's Southern Malay Force sail south from Indochina to intercept Force Z. Battleships *Haruna* and *Kongo*, three cruisers, and eight destroyers took up the hunt. More cruisers and destroyers were diverted to join in pursuit.

During the night of December 9, Force Z turned south to return to Singapore. Ozawa's ships were only about twenty miles away, searching in the dark.

Just before dawn on December 10, Admiral Phillips was informed of Japanese troops moving south down the peninsula from Kuantan toward Singapore. This was all the Royal Navy admiral needed to convince him to turn toward Malaya. But he chose not to radio his intentions, hoping to avoid it being picked up by the Japanese.

By mid-morning, Phillips was aware that Japanese long-range patrol planes were watching his ships, but he did not feel the need to inform RAAF command to send the fighters. Naval historians have long criticized this decision, but there is no way to know how the few Buffaloes would have done in a fight with the air strike being mounted against Force Z.

Shortly before 0800, having learned of the approximate location and course of Force Z, three groups of bombers left their Indochina bases near Saigon. The three waves of Nell and Betty bombers spotted the southbound ships at 1045 and fanned out for the attack. The high-level Bettys loaded with 250-kg bombs began dropping them in patterns on the *Repulse*, which twisted in tight turns. Most bombs missed, exploding in tall waterspouts around her curving wake. One bomb struck aft, killing about twenty men on the seaplane catapults. The harsh bang of the 2-pounders and shatter of smaller Vickers rapid-fire guns was a constant roar over the ships. The destroyers, whose captains noticed that the bombers were only interested in *Repulse* and *Prince of Wales*, bravely moved in to add their own deadly umbrella of fire into the sky. Shrapnel and bullets rained down upon the blue sea.

Then seventeen low-flying Nells, each carrying two torpedoes, came in from the west. Nine concentrated on Admiral Phillips's flagship. The hulking *Prince of Wales* turned to avoid the planes, but they bored in on both port and starboard, making evasion difficult. This was one time when her 14-inch guns were of absolutely no use. One of the Type 91 aerial torpedoes slammed into her stern, jamming one rudder and flooding the engine room. Ironically, this was the same damage sustained by *Bismarck* when she was attacked by British torpedo planes, dooming the German titan.

While it was commonly believed that *Prince of Wales* had been hit twice, a survey by divers in 2007 proved that only one torpedo fatally wounded the ship.

The newest battleship in the Royal Navy began a series of uncontrollable circles and listed to port as her damage control parties struggled to fix the rudder. *Repulse* was targeted by eight of the torpedo-carrying Nells. Maneuvering wildly, the battle cruiser avoided at least nineteen torpedoes, but she was finally hit, causing her to slow, allowing three more to strike. *Repulse* heeled over in a steep list. It was immediately apparent to Captain William Tennant that his ship was sinking. He ordered her abandoned before the battle cruiser turned belly up. Her crew of 700 officers and men went over the side, wallowing in the oil-choked water. *Repulse* sank by the stern, her sleek clipper bow rising straight into the sky. She went down at 1245, having lasted just ninety minutes.

Prince of Wales was now the single target. A Betty bomber hit her amidships with a 500-kg (1,150-pound) armor-piercing bomb. The blast did horrific damage, hurling steel, wood, and bodies hundreds of feet into the air.

The destroyer *Express* moved in to pick up survivors as the battleship began to roll over. For a few minutes, her dull red hull glistened in the sun and then she sank at 1318.

Admiral Ozawa's well-trained air crews had managed four hits on each ship, out of forty-nine bombs and torpedoes dropped. Three of the bombers were lost.

At the moment *Prince of Wales* foundered, ten RAAF Buffaloes arrived, but they could do nothing. One of the withdrawing bombers sent a radio message to the remains of Force Z in English: "Our job is done. Carry on."

Total casualties were 840 dead. Vice Admiral Sir Thomas Phillips went down with his command, as did Captain John Leach. Leach had watched *Hood* explode in May 1941. He had been in command when *Prince of Wales* carried Prime Minister Winston Churchill to his historic meeting with Franklin Roosevelt at Newfoundland in August 1941 for the Atlantic Charter Conference.

At No. 10 Downing Street, Winston Churchill was awakened by a call from First Sea Lord Admiral Dudley Pound, who informed him of the loss of *Repulse* and *Prince of Wales*. The prime minister later admitted that it was the "worst day of the war for me."

He reported the loss to the House of Commons the following day, and said, "There are no British capital ships in the Pacific." Singapore was now cut off without any strong naval support. The end was only a matter of time.

What the sinkings meant on a larger scale, even more than Pearl Harbor, was that battleships were now proven defenseless against air attack. Their role could no longer follow the old Alfred Thayer Mahan concept of big-gun duels. The primacy of the battleship was over.

MARINE BULLDOGS ON WAKE

The news of Pearl Harbor reached the garrison at Wake Island almost immediately after the attack began. The navy and Marine commanders on the tiny atoll knew how close they were to enemy territory. Wake was actually closer to Tokyo than Honolulu, more than 2,300 miles to the east. The Marshalls were 500 miles southeast. West of the International Date Line, Wake was eleven hours behind the U.S. West Coast. The tiny dot on the ocean was the most isolated place on Earth.

After the end of the Spanish-American War in 1898, the U.S. added Wake to its possessions, seeing its location halfway between Hawaii and Manila as useful for a coaling station. In January 1899, the United States annexed the islands. Little of note took place for the next thirty years until Japan withdrew from the League of Nations and began fortifying the Marshalls in the 1930s.

Wake was almost forgotten by the United States. But its location made it a threat to Japan, being close to the Home Islands and the Marshalls.

Wake Island was actually the eroded crest of an ancient volcano that rose steeply up from the deep ocean floor. Three long islands—Wake, Peale, and Wilkes—formed a blunt arrowhead pointed east-southeast. A nearly complete coral reef encircled the island, and strong currents swept over the low land, white beaches, scrub brush, and rocky hills. Comprising just over 1,780 acres, the land rose only twenty feet above sea level. Wake was hardly a place of beauty. It had been described as inhospitable, unwelcome, desolate, and barren.

The Navy Department knew of the build-up of Japanese military strength, and in 1935 a serious survey was conducted for a navy base to oversee the region. Meanwhile, Juan Tripp of Pan American Airways (PAA) was looking for a China Clipper flying boat stop between Midway and Guam. Wake was the place.

This was not lost on the Japanese, who knew that after the Pan American Clippers would come U.S. Navy PBY Catalinas and probably U.S. Army long-range Flying Fortress bombers. In short, Wake would be an American knife embedded deep in the flank of the Japanese empire. As early as 1935, the Imperial Navy General Staff revised its plans to include an attack and invasion of Wake in the first week of a war. Pearl Harbor was more than six years away, but the long fuse was already burning.

After securing the rights, in 1935 PAA began constructing a fueling and maintenance hangar as well as a prefabricated forty-five-room Pan Am Inn on Peale Island. Another hotel was constructed on Midway, which quickly gained the name "Gooneyville Lodge."

The reef around Wilkes and Peale had been blasted in several areas to permit ships to enter the lagoon. A 400-foot redwood ramp was constructed for the flying boats, as well as two fifty-foot antennas to help aircraft find the tiny island. They could pick up radio signals as far as two thousand miles away. Soon the entire facility was being called "PAA-Ville." By late 1935, the big Pan Am Martin and Boeing Clippers stopped at Wake twice a week, one coming from and one leaving the Orient. One of the navigators of the first scheduled flight was Fred Noonan, who would be lost with Amelia Earhart in July 1937.

A rash of defense-related projects in early 1940 allowed the navy to do something about Wake's weak position. A $7.6 million appropriation was passed for Naval Air Station Wake for "aviation shore facilities, buildings, accessories, and defense facilities." This was purposely written in vague terms in order to get by the isolationist watchdogs who were still trying to keep Roosevelt from "leading the nation into another war."

The U.S. Navy took the lead and, within weeks, contracted with several construction companies to get to work on Wake.

Under Lieutenant Commander Winfield Scott Cunningham, there were seventy naval personnel and over 1,200 Morrison-Knudsen civilian construction workers. Morrison-Knudsen had been one of the six companies employed in the building of Hoover Dam in the 1930s. Pan American employed about forty men from Guam.

But time was running out. Two crucial years had been lost to isolationist interference, and there was no way to make Wake Island a stronghold capable of resisting a determined Japanese attack.

In February 1941, FDR authorized the Wake Island Defense Zone, and by August, Wake became the home of the First Marine Defense Battalion, consisting of almost 450 officers and men. The Marine commander was Major James Devereux. But they were not equipped for any serious defense, having yet to receive one of the mobile SCR-270B radar units. *Enterprise* had delivered twelve Grumman F4F Wildcats of VMF-211 with Major Paul Putnam as squadron commander. Wake's defenses consisted of six 5-inch coast guns salvaged from the pre-WWI battleship *Texas*, and a dozen 3-inch AAA guns. Eighteen .50-caliber and thirty .30-caliber machine guns were situated around the buildings and airfield. But there was little else, and no one was fooled into believing Wake could hold off a Japanese air and land assault.

The Marines and sailors worked almost around the clock, waking for a hasty breakfast at 0500 in the dark and setting up fortifications, laying out communication wire, digging trenches, filling and stacking sandbags, pouring concrete, blasting out boulders and gaps in the reef, and setting up the guns, until well into the evening.

When the island radio picked up the report of Pearl Harbor, Cunningham and Devereux went on alert, but the Marines were still not mentally prepared for war.

Six hundred miles to the southeast on Kwajalein, the troops of the Special Landing Force were almost ready. Rear Admiral Sadamichi Kajioka had four cruisers, a half-dozen destroyers, and two older destroyers modified to serve as landing craft. His troops numbered 425 men, almost exactly the same as those under Devereux.

The sky was hazy with an approaching rain squall as the tiny dots of thirty-six Nell medium bombers appeared from the southeast at 1158 hours. Unescorted by Zeroes, the bombers were nearly at the limit of their fuel in the flight from the Marshalls.

As they swept over the narrow islands, 250-kg bombs began falling on the airfield. Eight of the Wildcats were parked at fifty-yard intervals on the tarmac, with the other four on patrol. All eight were destroyed. Unfortunately the four patrolling fighters failed to sight the enemy bombers due to the poor visibility. In one stroke, two-thirds of Wake's fighter strength was wiped out. It was a dramatic example of how radar might have saved the day.

Since the raid focused on the airfield, planes, and hangar, the coastal and AAA guns were left undamaged. The two 412,000-gallon aviation fuel tanks were burning, and more than twenty men were killed. Pan Am evacuated their personnel by plane.

It was only the beginning.

Cunningham and Devereux, along with Putnam, now down to four Wildcats, worked feverishly to consolidate their defenses. A call for reinforcements, planes, and more guns went out to Pearl, but they knew Kimmel was busy with the defense of Hawaii. The civilian engineers and workers bent to the task of digging trenches, using their concrete for dugouts and blast walls. Cunningham urged them to work faster while others were ordered to join the gun crews.

The following day, the bombers returned, but this time, the four remaining Wildcats were ready and shot down two of the Nells. The hotel and hospital were seriously damaged. On December 10, the raid aimed for the AAA guns on Wilkes, but they had been moved and replaced by wooden dummies, which were bombed instead. However, fate dealt a bad hand to Devereux's defenses when a bomb set off the AAA ammunition on Wilkes, leaving the guns useless.

On the morning of December 11, the leading Japanese ships arrived and began to deploy along the south shore of Wake. Kajioka's ships deployed to cover the landing of the two boats carrying the landing force. Submarines patrolled the perimeter. Devereux told his gunners to hold their fire until the ships were close enough to ensure direct hits, just as Simard had done at Midway three days earlier.

The first to come under Marine fire was the destroyer *Hayate*, which was hit several times by heavy 5-inch shells at a range of 4,000 yards. She sank in two minutes, raising hopes on the island. *Hayate* was the first Imperial Japanese Navy surface warship to be sunk in the war.

The cruiser *Yubari* was straddled but apparently not hit. The landing ships came closer, and when Putnam's four bomb-carrying Wildcats pounced on the destroyers, Captain Henry Elrod dropped one on the *Kisaragi*, which caused her depth charge racks to explode, sinking her with all hands. Elrod was given the nickname "Hammering Hank." Admiral Kajioka chose to withdraw, having suffered Japan's first defeat at American hands.

News reports swept through the United States of the heroic defense of the island. Cunningham is erroneously reported to have said, "Send us more Japs!" His real concern, though, was a shortage of ammunition, fuel, guns, radar, and men.

At Pearl on December 16, Admiral Kimmel hastily ordered the carrier *Saratoga*'s TF 14, under Rear Admiral Frank Fletcher, to sail to Wake as soon as possible. TF 12, with *Lexington*, under Rear Admiral Wilson Brown, was to move into the Marshalls and launch air strikes on Jaluit as a diversion. Halsey's TF 8 with *Enterprise* would support the other two forces. Vice Admiral William Pye, who was soon to be named acting CINCPAC, disagreed with the raid. It was too soon and no one knew where the First Air Fleet was.

Saratoga, with the heavy cruisers *Astoria*, *Minneapolis*, and *San Francisco*, along with fleet oiler *Neches*, the seaplane tender *Tangier*, and eight destroyers, would attempt to reach the beleaguered Wake Island Marines and sailors before the Japanese made another, potentially stronger landing attempt. There was no doubt the bombers would be back to erase every gun and plane on Wake.

Fletcher's task force carried VMF-221's twelve Brewster F2A Buffalo fighters, two batteries with two 5-inch and four 3-inch AAA guns, full fire-control systems for the guns, two radar sets for air and shore defense, and more than 21,000 shells for the guns. Three million more bullets for the machine guns were on board, along with more Marines to man them.

The following day, the fighters went up again to attack the bombers. In the evening, Lieutenant David Kliewer spotted one of the patrolling submarines and sank it with a single bomb.

Bad weather delayed the *Saratoga* relief force due to the lagging oiler *Neches*. Then Navy Intelligence at Pearl notified Admiral Pye that Nagumo's Second Carrier Division, which included *Soryu* and *Hiryu*, was spotted west of Wake. The risk was too high, and Pye ordered Fletcher and Brown back to Pearl.

On *Saratoga*, Fletcher threw down his cap in disgust. Some of his officers begged him to disobey orders and continue to Wake. But the admiral knew he could not risk his carrier against two Japanese flattops. Deeply ashamed, he ordered his task force to turn back. But this was the right decision since TF 14 could not reach Wake until December 24.

Meanwhile, Cunningham, Devereux, Putnam, and the garrison continued to fight against increasing odds, using up ammunition and losing men. The bombers came back day after day, and the F4F ground crews struggled to keep the weary fighters flying. They cannibalized spare parts from the destroyed Wildcats and patched up the damage as best they could. It was a battle they would ultimately lose.

Admiral Tamon Yamaguchi's Second Carrier Division was now in support of Admiral Kajioka's landing force. With the two carriers were the heavy cruisers *Chikuma* and *Tone*, along with a destroyer division. Every one of Admiral Yamaguchi's ships was a veteran of the attacks on Guam and Pearl Harbor. Kajioka would not fail again.

By this time, Putnam's Wildcats had been shot down or rendered unflyable. The plucky VMF-211 pilots were forced to fight on the ground with rifles. After a sustained bombardment by the cruisers and destroyers on the morning of December 23, the landing ships moved in to hit the beaches from north and south. This time, Kajioka had included 1,500 Japanese Marines to go in with his Special Landing Force. The weary American Marines and sailors, along with the civilians who could handle a gun, put up a fierce defense, in some cases forcing enemy troops to withdraw. The assault was in a shambles as Devereux's men moved and fired from hidden defenses.

But it was a lost cause. Eventually the Japanese Marines cut off all communication between Cunningham and Devereux. There was confusion at the navy base while the U.S. Marines temporarily gained the upper hand. But Cunningham, seeing a hopeless situation, finally agreed to surrender the island to Admiral Kajioka.

Devereux and his surviving Marines were furious at what they considered cowardice and betrayal. Putnam was on the ground, helping one of the 3-inch AAA gun crews when the island fell. Marine losses were 49 killed and 49 wounded. Civilian wounded numbered 12. The Japanese captured 433 American Marines and sailors and all of the civilian workers.

But the defenders on Wake gave better than they took, killing and wounding more than 150 Japanese and shooting down at least twenty Nells and carrier planes. The fall of Wake sent deep gloom through the country but gave birth to a legend. To this day, the fifteen-day defense of Wake Island has gone down in history with Thermopylae and Roarke's Drift.

The U.S. Marines were included in both the 1942 and 1943 shipments of POWs to Japan, along with those captured in Peking. As on Guam, the men who were captured endured horrible treatment, starvation, and murder.

The loss of the aircraft in the Philippines and Malaya had more far-reaching consequences than Pearl Harbor. It led directly to the fall of the Philippines, Singapore, and later, Burma. The simultaneous and disastrous attacks forced

American and British officers to accept the hard fact that Pearl Harbor was not a lucky fluke that could not be repeated. It was increasingly obvious that Pearl Harbor was only a move to put the U.S. Pacific Fleet out of action while the Imperial Navy and Army swept unchallenged across the Far East. It was a bitter pill to swallow, and it was only the beginning.

The long-feared war with Japan had been unleashed.

By the spring of 1942, Japan had defeated or destroyed the fleets of four Allied nations and killed or captured half a million Allied troops. Japan controlled an area as large as the western United States and the lives of over 150 million people, equal to the entire U.S. population.

The job facing the United States and its army, navy, and Marines was to determine what was left to fight with, and get down to work.

CHAPTER 8

NIMITZ TAKES COMMAND

"Victory usually goes to the army who has better trained officers and men." —Sun Tzu

Chester William Nimitz was born in Fredericksburg, Texas, in 1885, descended from Saxon German nobility and the Knights of the Sword in the seventeenth century. When Swedish King Gustavus II Adolf, coincidentally an ancestor of mine, invaded Saxony in 1621, the Nimitzes fought alongside the Swedish Army during his invasion of Pomerania in 1630. When the Peace of Westphalia was signed in 1644, thus ending the bloody Thirty Years' War, the Nimitz family settled in northwest Germany near Hannover. They sailed to Charleston, South Carolina, in 1840 and later moved to Texas. It was there that young Chester was born. His paternal grandfather had a profound influence on the boy. The old man taught him the lesson by which he governed his later life.

"The sea, like life itself—is a stern taskmaster. The best way to get along is to learn all you can, then do your best and don't worry, especially about things over which you have no control."

Nimitz carried those words in his mind as he entered the U.S. Naval Academy in 1901, coincidentally the same year Yamamoto went to Eta Jima.

In fact, there were several similarities between Nimitz and Yamamoto. They were each born of small rural families only a year apart, and both were drawn by the lure of the sea.

The United States Navy was undergoing a renaissance between 1880 and 1905. During that time, the navy left behind its old wood and broadside fleet and began building steel warships, the pioneers of the modern navy. With the victories over the Spanish at Manila and Santiago, Congress voted for an expansion of the fleet. This was the navy that Chester Nimitz and his Annapolis classmates would inherit. President Theodore Roosevelt, himself a disciple of Captain Alfred Thayer Mahan's vision of naval power and one of the most influential supporters of using the navy to project American interest on a global scale, built both a new navy and the Panama Canal to that end. When he was still Assistant Secretary of the Navy, Roosevelt wrote, "If only the people who are ignorant about our navy could see these great warships in all their majesty and beauty, and could realize how well-fitted they are to uphold the honor of America."

From 1898 to 1916, Congress authorized building one new battleship each year, along with several cruisers. The Annapolis class of 1905 numbered 131 cadets, by far the largest ever, to man those new ships.

Cadet Nimitz learned the ropes of sailing and seamanship on the old square-rigger *Chesapeake* in the vast bay of the same name. Her captain was Commander William Fredrick Halsey, Sr., the father of the future admiral and one of Nimitz's friends, who graduated in 1904.

Other future admirals and men who would become synonymous with the Pacific War, who graduated before or with Nimitz, were Ernest J. King, William Pye, Harold Stark, Husband Kimmel, Robert Gormley, Frank Fletcher, Raymond Spruance, John Towers, John S. McCain, and Richmond K. Turner, to name a few. The Annapolis classes of 1904 and 1905 were known as the "Admiral Classes."

Nimitz distinguished himself at Annapolis and graduated seventh in his class on January 30, 1905. Still a midshipman, he would have to serve for two years before being promoted to ensign. He was tall, well built, and handsome, with a pink face, an easy smile, and white-blond hair. He exuded confidence, efficiency, integrity, and a quiet, good humor. He made friends easily and, even more importantly, allies in the officer and enlisted ranks. Never one to flaunt his rank, he preferred to learn rather than teach, and find the best way to do his duty. His first assignment was on the battleship *Ohio*, one of the four capital ships authorized in 1898. She had just completed her trials and was headed for the Pacific from San Francisco, a city Nimitz would one day call home. USS *Ohio* was to take her place as flagship of the Asiatic Fleet, based in the Philippines. This was during the climax of the Russo-Japanese War when Togo defeated the Russian Fleet at Tsushima.

The Japanese emperor hosted a victory garden party at the Imperial Palace. American naval officers were invited, but only Nimitz and a few midshipmen attended. There the new officer met and talked with Admiral Heihachiro Togo himself. The short but captivating Japanese officer with piercing black eyes spoke excellent English, and Nimitz never forgot the event.

When *Ohio* returned to the States in 1906, Nimitz and several other officers were transferred to the cruiser *Baltimore*, which had been with Commodore

George Dewey in the May 1898 Battle of Manila. Nimitz's first command as a midshipman was the Spanish-built gunboat *Panay*, which he and another future admiral, John S. McCain, used on patrols around Mindanao in 1905. This was not the same *Panay* that would be attacked by the Japanese on the Yangtze River in 1937.

During the years after Theodore Roosevelt mediated the end of the Russo-Japanese War, there was great concern that Japan might invade the nearly defenseless Philippine islands. Nimitz and McCain patrolled the waters around the archipelago, but tensions soon abated. After being promoted to ensign on January 31, 1907, Nimitz used his time on *Panay* to his advantage. Not only did he like having a small vessel to learn as much about command and ship handling as possible, but he also made several contacts among officers and enlisted men who proved useful in future assignments, duties, or commands.

Nimitz's career was a nearly spotless series of accomplishments and steady advances. He commanded destroyers and submarines but never had the chance to command a battleship. Much of his service after *Ohio* and *Baltimore* was in subs, beginning with the U.S. Navy's first submarine, *Holland*, during his time at Annapolis. Curiously, he did not recognize the future value of the submarine as an offensive weapon of war, and would have been shocked to learn their greatest value was in sinking unarmed merchant ships. He commanded three of the early boats, *Plunger*, *Snapper*, and *Narwhal*, and briefly commanded Submarine Division 3 until 1911. It was during this time the young officer Nimitz played an important role in a development that would reap healthy dividends in the Second World War.

The subs serving the navy in the first decade of the century were powered by gasoline engines, which were underpowered, noxious, and highly volatile. Knowing that diesel engines promised more power and greater safety and reliability, Nimitz traveled on assignment to study German diesel technology. In 1913, shortly after marrying Katherine Freeman, who was fluent in German, the newly promoted lieutenant learned all he could about the excellent German diesel industry. He soon became the U.S. Navy's expert on the new and powerful form of propulsion. Diesel would soon be the prime driving force in locomotives, small craft, and, of course, submarines. In 1915, he was courted by a diesel manufacturer at a very good salary if he left the navy, which he refused to do.

One of the diesels he helped design and build for submarines was used to familiarize Annapolis cadets with the emerging technology. It nearly cost Nimitz his hand and career. In 1915, while demonstrating the engine to a group of engineers, he moved his gloved hand too close to a set of gnashing gears, pulling his hand into their whirling teeth. Only his Annapolis ring saved his hand, but half of the ring finger was torn off. Nimitz was able to stay in the navy, but it had been a close call. It is a curious coincidence that both Nimitz and Yamamoto had lost fingers while on duty.

Prescient and hard-working, Nimitz benefited from being in the right place at the right time. He well understood the value of doing his best, but luck and chance were as much a factor in victory as might. By the end of 1941, Nimitz had served in nearly every department of the navy. When the United States declared war on Imperial Germany in April 1917, Nimitz was serving on *Maumee*, a diesel-powered oiler. As the ship's engineering officer, he helped develop the navy's first practical system of underway replenishment. Tankers carried oil to a port destination, while oilers refueled ships. Six destroyers, the first U.S. Navy ships ever deployed to a war zone, were refueled by *Maumee*. It was the first time in history this procedure had been done. Like the improvement in diesel engines, the underway refueling of warships would be one of the most important advances in naval warfare in the years to come. Chester Nimitz was at the center of both projects, although he never took full credit, insisting that he had only been one member of the teams involved. This trait in itself was unusual in a service with more than its share of primadonnas and backstabbers.

By the time the war ended in November 1918, Nimitz had completed serving as chief of staff to Admiral Samuel Robinson, Commander, Submarines, Atlantic, or COMSUBLANT. He finally got his wish to serve on battleships, becoming the executive officer of the *South Carolina* and then captain of the heavy cruiser *Chicago*. Later he went to Hawaii, where he oversaw the construction of the submarine base, bringing the project in on time and under budget. He was then the commander of Submarine Squadron 14.

After completing studies at the Naval War College in Newport, Rhode Island, he went on to serve under the commander of Battle Fleet and commander in chief of the U.S. Fleet. At the University of California at Berkeley in September 1929, he was instrumental in setting up the first Naval Reserve Officer Training Corps, helping to expand the pool of college-educated men for naval service.

Commanding the cruiser *Augusta* in the Far East gave Captain Nimitz more experience in ship handling, command, and administration problems in far-flung parts of the world. His time in small and large craft, submarines, and engineering made him a well-rounded naval officer. He never failed to complete an assignment, and was praised and recognized at the highest levels for his excellent performance, again another parallel with Yamamoto.

In 1935, he returned to the States to become Assistant Chief of the Bureau of Navigation, then on to commanding Cruiser Division 2 and Battleship Division 1. It was in 1938 that he resumed improving the technique of underway refueling of capital ships, a major step up from the system for fueling destroyers. In 1939, Rear Admiral Chester Nimitz was made chief of the Bureau of Navigation, BuNav, the navy's personnel department. He was on this duty when Pearl Harbor was attacked.

The Bureau of Navigation was concerned with the procurement, training, promotion, assignments, discipline, and morale of officers and enlisted men. While being the head of BuNav was a desk job, and hardly the stuff of which important naval careers were made, Nimitz took the job seriously, giving it the same attention to detail and improvement he had shown with all his previous duties. As bureau chief, he was in a unique position to advance the careers of men with whom he had worked, whose past work proved worthy of promotion and important assignments. In doing this, he helped build the nucleus of the officer corps for the Second World War.

As early as 1930, Nimitz had predicted the United States would be at war with Germany and Japan and that the war would begin with a devastating attack on the army and navy. This was six years before the China Problem and the *Panay* Incident.

Nimitz was in his apartment in Washington, listening to a concert on the radio with his wife, when the broadcast was interrupted at 1500 hours with the announcement of the Pearl Harbor attack. He rose and put on his navy greatcoat, knowing he had to be at the office. His aide came and drove him to the main Navy Department building on the Washington Mall. Hastily constructed during the Great War, the three-story concrete and brick edifice was connected by a covered walkway to the munitions building near the Lincoln Memorial. Torn down in 1970, it is now the site of the Vietnam Veteran's Memorial.

There, Secretary of the Navy Frank Knox called for a meeting at the office of CNO, Admiral Stark. Attending the hasty meeting were Navy Undersecretary James Forrestal, Stark, Admiral Artemis Gate, Assistant Secretary for Air Rear Admiral John Towers, Chief of the Bureau of Aeronautics, and other men whose names would become known to the public in the coming years. Towers' career went back to 1911, when he was the second officer to receive the coveted wings of gold.

There they heard the first reports of the damage.

Knox was already looking at Kimmel as the scapegoat. He planned to fly to Hawaii and personally assess the damage and fix the blame. Always one to jump to conclusions, he was eager to put someone else in charge of the Pacific Fleet.

When Congress voted for the declaration of war, Knox's first order to the Pacific and Asiatic Fleets was to "Conduct unrestricted air and submarine warfare against Japan." The wording of this message is significant. It specifically meant carrier and submarine forces, all that was left to fight with.

A curiously amusing incident occurred the following day when Nimitz's daughter was walking their cocker spaniel. They were passing the Japanese Embassy on Massachusetts Avenue, where hundreds of angry citizens and reporters were gathered. Suddenly the normally sweet-tempered dog broke away from its minder and ducked under the fence surrounding the embassy ground. There the dog left a steaming load of feces on Japanese soil.

Nimitz was busy over the next week. His department had the unenviable task of informing the families of the dead and wounded, identifying bodies, and finding men to fill out the decimated crews of ships and squadrons. The men who had lost everything they owned when their ships sank had to be provided with new uniforms and supplies. A thousand details had to be taken care of, and Nimitz was busy signing orders, taking phone calls, and approving contracts. Volunteer enlistments skyrocketed, and they had to be included in the budget.

On December 9, Knox flew to Hawaii to confer with Kimmel and assess the damage to his fleet. Knox was not impressed with CINCPAC, and his demeanor showed it. Upon returning to Washington on December 13, he met with Roosevelt and recommended Kimmel be immediately relieved. Roosevelt agreed, but they took a day to decide on the replacement. In the meantime, Admiral William Pye would act as interim CINCPAC.

On December 16, Knox, Forrestal, Stark, Marshall, and King unanimously agreed on Rear Admiral Chester W. Nimitz for the new CINCPAC. The president said to Knox, "Tell Nimitz to get the hell out to Pearl and stay there until the war is won."

The secretary of the navy ordered Nimitz to his office and bluntly asked, "How soon can you be ready to travel?"

The admiral, tired from over a week of solid work, replied crossly, "Depends on where I'm going and how long I'll be away."

"You're going to take command of the Pacific Fleet, and you'll be gone for a long time."

Nimitz was chagrined at having to relieve Kimmel, an old friend, of command, but orders were orders.

The next matter led to the first decision the newly frocked CINCPAC made. He wanted Captain Randall Jacobs, his assistant chief, to take over BuNav.

"You can't have him," Knox said bluntly. "FDR doesn't like him."

Nimitz glared at Knox, suddenly angry at the stupidity of political machinations at such a dire time. "Goddamnit! He's the only man that can do the job."

Knox gave in. "Okay. Jacobs will take over. Now get going!"

Before he could head for his new command, Nimitz had to meet with Stark and King to decide what could be done with the remains of the Pacific Fleet. With the battleships out of action for the present, the fleet now consisted of three carrier task forces with *Enterprise*, *Lexington*, and *Saratoga*. On December 16, the same day Knox recommended that he be relieved, Kimmel had sent *Saratoga* to support Wake Island, which had been under nearly constant attack since December 8.

Other considerations had to be addressed. Roosevelt and Marshall had long since believed Hitler to be the more dangerous enemy. Plans to support Great Britain were in place, but with the sudden catastrophic blow in the Pacific, keeping every available asset from being sent to the Atlantic was more important. In fact, King and Knox were planning to send the carrier *Yorktown* back to Pearl. King, meanwhile, was told he would be appointed commander in chief of the United States Navy, with the unfortunate title of CINCUS. He would also take the role of chief of naval operations, CNO, previously held by Stark. Roosevelt intended to send Stark to England, where he would be commander in chief of U.S. Naval Forces in Europe. This was a convenient way to get Stark, whom FDR regarded as a bit of an embarrassment, out of Washington.

After packing for his new command, Nimitz boarded the Baltimore & Ohio's Capital Limited on December 19. He wanted to take the train to have time to catch up on all the sleep he had lost in the past ten days. He read over dispatches, letters, and reports of the current state of the navy. These had been handed to him by Stark in a large leather case. "Don't let this out of your sight, and don't open it until you are well on your way."

Precautions were taken to keep Nimitz's name and new assignment out of the press. In Chicago, he boarded the Santa Fe's Super Chief and headed west to Los Angeles's Union Station. From there he traveled to San Diego, where he boarded a Navy PBY Catalina flying boat that took off from San Diego Bay at 1600 hours on December 23. That same day, the *San Diego Union* reported the fall of Wake Island to a Japanese invasion force. Nimitz wondered what kept the relief force from reaching Wake as his plane winged its way southwest toward the setting sun.

He had written a last letter to his wife before takeoff. "I only hope I can live up to the expectations of you, the President, and the Department. I will faithfully promise to do my best."

He apologized to the PBY's crew for taking them away from their families at Christmas, but they all assured him they were honored to take him to Hawaii. Wildcat fighters met the Catalina as it approached Pearl Harbor. Nimitz asked the pilot to orbit the harbor while he looked down through the waist blister windows. Even though he had read the official reports, Nimitz was shocked at what he saw below the PBY. The harbor was no longer neat and orderly. The once blue-green waters were lakes of black and iridescent oil. Battleship Row was a riot of destroyed and overturned ships. Scores of launches and small craft crisscrossed the murky water among the sunken ships and lochs. Ford Island had burned-out buildings and shattered hangars. The wrecks of scores of planes had been bulldozed off the bullet-pocked runways. The Southeast Loch was choked with oil and ships that bombs had savaged.

The Navy Yard, he was glad to see, was in full operation, the huge crane swinging back and forth over the ships in dry docks. *Pennsylvania*, *Cassin*, *Downes*, *Shaw*, and a dozen other ships awaited repair.

West Virginia and *California* were sunk up to their main decks, while *Nevada* was being repaired where she had been beached. *Oklahoma*'s hull was a dusky red whale amid the bleak gray and black scene. *Utah* was also overturned, while *Detroit* and *Raleigh* remained at their berths. The sunken *Arizona* was a blackened citadel of scorched, torn steel. Her entire foredeck and turrets were awash. Yard boats, tenders, and barges were tied up beside the once-majestic battle fleet.

Hickam and Bellows Fields were in the same shape as Ford Island, with bulldozed planes and shredded hangars. Dozens of bomb craters pockmarked the concrete and surrounding land. Ewa Mooring Mast Field and Wheeler were no different. Here and there Nimitz noted a B-17 among the wreckage, including one broken clean in two. But there were dozens of fighters and patrol planes being serviced, and he saw more PBYs from Kaneohe heading out for long-range patrols. Pearl Harbor's barn door had been locked after the Japanese horse got away.

His PBY touched down on the water at 0700 and taxied to the ramp at the south end of Ford Island. The air still reeked of burned oil and scorched metal.

He was met by Rear Admiral Pat Bellinger, chief of the navy's Hawaiian air forces, and the chiefs of staff for Admiral's Kimmel and Pye. It was then he was informed that the Wake Island relief force had been recalled by Pye since there had been no chance of the task force reaching the Marines in time. There were reports of Japanese aircraft carriers to the west of Wake.

The boat carrying Nimitz and the other officers was filthy with oil and debris, and they all stood to keep from having their uniforms soiled. Occasionally they passed a yard boat pulling a bloated body from the water.

Wearing only the two stars of a vice admiral, Kimmel met Nimitz at the submarine base and the men shook hands. Once stout and erect, Kimmel looked as if he had shrunk and aged twenty years. Nimitz gave his old friend a sad smile. "You have my sympathy, Kim. The same thing could have happened to any of us."

Nimitz had Christmas dinner with Kimmel, Pye, and Mrs. Pye, after which the incoming commander received a gift from the officers and enlisted men of the submarine base, the facility he had constructed years before—a pair of four-star shoulder boards.

There is an interesting account of the day Nimitz toured the harbor, written by an enlisted man after the war. While it is difficult to confirm, I am including it since it fits Nimitz's character.

On Christmas Day, Nimitz toured the harbor on a newly scrubbed launch. The coxswain, standing behind the admiral, showed his dismay at the sight of the shattered fleet. Sunken battleships and navy vessels cluttered the waters everywhere they looked. As the launch returned to dock, the young coxswain asked, "Well Admiral, what do you think after seeing all this destruction?"

Nimitz, with his characteristically quiet voice, replied, "The Japanese made three of the biggest mistakes an attack force could ever make." He explained, "The Japanese attacked on Sunday morning. Ninety percent of the ships' crewmen were ashore on leave. If those same ships had been lured to sea and sunk—we would have lost 38,000 men instead of 3,800.

"When the Japanese saw all those battleships in a row, they got so carried away sinking them, they never once bombed our drydocks. If they had destroyed those, we would have had to tow every one of those ships to the West Coast for repairs. As it is now, the ships are in shallow water and can be raised. Also, every drop of fuel in the Pacific is in the ground storage tanks five miles away over that hill. One attack plane could have strafed those tanks and destroyed 4,500,000 barrels of fuel. Every drop has to be brought from the mainland."

He concluded with, "Since the Japanese did not return and complete the job, that was the greatest help to us. They left their principal enemy with the time to catch his breath, restore his morale, and rebuild his forces."

On the morning of December 31, 1941, Nimitz read the orders giving him command of the U.S. Pacific Fleet aboard the submarine *Grayling*. While it is said that the sub was the only undamaged ship in the harbor, the truth is more prosaic. Nimitz wore the coveted dolphins of the submarine force. To the new CINCPAC, one of the three fleet commanders in the navy, it was a means of returning to the fleet he knew and loved.

From that point on, Chester Nimitz was busy with inspections, meetings, and tours of the island. He intended to retain Kimmel's staff and officers for the foreseeable future since they were intimately familiar with the Pacific and Asiatic Fleets. His headquarters was in the sub base. The room was spartan and clean, with no certificates or photos of elected officials.

In addition to his staff, Nimitz had several flag officers who commanded task forces in the Pacific. Along with Admiral William "Bull" Halsey," were Admiral Richmond K. "Terrible" Turner, and General Holland "Howling Mad" Smith, who commanded the amphibious forces. Those men would earn those nicknames in the months and years to come. Nimitz continued to meet with Kimmel and Pye, as well as the CINCPAC staff. Seated in the chair recently occupied by Kimmel, he went right to work. Chester Nimitz was a busy man. Although he occasionally broke away from the office to take long walks or play tennis and horseshoes or a game of bridge, his ever-active mind was reviewing facts and figures, personnel, ship and aircraft availability, and pondering the latest intelligence reports from Captain Edwin Layton.

While Nimitz and Yamamoto shared certain traits and backgrounds, their personal habits diverged in one respect. Yamamoto was a gambler, never happier than when at a card game with a stack of chips. He liked to pit himself against other players, using his poker face and skill with cards to win the pot. He played against others and was not afraid to bet it all on a turn of a card.

Nimitz, on the other hand, preferred doubles in tennis and bridge. He liked to win as part of a team. He did enjoy target shooting with a pistol, one of the only pursuits in which he was his own opponent. Where Yamamoto worked and played alone, Nimitz was a member of a team. While only in his mid-fifties, his thinning white-blond hair and weathered face made him seem much older, a grandfatherly type a man could not help but trust.

In Washington, Admiral Ernest King quickly changed his acronym to COMINCH. His assistant chief of staff was the newly frocked Rear Admiral

Richmond K. Turner. While Halsey was certainly the most aggressive of the Pacific Fleet's flag officers, Turner was probably the most brilliant and effective. Back in late 1939, Captain Turner had the job of bearing the ashes of the late Japanese ambassador to the United States, Hiroshi Saito, to Japan on his ship, the heavy cruiser *Astoria*. Turner was well acquainted with the Japanese and the Imperial Navy. While in Japan, he met with many officers, including Yamamoto, who impressed him. Turner had predicted a war between Japan and the U.S. as far back as 1935 and was certain Yamamoto would be at the head of the Imperial Navy.

By the time Turner and his ship had returned to the United States, Hitler had invaded Poland, igniting the first fire of the Second World War.

Astoria was with Rear Admiral Wilson Brown's TF 12 when the *Lexington* reinforced Wake Island. Brown was ordered to Midway, thus avoiding being hit by Nagumo's bombers on December 7. *Astoria*, which had the distinction of being the last American warship to visit Japan before the war, would be sunk on the night of August 8, 1942, at the disastrous battle of Savo Island in the Solomons.

Now Turner was a rear admiral and the chief of war plans under King and Knox. King became one of the Joint Chiefs of Staff, JCS, joining General George Marshall, Air Corps Chief General Henry "Hap" Arnold, and Admiral William Leahy, who was FDR's chief of staff. They were the four most senior uniformed officers in the country. While the British and Americans jointly oversaw all Atlantic and European theater operations, JCS alone directed the Pacific.

For most of the next three years, the main strategies and campaigns of the Pacific War would be directed by King and Nimitz, who had only held their new posts for a matter of days. In style and demeanor, they were total opposites, except in their devotion to winning the war. Where Nimitz was democratic, King was autocratic. Nimitz rarely lost his temper and credited others, while King was caustic and often berated subordinates for his mistakes. But they made a good team, even if they frequently clashed on matters. When telegrams and telephone exchanges were insufficient, they met in San Francisco. King made good use of the links between Washington and Hawaii, often sending a dozen messages a day. Nimitz was less verbose and only sent replies he felt were necessary to appease the CNO.

Nimitz was considerate to his old friend Kimmel and attempted to have him reassigned to another post. But Knox was determined to have Kimmel and Short appear before a congressional committee to find and place blame for the Pearl Harbor attack. Nimitz was not in favor of this, believing that Pearl would have been hit regardless of who was in command.

CINCPAC's experienced staff, most of whom had been with Kimmel, was ready to assist and advise. Unlike most high-ranking flag officers, Nimitz listened to and took the advice of his subordinates. The task before Admiral Nimitz and the Pacific Fleet was immense: to assess the situation, enemy capabilities and intentions, and draft plans to take control from the Japanese.

Nimitz had the United States Navy and Marines at his disposal. Every carrier, battleship, cruiser, destroyer, oiler, minesweeper, transport, aircraft, and man was a part of what would become the mightiest naval and amphibious force on Earth.

But it would take time. The battleships *Maryland*, *Pennsylvania*, and *Tennessee*, having received temporary repairs, were on their way to the West Coast for more extensive work and would be returned to the fleet. But what Nimitz and some farsighted officers realized, even if most Americans did not, was that battleships had become redundant. The old way of fighting naval battles with two lines of big-gun warships battering away at one another was wasteful in lives and ships. It rarely decided the outcome of a war, especially at Jutland in 1916. They were too slow to keep up with the fast carriers, used too much fuel, could not project their power farther than twenty miles, and were too vulnerable to air and submarine attacks.

Nimitz intended to find better employment for his battleships. Aircraft carriers and submarines would strike the first blows at Japan.

King was concerned with the deteriorating situation in the western and southern Pacific. The small Asiatic Fleet had retreated into the Java Sea and toward Australia when a Japanese air attack severely damaged the naval base at Cavite. The Japanese had already started bombing the vital Burma Road at Rangoon in Burma, had occupied Hong Kong and Manila, and were advancing on the last British bastion in the Far East, Singapore. Moving out from the Marshalls, the enemy fleet moved in to seize the British islands of the Gilberts and bombed Johnston and Palmyra Islands between the Gilberts and Pearl Harbor. It appeared that the Imperial Navy and Army had unlimited resources. But it was increasingly obvious to the JCS that Yamamoto had his sights on the southwest Pacific, New Guinea, and possibly Australia. From Samoa, the enemy could interdict the vital shipping lanes between the United States and Australia. King was also concerned with the Japanese submarine activity in the Hawaiian Islands.

There was every chance Yamamoto would move against Hawaii and possibly invade. That could not be permitted. Samoa and the nearby island groups were the key.

The first order sent by King to Nimitz was in the form of a reminder that CINCPAC's first and most overriding job was to protect Hawaii and the shipping lanes between the U.S. and the western Pacific. That was one order Nimitz did not need to hear. He was well aware of his priorities. But in his introspective way, Nimitz understood King's need to manage everything.

Nimitz could not protect every Allied island and base in the Pacific. He well knew some places would have to fall while others had to be defended at all costs. But which? That would have to be determined using logic and a careful assessment of what could or could not be done. As Frederick the Great said, "To attempt to defend everything is to defend nothing."

What resulted from the early exchanges between the CNO and CINCPAC was the first U.S. amphibious operation in the war, to be followed by the first offensive attack on Japanese-held soil.

Transports would carry a brigade of 5,000 Marines from San Diego to Samoa, escorted by the carriers *Enterprise* and *Yorktown*. Their goal was to hold the island against Japanese occupation. But more had to be done to stem the tide of enemy forces into the South Pacific. The Australian government, recognizing that the Royal Navy had its hands full in the Atlantic, was asking for the U.S. to guard the sea routes. The island groups south of Samoa, the New Hebrides, Fijis, and New Caledonia, also had to be protected from enemy invasion.

One of the first things Nimitz did was send the newly formed navy construction battalions, the Seabees, to Palmyra and Johnston Islands to build air bases and port facilities. From there the navy could patrol with aircraft over the shipping lanes to Australia. At the same time he sent his submarines out to patrol the Marshalls and ascertain the strength of Japanese fortifications and defenses. This would help determine what targets should be hit first.

At present, Nimitz had three carrier task forces available. The *Saratoga*'s TF 14 under Vice Admiral Fairfax Leary; TF 11 with *Saratoga*'s sister, *Lexington*, under Vice Admiral Wilson Brown; and TF 8 with Halsey and *Enterprise*. TF 17 with *Yorktown* under Vice Admiral Frank Fletcher was still coming from the States with the Marines from San Diego. Each task force was escorted by at least two heavy cruisers and six destroyers. Fortunately, destroyers were not in short supply, although many were out-of-date World War I types.

For the first month after Pearl Harbor, *Enterprise* was on constant patrol between Hawaii and Wake, careful not to stray too close to Japanese land-based air cover. This rankled the aggressive Halsey, but his duty was to make sure Nagumo did not come back to Pearl to finish the job. His task force had the cruisers *Northampton*, *Salt Lake City*, and *Chester*, along with six destroyers.

They were on constant watch for aircraft and submarines. Of the latter, there were scores, at least to judge by the number of periscopes and torpedoes sighted by the green and hyperalert lookouts. The destroyers followed up every "sighting" and dropped depth charges on suspected sonar contacts.

The operation to Samoa and the Marshalls would be the first real attack on the Japanese, and a great morale booster for the country. The follow-up air strikes on the Marshalls had to be planned very carefully. Nimitz was acutely conscious that he had only four carriers, and if those were lost or damaged, the Japanese could attack Hawaii and even the West Coast at will. In a very real sense, Chester Nimitz was a man who could lose the war in a single day. On January 2, he met with Admiral William Pye and Rear Admiral Claude Bloch, commandant of the Fourteenth Naval District, which included Pearl Harbor, Midway, Wake, Johnston, and Palmyra Islands. Bloch strongly opposed any offensive operations, stating that it was too soon and the navy was not ready. Having watched Kimmel lose the fleet to air attack, Bloch was not about to let it happen again. It was Bloch's staff that had failed to recognize the import of *Ward*'s attack on the midget submarine on the morning of December 7, but he did not mention this oversight to Nimitz.

Nimitz had other detractors, mainly Rear Admiral Pat Bellinger, chief of the navy's Hawaiian air forces, who considered the new CINCPAC to be another battleship-minded sailor. But in this, Bellinger was overruled by Halsey. When he barged into a staff meeting after *Enterprise* arrived at Pearl on January 7, he immediately began growling about the defeated spirit at CINCPAC headquarters. But when Nimitz informed his old friend about the Marshalls operation, Halsey's dour look changed to a broad, if pugnacious, smile. He was delighted at the chance to hit the enemy as hard as he could.

In his post as vice admiral, and commander of aircraft for Battle Force, Halsey's opinion carried weight and soon dispelled the caution among Bloch and the other admirals. This meant a great deal to Nimitz, and he never forgot Halsey's support in the darkest days of the war.

Nimitz began by detailing the proposed Marshalls campaign, and the discussion that followed was both spirited and somber. Task Force 8 with *Enterprise* was to be joined by TF 17 with *Yorktown* to bring the Marines to Samoa and see they had all the support they needed to fortify and hold the island. Then the combined TFs 8 and 17, under Halsey's command, would head to the Marshalls and Gilberts to launch air strikes against Kwajalein, Roi, Makin, Jaluit, Wotje, and other Japanese bases in the area.

While there was little chance of doing great damage to the Japanese, the strikes would not only disrupt and possibly postpone further enemy moves into the southern Pacific, it would be a great morale booster. Nimitz had been plagued by reporters whose papers and radio networks constantly asked, "Where is the Navy? When are they going to fight back?"

Nimitz, well aware Navy Secretary Frank Knox was the publisher of the *Chicago Daily News*, one of the most influential papers in the country, knew the value of secrecy. The real damage to the fleet had to be kept from the enemy as long as possible, but the American people deserved information. Nimitz, treading lightly, met with a group of reporters and explained the need for keeping certain data from reaching Tokyo. He said his staff would provide information when available and the reporters would be permitted to go with the fleet to be on hand when news was made.

Meanwhile, *Enterprise* was being, as one Fighting 6 pilot later said, "loaded for bear." More fuel oil and aviation gasoline than usual was loaded into her tanks. Crates of shells for the ship's AAA guns and bullets for the planes were carried down to the magazines deep in the hull. Lines of sailors moved tons of extra food, spare parts, and medical supplies to fill storage lockers. The crew knew something big was up.

At noon on January 11, the fully loaded *Enterprise* headed down the channel to the open sea, escorted by destroyers *Balch*, *Moury*, *Dunlap*, *Ralph Talbot*, *Blue*, and *McCall*, heavy cruisers *Northampton*, *Chester* and *Salt Lake City*, and fleet oiler *Platte*. In command of Cruiser Division 6 was Rear Admiral Raymond Spruance, who had been following Halsey's carrier since early 1941. Every eye in Pearl watched the carrier leave, and most thought she would never return.

There was reason for concern. The cryptanalysts in Pearl learned that Nagumo's six carriers had left Japan on January 6, destination unknown. The Philippines, Fiji, Samoa, Wake, Midway, or Hawaii might be their target. In any case, Halsey's carriers would have to be alert for them. When TF 17 joined with Halsey's force, they turned southwest to Samoa. At that moment, the two flattops were the most powerful American Naval striking force in the Pacific.

Then disaster struck when *Saratoga*, patrolling 400 miles south of Oahu, was hit by a submarine torpedo. The carrier was badly damaged but remained afloat as her escorts brutally depth-charged the sub. She returned to the States for major repairs. In one blow, a quarter of Nimitz's carrier strength was out of action.

Nimitz likely considered recalling Halsey, but he trusted the aggressive carrier commander. It was all in the hands of the men at sea. All he could do was wait and hope.

On board *Enterprise*, *Yorktown*, and their escorts, morale ran high. At last they were going to hit the Japs and begin payback for Pearl Harbor. Every man had known sailors who had died from Japanese bombs. The taste of revenge was in the salt-laden air. Halsey and Fletcher conferred daily on the conditions in the Marshalls from submarine reconnaissance.

On January 18, the two task forces began running along a north-south line a hundred miles north of Samoa to protect the landing force from surprise enemy air or sea attacks. Wildcat fighters patrolled in a wide arc from east to west while the Marines landed at Pago-Pago. There was no enemy opposition, but no one doubted the Imperial Navy and Army were out there and would come as soon as word reached Tokyo.

On January 22, Nimitz sent Rear Admiral Wilson Brown and the *Lexington* task force, then cruising 500 miles southwest of Oahu, to steam north to bomb Wake Island. But when a Japanese sub sank an oiler, he canceled the raid and ordered Brown back to Pearl.

When the Marines were safely ashore on Samoa and the Seabees began constructing runways and piers, the two carriers turned northwest. It was time to strike back. Taking the initiative away from Yamamoto was the most important element of the attack, but its objective was as much psychological as tactical.

Fletcher, aboard *Yorktown*, was assigned to hit Jaluit and Mele in the southern Marshalls and Makin in the northern Gilberts.

Halsey, using the commander's prerogative, took the more important targets of Wotje, Maloelap, and Taroa in the northern Marshalls. A report radioed from the sub *Dolphin* revealed the islands were not nearly as well fortified as reported by Naval Intelligence. With his eyes gleaming under bushy brows, Halsey planned strikes on Roi and Kwajalein, the latter the largest Japanese base in the region. This was a gutsy move since Kwajalein was in the geographic center of Japanese-held territory.

For the next five days, the two task forces moved closer and deeper into enemy waters. There was a real danger. Since the Japanese had withdrawn from the League of Nations in 1931 and refused any foreign shipping to enter the area, there were no recent charts. Every hour increased the risk of being sighted by a patrol plane. If that happened, not only would Task Forces 8 and 17 lose surprise, but they would likely meet a violent end.

At dawn on January 28, the oiler *Platte* began refueling first the destroyers and then the cruisers of Halsey's force. On the horizon, Fletcher's TF 17 was doing the same from its own oiler. It took hours, while patrols cast their eyes far and wide to spot any Japanese plane, ship, or sub. It was after 2000 hours when the Big E moved close to the smaller oiler and heavy hoses were swung out and fitted. In total darkness, two alert helmsmen watched the waves to prevent a disastrous collision. It took five stressful hours. When it was finally over, Task

Forces 8 and 17 were ready. Thanks to the then-captain Chester Nimitz and his team, the United States Navy had at last used his underway replenishment system to refuel warships on the eve of a major battle.

As risky as the job had been, it was well worth it. Now the two carrier forces could race in under the cover of the predawn, launch their planes, maneuver during flight operations, and withdraw at full speed to avoid counterattack by land-based Japanese aircraft. Only full bunkers made this possible.

There was no concern about any enemy carriers in the area. Intelligence reported that Nagumo's carriers were busy supporting the landings on New Britain in the Bismarck Archipelago. Japanese bombers and landing forces had been hitting the island since January 4 to capture the excellent deep harbor of Rabaul from the Australians.

Each American carrier had about fifty dive and scout bombers, eighteen torpedo bombers, and eighteen fighters, as well as several spares in storage.

On the hangar decks of *Yorktown* and *Enterprise*, preparations were underway for the coming air strikes. Only a CAP would remain over the fleet. All the Douglas SBD Dauntless dive bombers of the scout and bombing squadrons would launch, while most of the Douglas TBD Devastator torpedo bombers were to go. Some were to remain behind to be launched if enemy ships were sighted. The Grumman F4F Wildcat fighters had been fitted with boilerplate armor behind the pilot seats, something that would become standard in the years to come. Guns were loaded, bombs fitted, and fuel topped off. Medical supplies, gallons of coffee, and mountains of sandwiches were readied for a full day of combat. On the escorts, the new Mark 37 analog gun control system was powered up and linked to the SD high-frequency surface radar. Damage control parties equipped themselves with lanterns, fire extinguishers, and breathing apparatuses. Towing hawsers were coiled on bows and sterns for immediate use in case a ship took damage.

For the first time since the Great War, the United States Navy was about to launch an attack on a foreign power.

On the afternoon of January 29, *Enterprise*'s radar picked up a blip far astern. It was not one of the CAP, so it had to be an enemy plane. Operators watched the blip with trepidation as it came to within thirty miles. There was no way the enemy pilot could fail to see the Big E's wake, like a foaming white arrow pointed right at the carrier's stern. All they could do was watch and pray.

Then it was gone. No other blips appeared. Halsey was both delighted and relieved. He had a Japanese-speaking staff officer write a note to be dropped on

Kwajalein, thanking the pilot who "did not see us coming." That was Halsey's style. Vice Admiral Shigeyoshi Inoue, who commanded the Fourth Fleet in the area, would not be pleased with the missed opportunity.

In the squadron ready rooms, pilots were briefed on their timetable and targets. The SBDs were to be fully loaded with two 200-pound general-purpose bombs on the wing hardpoints and a single 500-pound bomb on the centerline. The smaller bombs would be used on light structures and fuel tanks, while the larger bombs were saved for key targets. Every plane was to strafe anything that moved or could be torn apart by bullets.

They were to hit aircraft, fields, fuel tanks, ammunition dumps, hangars, powerhouses, weather and radio stations, port facilities and docks—in short, anything of use to the Japanese. The radio station had to be destroyed quickly to prevent a call going out to other bases and to Tokyo. Shore guns and AAA batteries also had a high priority. But without aerial photos or detailed maps, every target had to be found and identified before it could be bombed. The bases were to be hit simultaneously, and with only about eighty-five aircraft from each carrier in the strikes, every bomb and bullet counted. Halsey planned for the planes to approach their objectives from the east and southeast at 0658 hours, exactly fifteen minutes before sunrise, so they would have the sun behind them. Ironically, the Japanese defenders would be blinded by the rising sun. Fortunately they had not yet adopted radar. The only way Japanese forces would know of the incoming raid was by sight or sheer luck. Halsey was eager to keep luck on his side, but his planes would be facing the Imperial Navy's 24th Air Flotilla, an experienced unit composed of Mitsubishi and Nakajima fighters.

In the predawn gloom at 0443, the first SBD, piloted by Lieutenant Commander Howard Young of Scouting 6, roared up the flight deck, blue flames pulsing from its exhaust as it clawed its way into the sky. It was followed by forty-six more at eight- to ten-second intervals. They formed up at about a thousand feet over the task force and took their position in the formation. Each squadron turned west and climbed. The fighters took their position above while the TBDs remained low. It was a delicate balance to maneuver and coordinate the planes in the dark without radios, but they managed it. Every pilot followed the small white light on the tail of the plane ahead. It was all they had until dawn broke behind them.

When the purple glow in the east allowed better visibility, the bombers slid into "V" formations. Roi and Kwajalein were only 150 miles away.

As soon as the last plane left the flight deck, Captain George Murray ordered *Enterprise* to steam at 30 knots to close on the island targets. The cruisers and destroyers followed, their main gun crews ready.

At 0650, the thin, dark, foreshortened ring of Kwajalein's islands and reefs appeared over the blue horizon. Young signaled the Dauntlesses to break into their six-plane formations to dive on their targets. But even at this early hour, Inoue's AAA guns were alert. Long orange tracers laced the sky and bright yellow flashes marked the bursts of exploding shells. But hitting a diving SBD was nearly impossible as they screamed from the sky. At the airfield on Roi, the Second World War's first American bomb dropped on Japanese soil and tore a giant hole into the runway. On Kwajalein, Zero fighters were already turning onto the runway as Young's SBDs released the first bombs on the concrete. Pale yellow and gray explosions erupted and crated the airfield, causing some fighters to crash. But others made it into the air and turned to move in on the Dauntlesses. Commander Wade McCluskey's Fighting 6 screamed down and opened fire on the Zeroes. The SBDs banked away from their first pass. They still carried the 500-pound bombs and started looking for good targets.

The Wildcats did great damage to trucks, planes, fuel tanks, and men, but their six .50-caliber Browning machine guns only carried enough ammunition for about thirty seconds of firing. The pilots used short bursts.

Young called on the radio that he had found targets suitable for the heavy bombs at the Kwajalein anchorage. The Dauntlesses of Bombing and Scouting 6 turned while Lieutenant Commander Gene Lindsey of Torpedo 6 led nine bomb-laden TBD Devastators to dive on a cruiser, five submarines, and a few merchant ships. The SBDs, having climbed to more than 10,000 feet, opened their perforated dive brakes and aimed at the ships with their big bombs.

Flak bursts and tracers peppered the dawn sky as bombs rained down. Most missed, raising tall white columns of dirty water, but some hit.

When Lieutenant Commander Lem Massey arrived with the nine Devastators with Mark 10 aerial torpedoes fifty minutes later, they found confusion and rising smoke above the anchored ships. They got in each other's way as they headed for the largest ships. Massey's pilots hit two tankers, setting them afire, and one large merchantman. The light cruiser *Katori*, which had managed to raise steam, was racing for the harbor entrance, but two more torpedoes slammed into her hull. Six other ships were also hit and sunk.

At Maloelap, Jim Gray's Wildcats, which each carried two 100-pound bombs, found little of value to bomb. Then they came to Taroa, where they found two newly completed 5,000-foot runways, two hangars, a fully operational navy yard, and a radio station. Parked along the runways were at least thirty Betty twin-engine bombers. There were also Mitsubishi AM5 Claudes, the forerunner of the Zero, in the air, ready to defend their base.

Gray, knowing the danger those bombers posed to his ship, led the fighters in to drop their bombs on the parked planes. But try as they might in pass after pass, they only managed to set one afire and peppered the rest with .50-caliber bullets. The fighters came in and a low-level dogfight ensued with little real effect on either side. At that point, four floatplanes from the cruiser *Chester* arrived while the ship began shelling from maximum range with her 8-inch guns. This gave the Wildcats the chance to withdraw with their empty ammunition trays.

At Wotje, more of Fighting 6's Wildcats screamed over the island. Bombs and bullets tore into everything of value as Japanese soldiers and airmen ran for cover. *Northampton* and *Salt Lake City*'s big guns added more destruction to the base. The destroyers, racing in fast, fired their 5-inch .38-caliber guns at the port facilities and fuel tanks. Several times a peculiar characteristic of the gun resulted in a perfect yellow smoke ring expanding outward like a snake biting its tail. The crew never tired of this phenomenon. Raging orange fires raised black smoke into the clear morning sky so high that it was seen from the carriers, now fifty miles offshore. *Enterprise* was steaming in an oval, twenty by five miles, so damaged planes could land.

The first bombers landed and were immediately refueled and rearmed. The pilots detailed what they had seen to officers who ran into the island superstructure to report. Taroa was chosen as the most critical target, and the bombers took off to finish what Gray's fighters had seen.

The second raid tore into the parked bombers and hangars. Lieutenant Richard Best led nine more SBDs loaded with 200-pound and 500-pound bombs, which wrecked most of the base facilities and cratered the runway. But by then, enraged AAA gunners were scoring hits on the Americans. Rear gunners dueled with the fighters while the pilots tried to do the most damage with their bombs and machine guns. *Enterprise* was just over the horizon by then, and her escorts were shelling Taroa's buildings and docks. Three bombs destroyed the radio station, administration building, and a fuel dump, all from one Dauntless piloted by Ensign Buck Walters. Ensign Jack Dougherty was lost when he was set on by three Claude fighters. His last words were, "These goddamned Japs will never get me!"

Yorktown's bombers and fighters had much the same story at Jaluit, Makin, and Mele, coming in just as dawn was breaking. The cruiser *Louisville* and her consorts shelled Makin and Jaluit. While their targets were less important than those hit by *Enterprise*'s strike, they contributed to the overall destruction of Admiral Inoue's airfields and ports. *Yorktown* lost seven planes, while *Enterprise*'s air wing was six planes short when the attack ended at 1300 hours.

As the bombers and fighters came in for landing, the plane handlers quickly disengaged them from the arrestor wires and lowered them by the forward elevator to the hangar deck for needed repairs. The fighters were refueled to augment the CAP in case any enemy bombers showed up. Halsey would not wait around for that. He had pushed his luck far enough. *Enterprise* and her screen left long foaming wakes as they retreated at full speed to the northeast. This gave rise to the soon-to-be-familiar phrase, "Haul ass with Halsey!"

Radar antennas rotated while every gunner watched the clear blue sky for an attack. Far in the rear, dozens of hazy gray pillars of smoke left no doubt that their ships had at last hit the Japs hard. The Gilberts and Marshalls raids on February 1 did not put Admiral Inoue's Fourth Fleet out of business, but he would find his job of supporting the Philippines campaign harder to achieve.

The pilots were debriefed, giving Halsey a good idea of what had been done to the enemy bases. But at 1340 hours, radar picked up five incoming aircraft, which proved to be twin-engine bombers. In moments, every single AAA gun in TF 8 was hammering away at the enemy planes. But even though they filled the air with flak bursts and tracers, they were not yet experienced enough to hit anything. The bombers continued coming in at a low angle, jinking and bobbing to avoid the gunfire. McCluskey's Wildcats, which remained outside the barrage, called in advice to help the gunners as the planes released their bombs. The first fell into the sea, raising waterspouts as high as the carrier's bridge. All fifteen bombs missed, but the last one was close enough to damage a fueling system and kill one gunner.

What happened next was witnessed by dozens of men on the carrier. The last bomber, hit by AAA fire, turned back and attempted to crash into the carrier's deck. Captain Murray ordered the helm hard over, but an intrepid gunner named Bruno Peter Guido leaped into the aftermost SBD and aimed the twin .30-caliber machine guns into the approaching bomber. He was not alone in firing at the plane, but his bullets ripped into the bomber's cockpit, causing it to veer off. The port wing separated and cut Guido's SBD in two just behind where he was standing. The rest of the plane crashed into the ship's curving wake. Burning fuel from the bomber splashed across the deck while the SBD skidded into the port side catwalk. Incredibly, Guido continued to hammer away at the sinking plane.

Another raid came in, but this time, the AAA gunners and fighters killed half the planes and drove the rest away.

The day's action was over. By 1600 hours, there were sixty more miles between the task forces and the enemy islands. As dusk fell, the ships came off battle stations while the radar swept the seas and sky. A low storm front was sighted, and the two carrier groups headed into it, knowing they were at last safe from Japanese air attack. A submarine was sighted the following day, which was bombed and strafed by a Scouting 6 SBD. A destroyer moved in to drop depth charges. A spreading stain of iridescent oil coated the surface. It was counted as a probable kill.

On February 5, *Enterprise*, followed by *Yorktown* and the escorts, steamed past Fort Kamehameha, Hospital Point, and Hickam Field into Pearl Harbor with her biggest battle flag flying. The bright red, white, and blue bunting caught the eye of every sailor, airman, Marine, soldier, and civilian. The Big E had not only returned safely, she and *Yorktown* had at last struck back at the Japs less than two months after the U.S. Pacific Fleet had been savaged.

Thousands of men and women cheered and waved at the victors. The bombers and fighters from the two carriers swept over the ships before landing at Ford Island. Sirens and whistles blew, bands played, and flags flapped.

As Vice Admiral William Halsey watched his white-clad crew wave at the people on shore, he smiled and let them enjoy their well-earned triumph. While he knew the raid had not done significant damage to the Japanese, it was still important. The United States Navy had at last fought back.

Nimitz was waiting when Halsey came ashore and warmly greeted him. "Welcome back, Bill," he said. "Great work."

As usual, Halsey waved it off. The credit went to his staff, pilots, and crews. It was time to get on with the war.

CHAPTER 9

VICTORY DISEASE

"The battlefield is a scene of constant chaos. The winner will be the one who controls that chaos." —Napoleon Bonaparte

During the first two weeks of the Pacific War, Japan swept virtually unchallenged over a 6,000-mile front from Wake Island to the Australian coast. In its encircling tentacles were a dozen island groups, encompassing more area than all of the United States west of the Mississippi River. A hundred million people would end up under brutal Japanese domination. In Washington and Pearl Harbor, London and Singapore, Canberra and Manila, the Allies desperately tried to assemble enough forces to slow the relentless advance of Japanese bombers, fighters, warships, transports, and troops. There seemed to be no end to them and no stopping them.

From December 10, 1941, when Guam fell, until May 1942, when General Jonathan Wainwright surrendered his battered and starved forces on Corregidor, headlines across America only reported bad news. But there was one shining ray of success from China—the AVG, now known as the Flying Tigers, having painted fanged shark mouths on their Curtiss P-40s, had been racking up a continuous string of kills against the Japanese air forces flying out of Thailand. From December 1941 to July 1942, the AVG, always outnumbered by the Japanese Mitsubishi bombers and Nakajima fighters over China and Burma, brought down nearly 300 enemy planes and damaged another 300. They suffered twelve of their own losses to the Japanese. The Flying Tigers' exploits proved that Americans could and did fight back against the supposedly unstoppable Sons of Nippon.

One element of their story that would be repeated many times all over the Pacific during the war was the dedicated and exhausting work by the mechanics, armorers, and crews that kept the planes in the air and armed. Against all odds, they often built serviceable planes out of near scrap. On carrier hangar decks and island airstrips, in jungles and on burning air bases, they did vital service to the men who flew the planes.

In Washington, the Joint Chiefs met to discuss the next move. With Japan already moving against the Far East, it was obvious they had no intention of slowing down. With members of the British Chiefs of Staff in Washington, it was decided to form ABDACOM—American, British, Dutch, and Australian Command—a cooperative air, sea, and land force to combat the Japanese in the Far East. ABDACOM would cover everything from Burma to the Dutch East Indies, which included the Java Sea, western New Guinea, northwest Australia, and the Philippines. It was a huge area to cover.

The first issue was deciding who would command the ad hoc ABDACOM fleet. Marshall and King, in particular, did not want an American in command since they knew victory was highly unlikely, and having a Royal Navy admiral who would probably focus on British colonial possessions was not much better. So a Royal Netherlands Navy admiral, whose Dutch East Indies were in Japan's crosshairs, was chosen. Bluntly put, the U.S. and Royal Navy high command wanted a foreign admiral to blame for the inevitable defeat. This was certainly a defeatist and somewhat politically motivated view, but there was no disputing that the ABDACOM fleet was scraping the bottom of the barrel. Their enemy was the largest and most powerful fleet in the Pacific.

Originally it was a polyglot command, with Asiatic Fleet commander Admiral Thomas Hart as the naval commander, a Dutch general as the ground forces commander, and a Royal Air Force general in command of all ABDACOM air forces. Since the United States had no colonies in the region other than the Commonwealth of the Philippines, the Royal Dutch Navy high command did not feel Hart was as committed to their common goal as the other members. It was a strange organization. The ABDACOM would have a short, violent, and ultimately unsuccessful life.

On the other side of the Pacific, the West Coast was in a state of near panic as Japan ran unchecked. There seemed no stopping the Imperial Navy.

On Monday, December 8, there were reports of unidentified aircraft off Long Island, and air raid sirens blared all over Manhattan. Bombers were seen heading for the Brooklyn Navy Yard and Norfolk Navy Base. Companies of army soldiers patrolled the beaches from Seattle to San Diego, from Maine to Florida, and along the major rivers.

Practice blackouts were announced while homeowners and businesses were instructed how to cover their windows and automobile headlights from being seen from the air. Vigilante groups of men carrying guns and baseball bats and wearing old helmets prowled streets at night, breaking the headlights and windows of anyone who did not follow the blackout rules. Schoolchildren, teachers, and office workers learned what to do in the event of an air raid or invasion. California, Oregon, Washington, and even Alaska suddenly became kindred spirits in a common bond of fear and uncertainty.

The U.S. Army Air Corps reported that fifty Japanese aircraft were seen closing in on the Golden Gate Bridge shortly after nightfall on December 8. They were shot down or driven off by American fighters. The supposed sighting was pure "war nerves," indicating how far the hysteria was spreading.

Lieutenant General John DeWitt, commanding the Fourth Army at the Presidio, said "death and destruction is likely to come to this city at any moment. But the people of San Francisco seem unable to appreciate we are at war. Those planes were over our community. They were enemy planes; I mean Japanese planes. They were tracked out at sea. Why bombs were not dropped I do not know."

DeWitt was not one to hide his light under a bushel. "It might have been better if some bombs were dropped to awaken this city. If I can't knock some sense into your heads with words, I'll turn it over to the police, and let them knock sense into you with clubs."

Such obviously bellicose posturing is hard to credit today, and DeWitt's statements had an almost fascist flavor, only matched later by General George Patton.

The only voice of calm was from the president during his December 9 Fireside Chat. In his avuncular, soothing voice, FDR said that Japan and its Axis allies were a league of thugs to be defeated by the law-abiding, decent nations of the world. "We must be set to face a long war against crafty and powerful bandits," he continued. "There is to be a massive increase in war production, with a seven-day week, to support not only America's military forces, but of those of our Allies." He acknowledged that the American people had the right and need to know what was happening in the Pacific, but a news blackout was enforced to prevent vital information from leaking to the enemy. Pearl Harbor had been badly damaged, but the U.S. Pacific Fleet was not destroyed. Guam, Wake, and the Philippines were under attack and may fall. Then he made the profound statement that the American people should not believe half the rumors flying around. This soothed many Americans who saw FDR as the voice of reason. A near-record fifty million listeners heard FDR's voice over the radio.

The Imperial General Staff and Combined Fleet Headquarters were pleased and amazed at how well the new war was progressing. The victories in the Far

East, which led to the fall of Singapore on February 15, and the continued advances in the Philippines prompted the high command to move their original timetable up. Instead of waiting, they chose to move ahead for their ultimate goal in the South Seas.

Located between Australia to the south and Asia to the north, by India to the west and the Solomons to the east, an area of over 740,000 square miles, the Dutch East Indies, now Indonesia, was Japan's next major objective.

The major islands of Java, Borneo, Timor, Bali, Sumatra, New Guinea, New Britain, and more than a thousand others were home to over sixty million people. What Imperial Japan wanted from the region was its bonanza of iron ore, rubber, rice, timber, and, most important of all, oil. Japan, a land with few natural resources beyond coal, needed the rich mineral and natural wealth of the Dutch East Indies. In a sense, they were the real reason Japan went to war.

The Dutch East India Company's ships first surveyed and colonized the region in the late 1500s. While the indigenous peoples made total Dutch control of the islands questionable, the rich resources were enough to keep real revolution from being a problem. The Dutch maintained a major military presence on both land and sea. Java was the centerpiece of the Dutch government, but Bali, Sumatra, and Borneo remained Indonesian.

The last governor-general of the Dutch East Indies knew his far-flung dominion would be a Japanese target. But the Royal Dutch Army, Air Force, and Navy were hardly up to the task of resisting, let alone stopping the inevitable Japanese blitzkrieg.

So it was that two huge Japanese combined sea, air, and land forces drove into and enveloped the East Indies like a wrestler's muscular arms. From Indochina and down the South China Sea, one arm circled to take Borneo and Sumatra. Another combined force encircled East Borneo, Timor, and Bali.

The flagship of the Asiatic Fleet was the heavy cruiser *Houston*, a *Northampton*-class ship from Newport News Shipbuilding in 1930. She had carried President Roosevelt on a 12,000-mile cruise from Virginia to Pearl Harbor and Seattle in 1935. Roosevelt considered her his favorite ship. Attached to the Asiatic Fleet in 1940, *Houston* became Admiral Thomas Hart's flagship based at Cavite in Manila.

Under orders from Knox and MacArthur, Hart had pulled his fleet out of the Philippines before the Japanese could destroy it, and made for Australia.

There *Houston*, the light cruiser *Marblehead*, and thirteen destroyers joined the ad-hoc Naval Striking Force in Palembang in western Indonesia. By January

27, most of the ABDACOM American and Dutch warships were escorting convoys to reinforce the East Indies islands most in danger of invasion.

Hart sent four of his destroyers, old WWI four-pipers like the *Ward*, to intercept a Japanese troop convoy approaching Balikpapan on Borneo on January 23. The blacked-out cans launched a torpedo strike on the transports, sinking four. It was the first United States Navy surface battle of the Second World War. The sinking of four enemy ships by a torpedo attack was more luck than planned. At that time, the Mark 14 torpedo was unreliable, a problem that would not be resolved until October 1943.

The Japanese tactics to take the Dutch East Indies were simple in context and well rehearsed. First a group of Nell and Betty bombers, escorted by fighters, swept in in the morning and pounded the landing area, totally disrupting any land or air resistance. Once the beachhead was secure, the heavily loaded flat-bottom boats moved in with cruiser and destroyer support, and the troops charged ashore, overwhelming the shocked and numbed defenders. Once that objective was taken, a hasty airfield was constructed and used as a forward base for the next island. This way, the shorter-range Zeroes could maintain constant cover over the bombers and strafe Royal Dutch Army and Air Force bases.

In one case, twenty-four Mitsubishi Zeroes flew an astonishing 1,200 miles to land at a new air base. The Zero normally had a maximum range of 900 miles, but with extra tanks and careful adjustments of fuel mixtures, the air group reached the new base to add their striking power to the onslaught. It was an excellent example of the careful planning for the South Seas campaigns.

One by one, the key islands were attacked and fell.

On February 1, Hart sent four cruisers and two dozen destroyers into the Bali Sea to intercept a Japanese convoy of twenty-two transports, three cruisers, and thirteen destroyers headed for Surabaya. The Japanese had already taken Borneo, Maluku, and Tarakan. Hart sent his force toward the Makassar Strait, hoping to cut off the Japanese advance. With the imminent arrival of three more Japanese cruisers and eighteen destroyers under Rear Admiral Takeo Takagi, the odds were highly against the ABDACOM ships.

Again the ubiquitous Betty bombers found them and began hitting the ships. *Houston* was hit on her after turret, putting it permanently out of action and killing forty-eight men. *Marblehead* was so badly hit she had to retire to the west.

The bomber crews reported sinking three cruisers, another indicator of their overconfidence. The Makassar Strait and the Molucca Sea beyond were now under Imperial Navy control, tightening the noose on the western Java Sea.

The battered ABDACOM force still had some fight in it, however. *Houston* effected repairs and left for Darwin to escort troop transports headed to help defend Timor. During the voyage, the small ABDACOM force of *Houston* and five destroyers and patrol boats were hit by a wave of forty-four medium bombers. The cruiser put up such a hail of AAA that she appeared to be on fire. Seven of the bombers were shot down. But Australian naval intelligence picked up indications of at least two of Nagumo's carriers in the area along with a task force to support an amphibious landing. This was too large a force for the *Houston*, which still lacked the use of her after turret. The ships turned back to Darwin.

Admiral Nagumo's First and Second Carrier Divisions of *Akagi, Kaga, Soryu, Hiryu*, and supporting ships were approaching Darwin on February 18. His orders were to bomb the port. While Darwin was a small port, far from the big Australian cities, it was the southern terminus of the air route between the island continent and the Philippines. It was also where most of the convoys congregated.

At dawn on February 19, in a replay of Pearl Harbor, Commander Mitsuo Fuchida led 188 bombers and fighters to hit Darwin's port facilities and any ships in the harbor. At that time there were sixty-five Allied ships, mostly freighters and destroyers, the latter putting up a hail of AAA fire. The port had weak air defenses and the RAAF fighter squadrons were far inferior to the Zeroes. Two hours later, more than fifty Nell and Betty bombers arrived from the Celebes. The two strikes virtually flattened Darwin and proved that Pearl Harbor was not a lucky fluke.

Eleven ships were sunk, three beached, and twenty-five damaged. Thirty RAAF aircraft were lost, yet only three Japanese planes downed. Loss of life was 340 dead, with another 400 wounded. The most serious and long-lasting consequence for ABDACOM was that the main sea link between Australia and Java was cut.

Admiral Takagi now had the main island of Java as his next objective.

This led to the February 27 Battle of the Java Sea, the largest surface naval battle since Jutland in May 1916. Admiral Hart was relieved of command of the ABDACOM naval force. His replacement was the egotistical and brash Royal Dutch Navy Admiral Karel Willem Doorman. He only had *Houston* and four light cruisers from the Royal Navy, Royal Australian Navy, and Royal Dutch Navy and ten destroyers. One of the British cruisers was *Exeter*, which had pursued the German raider *Graf Spee* in the South Atlantic in December 1939.

During the late afternoon of February 27, Doorman and Takagi met. They were almost evenly matched, the Japanese having four cruisers and thirteen destroyers. But numbers are illusory. The Japanese heavy cruisers *Nachi* and

Haguro, each with ten 8-inch guns, also carried the excellent Type 93 torpedoes. These were better and more powerful than the American Mark 14. One of the destroyers, *Ushio*, was a veteran of the Midway Neutralization Force on December 8. *Houston* was handicapped by having only six of her 9-inch guns operable.

With the smaller ships laying a smokescreen, a common practice in the era before radar eliminated its effectiveness, the cruisers opened fire on each other at about 1620 hours. While *Exeter* had the new Type 284 fire-control radar, her older guns could not reach the enemy cruisers. Doorman's goal was to get past Takagi's screening force and reach the transports headed for Java. During the daylight hours, the ABDACOM fleet had air cover, but the fighting continued until almost midnight. The only saving grace was that the Japanese bombers were grounded by bad weather. While the ABDACOM cruisers put up a valiant fight, *Exeter* was badly hit by an 8-inch shell exploding in her boiler room.

Takagi's light cruisers and destroyers launched about ninety torpedoes on the Allied line, but only one scored a hit on the destroyer *Kortenaer*, which broke in two and sank. The *Electra*, a Royal Navy destroyer that had been with *Repulse* and *Prince of Wales*, was hit by shellfire and so damaged she was abandoned.

During the night, another gun duel erupted, with the Dutch *Java* and *Ruyter* being sunk. Among the dead was Admiral Doorman.

Houston and the Royal Australian Navy light cruiser *Perth* withdrew, out of ammunition. While being partially reprovisioned, they received orders to proceed to the Sunda Strait on February 28. There they came upon the Japanese amphibious force headed for Bantam Bay on Java.

Houston and *Perth*, the last cruisers of the ABDACOM force, managed to sink six transports but were set upon by enemy cruisers. At last, severely battered, with hundreds dead and wounded, *Houston*, the favorite of President Roosevelt, sank after midnight along with *Perth*. More than 600 Allied sailors were taken prisoner. Captain Albert Rooks of *Houston* posthumously received the Medal of Honor.

But not all the luck was on the Japanese side. During the furious night battle, some of the Type 93 torpedoes launched by the destroyers missed the ABDACOM ships and continued on to sink four transports and a minesweeper. General Hitoshi Imamura was on board the *Ryujo Maru*, which sank under him. He was later rescued.

The Battle of Sunda Strait was the final blow for the short-lived ABDACOM navy and the death knell for the Dutch East Indies. Java fell on March 1. They had managed to delay the Japanese landings by one day. The following day, Batavia and the oil-rich islands were under Japanese control.

To Nimitz and his intelligence chief, Edwin Layton, it was like watching dominos fall. Among Admiral Hart's remaining ships was the old *Langley*, the first aircraft carrier in the U.S. Navy. *Langley* was sent from Darwin to Freemantle in January to pick up thirty P-40s of the FEAF and twenty-seven in crates. Pilots and ground crew were shipped aboard the transport *Sea Witch*. Initially ordered to take the planes to Colombo, Ceylon, they were redirected to Java.

On February 27, two U.S. destroyers met the two ships. Then a flight of sixteen Betty bombers from the new Japanese air base on Bali arrived and began targeting the ships. *Langley* avoided the first two patterns of bombs but was hit five times in the third pass. The old carrier, which had begun life as the collier *Jupiter*, had little chance of surviving combat damage. She listed steeply while her surviving crew boarded the destroyers. Then the old ship was sunk by gunfire and torpedoes to prevent her from being captured by the Japanese. The ship which had given the American Navy its first boost into the sky was gone.

The commander of the Fourth Fleet, Vice Admiral Shigeyoshi Inoue, who had recently been bombed by Halsey, supported the landing of the South Seas Detachment on the eastern and northern coasts of New Guinea. The strategic port of Lae, which, in 1937, had been where Amelia Earhart took off for her ill-fated flight to Howland Island, now gave Japan a launching point to support further campaigns from the Marianas and the huge naval base at Truk in the Caroline Islands. One by one, the Japanese took the Bismarck Archipelago, the Admiralty Islands, and the Solomons. The large island of New Britain in the Bismarck Sea had a superb deep-water harbor, Rabaul, which Australian troops savagely defended only to be overwhelmed by General Hitoshi Imamura's Eighteenth Army. Rabaul became a cornerstone of Japan's domination of New Guinea and the Solomons.

The wildly successful string of conquests had given birth to what would later be termed "Victory Disease." Defeating American, British, Dutch, and Australian land, air, and naval forces convinced the Japanese high command that Western nations were weak and not to be taken seriously as warriors. This was much the same opinion that had prevailed about Japan in the United States and Britain in the years before Pearl Harbor. That ill-advised view had been erased in just a few weeks.

Nimitz and King were convinced Yamamoto's next objective was Australia. The Royal Australian Army was weak since so many of its divisions were fighting alongside British troops in North Africa. But Yamamoto had never intended to invade the island continent. His plan was already achieved with the fall of the Dutch East Indies. From Java, Borneo, New Guinea, Rabaul, and the Solomons, they could cut off the vital sea lanes between the United States and the southern Pacific. With the Philippines under constant siege, Generals MacArthur and Wainwright could not launch any offenses to the south.

Yamamoto saw a campaign against Australia as the key to maintaining the Greater East Asia Co-prosperity Sphere, the term that applied to the eastern half of Asia and the western Pacific. By staging bombing raids on Australia's northern ports and bases, Japan could prevent the Allies from consolidating and launching a coordinated campaign on Japan's southern flank.

But India, the Crown Jewel of the British Empire, was also under threat of Japanese attack and control. The timing was bad for Great Britain, as anti-colonial resentment was high in the sub-continent in 1941. If Japan were to take Burma and India, it could not only cut off the vital supply lines from Europe to the Far East, but it could link up with German armies in North Africa and the Mediterranean. That scenario was too ghastly to allow.

Yet, unknown to the Allies, there was little chance of any direct military cooperation between Japan and Germany. The Tripartite Pact of September 1940 stipulated that each signatory would be supported by the others in case of attack by an outside nation. But since both Germany and Japan had initiated hostilities outside their own borders, this muddied the diplomatic waters. Japan was already at war with the ABDA powers, while Germany, after declaring war on the U.S. on December 11, 1941, was at war with Great Britain, the Soviet Union, and the other Allied powers. Hitler was confident his forces could handle the North African and Mediterranean theaters, as well as hold Europe and succeed in the invasion of the Soviet Union. In reality, Germany had far overreached its military and economic limits.

Yamamoto had never trusted Hitler; in fact, he had refused to meet with the chancellor when in Europe some years before. Yamamoto never believed Germany would come to Japan's aid. Yet the Imperial General Staff were counting on Germany to keep Stalinist Russia occupied while Japan maintained control of China and Manchuria and planned an eventual invasion of the Soviet Union. The rich mineral resources of eastern Siberia would provide Japan with all it needed to move west. But Stalin's Red Army was holding fast. Hitler refused to listen to his field commanders, who insisted the Soviet Union could not be conquered.

Furthermore, the insidious guerilla campaign by China's nationalist armies forced Japan to maintain the bulk of its army in China, where they would be of no use when the Western Allies began their drive to take back the Pacific.

The Dutch East Indies were Japan's last conquest in Asia. The Philippines were already under Japanese control except for the small beleaguered garrison holding out on the Bataan Peninsula and Corregidor.

As it was, the eastern and western Axis powers never cooperated beyond an exchange of engineering and technology, and did not participate in even one joint military operation.

In the first uncertain and terrifying days after Pearl Harbor, the port cities of Juneau, Seattle, San Francisco, San Pedro, and San Diego were on high alert, with armed patrols watching the beaches and cliffs for the sight of a Japanese fleet approaching. Air and coastal defense stations were trained to react immediately if an alert sounded.

The Western Defense Command's Fourth Army, under the command of General John DeWitt, headquartered at the Presidio in San Francisco, had six divisions, a full cavalry brigade, and fourteen AAA regiments from Canada to Mexico. This totaled over 200,000 men, half of whom manned and supported the AAA batteries. Coastal defense guns at Fort MacArthur and Point Loma in San Diego were on full alert.

Blackouts were imposed and curfews enforced. Citizens were instructed to drive as little as possible at night, and taught to cover their windows with heavy drapes to prevent lights from being seen out to sea or from the air. Anti-aircraft guns were mounted at or near aircraft factories, oil refineries, and other critical defense plants.

Added to this were reports of American merchant ships being torpedoed off the coast. Apparently more than a dozen were sunk or damaged, and this seemed to be a precursor to invasion. In reality, there was no danger of an invasion of or an attack on the West Coast. The Imperial Navy had overstretched its resources. But no amount of logic or reason would calm the jumpy populace.

Naturally there were false alarms and jittery citizens and homeowners along the thousand miles from Mexico to Canada, with reports of mysterious lights out to sea, periscopes creeping along the beach, or hordes of enemy planes overhead. But as the weeks passed with no attack, a measure of tense calm settled in. News stories of the Japanese invading the Philippines and taking Wake and Guam were far, far away.

This changed on the night of February 23, 1942. Ironically it was during one of President Roosevelt's radio Fireside Chats when the enemy struck directly at the coast of the United States. While FDR was relating the importance of fighting the Nazis and Japanese as far from American shores as possible, a Japanese submarine was surfacing off the coast of Santa Barbara.

"If we lost communication with the southwest Pacific," the president was saying, "and Australia and New Zealand, the West would fall under Japanese domination. Japan, in such a case, could release great numbers of ships to launch attacks on a large scale on the Western Hemispheres, South America, Central America, and the United States."

Roosevelt's words were prophetic.

As the sun set over the Pacific, the submarine's deck hatches opened and several men came out and took positions on the bridge and at the 4.5-inch deck gun. Binoculars to his eyes, the *I-17*'s commander, Kozo Nishino, peered at his target in the fading sunset. The sub was only 200 yards off the beach. In light of the alertness of Californians, it was remarkable that no one saw the low black silhouette of the big sub.

The *I-17* was one of the largest submarines in the world, built at the Yokosuka Navy Yard and launched in July 1939. She was commissioned just eleven months before Pearl Harbor. At 352 feet long and displacing 2,500 tons, *I-17* and her crew of 93 officers and enlisted men could take her across the Pacific and back without refueling. She was based at Kwajalein in the Marshall Islands.

On February 19, Nishino, unsure of his location, crept up to the shore of Point Loma at the entrance to San Diego Bay. Spotting the darkened lighthouse, he determined his position and moved out to sea, turning north along the coast past the sprawling expanse of Camp Pendleton Marine Base.

On the afternoon of February 23, he raised the periscope and saw that his sub was close to Santa Barbara. This was exactly where he intended to be. Alerting his crew, he waited for sunset. The coast would be illuminated by the setting sun behind him. Nishino was about to get his revenge against the Americans.

While commanding a Japanese-flag oil tanker in the late 1930s, Nishino had been invited to tour the large Elwood Oil Refinery on the Santa Barbara coast. While walking with his crew up a steep hill to where a reception committee was waiting, he slipped and fell into a prickly pear cactus. The American oil workers laughed. Hurt and humiliated, Nishino vowed to have his revenge. The story may be apocryphal, but it was the Elwood plant and Bankland that he chose to fire upon. Considering how many other important targets and defense plants were within range of his gun, it is interesting that Nishino chose to revisit the scene of his mortification.

After surfacing just off the Coal Oil Point near Elwood, he ordered his gun crew to aim at the large tanks on the bluff. These were the Bankline Company's aviation fuel tanks, containing over 100,000 gallons of highly volatile fuel.

At 1900 hours, he gave the order to fire, making *I-17* the first Axis warship to attack the United States mainland.

Seventeen 83-pound shells arced into the night sky and landed on Nishino's target. But they seemed to have little effect. There was no explosion, no inferno of burning fuel. In fact, except for sirens and the dark figures of running men, nothing happened at all. Only one of the 5.5-inch projectiles did any damage. The total cost to repair the damage from Nishino's revenge attack came to less than $600. Knowing his sub was now vulnerable, Nishino ceased fire and turned *I-17* seaward.

While the shelling did no damage, the press made the event into the precursor of a major invasion. For the first time since Pearl Harbor, a direct act of war had hit America. But no one, least of all the panicked citizens of the Los Angeles area, would ever have believed that it was only the spiteful act of a single submarine captain.

San Francisco Chronicle's February 24 banner headline read, "SUB SHELLS California!"

"Army says alarm real," blared the *Los Angeles Times*. "Roaring guns mark blackout."

DeWitt's Fourth Army went on immediate alert from Mexico to San Luis Obispo. Every AAA battery was ready for a major air assault. To make matters worse, the Office of Naval Intelligence in Washington issued a statement that California could be attacked within the next twelve hours. There is no record of how the ONI reached this conclusion, but it might have been a case of "better to be safe than sorry."

General DeWitt was also deeply concerned about sabotage by Japanese Americans. It was he who instituted the forced relocation of any person of Japanese descent into the infamous internment camps.

Even though Nishino had long since left California behind, never to return, the hysteria had not yet reached its peak. That would come thirty-six hours after the last shell landed on American soil.

Things had not settled down on the evening of February 24, when a single Douglas B-18 Bolo medium bomber lifted off the runway at Travis Army Air Base near Sacramento and headed west toward San Francisco. The city was nearly all blacked out, but the SCR-270 mobile radar unit on the coast detected the westbound plane, which triggered no alert.

Aboard the bomber were a young United States Army Air Corps pilot, Second Lieutenant Harry Kane Jr. of the 396th Medium Bomb Squadron, and his crew. Kane, a twenty-two-year-old New Yorker, knew every man on board, from his co-pilot and bombardier to the three gunners. But he had a new trainee navigator aboard, and for this reason, Kane and his Bolo were flying west on the night of February 24.

"It was supposed to be a routine training mission," Kane said in an interview years later. The training for the new navigators involved a long overwater flight to give them some real experience.

After leaving behind the nearly blacked-out city of San Francisco, the B-18 flew straight west for 200 miles, then turned south for another 360 miles. That would put the plane almost directly west of Santa Monica. The new navigator was to recommend when Kane should turn east on a heading of 074 degrees, which would take them to March Air Field, sixty-five miles southeast of Los Angeles. Even though the course would take them directly over the shipyards, aircraft plants, and the Long Beach Naval Air Station, Kane was not concerned. He knew the dispatchers back in Sacramento had alerted Western Defense Air Command of his arrival and flight to March. So even though the AAA gunners and spotters were still on high alert after the Elwood shelling, his single plane would be able to fly over the city unmolested.

Shortly after turning east, Kane saw a thick cloud bank ahead of the bomber. Just to be certain, he told the navigator to take radio direction fixes on the commercial radio stations. This was a common practice, and in fact, the Pearl Harbor attack force had used the broadcast from Honolulu's KGMB to home in on Oahu. But Kane became perplexed when they found that all the stations between Santa Barbara and San Diego were off the air. He assumed it was the result of the recent panic after the submarine attack. Descending to a lower altitude in order to see the coast, Kane gave up and flew over the cloud bank again. There was a danger of crashing into the blacked-out Channel Islands off the coast.

The coast passed under the B-18's wings. They flew over the very plant where the plane had been built, Douglas Aircraft in Santa Monica, and the nearby Lockheed plant in Burbank. A few minutes later, they passed over North American Aircraft in Inglewood. "A lot of new warplanes were being rolled off the assembly lines down there." He hoped to one day fly something better than the Bolo. Maybe the fast new North American B-25 Mitchell bomber.

Two hours after turning east, Kane and his co-pilot made their final approach into March Army Air Field. It had been a perfect flight and the navigator had done well. It was just after 2200 hours when Kane was lowering the landing gear and a stern voice came over his headphones from the March control tower. "Lieutenant Kane, you are directed to land immediately. The commanding general wants to see you at once."

Kane and his co-pilot exchanged surprised glances. That was highly unusual. Normally the tower controller would use the plane's tail number, but this call had been for him personally.

Shrugging, Kane touched the plane down and taxied to the ramp. After shutting down the engines, he climbed out of the plane and was told by a ground crewman to report to the administration building. Still confused, Kane walked in and was suddenly facing the furious Fourth Air Force commander, Major General Jacob Fickel. Kane snapped to attention.

The red-faced officer yelled at him at full volume. "You stupid bastard! Do you realize what happened?"

"N-no, sir," Kane replied in a shaky voice.

"You were an unidentified aircraft, and you blacked out all of Los Angeles and San Diego, and put all the radio stations off the air!"

Kane suddenly remembered not being able to pick up any broadcasts. He tried to reply, but Fickel cut him off. "And I sent four P-38s up looking for you with instructions to shoot you down!"

Soon the truth came out. Back in Sacramento, the air dispatchers had failed to contact the Fourth Air Force Command of his incoming flight. When the SCR-270 radar at Santa Monica had detected the B-18 coming in from the open ocean, they alerted Air Defense Command, which then went on alert. The city was blacked out and all radio stations silenced.

The previous twenty-four hours had been a strain on the defenders of the Los Angeles region. Waiting for the order to fire, they watched the darkened skies with exhausted senses. The army's P-38 Lightnings were searching for the lone unidentified plane, so the AAA gunners held their fire. Searchlights swept the skies but Kane's plane was already past, innocently headed for March.

The alert passed, but the tension did not abate. Four hours after Kane had been chewed out by the general, all was quiet. Until 0220. What triggered the second alert has never been determined. It may have been a private plane or a series of lights flashing in the hills to the east, but suddenly the sky over the darkened city erupted. First a few tracers streaked up from Long Beach, followed by more from Fort MacArthur, then over Santa Monica and Los Angeles. These were from a few air bursts of exploding AAA shells, then a few larger caliber explosions. In moments, the jittery, tired anti-aircraft gunners, believing that a real air raid was in progress, opened up with everything they had. It was a perfect case of a runaway chain reaction. In moments, the entire area was strobed by the bursts in the sky as dozens of searchlights waved back and forth in a fruitless hunt for Japanese bombers.

Citizens ran into their homes to turn out the lights. Thousands of cars pulled off the roads. Pieces of hot shrapnel and dud shells rained down on the city. Phones rang and teletypes chattered in every government and military office on the West Coast. "The Japs are coming! Be on the alert!" Panicked citizens reported seeing dozens of planes flying over and strange lights in the hills. More submarines were seen off the coast.

From Alaska to Mexico, the entire Western Defense Command mobilized as tens of thousands of soldiers and airmen rushed to their stations to repel an invasion. But nothing happened. For five hours, the brilliant flashes of air bursts continued, then subsided. Then all was quiet. While the searchlights continued probing, there were no more sirens or explosions.

Dawn rose from the east and Angelinos crept out of their homes and cars to look up at the empty morning sky.

Three people had died from auto accidents, and dozens more were injured by falling shrapnel. Over 1,400 AAA shells had been fired, along with God only knew how many machine gun rounds. Many citizens shot into the air with their hunting rifles and shotguns. The streets and rooftops were littered with bits of twisted metal and fragments of shells. There was widespread property damage. But not a single downed Japanese plane was found.

"It was the first real show of the Second World War on the American continent," said one radio broadcast later that day.

To this day, the exact cause of the "Battle of Los Angeles" has never been determined. But even though the precise trigger will probably never be known, it was certainly a combination of the *I-17* attack on Santa Barbara, the day-long alert, the report from the Office of Naval Intelligence, and Kane's unannounced flight from over the open ocean. Some of the blame must be attributed to the failure of the Air Corps dispatchers in Sacramento to inform the Fourth Air Force of the incoming flight.

The event predicated the darker side of white Americans' need to accuse innocent Japanese Americans of sabotage, suggesting these citizens were helping the Imperial Navy to invade the United States. Hundreds of thousands of Japanese Americans were rounded up from their homes, farms, and businesses to be herded into internment camps. The Western Defense Command reported that twenty suspected Japanese saboteurs had been arrested. Henry Stimson, the Secretary of War, issued a statement on February 26 that the alert might have been caused by low-flying aircraft chartered by enemy agents of the Japanese government. It was a way to locate and evaluate the air defense batteries. This was pure spin control, intended to appease the edgy and vengeful citizenry. Frank Knox said it was merely a false alarm.

But Kane's story was not quite over.

On the morning of July 7, 1942, off South Carolina's Cape Hatteras, the German Type VIIC submarine *U-701* was prowling under the calm blue waters of the Atlantic. The sub, having been commissioned into the *Kriegsmarine* just a year earlier, was one of the most successful U-boats of Admiral Karl Doenitz's Operation Drumbeat, the wholesale attacks on Allied and American shipping on the East Coast. On three patrols, Kapitanleutnant Horst Degen and his fifty-man crew sank five ships and laid mines, which sank and damaged at least three more. Degen was waiting for night to fall so he could surface and begin hunting again.

At the same time, the crew of a Lockheed Hudson A-29 medium bomber, No. 929322 of the 396th Bombardment Squadron, based at Marine Corps Air Station Cherry Point, was headed east to begin another long anti-submarine patrol over the Eastern Sea Frontier. Aboard the plane were an officer and four enlisted men, one of whom was Corporal George Bellamy, the bombardier. This was their eleventh patrol since arriving at the station in May.

While the plane was based at a Marine air station, the anti-submarine patrols were conducted by U.S. Army Air Corps crews. Bellamy settled into his seat in the plane's greenhouse nose while navigator Lieutenant Lyn Murray and radio operator Corporal Leo Flowers climbed into their stations. The engines sputtered as they warmed up. It would be another hot summer day in the oven of the aluminum and glass aircraft. Taxiing to the runway, the pilot pushed the throttles to full power and released the brakes. The Hudson climbed into the humid coastal air and banked southeast to begin its patrol.

At 1400 hours, Horst Degen brought the *U-701* to periscope depth and took a look around. The air was empty of aircraft, and his hydrophone operator assured him there were no patrol craft in the area. Needing to ventilate the boat of carbon dioxide that had built up during the morning submergence, Degen decided to surface for a short time and open the hatches. When *U-701* broke the surface, his lookouts scrambled to the bridge and the diesels thrummed to life. They were about thirty miles off the Outer Banks. The sub's hull was still submerged, only the conning tower exposed.

Four hours into its patrol, the Lockheed Hudson and its crew were flying at 1,500 feet, just above a layer of broken cloud. At 1410 hours, the pilot saw a thin feather of white water ten miles away and banked in that direction. He reduced power to lessen the engine noise.

Degen and his lookouts were scanning the sky with binoculars. Just then, the watch officer in the control room said the boat was ventilated. Degen ordered the sub to dive. With their attention on the dive, the lookouts failed to see the Hudson coming at them from the port quarter. One man spotted it and called out. But it was too late. Degen was horrified at being caught on the surface in daylight.

The sub was almost down as the Lockheed's bomb bay doors opened. It was diving at the U-boat at 220 knots, fifty feet over the water. As the plane passed over the sub, Bellamy stabbed the release button and three Mark 17 300-pound depth charges fell away. The pilot banked hard and watched as the three bombs fell. One missed astern but the others straddled the sub's hull behind the conning tower. As they exploded, the force crushed the hull's steel plating like paper, and in moments the *U-701* began to sink. Huge billows of froth, bubbles, and fuel oil came to the surface. Seventeen of the crew survived the sinking, but only seven, including Degen, lived to be taken prisoner.

The attack on *U-701* was the first confirmed sinking of a German U-boat by a U.S. Air Corps bomber crew in the war. The pilot of the Lockheed Hudson was Lieutenant Harry Kane.

In the Philippines, General Douglas MacArthur's hold was in jeopardy as General Masaharu Homma's Fourteenth Army came ashore at Lingayen Gulf on the morning of December 22. With the withdrawal of Admiral Hart's Asiatic Fleet to Australia and the complete destruction of the Far East Air Force, there was virtually nothing to stop the Japanese from taking Leyte, Mindanao, and Luzon. The surviving B-17s had little success. Hart's twenty-seven submarines made forty attacks on Japanese ships in December. They fired more than ninety torpedoes, achieving eight hits and sinking three transports. The *Sargo* attacked in Indochina's Cam Rahm Bay, firing thirteen Mark 14s without a single one exploding.

The Mark 14's flaws were becoming apparent to the navy.

MacArthur, who refused to surrender, consolidated the USAFFE and IV Corps and four Philippine divisions into a single unit, with General Jonathan Wainwright in command of the ground forces. Starting in early January, this began three months of desperate and savage fighting while withdrawing south down the long Bataan Peninsula. Wainwright and IV Corps established five defensive lines across the main road and held until strong enemy forces overwhelmed them. Then they moved back to another line of defense. The bloody defense on Bataan has gone down in history, along with Thermopylae and Bastogne, as one of the most superbly conducted retreats in military history.

On March 12, Army Chief of Staff General Marshall in Washington ordered MacArthur, his family, key Air Corps officers, and staff to leave Corregidor on four PT boats for Mindanao, where they would fly to Australia to regroup and plan a return to the Philippines.

At this point, Major General Wainwright was promoted to lieutenant general and given command of the newly established, if somewhat pointless, United States Forces in the Philippines, or USFIP. With no hope of reinforcements from Australia or the States, the newly formed army was essentially doomed.

Early April was a dark time for the Royal Navy as well. On April 5, cruisers *Dorsetshire*, the ship that had fired the torpedoes that sank the German battleship *Bismarck*, and *Cornwall* were sunk by Japanese planes in the Indian Ocean. Two days later, the carrier *Hermes*, accompanied by Australian cruiser *Vampire*, was spotted off Ceylon and sunk by planes from Nagumo's carriers.

Wainwright established his headquarters in the huge Malinta Tunnel on Corregidor. During Easter Week of April 1942, the Japanese shelled the last resistance with a hundred guns while bombers swept unchallenged over the peninsula.

Even though they knew they would not be relieved or rescued, the beleaguered troops fought on, recovering their wounded to be taken by private craft and PT boat to the island stronghold of Corregidor. With a trickle of supplies and ammunition brought in by night on submarines and PT boats, Wainwright's army held out until early April. Beaten, starved, riddled with tropical disease, and out of food and ammunition, the men who later became famous as the "Battered Bastards of Bataan" surrendered on April 9. Eighty percent were suffering from malaria, beriberi, and dysentery. More than 76,000 men surrendered, both American and Filipino, marking the largest defeat in U.S. history. They were subjected to the ordeal of the Bataan Death March, in which thousands, already wounded or weak from malnutrition, exposure, and disease, died or were killed by brutal Japanese soldiers. They endured three and a half years of inhuman conditions in POW camps.

All that was left was the garrison on Corregidor. Just 1.8 miles south of the Bataan Peninsula at the entrance to Manila Bay, Corregidor covered about 2,000 acres and was just over 500 feet high, with steep rocky walls and deep ravines.

Only 13,000 soldiers, many of them wounded from the Bataan fighting, and hundreds of Army nurses remained on Corregidor. Wainwright knew the island was the last Allied bastion in the Philippines. It was only a matter of time before he would be forced to surrender. Then hoards of enemy troops, siege artillery, and aircraft surrounded Corregidor. The Japanese began a month-long siege of the rocky island.

On May 5, Major General Kureo Taniguchi landed troops on the battered island.

While the massive Malinta Tunnel and its many laterals was impervious to bombs and shells, it was poorly ventilated, and the water and power were inadequate for the number of people inside. Reports came in of thousands of Japanese troops moving up the winding roads and approaching the tunnel and fort buildings. As the shelling increased, hundreds of wounded and dying men were brought in to be cared for by the nurses who never faltered in their brave duty.

Corregidor's solid rock shook with the detonations of heavy mortar shells as Wainwright sent radio reports to Australia. Food, water, and medical supplies ran critically short. By the afternoon of May 6, Wainwright had no choice. He had to surrender his brave but hopeless defense. He sent a courier under a white flag to find the Japanese commander to discuss surrender.

In Lateral 12 of the Malinta Tunnel was the sending and receiving set of the 228th Signal Company of the Signal Corps. Corporal Irving Strobing, a twenty-two-year-old from Brooklyn who had joined the army in 1939, was at the set. Strobing had been keeping the line to Australia and other Allied bases open. His Morse messages would be the last anyone heard from Corregidor. Spelling is as in the original text.

> they're not here yet. We are waiting for God knows what. How about a chocolate soda? Not many. Not here yet. Lots of heavy fighting going on. We've only got about one hour twenty minutes before . . . we may have to give up by noon. We don't know yet. They are throwing cannon shells at us and we may not be able to stand it. They have shelling us faster than you can count.

A pause silenced the message. Radio operators across the Pacific waited with clenched teeth to hear the next words from the Malinta Tunnel.

> We've got about fifty-five minutes and I am sick at my stomach. I am really low down. They are around now and smashing rifles. They bring the wounded in every minute. It is a horrible sight. We will be waiting for you guys to come and help.
>
> This is the only thing I guess that can be done. General Wainwright is a right guy. And we are willing to go on for him. But shells were dropping all night . . . faster than hell. Damage terrific. Too much for guys to take. Enemy strong shelling and bombing.

They have us all around and from sky. From here it looks like firing ceased on both sides. Men here are all feeling bad because of terrific nervous strain of the siege. Corregidor used to be a nice place. It is haunted now. Withstood a terrific pounding. Just made broadcast to Manila to arrange meeting for surrender. I can't say much. Can't think at all. I can hardly think.

Say I have sixty Pesos you can have for this weeken.

At this point, Strobing paused. He heard shouting and wailing. Wainwright had surrendered.

The white flag is up. Everybody is bawling like a baby. They are piling dead wounded soldiers in our tunnel. I'm vomiting. I'm weak from pounding keys long hours. No rest. Short rations. Tired.

I know now how a mouse feels caught in a trap. Waiting for guys to come along finish it up. Got a treat. Canned pineapple. Opening it with a Signal Corps knife.

The last part of the transmission was a message to his mother.

My name Irving Strobing. Get this to my mother Mrs. Minnie Strobing 605 Barbey street, Brooklyn New York. They are to get along okay. Get in touch with them soon as possible.

Message: My love to Pa Joe Sue Harry Joy and Paul. Also to all family and friends. God bless em all. Folks may be there when I come home.

Tell Joe wherever he is give em hell for us. My love to all. God bless and keep you.

Love. Signed my name and tell my mother how you heard from me.

Then the very last dot and dash came from the Philippines.
"Stand by."

The USAFIP had surrendered to the Japanese. It was over. The last Allied bastion had fallen to Japan. The empire controlled the entire western Pacific and the Far East, all the way to Burma and up to the Soviet border.

In all, more than twenty large Allied ships had been lost in the Dutch East Indies.

As for Japan, her total losses by May 1 were less than two dozen small warships, about 300,000 tons of merchant ships, 300 aircraft, and fewer than 4,000 men. To Yamamoto and the Combined Fleet, the gains were well worth the cost. Their next objective was the line between Fiji, New Caledonia, and Samoa, cutting Australia off from any hope of reinforcement from the United States.

But on the very day Wainwright surrendered to General Taniguchi, a battle that would at last dent the armor of Japanese invulnerability was being fought in the Coral Sea.

CHAPTER 10

THE NAVIES

"To know thy enemy is to win half the battle." —Sun Tzu

Geographically and administratively, there were four commands in the Pacific. The Northern Area covered the ocean north from 40 degrees North Latitude, a line running roughly between San Francisco and Vladivostok, Russia. The Central area stretched westward to Hong Kong and down to the equator at 0 degrees Latitude. From the equator south and west to Australia was the Southern Area. Each area had its own commanding admiral, who reported to Nimitz, the commander of the Pacific Ocean Area, who then reported to King and the Joint Chiefs, who had the final say in any operational decision.

The most potentially serious problem was duplication of effort or, worse, a turf fight among area commanders. But the navy admirals were of like mind and goals, whatever their personalities and egos. This, however, did not apply to General Douglas MacArthur.

MacArthur commanded the Southwest Pacific Area, which included Australia, the Philippines, the Solomons, New Guinea, the Bismarck Archipelago, Borneo, and the Dutch East Indies. Of course, all but Australia was in Japanese hands, but that would be dealt with in time.

General Douglas MacArthur was almost a mythical hero with unparalleled status in the United States, the Philippines, and Australia. Some members of Congress were considering him for supreme commander, U.S. Army and Navy. MacArthur, with his overblown ego and sense of importance, would be more than glad to accept. But saner heads prevailed. He would receive command of the Southwest Pacific, that is, the United States Army in that area. The Navy Department and King were not about to give a fleet to an army general. Therefore, MacArthur and Nimitz would share the vast Pacific Ocean.

The Australians, while willing to accept an American in command of all the military forces, were not about to let an admiral in Pearl Harbor run things from five thousand miles away. After reaching Australia from besieged Manila, MacArthur made his famous "I shall return" speech over the radio to the Philippines and, of course, the world.

The Joint Chiefs told both Nimitz and MacArthur to prepare for offensive operations. But first, they had to stop Yamamoto, who showed no signs of slowing. The only Pacific commander who had the means to do so was Nimitz.

Even with the reduced force left over after Pearl Harbor, which was being reinforced by ships from the Atlantic and new hulls under construction, Admiral Nimitz had a reputation as a man who could "do much with very little," as King put it. Nimitz had proven it, time and time again, during his career, and now it would stand him in good stead. As CINCPAC, CINCPACFLET, and commander of the Pacific Ocean Areas, Nimitz was responsible for the largest geographic area in the entire world.

In temperament and leadership personality, Nimitz and MacArthur could not have been more different. Where the general was fond of grand gestures and making impulsive decisions, the admiral was quiet, introspective, and a team player. Where Nimitz led a team of dedicated officers, MacArthur held court with sycophants like General Sutherland, the man who refused to allow FEAF General Brereton to launch a preemptive strike on the Japanese at Formosa.

Among the navy brass, MacArthur had no shortage of critics. Almost immediately after the administrative divisions of the Pacific had been established, Admiral Richmond K. Turner, perhaps the navy's most brilliant tactician, warned Nimitz that MacArthur, who knew nothing of the navy way and did not care to learn, would use his naval and air forces in the "wrong manner, because of his unfamiliarity with proper navy and air functions."

Conversely, Nimitz had absorbed a great deal about land and air tactics and operations during his long career. Yet he knew enough to understand that he needed to learn more, and fast. He read every book he could find on army and air operations, equipment, tactics, and history. Nimitz spent most of his time meeting with his commanders and learning everything he could about his fleet. He studied carrier tactics and read reports listing the gunnery scores of his surface types, the destroyers, light and heavy cruisers, and battleships. Overall, they were good, but the scores represented shooting at towed targets, not enemy warships that shot back. He learned about the emerging technology of radar and the fire-control systems installed on new ships.

He recognized the need for land- and ship-based radar sets, but the annual navy budget of $500 million was insufficient to have more in service by January

1942. The problems with the Mark 14 torpedo were becoming a serious issue because, at $10,000 each, they had been deemed too expensive to waste in live-fire training. His submarines were well built and capable, but their commanders had a lot to learn about the kind of warfare that would bring Japan to its knees. German U-boats were doing just that to Britain.

The standard 1.1-inch AAA guns and water-cooled .50-caliber machine guns were inadequate, something made clear at Pearl Harbor and the Philippines. Nimitz ordered huge stocks of fast Oerlikon 20mm and Bofores 40mm guns for his ships. Sixteen for each battleship, twelve for cruisers, and four on the destroyers. Carriers, the new queens of the navy, were each fitted with twenty-four of the excellent guns.

Then there was the problem of landing amphibious troops on an enemy shore. What kind of craft would serve the needs of the army and Marines on low beaches or reefs, and how could heavy equipment and tanks come ashore? Would Marine aviators fill the increasing need for fighter and bomber crews? Which of his carrier planes needed to be replaced? How many would be needed for the new carriers coming into service? The normal air group for the carriers consisted of thirty-four SBD dive bombers, eighteen TBD torpedo bombers, and eighteen F4F fighters, with at least a dozen spares, plus engines and parts.

Nimitz considered the vastly increased number of men to crew his ships, fly his planes, carry his cargo, and fight the Japanese. New training camps and stations would have to be built all over the United States, and somehow those hundreds of thousands of new men had to be fed, clothed, trained, and shipped to the Pacific. Bit by bit, report by report, meeting by meeting, the new United States Navy was being born.

When Pearl Harbor was attacked, the United States Navy numbered 374,070 officers and men. Two years later, it boasted more than two million, nearly all volunteers.

> "Ships ran on fuel oil, and airplanes flew on aviation gasoline, but the men who won the war in the Pacific were fueled by coffee."
> —ADMIRAL JAMES D. "JIG DOG" RAMAGE

The men and boys who wore navy blue came from fields and farms, factories and ball fields, cities and small towns, from the plains, mountains, and fertile valleys all across America. They came down from the Appalachians, Rockies, Blue Ridge, Sierras, and Ozarks. Their homes were in towns and cities along the Mississippi, Missouri, Ohio, Hudson, Rio Grande, and Columbia. Many came from tenements in New York, Brooklyn, Chicago, St. Louis, Philadelphia, Boston, and a hundred other cities.

They had names that ran from Abrams to Zamorsky, with a liberal dose of Smiths, Joneses, and Browns. There were more than a few Irish, Italian, German, Polish, and Eastern Europeans among them, along with a livening of Jews, Frenchmen, and Greeks. In other words, every name in the Chicago and New York phone books.

They were Catholic, Protestant, Jewish, Methodist, Baptist, atheist, agnostic, racist, and nondenominational. There were saloon brawlers, baseball players, college dropouts, plumbers, accountants, mailmen, policemen, firemen, lifeguards, bus drivers, lawyers, taxi drivers, lumberjacks, coal miners, waiters, bartenders, and theater managers. Coming from poor, middle-class, and wealthy families, they all went to movies and dances, learned to drive at sixteen, played baseball and football for their school teams or state universities. They averaged five feet, ten inches in height, weighed about 140 pounds, and had red, brown, auburn, blond, black, and sandy hair. Some had little more than a sixth-grade education, most were high school graduates, while others had college degrees and PhDs. They spoke every dialect and accent from California to Maine, from Alaska to Puerto Rico, in slow Alabama drawls, Nebraska twangs, New England sass, and Missouri rasp.

About a third were married, while the rest had sweethearts back home. Most began smoking at fifteen, drank beer and whiskey, often got drunk on leave, or lost their pay on a game of craps. While all ranks enjoyed beer or a rare Coca-Cola in the war zones, the predominant drink was coffee. Navy coffee was always black and hot. Every meeting among officers and around the table in the crew's mess was accompanied by the aroma of fresh coffee in the air. It has often been said that the war was won on coffee, and that is no exaggeration. A battleship or carrier crew drank about 300 gallons a day.

The navy's white enlisted ranks were leavened by dark-skinned Filipino, black, or Latino stewards. A derogatory term for those men was "burnt cork."

They had to learn a new language. Floors, stairs, bathrooms, elevators, were now decks, ladders, heads and hoists. Ropes were lines, and every sailor had to "Learn the ropes," a leftover from the days of sail.

On shore leave or liberty in a friendly port, virtually every man was out to find a willing female companion, preferably one who could be talked into bed. But paying for it was understood.

Navy men tended to be superstitious, carrying good luck charms or a favored family keepsake. They believed in good luck ships and hoodoo or jinxed ships.

Medically they were healthy and tended to be slim or wiry. Soda pop, gum, candy bars, and ice cream were favorite treats, as much loved as creamed chipped beef on toast, commonly known as "shit on a shingle," was universally hated. Sailors collected pin-ups of Betty Grable, Ann Sheridan, and Veronica Lake to put over their bunks. Musical tastes ranged from jazz, big band, and swing, to songs by Bing Crosby and the Andrews Sisters. Wardroom and Crew's Mess radios were tuned to Armed Forces Network to pull in Benny Goodman, Tommy Dorsey, and Glenn Miller. Bob Hope and Jack Benny were favorites, as were Abbott & Costello and the always-popular Amos 'n' Andy. Later in the war, they laughed and jeered at the weekly pronouncements of doom predicted by the honey-voiced Japanese propagandist, Tokyo Rose.

They had grown up during the Great Depression and worked hard to help feed the family. In fact, many joined the navy to send money home. Often, $10,000 life insurance policies were purchased by sailors, and was used to pay off the mortgage on the family farm. This led to the common euphemism, "He bought the farm."

As with any large institution, there were troublemakers. They were put on report and were ordered for "shit details," like scrubbing out the heads or kitchen duty. Even the most difficult malcontents were there to do the job when the ship was in battle. A few of the worst even won medals for meritorious conduct.

In short, they were a microcosm of American men of the early 1940s.

What did they all have in common? Almost nothing, except that they were all volunteers, eager to leave home and hearth to fight the Germans and Japanese, the latter being the preferred choice. The United States sailors were the best trained, best fed, best equipped, and most motivated seamen in the entire world. The young men who rushed to the navy recruiters after Pearl Harbor and for years afterward had been toughened by the Great Depression, knew the value of a hard day's work, and wanted revenge on the Japs.

They were facing the two most deadly and implacable enemies—Japan and the sea. Most had never left their hometowns, let alone voyaged halfway around the world to fight in places like the Coral Sea, Java Sea, Midway, the Marshalls, the Gilberts, and Guadalcanal. Few sailors could find those places on a map. But they went, spending most of their time scraping rust, cleaning equipment, loading supplies, and painting gray everything that did not move. Many did not return from the war, and those who did were changed forever, both physically and emotionally. But few would have had it any other way. They fought the enemy that could not be beaten and came home as heroes.

As for officers, the young men who passed the rigorous entrance exam and survived the daunting selection process entered the Naval Academy at Annapolis or the many new midshipman colleges around the country. They were middle-class and Protestant almost to a man. A few were Catholic and Jewish, one being Hyman Rickover, the acerbic and brilliant father of the postwar nuclear navy.

While some were the sons and grandfathers of naval officers, they came from all over the country. Yet four years of hazing, instructing, and training leached out nearly every trace of regional accents. This is why all naval officers sounded alike, whether from Alabama or Massachusetts. They were soon immersed in a world where academic standing and rank were inviolate. The cadets woke at 0630 hours and drilled, marched, exercised, studied, and trained without letup until lights out at 2130.

Surprisingly, the most important standard for the cadets was not academic brilliance or seamanship but character and integrity. They were never allowed to forget they were part of a great warrior tradition, with tradition being the key element in their roles as officers. They were expected to revere and emulate men like Decatur, Porter, Preble, Farragut, Dewey, and Sims.

One small but important part of the training was how to write clear and concise dispatches and messages, a skill as important as knowing how to navigate or fire naval guns.

The Annapolis curriculum was brutal and unforgiving, but it created the best-trained and prepared midshipmen in the world. They took immense pride in their graduating class and maintained associations and friendships that aided greatly in furthering their naval careers.

The officers who joined the fleet were thought of by their crews as either cast-iron bastards or the greatest guys on earth. Most captains had served for several years, having moved up from the junior ranks after graduating from Annapolis or midshipman colleges. There was certainly a wide spectrum of commanding officers. Some were like Lieutenant Doug Roberts, played by Henry Fonda, and a fair number of Captain Queegs of the *Caine*. Most fell in between, being solid and reliable. More than a few were petty, overbearing, and gave more punishment than praise. These officers had the collective label "chickenshit," meaning they were small-minded, making more of the trivial than the significant. Fortunately they were in the minority.

Sailors gave their ships pet names, like the battleship *West Virginia*, known to her crew as the "Wee Vee." Some loved their ships and took immense pride in serving. The big carrier *Lexington*, the "Lady Lex," was a favorite. But for some reason, her identical sister, *Saratoga*, was never a favorite. The "Big E," Halsey's *Enterprise*, never lost her place at the top of the carrier pantheon, even when replaced by far more advanced vessels.

Cruisers and destroyers, with their smaller, close-knit crews, were respected all over the navy for their role in protecting the bigger ships.

Even sailors serving on oilers or landing ships, minesweepers and destroyer escorts, considered themselves part of a team. Destroyers and destroyer escorts, commonly known as "Tin Cans," or just "Cans," were the scouts and cavalry of the fleet. Some destroyers achieved posthumous fame, such as the *Samuel B. Roberts* and *Johnston*, both of which were sunk after furious fighting at the October 1944 Battle of Samar.

Every ship printed a newspaper, which reported not only shipboard gossip but national and world news. A new sailor, having been assigned to a destroyer escort, asked his captain, "Sir, how often does a ship this size sink?"

His commander, understanding the new crewman's concerns about serving on a ship hardly 300 feet long, replied, "Usually only once."

Along with their uniform, underwear, shaving kit, and personal gear, every sailor had a book in his seabag. Known as *The Bluejacket's Manual*, this book, reprinted and updated annually, was the sailor's bible. It provided everything a new "boot" should know, from how to salute to the proper way to shine their shoes, from the signal flag alphabet to how to fight shipboard fires, from understanding watches to shipboard etiquette—the book had it all. The rest was provided by experience and pride.

Sailors quickly took offense when hearing a disparaging comment about their ships. It was not uncommon in liberty ports to see gangs of blue-suited swabbies slugging it out for the honor of their ships, even those who spent most of their shipboard time griping about being assigned to "this old tub." They also defended their seaborne service when insulted by their traditional rivals, the U.S. Army.

Warfare at sea had changed long before the United States and Japan came to blows in the Pacific. In a little more than seventy years, from about 1855 to 1925, warships underwent a dynamic evolution from sail-driven wooden broadside ships to steam-powered steel ships with turreted guns.

If we accept that the first major revolution in naval warfare was the change from sail to steam, and the second being the far faster evolution from wood to steel, it is safe to say the invention and development of submarines and aircraft carriers to be the third revolution. Their parallel evolution from birth to maturity took place in the first three decades of the twentieth century, entirely independent of one another. Other than the medium each called home, they had absolutely nothing in common except that the traditional surface fleet navy distrusted and scorned both.

The fleet consisted of several types of ships. Submarines, destroyers, light and heavy cruisers, battleships, and aircraft carriers. While submarines had proved their value as early as 1915, it would be another decade before *Langley* showed the utility of launching aircraft far out to sea. Yet one more decade would pass before early glimpses of what naval airpower could do were recognized by the United States and Japan. The Royal Navy made limited use of carriers in the Second World War, while Germany, with its limited coastline and access to the open sea, could not deploy a carrier fleet.

The big gun had reigned at sea since the Spanish Armada. As ships became bigger, better armed, faster, and evolved into steam-powered ironclads, they were the ultimate icons of a nation's will and policy. That is, until the coming of the airplane.

While the first flimsy, wood-and-fabric biplanes promised nothing in the way of a threat to naval power, that day came when General William Mitchell demonstrated in 1921 that airplanes could sink warships. Mitchell was only interested in advancing army air power, yet he was ultimately responsible for the United States Navy's first aircraft carrier. Farsighted naval officers saw the writing on the wall for surface warships and chose to add the arrow of naval aviation to its quiver. As for aircraft, other than the limited use of seaplane tenders by the Royal Navy in the North Sea, the aircraft carrier did not come of age until the late 1920s. It was a slow and uncertain progression to mate aircraft and ships. In the meantime, the big guns of the battle line held the lead role of sea power.

It could be said that the last time in history a fleet of big-gun warships made a momentous contribution to the outcome of a war would either have been at the Battle of Manila Bay in May 1898, or Tsushima in 1905. The Spanish-American War and the Russo-Japanese War ended rapidly with the destruction of the Spanish and Russian fleets.

The real moment that marked the end of the battleship's primacy in the seas was on that Sunday morning in December 1941 at Pearl Harbor.

While there is no argument that the attack on Pearl Harbor was devastating to the U.S. Navy, in retrospect it proved to be the biggest mistake the Imperial Japanese Navy ever made. In other words, it was a tactical win for Japan that led to the strategic victory for America.

Even the largest and most powerful battleships had some major limitations. They were slow, burned immense amounts of fuel, and could only project their power as far as the range of their guns. In other words, a battleship's reach was only about twenty-five miles. As long as an enemy remained out of the battleship's reach, it was impervious. Battleships had remained largely unchanged in every aspect except size and firepower, but even though their big guns rarely fired at other battleships, they would eventually find a useful role in pre-invasion bombardment for amphibious landings. Their heavy shells would soon pound Japanese troops and defenses on a hundred beaches from Guadalcanal to Okinawa. Then the LSTs, LCIs, and LCVPs, manned by navy crews, carried the soldiers and Marines to the battered but still deadly shores.

The real job of the navy was to support the ground troops. No war can be won without men taking enemy tactical and strategic objectives. The warships protected and supported the ships and craft that put the soldiers and Marines on beaches held by the enemy.

When aircraft carriers became the nucleus of American task forces, the flattops were placed at the center of concentric rings of cruisers and destroyers. This was already standard doctrine by 1941, the only difference being that battleships were not the ships being protected, but rather part of the defensive screen. The defensive ring also surrounded the all-important oilers, without which the task force could not reach distant objectives. This was when the navy began building specialized anti-aircraft cruisers, such as the *Atlanta*-class, which would be the first new ship commissioned into the navy in May 1942. *Atlanta* would be christened by the author of *Gone With the Wind*, Margaret Mitchell.

The cruisers and destroyers were there to protect the carriers, providing a dense cloud of AAA fire, augmented, in some ships, by the first use of fire-control radar. The outlying destroyers also provided anti-submarine coverage, listening for the sound of enemy subs. They were armed with depth charges in addition to torpedoes in swiveling mounts on the superstructure.

The other vessel that emerged from the chrysalis of the Third Revolution was the submarine. Its history has its roots in the American Revolution when David Bushnell built the wooden *Turtle* which unsuccessfully attacked the Royal Navy warship *Eagle* in New York Harbor in 1776. The Confederacy built the *Hunley* in 1863, the first submersible craft to sink an enemy warship.

Irish-American inventor John Holland designed the first practical submarine in 1900, and it was the basis for the subs of the First and Second World Wars after being vastly improved by Nimitz's work with diesels.

One of the first orders given to the fleet by the new CINCPAC after taking command was to the submarine fleet. They would begin unrestricted submarine warfare on Japan's navy and merchant fleet.

Before the war, American submarines were named "Fleet Submarines," denoting their role as escorts to the battle fleet. But by the end of 1941, there was no denying that German U-boats were coming close to strangling Great Britain by sinking unarmed freighters, tankers, and merchantmen. British Prime Minister Winston Churchill admitted he feared the U-boats above all else. German subs occasionally found and sank Royal Navy warships, but they were far more effective in sinking convoys and transports.

It was not a big leap for the United States Navy to see the light and send its own subs to the Pacific to cut Japan off from her sea trade. Japan and Great Britain, being island nations, were dependent on shipping to survive.

American subs were to operate independently, prowling in specific areas to interdict and sink any and all Japanese merchant ships. As mentioned in Chapter Four, the Japanese merchant fleet had been recalled to the Home Islands by November 1941. This was not only to protect them against submarine attack—they were to be employed carrying vital raw materials to Japan and war supplies to the armies in the Philippines and Far East. This gave Nimitz and his submarine force commanders, Admirals Robert English and, later, Charles Lockwood, an easier job since all the IJN's most vulnerable eggs would be in one basket, so to speak. The *Marus* would be in convoys, running between Japan, China, the Mandate Islands, and the South China Sea. While they would be escorted by destroyers, that left fewer of those to protect the task forces.

Unlike surface warships that moved along a horizontal plane, subs added the vertical dimension to that equation. They were designed to sink and operate in an environment totally hostile to humans. A sub skipper had to handle problems and situations no surface commander faced. Submarines were virtually autonomous units, often operating as lone wolves prowling the seas for prey, so a sub skipper often operated without any direct orders from higher command. Submarine skippers had to be among the best and most independent of naval commanders. An entire crew could die from one serious error inside a submerged submarine.

For that reason there was another layer of operational training for any man, both officer and enlisted, who volunteered for the sub service. First, they trained to work in a confined, even claustrophobic, steel cylinder hundreds of feet under the surface of the ocean. Submarine crews had to qualify to serve in the boats. In other words, in addition to the intense training they had to undergo at the submarine school in New London, Connecticut, they had to study and master virtually every piece of equipment and device on board a sub.

They had to know every detail of the hydraulics that operated the vents and pumps, the complex wiring and compressed air schematics, how the ballast and trim tanks, engines, batteries, electric motors, and torpedo tubes worked. Every crewman was expected to handle and operate every system on their sub and pass a rigorous test by a board of the boat's chiefs and officers before he was allowed to wear the coveted "dolphins" of the sub service.

Submarine crews were tightly-knit and loyal to each other in a way not often seen on surface ships. Unlike surface ships, when a sub went down from enemy action, it usually meant the loss of the entire crew.

A German word, *Schicksalsgemeinschaft*, which meant a community bound by a common fate, exactly fit life and death on a sub.

Officers mastered navigation, gunnery, torpedoes, communications, engineering, and diving, then had to conduct a successful approach on a target before being considered for command of a sub. Surface ship officers often spent their entire careers in one department, such as navigation, engineering, or gunnery. A submarine officer had to be a jack of all trades.

Many Hollywood films told stories of the submarine navy, but few could convey the dark, smelly, cramped, humid life aboard a 300-foot-long steel tube on patrol. Several classes of subs went into service before and during the war and had the highest attrition rate of any service, even the Army Air Forces. Of the more than 300 U.S. submarines that went to war, fifty-three did not return. But they accounted for nearly half of all Japanese warships and merchant vessels sunk during the war.

Destroyers and their smaller cousins, the destroyer escorts, acted as bodyguards, protecting the capital ships from air and submarine attack. No large task force dared venture out into the broad, dangerous ocean without the smaller ships to provide an outer ring of security. Scores of the old four-piper 1,200-ton World War I destroyers were converted into minesweepers or fast couriers to carry aviation fuel, weapons, troops, and medical supplies to widespread areas of the Pacific. While they carried no armor, their high speed, maneuverability, accurate and fast-loading 5-inch guns, deck-mounted torpedo tubes, and dense smoke screens made the "cans" indispensable as they darted like hyenas among the bigger ships.

There were other types of ships that rarely generated headlines or Hollywood films. They were the minesweepers, destroyer and seaplane tenders, minelayers, and support ships. Patrol craft and torpedo boats played their role in the navy. To operate, maintain, repair, and supply these ships was the job of the American sailor.

In Warner Brothers' 1943 film *Action in the North Atlantic*, Humphrey Bogart, portraying a Liberty Ship officer, tells his crew, "There's no job bigger than this. No matter how many planes and tanks and guns you fire up, no matter how many men you got. It doesn't mean a thing unless the men get the stuff when they need it. It's our job to see they get it."

Bogie had it right. The thousands of C-47 and hundreds of transports, freighters, and tankers carried vital war materiel to the far-flung fronts around the world. They carried not only food, medical supplies, ammunition, weapons, clothing, bombs, and fuel but also morale-boosting ice cream, Coca-Cola, beer, chewing gum, Lucky Strike cigarettes, soap, chocolate, movies, magazines, phonograph records, letters from home, hometown newspapers, and countless other items the fighting men needed. They were as crucial to Allied victory as radar, codebreaking, and training.

> "The good fighters of old first put themselves beyond the possibility of defeat, and then waited for an opportunity of defeating the enemy." —Sun Tzu

The Imperial Japanese Navy was born in 1868, little more than a decade after Commodore Matthew Perry forced Japan to abandon its isolation. By 1869, an early naval academy was established near Tokyo, and in 1880, it was moved to Eta Jima near Hiroshima. In the first year of officer training, loyalty was to their domain of origin rather than to the navy as a whole. This led to changes in the recruitment policy. To counter this, candidates had to pass an entrance exam before being accepted. The navy also put out the word that anyone wanting a navy career was welcome, regardless of social standing or regional origin. This led to a rapid increase in applicants from the commoner classes.

Cadets learned history, science, engineering, navigation, mathematics, and languages. Every cadet had to endure tough physical training and learn the core values of loyalty, duty, obedience, valor, courtesy, and ambition.

After graduating from Eta Jima as midshipmen, the new officers were assigned to training ships for about a year, after which, as new sub-lieutenants, they began specialized training in gunnery, torpedoes, engineering, or navigation, the most important disciplines in any navy. The new second lieutenants entered line service with the fleet. Unlike Western navies, officers received department training before learning to sail and command ships.

However, a board of reviewing officers could directly promote exceptional officers into line service. From the rank of lieutenant commander, competition for the rank of commander was intense. This was the usual "make or break" point at which many officers either pushed harder or remained at the mid-level rank. Further promotion was granted after four or five years in each grade, from commander, to captain, to rear admiral.

The flag rank of vice admiral was the highest any regular officer could reach without Ministry approval, which was often contingent on connections or recognition by the Navy Ministry. For wartime, good officers moved up the ranks in less time, often when higher-ranking officers were killed in combat.

As for the enlisted ranks, sailors were allowed to enlist rather than conscripted as in the army. Preference went to those who already possessed knowledge of the sea, such as fishermen and coastal steamer crews. They were taught traditional military values and the pride endemic in the navy. They were driven more by ideological brainwashing from youth than pure patriotism. They were trained at four regional navy centers at Maizuru, Kure, Yokosuka, and Sasebo for a term of four months. These centers turned out the men who would be the noncommissioned chiefs and ratings as the new century began. Emerging as third-class seamen, they were assigned as gunners, electricians, machinists, firemen, and the other ratings needed on a warship. The most qualified were selected as third-class petty officers, the backbone of any navy. Rising through the three grades of petty officers led to warrant officer rank and up to sublieutenant, the rough equivalent of an ensign in the United States Navy.

The merit system soon led to the Imperial Navy having the highest morale, training, devotion to duty, and discipline in the world.

One thing virtually all Japanese sailors, from the officer corps to the lowliest seaman, had in common was a rabid feeling of cultural and racial superiority to all other nations, particularly the polyglot British and Americans. Most Japanese military men were taught to believe all non-Japanese races were inferior and even subhuman. This brainwashing was prevalent in the early years of the war and emerged in the way Japanese sailors, soldiers, and airmen treated conquered peoples and enemies.

In the matter of building a real fleet, the IJN was influenced by Western navies. In 1873, thirty Royal Navy officers traveled to Japan to advise the Meiji Naval Ministry on building a fleet. This is why the later IJN was so like the Royal Navy in rank structure, administration, and tradition.

In the 1870s, the IJN contracted three large, modern ironclad warships to be constructed in England—the *Ie, Kongo,* and *Fuso*—the first to be built for the new navy outside Japan. The growth continued with the 1883 naval expansion budget, which was larger than the entire expenditure for the navy during the past decade.

With that completed, an even more ambitious building program was proposed in 1895, which stipulated more than 250,000 tons of new ships constructed in England. This would make the Imperial Japanese Navy the fourth-largest navy in the world. It consisted of six pre-dreadnought battleships, eight cruisers, twenty-four destroyers, and sixty-eight torpedo boats. Some were built and launched in England, while the rest were constructed in Germany, Italy, and Japan. A few were even launched in San Francisco. Some of these were present at Tsushima, demonstrating the superiority of the new navy.

Tsushima was among the most one-sided naval engagements in history. Of the thirty-eight ships in the Russian Baltic fleet, twenty-one were sunk, seven captured, and six more put out of action. Nearly 10,000 Russian sailors and officers were killed or captured. Japan's losses were three torpedo boats and less than 150 men killed. Among the wounded was Isoroku Yamamoto.

The IJN also purchased five Holland submarines from Electric Boat in Groton, Connecticut, in 1905. While history records that HMS *Dreadnought* was the world's first all-big-gun battleship in 1906, Japan in fact had ordered the *Satsuma* the year before. At 485 feet long and 19,500 tons, *Satsuma* carried four 12-inch and twelve 10-inch guns, making her the lead ship of a class of the so-called semi-dreadnoughts. The IJN was the first navy in the world to adopt the Marconi Wireless for communication.

By 1914, Japan possessed the most modern fleet in the world.

When the Great War began in August 1914, Japan was allied with Great Britain. Seizing the chance to take control of the German colony of Tsingtao, the new Imperial Navy conducted the first sea-launched air raid from the seaplane tender *Wakamiya* in September. The world's first air-sea battle damaged the German cruiser *Kaiserin Elisabeth*. This predated the December 1914 Royal Navy air raid on the Cuxhafen Zeppelin sheds. It was a harbinger of things to come.

By 1921, Japan had begun building its own capital ships, including the first real dreadnought *Nagato*, a 32,000-ton monster with eight 16-inch guns. At that time, *Nagato* was the most powerfully armed warship in the world. Ironically, she was the sole IJN battleship to survive the war, being sunk during the 1946 Bikini Atoll Atomic Bomb tests of Operation Crossroads.

Sato Tetsutaro, Japan's version of naval prophet Alfred Thayer Mahan, urged his nation to build a fleet specifically to challenge and defeat the Royal and United States Navies. He proposed a fleet centered around eight battleships and eight fast battle cruisers. The 1922 Washington Naval Treaty initially foiled this plan but did not stop the rapid build-up.

In 1928, the IJN launched the new, fast, powerful *Fubuki*-class destroyers, the first to mount enclosed turrets for 5-inch guns. Another IJN innovation quickly copied by other navies was the deck-mounted torpedo launcher, giving the ship immensely greater firepower. Japan would rely heavily on these during the war, to great effect.

Four building plans, called *Maru Keikaku*, were laid out for 1931, 1934, 1937, and 1939. The first was to lay down and launch thirty-nine new ships centered on the powerful *Mogami*-class heavy cruisers. But due to a basic flaw of overloading with more armor and weapons than the hull was designed to carry, some ships capsized after being fitted out. Majority of the 1931–1933 budget went to correcting the flaws in the existing ships. In 1934, the plan called for forty-eight new ships, including the superb *Tone*-class heavy cruiser and the new carriers *Hiryu* and *Soryu*.

With Japan's rejection of the 1930 London Naval Treaty, building new ships proceeded at a feverish pace, leading to the two most powerful warships in the world—the proposed *Yamato*-class super battleships. Also under construction were the big, fast carriers *Shokaku* and *Zuikaku*, which would fill out the First Air Fleet in December 1941. Another sixty-four ships were to be put into service by 1939. In addition, a dozen new air groups were formed, along with land bases for training.

By 1941, the Imperial Navy boasted ten battleships, twelve carriers, nearly forty modern and fast cruisers, more than a hundred destroyers, sixty submarines, and hundreds of support and auxiliary ships.

Compared to the Western navies, the bulk of these ships were more modern, faster, better armed, and technically superior to anything in the United States and Royal Navies. Yet with this mighty fleet, Japan was both narrow-minded and shortsighted in its use of those ships.

Like Great Britain, Japan was heavily dependent on foreign oil sources, and this was one reason the IJN opted for bigger and longer-ranging ships. They had to be capable of mounting campaigns of conquest as far away as Australia, the Java Sea, India, and New Guinea. Thus the navy had already committed its fleets to fight the three nations most likely to oppose them: the Dutch, Great Britain, and the United States. In essence, the modern Imperial Navy was custom-built to fight the Allies, possessing better equipment combined with the biggest and best warships in the world.

But the Code of Bushido was prevalent in how the Imperial Navy planned their naval campaigns and fought their battles. Battleships were still the dominant force in naval warfare, even while the carrier was asserting its preeminence. The superb and numerous destroyers and cruisers were the modern sword in the hands of their captains. But the way the Imperial Navy wasted its excellent submarines was another example of the ancient Samurai code dominating modern naval tactics. Unlike the Germans and Americans, which devoted their submarine forces to sink enemy sea commerce, Japanese submarine commanders were ordered to find and sink American warships, even if this meant leaving vulnerable oilers, tankers, transports, and freighters untouched. They were trained that an armed enemy ship was more worthy than an unarmed one.

The United States Navy, while being at a great disadvantage in the first months of the war, had one thing in its favor: His name was Admiral Chester William Nimitz.

CHAPTER 11

STRIKING BACK—THE DOOLITTLE RAID AND THE CORAL SEA

"There is nothing impossible to him who will try."
—Alexander the Great

While there is no disputing that the U.S. Navy did plan and execute offensive operations in 1942, there was always a defensive element to the planning. It was the old story that a cornered mouse will fight like a tiger, and the Americans knew they were at a disadvantage.

During the months after the fall of Wake and the Battle of the Java Sea, Nimitz was playing a balancing act with his fleet. One serious issue was the shortage of oilers. The man who had helped perfect underway refueling had few oilers in the Pacific. Most had been sent to Iceland to support the Atlantic convoy routes. Each carrier task force was accompanied by an oiler, but it stretched things too thin if more than two task forces were at sea at the same time. Even after insisting on the return of the oilers sent to the Atlantic in 1941, Nimitz would only have seven to work with. The seven battleships of TF 1 on the West Coast consumed 300,000 tons of bunker fuel per month, the maximum available at Pearl. It was a simple decision. He would have enough fuel for either the battleships or the carriers. The carriers won.

On January 31, Admiral Wilson Brown's TF 14 left Pearl to take the oiler *Neosho*, a survivor of the attack on Battleship Row, to refuel Halsey's TF 8, which was west of Hawaii undergoing combat readiness drills before heading to attack the new Japanese base on Wake Island. Two days out, Brown learned that Halsey would not need the fuel, so TF 14 would prepare for a raid on the base at Rabaul on New Britain. Brown's ships began refueling from *Neosho* on February 13, but the cruisers could only fuel to 75 percent. Another problem was communications. Wanting to ensure the Japanese could not detect the task force near Rabaul by its radio messages, Brown had two officers flown to an Allied base to report to Nimitz and King. Brown turned his force to the northwest, intending to hit

Rabaul from the northeast and conceal his location. On February 20, while still 400 miles from their target, TF 14 was attacked by eighteen Betty bombers. The ships evaded all the bombs, and about fifteen bombers were shot down. Now that the element of surprise was lost, Brown chose to head south to support the Australian and New Zealand landings in the Solomons. Brown later wrote that the limiting factor in any fast carrier task force was fuel.

Nimitz absorbed this as he had everything else in his new command. Another part of the fuel problem was the battleships. Pearl Harbor had only enough ready fuel oil for the surviving battleships to reach the Marianas and return. This was far short of what was needed to sustain major fleet campaigns in the Far East.

Halsey, with his task force now redesignated as TF 16, was moving north to Wake Island. Rear Admiral Raymond Spruance, who commanded the cruisers, would take *Northampton*, *Salt Lake City*, and two destroyers to hit Wake from the west, while *Enterprise* and the other destroyers launched an air strike from the north at dawn on February 24.

The cruisers would open fire at the moment the first bomb fell on the former American Marine base. TF 16's officers, pilots, and crew were determined to make the Japs pay dearly for taking the island.

Low overcast and thick mist hampered the pre-dawn launch, so it was nearly 0650 hours before the strike left the carrier and turned south. Wake Island was 100 miles away. Eighteen Bombing 6 SBDs, eighteen Scouting 6 SBDs, and nine Torpedo 6 TBDs with bombs were escorted by six Fighting 6 F4Fs. It was exactly two months and one day since Wake's Marines had been forced to surrender.

Peale Island on the north held the seaplane ramp and PAA hangars, while Wilkes to the south had the runway, oil, and fuel tanks. Commander Young, the raid leader, was to avoid hitting the tent city on Wilkes, just in case the Marines and civilians were still being held there.

At about 0755, he radioed, "Attack! Attack!"

The Dauntless dive bombers planted their 500-pound bombs into the runway, hangars, and AAA guns. The Devastator level bombers destroyed seven of the fuel tanks, which went up in bright orange fireballs.

The SBDs then used their smaller 60-pound bombs on soft targets. There was no fighter cover, and McCluskey's Wildcats only had to watch for enemy planes arriving from the west. One big Kawanishi flying boat had managed to take off, and the Wildcats brought it down. Meanwhile, Spruance's cruisers shelled the western end of the island with their heavy 8-inch guns.

When the planes landed on the Big E at 0945, Wake Island had suffered serious damage. As intended, Halsey had put it out of action for at least three months; in fact, the Japanese occupation of Wake was already turning out to be a liability for the Imperial Navy.

As TF 16 regrouped, Halsey received a message from Nimitz. CINCPAC asked if TF 16 could launch a strike on Marcus Island, 650 miles farther west.

Marcus, or to use its Japanese name, *Minamitorishima*, was only a thousand miles from Tokyo. It would be the closest any task force had gotten to the Home Islands so far in the war. Because the oiler *Sabine* could not fully refuel the big ships and destroyers, Halsey chose to leave them behind. It was a risky decision.

While Halsey raced west with the two cruisers, deep into enemy territory, word came of the battle in the Java Sea. *Houston* had been sunk. This was bad news for Spruance, who was, by choice, a cruiser commander. The additional news that the old carrier *Langley* was lost put a pall on the aviator. It was up to them to avenge the first American carrier to be sunk.

At 0455 on March 4, thirty-eight bombers and fighters roared off the Big E's flight deck and headed southwest for the small island. While the attack was only another spoiling raid, the pilots and deck crew were now veterans. They had launched successful strikes on the Marshalls and Wake. They were learning fast.

It was still dark and the low cloud layer prevented any visual sighting of their target. For the first time in an air strike, radar played a role. Back on *Enterprise*, the radar operator had drawn a line on his scope denoting the course to the tiny island, whose total land area was less than a square mile. When he saw the radar blip showing the planes heading slightly right of his line, he sent a coded Morse message that told Commander Young to alter course slightly to port. This brought the planes right on target.

The SBDs pasted the runway and hangar. The Zero fighters were ripped apart in the blasts while the surprised AAA gunners began firing into the still-dark sky. One Dauntless was hit and the crew ditched to be taken prisoner.

In Hawaii, Nimitz was pleased with the results of the two air raids. Admittedly they were not on the scale of anything the Japanese Imperial Navy had done in the last two months, but they were significant. He knew the Pacific Fleet needed more oilers. Having at least two with each task force would cut in half the time needed for underway refueling, and there would be less risk of leaving some ships without enough fuel for fast operations. In naval warfare, speed was the key to survival, especially when dealing with the air threat.

The raid had one negative effect on the defenses of the Home Islands. Marcus Island was one of the links in the long defense and communications chain encircling Japan. Now there was a break in that chain, and the Imperial Navy's ability to protect Japan came under criticism.

Marcus Island was a tiny, insignificant dot in the vast ocean and certainly not worth risking one of his valuable carriers. There was now a gap aimed directly at Tokyo.

THE DOOLITTLE RAID

"If your opponent is of choleric temper, irritate him." —SUN TZU

Unbeknownst to Halsey, Admiral King and Army Air Forces General Henry Arnold were hatching an audacious scheme to hit Japan itself. Aviation Project No. 1 was the brainchild of Captain Francis Low. Eager to find a way to "avenge Pearl Harbor," Low believed that North American B-25 Mitchell medium bombers, the far superior American counterpart to the Betty, could be launched off a carrier. While unable to land on a carrier deck, they could fly farther with a heavier bomb load and perhaps land in China. This was the origin of the famous Doolittle Raid.

With remarkable inter-service cooperation between the traditionally contentious U.S. Army and Navy, King and Arnold pulled together a team of skilled and clever officers. The first was Lieutenant Colonel James H. Doolittle, who had long since won fame for air races and setting records, as well as developing early instruments for blind flying and formulating new high-octane fuels.

He was chosen to plan, coordinate, and lead the audacious raid.

Halsey's *Enterprise* and the new *Yorktown*-class *Hornet*, now transiting the Panama Canal on her way to San Francisco, would be the core of the newly designated TF 18.

The 17th Medium Bomb Group based in Oregon was asked to volunteer for the mission but not told what they would be doing. Every one of the twenty-four aircraft crews volunteered and flew their B-25s to Eglin Field in Florida. Eglin was perfect for the secret training, being far away from populated areas.

There they learned how to lift their 15-ton bombers into the air in less than 500 feet.

After weeks of secret training, the men flew twenty-two bombers to NAS Alameda near Oakland, California, where sixteen planes, all that fit on the flight deck, were hoisted aboard the *Hornet*. The ship sailed under the Golden Gate Bridge at 1200 hours on April 2. Aft of *Hornet*'s island superstructure was a sight never before seen in the history of aviation: Sixteen bombers were parked in neat herringbone rows all the way to the fantail. The last of the huge planes, which looked far too big to fit on a carrier, hung over the water.

While there was no way to conceal the odd sight of a carrier loaded with the brown twin-engine bombers, it was not uncommon for the flattops to ferry planes to the war zone.

Hornet sped westward with her escort, the heavy cruiser *Vincennes*, light cruiser *Nashville*, and four destroyers.

On April 8, *Enterprise* and her escorts left Pearl and headed northwest. Her air group flew out from Hawaii to land on their ships. The new F4F-4 Wildcats were the first to have folding wings and self-sealing fuel tanks. New Grumman TBF Avenger torpedo bombers would soon arrive, but for now, *Enterprise* still carried the old, slow TBD Devastator. *Enterprise* and *Hornet* were the first carriers to be fitted with the new Oerlikon 20mm twin gun mounts, and their crews practiced in anticipation of shooting down hordes of Japanese bombers.

Only after they were well out to sea were the men told of their mission. They were on the way to bomb Tokyo, Yokohama, and Kobe.

On April 9, the ship's paper reported the fall of Bataan, making the navy men more determined than ever to hit the Japanese where it hurt most.

The two task forces joined at 39 degrees North Latitude and 180 degrees Longitude. The cruisers and destroyers formed a protective arc ahead of the two carriers. As the task force raced westward at 20 knots in cold and damp weather, the usually confident and cocky army bomber crews were subdued by the maze of corridors and thousands of rooms on the huge ship. Relations between the army and navy had always been antagonistic, but upon hearing of their mission, the navy crewmen welcomed the army fliers with warmth, respect, and even a little envy.

After refueling from the oilers *Cimmaron* and *Sabine*, the two carriers and their cruisers left the destroyers behind and raced at full speed to the launch point. The men of TF 18 eagerly waited for the moment when their labors would be rewarded. The bombers were inspected and tuned up to ensure every engine ran smoothly, every system was perfect, and each instrument was calibrated. They were to launch at dusk 400 miles from the Japanese coast, bomb their targets in the predawn, and fly 1,400 miles across the East China Sea to prepared bases near Kunming, China. There the bombers would be incorporated into the new Tenth Air Force. There they were to join with the famous Flying Tigers of the American Volunteer Group, or AVG. Doolittle was to take off at 1400 hours on April 18, in advance of the other fifteen planes, to drop

STRIKING BACK—THE DOOLITTLE RAID AND THE CORAL SEA

incendiaries on the targets. The other planes, launching at dusk, would have small fires to mark their targets.

In an interesting coincidence, Halsey had earned his wings in 1935 while a captain commanding NAS Pensacola. One of the naval aviation cadets under his tutelage was James Howard, who would become a double ace, first as one of the original Flying Tigers, then as a P-51 Mustang pilot in the Eighth Air Force in England. Howard was now in Kunming, China, one of the AVG pilots awaiting the arrival of Doolittle's force.

Onward TF 18 raced, covering 850 miles per day, while *Enterprise*'s scout bombers probed far ahead to spot any enemy ships or planes. On the early morning of April 18, the *Nitto Maru*, an armed Japanese picket boat 600 miles off the coast, spotted the *Hornet* and *Enterprise* steaming southwest toward Japan.

A furious fusillade from *Nashville* sank the small vessel, but not before it transmitted a warning to the Home Islands that an American naval force was heading their way.

The carefully laid plan would have to change. Halsey ordered his ships to flank speed, 23 knots, trying to gain a few more miles before launch. Despite knowing Japanese air defenses and fighters would be waiting for them, and they would have to try and land in China in the dark, the Raiders never hesitated.

Extra fuel was loaded on board each bomber. None carried more than the guns in the upper turret and nose. They would each bomb on their own, with no escort.

Their chances of reaching friendly bases in China were almost hopelessly remote.

From *Enterprise* a blinker light flashed at *Hornet*. "Launched planes. To Colonel Doolittle and his gallant command. Good luck and God Bless you. Halsey."

Doolittle, in Plane Number 1, revved his engines and rolled forward on the wet, pitching deck to the starting position beside the island. There were only 465 feet of deck ahead of the big bomber. The plane's 67-foot wingspan was six feet short of the steel superstructure. Navy crewmen stood alert for any signal from the officer standing by Doolittle's port wing as he listened to the sound of the Wright R-2600 1,700-hp radial engines.

If there was any indication of faltering engines or balky controls, they had orders to push the plane overboard to make room for the next one. There was no time for anything but getting those planes in the air. Halsey planned to turn east immediately after the last bomber lifted off.

When Doolittle's engines were roaring like banshees, the officer holding the flag watched the pitch of the deck until it was just dipping into a wave. Then he slapped the flag down and dove for cover. Doolittle and his co-pilot, Lieutenant Richard Cole, released the brakes and the heavy bomber, loaded with four 500-pound incendiary bombs, rolled along two white lines painted on the deck.

When the bow was just rising, the big bomber reached the end and clawed its way into the air. Doolittle struggled to gain altitude, not hearing the wild cheers of the thousands of men of TF 18. It was 0806.

Plane Number 2, piloted by Travis Hoover and Bill Fitzhugh, followed Doolittle's example. Then Planes 3, 4, 5, and the rest slowly moved forward to take their places on the white lines. Fifty-nine minutes after Doolittle took off, Plane Number 16 left the deck, headed into the morning sky and an unknown future.

TF 18 turned east at full speed. There was no need to remain. The bombers could not land on the carrier. Every plane and crew was on its own, but the last ones knew they would be flying over burning and alerted targets in a sky crawling with snarling Zeros and black with AAA fire.

The first planes were over Tokyo at 1200 local time, and climbed to about 1,500 feet. They had been specifically instructed not to bomb the Imperial Palace. The mission was not to assassinate Hirohito, regardless of how satisfying it might be. Bombing the palace would only serve to inflame the Japanese. The raid was to prove to the nation that they were vulnerable and that the United States was still capable of fighting back. They looked for their briefed targets with some success. The 500-pound general-purpose and incendiary bombs exploded on oil refineries, fuel tanks, factories, and powerhouses. Damage was minimal. The panic it caused was far greater. But even after the first several planes bombed their industrial targets, there was little opposition. The few fighters on routine training flights simply never saw the bombers flying low over the huge city.

Tokyo, Kobe, and Yokohama received moderate damage.

An hour later, the last plane, Number 16, left the city behind and put on full power to reach the coast and China before the sun set.

At that time, steaming north of Formosa, flushed with the heady string of victories, Admiral Nagumo's flagship, *Akagi*, and the Second Carrier Division of *Soryu* and *Hiryu* received a message ordering them to head for the east coast of Honshu and find the American carriers. With that, Yamamoto's carefully planned schedule was interrupted. Battleships, cruisers, and destroyers all around the Marianas, Carolines, Philippines, and China Sea, turned north to locate the enemy task force. On Shikoku, Honshu, and Hokkaido, squadrons of fighters and bombers screamed into the sky. It was assumed that the American ships would have another full day of steaming before they could launch. But Halsey was already headed home.

After leaving the coast of Japan behind, the B-25s went to full power to put as much distance between themselves and the angry enemy as possible. But luck ran out for some crews. Captain Edward York, piloting Plane 8, had been informed by his crew chief of a fuel leak and they would never reach the Chinese coast. York chose to turn west and try for the Soviet port of Vladivostok. He and his crew were interned by the neutral Russians for several months.

Plane 6 ditched in the dark off the Chinese coast, drowning two crewmen. The other three were captured. Only one survived the war.

Plane 16, the last to launch, ran out of fuel over China. The crew bailed out and was captured. Pilot Bill Farrow and engineer Hal Spaatz were executed in October.

Doolittle's crew bailed out and survived with the help of Chinese guerillas, as did most of the Raiders. Ted Lawson's Plane 7 crashed in the surf and all but one of the crew suffered terrible injuries. They were found by Chinese guerillas and eventually made it back to the States.

An unknown but clever sailor on *Enterprise* wrote a "business letter" to Prime Minister Hideki Tojo. It read, in part:

Americans Incorporated
United States of America
20 April 1942

Dishonorable Sir,

It gives me great pleasure to inform you, that in accordance with the terms of the contract accepted by us on 7 December 1941, the first consignment of scrap metal has been delivered to your city. You understand, delivery conditions being what they are, it is necessary for us to effect delivery by air. While we are cognizant of the fact that this method of delivery is not to your liking, nevertheless, we are required by the terms of the contract and will continue to effect delivery by any means at our disposal of all scrap metal contracted for.

As a concession, however, we will not ask for payment until such time as you inform us that you have received sufficient material to suit your needs. I wish to remind you that we are in a position to continue deliveries for years to come. We will, in the future, endeavor to spread same over as wide an area as possible in order that you receive the full benefit of this superior material.

You entered into this contract of your own volition, and must pay the price of same in full.

*John Q. Citizen, Representative,
Americans, Incorporated*

There are many other examples of the rising spirit of pride and devotion to duty, but this letter serves as good as any. The Doolittle Raid had virtually no tactical or strategic significance in the Pacific War, but it had far-reaching consequences on both sides of the ocean.

During a lecture detailing the immense value of codebreaking and traffic analysis, historian and author Stephen Ambrose was asked, "If it was so important, why didn't they use it to shorten the war?"

The answer, of course, was "They did."

The Office of Naval Security Communications at the Navy Department in Washington was designated OP-20G. This unit oversaw all the naval communications in both the Atlantic and Pacific.

There were several radio listening stations in a great arc across the Pacific, such as FOX in San Francisco, CAST on Corregidor in the Philippines, ITEM in Imperial Beach near San Diego, and others in Washington, Panama, Australia, and the Aleutians. For instance, each station was designated COM 12, 14, and 16, for the Twelfth, Fourteenth, and Sixteenth Naval Districts in San Francisco, Hawaii, and the Philippines.

When Singapore and the Philippines fell, the British moved their station to Columbo, Sri Lanka, and CAST was moved to Melbourne, Australia. The two relocated high-frequency radio direction finding stations provided valuable information on the First Air Fleet's movements in the Indian Ocean.

In the basement of the Fourteenth Naval District Headquarters in Pearl Harbor, close to the Navy Yard, was a large windowless room accessible only to those with the right credentials. Under buzzing fluorescent lighting were dozens of plain wooden desks in long, orderly rows. But the room's atmosphere—stuffy, reeking of cigarette smoke and stale sweat—was anything but orderly. At every desk sat either a man or woman in navy uniform, but few would have passed inspection. They were bent over typewriters and phones, poring through reams of papers, pulling open file cabinets, and living off cold coffee. It was the epitome of hectic disorder, but the Combat Intelligence Unit, CIU Station HYPO, was probably the most important room in the entire United States Navy. A score of yeomen inserted punch cards into the IBM 405 tabulators, the primitive forerunners of the computer, while others ran off mimeographs.

The constant chatter of typewriters, phones, and adding machines was music to the ears of Commander Joseph J. Rochefort, CINCPAC's codebreaking genius. Often sporting a stained smoking jacket or bathrobe and puffing on a cigarette, Rochefort rarely left the underground room except for important meetings with Layton or Nimitz. Other than rare showers at his quarters, which his staff insisted on, he spent critical periods in his domain, catching short naps on a cot and living on coffee and sandwiches.

COM 14's hand-picked team of cryptanalysts were not the stuff of heroic tales, but they were the men and women who listened to, decoded, translated, and interpreted the thousands of Japanese radio intercepts from all over the Pacific. To the harried but brilliant staff who worked in the CIU, it was called the Dungeon. Yet they knew what went on in that room was as vital to the war effort as building airplanes or landing on enemy beaches.

The primary Imperial Navy code was JN-25, the twenty-fifth in a series that began with JN-1 in the 1920s. Japanese diplomats used a separate code, known to the U.S. as Purple, decoded by the army and navy in 1940 using an electronic system coded MAGIC. The key to decoding JN-25 was the fact that the Japanese language uses syllabic ideographs rather than letters. For instance, Yamamoto is not made up of eight letters, but four syllables, Ya-ma-mo-to. This, along with the far smaller number of vowels compared to consonants, made breaking Japanese codes easier.

Based on roughly 45,000 five-number groups, the JN codes were essentially substitutions for specific words or phrases to be sent in a message. The only way to solve the code was to have a team of intelligent, quick-minded, highly curious men and women, the kind who, as one later said, "can do crossword puzzles in ink in ten minutes." They were people who did not mind working in the Dungeon, and could remember bits and pieces of messages from days or weeks ago, providing a clue to solving a word or sentence in a later message.

The process, commonly called cryptanalysis, was known as Signals Intelligence.

While extremely complex in practice, the process was simple in concept. The IBM tabulators made it somewhat easier, since they could run through and compare the more than one thousand IJN messages intercepted daily. The rattling machines were separated from the team by a soundproof wall.

When certain five-number groups turned up in more than one message, it could be compared with known transmissions, giving more clues as to its origin and meaning.

The CIU analysts soon learned to recognize the "fist" of certain Japanese senders. Some had a particular rhythm to their Morse code, as distinctive as fingerprints. Knowing what ship or base station that operator was assigned to gave Rochefort clues to further analysis. For example, if a radio operator known to be on *Akagi* suddenly transmitted from a location where *Akagi* was known not to be, it meant the radio operator had been assigned to a new ship, providing a clue to the composition of a task force. By using radio direction and triangulation, the CIU could roughly track ships and task forces on the move, giving more information to the analysts.

If a carrier division was paired with an amphibious unit, that meant a landing. Since most Japanese fleet divisions, with the exception of destroyers, usually remained together, knowing where *Soryu* was would probably also be the location of *Hiryu* and specific battleships and cruisers. Bit by bit, pieces of Yamamoto's complex puzzle came together until a picture began to emerge. Every snippet of information was saved and dissected for future use.

The communications blackout imposed by the new code when it was instituted just before Pearl Harbor caused the CIU team great worry. They were anxious to avoid any more disasters, and the string of Japanese victories only heightened the stress. Admiral Ernest King was concerned that Australia was Yamamoto's next target, so the CIU looked for signs of that being the case.

Then in mid-March, the IJN included additional additives to the JN-25, designated JN-25B, or Baker, by OP-20G. Because sending thousands of copies of the new code books to the ships, bases, and commands all over the widening Japanese sphere of influence was a huge task, not all the operators had the new code. At first JN-25B threw HYPO and OP-20G into turmoil until some Japanese radio operators began using the old and new codes together. Since HYPO could read most of the standard JN-25, it was a fairly simple matter to transpose it onto the new JN-25B messages.

By late March, CIU had decoded about ten percent of the JN-25B code. While this hardly allowed them to read IJN messages verbatim, it did give the men and women in the Dungeon some idea of what Yamamoto was planning. Several two-letter codes kept popping up, such as MO and a few others. It did not require much imagination to guess that MO stood for Port Moresby. From there Rochefort's team began looking through old messages for other occurrences of that code and, more importantly, what operations orders and fleets were associated with them. Since every ship had its own call sign, this gave solid data regarding which divisions and commanders were involved.

The value of such work has often been underrated by those who believe naval victories depend on having more ships, more planes, and bigger guns. But knowing where and when to send them was the key to victory.

The First Blow—Coral Sea

> "The battlefield is a scene of constant chaos. The winner will be the one who controls that chaos, both his own and the enemies."
> —NAPOLEON BONAPARTE

Admiral Wilson Brown's TF 11 launched air strikes on the newly established Japanese beachheads at Lae and Salamaua on New Guinea. Two days later, bombers and fighters from Australia flew over the towering Owen Stanley Range to bomb Rabaul, where they sank a minesweeper and two auxiliary ships.

On April 3, Nimitz relieved Brown of command of TF 11 and recalled him to Pearl for medical reasons. Rear Admiral Aubrey Fitch, who commanded *Saratoga* when the carrier was torpedoed on January 10, became the new commander. Unlike Brown and Fletcher, Fitch was an aviator, and like Halsey, he was suited to command a carrier task force.

Fitch was still in the southern Pacific, keeping clear of land-based air attacks, when, on April 19, Nimitz sent word to Fitch to join Admiral Jack Fletcher's TF 17 near New Caledonia.

Lexington and her escorts continued south across the equator, where the so-called Polliwogs, men who had never "crossed the Line" before, underwent an old and often bizarre ceremony to become "Exalted Shellbacks in King Neptune's Kingdom."

Now that they were in the South Pacific, the late-winter air grew warmer and more humid with each passing mile. The radars were on constant alert while the Wildcats flew patrols around the task force.

Rochefort, who reported to Captain Edwin Layton, Nimitz's intelligence chief, rarely had any contact with the Navy Department. So when he received direct communication from Admiral King in Washington in late April, he was astonished and not a little intimidated. King, in his usual direct style, went "under Nimitz and Layton to demand that the CIU provide a long-range estimate of Japanese intentions." Nimitz, aware of this, was piqued but chose not to make an issue of the irregular order. He too wanted that information, and it did not matter who originated the order.

Based on his team's work with the JN-25 and JN-25B codes, of which they could read as much as fifteen percent, Rochefort replied via Layton, that:

1. The air and amphibious fleets in the Indian Ocean were moving east.
2. That Australia did not appear to be at risk of invasion.
3. That an operation involving aircraft carriers, battleships, cruisers, and amphibious forces were converging around Rabaul on the northern tip of New Britain.
4. Further operations in the Central Pacific were being discussed but not yet known.

Rochefort was remarkably prophetic in his conclusions. Item number three was the planned strikes and landings at Port Moresby on the eastern tip of New Guinea. That was the "MO" his people had heard in several messages.

King was unconvinced, but Nimitz, the man who made the operational decisions in the Pacific, was. Port Moresby was only 300 miles from Australia, making it an important jumping-off point for further southwestern Pacific objectives.

Further intercepts revealed that at least one Japanese infantry division based at Truk in the Caroline Islands had left and appeared to be headed to Rabaul. The convergence of so much naval, air, and infantry strength indicated a major operation.

On April 29, TF 11 entered the northern Coral Sea, a body of water so azure it was considered the most beautiful ocean in the world. Nestled like a bright blue sapphire between New Guinea, the Solomons, and New Caledonia, the Coral Sea covered over 1.8 million square miles and included the lush green palm-shaded islands along Australia's Great Barrier Reef.

Rochefort uncovered an unexpected benefit of the Doolittle Raid. The ships sent on the fruitless chase for Halsey had to return to Japan to refuel, which left them out of the next operation. The only heavy carriers available were the Fifth Carrier Division with *Shokaku* and *Zuikaku*, sent along with the Fifth Cruiser Division to join Vice Admiral Shigeyoshi Inoue's Fourth Fleet at Rabaul. Further intercepts were picked up on April 24 concerning the MO Strike Force and the MO Occupation Force. It was almost definite that the big carriers would support landings at Port Moresby.

Then the CIU team examined another intercept from the Combined Fleet and decoded it almost completely. "The MO Striking Force will launch an attack from the southeast on bases in Moresby area on X-3 Day and X-2 Day. This order is in effect until the operation is successfully completed. Commence preparations."

By using data regarding the distance between Rabaul and Moresby and how fast the ships could travel, CIU deduced the attack would begin on May 10. The attack was actually scheduled for May 7, but the accuracy was uncanny.

Layton wrote, "If it had not been for radio intelligence, the first we would have learned of the Coral Sea would have been a victory broadcast from Tokyo."

Then on April 25, Nimitz was summoned to San Francisco for a face-to-face meeting with King. Annoyed at leaving at such a dangerous time, Nimitz flew to meet with the CNO. King expressed dissatisfaction with Jack Fletcher, who was to be in command of the newly constituted TF 17 with *Lexington* and *Yorktown*. King felt Fletcher, based on his lackluster performance at Jaluit in the Marshalls, was not aggressive enough.

Nimitz, who had to agree, said he could not remove Fletcher at this time. They would have to wait and see what happened. The CINCPAC immediately returned to Pearl and went into high gear, contacting Fitch and Fletcher on *Lexington* and *Yorktown*. He also sent Halsey a message to join with the others. But *Enterprise* and *Hornet*, which had returned to Pearl on April 25 after the Doolittle Raid, required five days of reprovisioning. Unable to leave Pearl until April 30, Halsey's two carriers would not join TF 17, more than 3,500 miles distant, until too late to affect the coming battle. While Nimitz was certain of what Rochefort had concluded, he was uncertain that two carriers would be enough to stop the Port Moresby invasion.

As naval historian Samuel Eliot Morison remarked, "to know your enemy's intentions is fine, but that does not always mean that you can stop him."

Nimitz considered contacting MacArthur in Brisbane to request that the more than 300 medium and heavy bombers in Australia be sent to find and bomb Inoue's invasion fleet. But Chief of Staff General Marshall had put them under MacArthur's control, who did not want to risk any of his air force for a navy operation. His sole objective was to land on New Guinea and begin his journey back to the Philippines.

In any case, high-altitude bombers were ill-suited for bombing fast-maneuvering warships. This was proven a month later at Midway, in stark contrast to the extravagant claims of the U.S. Army flyers.

Nimitz and his Pacific Fleet were on their own.

He did have some navy reconnaissance assets in the area and planned to use them. The seaplane tender *Tangiers*, with twelve PBY Catalinas, was at Numea in New Caledonia along with two squadrons of Army P-40 Warhawks. They had arrived in April with 22,000 troops to anchor this flank of the Australians in the Solomons.

More American troops were headed for Tonga, south of Samoa, where they, along with four New Zealand destroyers, would attempt to cut off any unexpected Japanese moves south. Even though he had never before juggled so many balls at one time, Nimitz managed well.

Meanwhile, Admiral Shigeyoshi Inoue planned to use the landings on New Guinea to act as bait for the single American carrier he believed was in the area. While he thought it to be *Yorktown*, it was in fact Fitch's *Lexington*.

With the two big carriers under Rear Admiral Chuichi Hara, *Zuikaku* and *Shokaku* on one flank and the light carrier *Shoho* under Rear Admiral Aritomo Goto on the other, he planned to catch the U.S. flattop in between. Of course he did not know Nimitz was already ahead of him and that two carriers were converging on his fleet. Had he known Halsey was also being readied to come to the party, he might have reconsidered. But the Bushido code would not have permitted that.

On the morning of May 1, at 16 degrees South Latitude and 162 degrees East Longitude, about 300 miles north of New Caledonia, *Yorktown* and *Lexington* rendezvoused at the location designated "Point Acorn."

Yorktown was the newer of the two carriers, yet the beloved Lady Lex was larger, with more aircraft. Together the newly designated TF 17 under Fletcher continued south to find the enemy invasion fleet. The excellent work at Station HYPO made it possible for TF 17 to be in place in the nick of time.

The next day, the Fifth Carrier Division left Truk Lagoon in the Caroline Islands, bound for the Coral Sea. With them were three heavy cruisers and seventeen destroyers. Auxiliary ships, minesweepers, submarines, seaplane tenders, sub chasers, and transports also accompanied the carriers.

That same day, Takeo Takagi was promoted to vice admiral and placed in overall command of Operation MO. Takagi was already infamous to the now-defunct ABDACOM. His ships had sunk the *Houston* and *Perth*.

Back in Pearl, Nimitz listened to Layton and Rochefort, who wore wrinkled but regulation khakis. They knew CINCPAC already had a lot on his mind—there were indications of something else in the wind. Rochefort was hearing the codes AO and MI in several intercepts at HYPO. It was like assembling a jigsaw puzzle but one in which the picture was a mystery. They discussed the possibilities. The Aleutians, probably, and the mention of that new super battleship *Yamato*, now serving as Yamamoto's flagship, was to be included. That was ominous. But for now, the Coral Sea occupied Nimitz.

Admiral King was not making his work any easier, literally "breathing down our necks every day," as Nimitz wrote later.

Vice Admiral Frank "Jack" Fletcher, a crusty Iowan with a pinched face like a bank examiner, had not impressed King. His less-than-spectacular conduct at Jaluit was only one strike against him. Fletcher had been in command of *Saratoga*'s task force to reinforce Wake Island and had not moved fast enough to reach the Marines before they were overrun. This was not totally his fault, since bad weather hampered underway refueling.

As commander of TF 17, he was poised for action in the northern Coral Sea. One option open to him was a preemptive air strike on Rabaul, where Vice Admiral Takagi's strike fleet was assembling. This might have forced the Japanese to alter or even cancel their plans for Port Moresby. But that was not Fletcher's way.

He preferred to let the enemy come to him. To be fair, Fletcher was an experienced blue-water sailor and a graduate of Annapolis and the Naval War College. He had served on all classes of surface ships but was not an aviator like Halsey and Fitch. He put his staff to the task of devising a battle plan when the enemy arrived.

Fletcher's greatest concern at the moment was fuel. Like any good commander, he wanted his ships to have plenty of fuel for any contingency. But to pump close to ten million gallons of oil into nearly twenty-five ships would take at least three days. He signaled the oilers *Neosho* and *Cimmaron* to begin with the carriers, then the cruisers, and finally the destroyers.

But Takagi and Inoue were not going to wait for their enemy to finish refueling, and on May 3, the first part of Operation MO went into effect as Japanese naval infantry landed at Tulagi in the Solomons. An airfield was constructed on Guadalcanal, from where the Imperial Army could patrol the Solomons.

The invasions were virtually uncontested by the Australians. Admiral Goto, with the light carrier *Shoho*, sent planes to mount air strikes on the Australian positions at Port Moresby, then returned to Bougainville to refuel.

After a successful landing, the army divisions would march west over the towering Owen Stanley Range to the west, where the Australians would be overwhelmed. Along with a landing at Tulagi in the Solomons, Operation MO would be supported by the big carriers *Shokaku* and *Zuikaku*. Takagi and Hara, with the three carriers, waited for the Americans to arrive and attack the Tulagi beachhead.

Fletcher finished refueling by May 5 and was ready to meet the enemy. When he learned from Nimitz of the possible landings on Tulagi, he chose to head south to a point a hundred miles off a jungle-choked malarial pesthole called Guadalcanal. Keeping radio silence, he could not inform Fitch on *Lexington* of his movement. Fitch, after finishing his own refueling, steamed to the previously agreed on rendezvous with Fletcher. He turned north, away from where Fletcher was headed. Therefore the two carrier forces were widely separated and unable to coordinate when the fighting started. It was only the first of many errors committed by both sides in what was about to become the Battle of the Coral Sea.

Fletcher was most concerned with keeping the enemy from learning where he was. When his scout bombers spotted and bombed a Japanese sub, he was certain the enemy now knew his location. But he was lucky. Bad weather hid the task force, and when Yorktown began launching planes at dawn on May 4, the carrier remained under a rain squall.

Three waves of sixty planes began bombing the amphibious ships at Tulagi, currently unprotected by *Shoho*. They sank a destroyer and three minesweepers.

On May 5, TF 17 and TF 11 joined up, now accompanied by a combined American-Australian light surface force, TF 44 under Royal Australian Navy Vice Admiral John Crace. With two cruisers, including the *Northampton*-class heavy cruiser *Chicago* and three destroyers, it was MacArthur's sole contribution to navy operations in the Coral Sea.

When Wildcats from TF 11 spotted a big Kawanishi flying boat less than twenty miles from their ship and shot it down, Fletcher again worried about his location being known. But the patrol plane had not been able to report its sighting.

Nimitz radioed Fletcher that Rochefort's CIU team had concluded the Port Moresby landings would be on May 10 with the carriers in support. Once again, Fletcher prudently refueled his ships on May 5 and turned north, leaving *Neosho* and the destroyer *Sims* to wait out of danger.

Inoue correctly assumed that the missing plane had been shot down by U.S. carrier planes. Meanwhile, Takagi's carriers steamed through the channel between Guadalcanal and Rennell, entering the Coral Sea.

The main players were in place. It was May 6, 1942. The first naval battle between aircraft carriers was about to begin.

Later that afternoon, another Kawanishi spotted TF 17 and reported its position to Takagi, who turned south when his own refueling was complete. At that moment he was more than 300 miles from the U.S. force, too far for an air strike. They would not be able to find and bomb them in darkness. He had to get closer and launch a strike at first light.

At dawn on May 7, Fletcher sent Crace's ships, now redesignated TF 17.3, to cover the channel near Jomard Island. While the cruisers would be without air cover and the carriers would lose some of their AAA defenses, Fletcher, in a move King would never have credited, was willing to take the risk. He assumed the Japanese ships were to his north, while Takagi put the Americans to his south. Takagi launched twelve Kates to search to the south and west, while Fletcher sent ten SBD Dauntless scouts to the north and east. The rest of the bombers and fighters prepared to launch at the moment the enemy was sighted. A dozen Betty bombers flew out of Rabaul to add their airborne eyes to the search.

One of *Shokaku*'s scouts, flying out on the western arc of its patrol, reported ships bearing slightly west of south. Takagi acted immediately. But what the scout plane saw were the *Neosho* and the *Sims*, an oiler and a destroyer Fletcher had sent south to await orders.

Eighteen Zeroes, twenty-four Kate torpedo bombers, and thirty-six Val dive bombers launched from *Shokaku* and *Zuikaku* and headed off to hit the enemy ship. At 0820 hours, another scout saw TF 17 and reported it to Inoue at Rabaul, who passed it on to Takagi. The Japanese had won the search race.

Ordering the strike force to continue onto the two ships to the south, Takagi moved the carriers northwest to close on TF 17. Meanwhile, Lieutenant Commander Kakuichi Takahashi, a veteran of Pearl Harbor, realized the two ships spotted earlier were not carriers. He left the dive bombers to deal with the oiler and destroyer while he turned back to his own task force.

Sims, while filling the sky with AAA bursts, was hit by three bombs and sank with only fourteen survivors. *Neosho*, now defenseless, was hit seven times and burned. Her captain radioed Fletcher that she was under attack, but a garbled transmission gave incorrect coordinates. The ship burned and wallowed for four days before the destroyer *Henley* rescued the 114 survivors. One of her crew, Chief Petty Officer Oscar Peterson, while badly wounded, worked tirelessly to save his ship. He posthumously received the Medal of Honor.

At 0824, a *Yorktown* scout spotted Goto's force, with *Shoho* screening the invasion force about 240 miles northwest of TF 17. But due to yet another communications error in coding from the scout, Fletcher thought his plane had found the *Zuikaku* and *Shokaku*.

This was one of the moments where both admirals made the same mistake.

Both *Lexington* and *Yorktown* launched their strike forces, consisting of eighteen Wildcats, twenty-two Devastators, and fifty-three Dauntlesses headed for that position at 1013 hours.

At that moment, Takagi's carrier force was well to the east of TF 17. The comedy of errors continued on both sides.

At 1047, the U.S. strike force found the small *Shoho* and deployed for the attack. The light carrier had six fighters up, but the rest of her air group was below on the hangar deck being readied for their own strike on the U.S. carriers. *Lexington*'s Dauntlesses and Devastators made a well-coordinated attack on the twisting carrier, putting four Mark 10 aerial torpedoes into her hull and two 500-pound bombs in the flight deck. This attack badly mauled *Shoho*, and *Yorktown*'s bombers moved in to finish the job.

At least eleven bombs struck the small carrier, along with two more torpedoes. *Shoho* was now a burning wreck that no longer resembled an aircraft carrier.

At this point one of the Second World War's most famous quotes was broadcast by Lieutenant Commander Robert Dixon of *Yorktown*'s Bombing 5: "Scratch one flattop! Signed, Bob."

Langley had been avenged. Japan had lost its first carrier.

By 1430, the bombers had landed, refueled, re-armed, and readied to launch a strike on Port Moresby. When Fletcher learned that his bombers had only found Goto's force and not Takagi's main striking force, he chose to remain under the thick rain squalls. Even if one of his scout planes found the flattops, it would be too late in the day to launch an effective attack.

At Rabaul, Vice Admiral Inoue told Goto to suspend the landings and withdraw to the north while Takagi waited for his bombers to return from the attack on *Sims* and *Neosho*.

Task Force 17 was now only 260 miles west of the two big Japanese carriers. The radio problems plaguing TF 17 were also active in the Japanese fleet. A plane from Rabaul found Crace's TF 17.3 and reported it to Inoue, but the message was garbled.

Takagi believed the American carriers were more than 400 miles away, too far for his planes to reach. Inoue, having at least learned of Crace's cruisers, sent twelve torpedo-armed Bettys, the same type that had sunk *Repulse* and *Prince of Wales*, and nineteen bomb-laden Nells to hit the smaller force.

Admiral Crace was lucky. The bombers moved in but missed with every torpedo and bomb. The bomber pilots claimed to have sunk a *California*-class battleship and damaged another battleship and a cruiser.

TF 17.3 moved south to increase the distance from Rabaul and still be close enough to intercept any surface force coming to aid Goto. But his cruisers were low on fuel. Fletcher, maintaining radio silence, did not tell Crace where he was or where the oiler *Cimmaron* was.

As with many aspects of this confusing battle, Takagi assumed the ships bombed by the Rabaul planes were Fletcher's carriers, and he estimated they would be within striking range around nightfall. He decided to launch and take the risk of his planes coming back in the dark.

At about 1520 hours, the dive bombers returned, and after a hasty refueling and re-arming, *Zuikaku* and *Shokaku* launched twelve dive bombers and fifteen torpedo planes to fly almost directly west at 277 degrees.

Fletcher's ships, still hiding under the rain squalls, picked up the incoming enemy planes on radar a few minutes before 1800 and turned south into the wind to launch eleven Wildcats. The AAA gunners went on full alert. Vectored by radar, the F4F-4s, the newest model, tore into the unsuspecting bombers. Seven Kates spun into the cold sea, followed by a Val. The remaining bombers, unable to see the American carriers in the gloom, turned back.

The confusion spread when the Japanese dive bombers, now flying in near darkness, lost their bearings and queued up to land on *Yorktown*. The AAA gunners corrected this notion, and the shocked pilots sped away to the east. Radar tracked them for about fifty miles, giving Fletcher some good data on the possible location of the enemy carriers.

Admiral Fletcher had had enough of feeling his way around in the dark and ordered Scouting 5 to be ready to conduct a 360-degree search at first light.

At that moment Inoue ordered Takagi to find and sink the U.S. carriers as soon as possible while he postponed the Port Moresby landings five more days to May 12. This in itself was a first—the Imperial Navy never postponed an amphibious campaign because of enemy action.

While the weary Japanese and American airmen tried to catch a few hours of sleep, the enemy admirals planned to find and sink their adversaries in the morning.

So far, the Battle of the Coral Sea was a study in confusion, missed opportunities, poor decisions, and just plain bad luck for both sides.

As the predawn sun turned the indigo sky over the azure sea a pale pink, seven Kates lifted off from *Zuikaku* near Rossel Island and began a sweep of the sea in an arc from 140 to 230 degrees, roughly southeast to southwest, to find the U.S. task force. It was 0615 hours on May 8. Also on the search were more Kawanishi flying boats from Rabaul and more floatplanes from Goto's cruisers.

Twenty minutes later, 180 miles to the southwest, TF 17 launched eighteen SBDs to conduct a thorough search of the area.

At 0820, things began to happen all at once. A Scouting 5 Dauntless spotted *Shokaku* and *Zuikaku* about 210 miles away and reported to Fletcher. Exactly two minutes later, a *Shokaku* Kate found *Lexington* and *Yorktown* and radioed to Hara on *Shokaku*.

At 0915, all four carriers launched their ready fighters and bombers. Lieutenant Commander Takahashi led eighteen Zeroes, thirty-three Vals, and eighteen Kates to the reported enemy position. *Yorktown* and *Lexington*'s fifteen Wildcats, thirty Dauntlesses, and twenty-four Devastators were in the air at the same moment. Identical takeoff times were rare even within a single carrier task force, and to have both fleets launch within moments of one another was remarkable.

An hour and fifteen minutes later, the leading SBD dive bombers found Hara's carriers. *Zuikaku* was under a low rain squall, but *Shokaku* was exposed in the open, about 10,000 yards away. The SBDs climbed to give the slower TBDs time to catch up while the F4Fs stayed close and watched for the Japanese Zeros.

The Dauntlesses screamed down from 12,000 feet and released their bombs on *Shokaku*, which was maneuvering wildly, leaving a long, curving wake and filling the sky with AAA bursts. Two 1,000-pound armor-piercing bombs slammed into her forward flight deck, exploding on the hangar deck below. Fanned by the bow wind, fires raged through the huge steel cavern, but her speed was undiminished. The *Yorktown* torpedo planes failed to hit the carrier. Then *Lexington*'s planes arrived, with one dive bomber hitting the carrier with another heavy bomb. The rest of the bombers went for *Zuikaku*, but none hit the ship lurking under the low cloud cover.

Shokaku could not conduct flight operations with three big holes in her flight deck. Her captain requested permission from the division commander, Hara, and fleet commander, Takagi, to withdraw. With two destroyers escorting her, the big *Shokaku* turned northwest, out of the battle.

Takagi had lost half his carrier strength, but *Zuikaku* could handle her sister's planes.

Two hundred miles away, at 1055 hours, *Lexington*'s radar picked up the incoming Japanese strike force at a range of 65 miles. Nine F4Fs were vectored to intercept, but in yet another error, the fighters were far lower than the Kate torpedo planes, which passed overhead and continued on to their target. Because of the heavy losses the previous night, Lieutenant Commander Shigekazu

Shimazaki, who had led the second wave at Pearl Harbor, could not conduct a normal coordinated attack.

He radioed his planes to split up, with fourteen heading for the larger and closer *Lexington* and four on *Yorktown*. Wildcats shot down one of Shimazaki's Kates, while SBDs brought down three more, a notable feat for a bomber. Zeroes shot down four Dauntlesses.

The Lady Lex came under attack at 1115. *Yorktown*, only 3,000 yards away, joined her consort with a hail of AAA fire from her new 20mm batteries.

Larger and with a bigger turning radius, *Lexington* was bracketed by eight Kates, which put two Type 91 aerial torpedoes into her hull. Three of her boilers were put out of action, and a rent in one of her aviation fuel tanks filled the lower spaces with volatile fumes. Still able to maintain a steady 24 knots, the carrier kept up the fire and shot down four more Kates. *Yorktown*, madly twisting and turning, was missed.

Then Takahashi's dive bombers arrived. Nineteen went for the damaged Lady Lex and fourteen more dove on *Yorktown*. *Lexington* took two bomb hits and several near misses, but *Yorktown*'s Wildcats managed to break up the Vals going for their ship.

Then *Yorktown*'s luck changed for the worse. A single armor-piercing 250-kg bomb tore into her flight deck and exploded four decks below, causing great internal damage. At least ten more bombs detonated close to the ship, denting and stoving in hull plates. Her boilers were damaged, and more than two dozen main hull frames were wrecked. But the carrier not only remained afloat, her gunners brought down two more of Takahashi's dive bombers.

The Japanese broke off, turning back to their own ships. At almost exactly 1200 hours, the fighters and bombers of both fleets passed each other and a fierce but brief air battle ensued. More American and Japanese planes fell, with Takahashi among the dead.

While both *Lexington* and *Yorktown* had been hit on their forward flight decks, they recovered the incoming planes. As for the Japanese, the survivors landed on the remaining *Zuikaku*. The two days of combat had shredded *Zuikaku*'s air group, leaving twenty-four Zeroes, eight Vals, and four Kate's still fit to fly. Takagi learned that his cruisers and destroyers were low on fuel. Ironically, Fletcher was then facing the same problem. But with the sinking of *Neosho*, he had only one oiler left to fuel three task forces.

In the space of three hours, both Fletcher and Takagi had inflicted serious damage to their enemy, shot down several planes, and been severely damaged in turn.

After her damage control crew performed heroic work, *Lexington* was able to steam and perform flight operations. But an explosion of aviation fuel fumes set off by a running generator ripped through her interior, forcing the engineers to head topside. Then two more explosions started huge fires, and by 1730, Captain Forrest Sherman ordered the carrier abandoned. The destroyer *Phelps* moved in to pick up survivors coming down lines to the sea. Admiral Fitch was also picked up. When it was obvious the gallant ship was doomed, Lady Lex was sunk by five torpedoes from the *Phelps*, going down shortly after 1900 hours. Of her crew, 215 went down with her, along with more than thirty planes that could not be launched from the stationary ship.

The most beloved carrier in the United States Navy, the proud Lady Lex, was gone.

Yorktown moved east at a reduced speed, leaving behind a long iridescent trail of oil. Fletcher, who had received a message from Nimitz that the CIU had hinted of possibly two more carriers in addition to the ones he knew of, was not about to tempt fate any longer. He chose to withdraw and link up with Crace's TF 17.3 and rendezvous with his only oiler, *Cimmaron*.

At Rabaul, Vice Admiral Inoue contemplated the ruin of his carefully planned Operation MO. With no carriers to support the landings, he postponed it to July 5. He ordered the damaged *Shokaku* to Japan and *Zuikaku*, with only a remnant of a single air group, back to Rabaul.

His next objective was the island of Nauru, Operation RY, but that would have to be postponed as well. But he believed his carriers had sunk *Yorktown* and a *Saratoga*-class carrier. No matter what, they were out of the way. Yamamoto would be pleased with that, at least.

But Inoue was badly mistaken. Yamamoto, from his new flagship *Yamato* at Hashirajima in Hiroshima Bay, ordered Inoue to turn *Zuikaku* and the remaining surface forces around and attack the U.S. ships. The commander-in-chief also ordered Goto to resume the Port Moresby invasion without naval air support, which was both reckless and desperate.

After refueling, Takagi and Goto spent a fruitless May 9 looking for TF 17. By then Fletcher and Crace had left the Coral Sea, heading east.

Continuing Operation RY to land on Nauru and Ocean Islands, Inoue was frustrated by an old U.S. submarine. The *S-47*, a remnant from the 1920s, sank one of his transports. He changed the date of the landings. With Takagi out looking for the enemy carriers, he had no way to support the Nauru assault.

Then on May 15, Halsey arrived with *Enterprise* and *Hornet*, intending to attack the Nauru invasion force. Nimitz then ordered Halsey to turn back to Pearl when it became apparent Inoue could not conduct the amphibious assault. By turning TF 16 around, Nimitz was sowing the seeds of his plan to protect Midway.

Coral Sea has long been a source of intense study and fascination for naval historians. There were surprising parallels for both sides: the confusion of the first day, launching air strikes on enemy ships that turned out to be something other than the expected carrier force, and the nearly simultaneous launching of aircraft and attacks on the opposing carrier forces. It was a strategic victory for Fletcher, since Inoue had to abandon the Port Moresby landings, and a tactical victory for Takagi since his planes had sunk a big fleet carrier.

But the most important aspect of Coral Sea was that Nagumo, who was even then preparing for the Midway operation, had lost *Shokaku* and virtually all of *Zuikaku*'s air group, reducing the First Air Fleet to four carriers. Yamamoto believed Takagi had sunk two big U.S. carriers, and with *Saratoga* still under repair, only *Enterprise* and *Hornet* remained in the Pacific Fleet.

CHAPTER 12

THE PRINCIPLE OF CALCULATED RISK

> "Never interrupt your enemy while he is making a mistake."
> —Napoleon Bonaparte

The first message Fletcher and Task Force 17 transmitted on the afternoon of May 8, while *Lexington* was still afloat, was "First enemy attack completed, no vital damage our force." That was good news, but soon enough, CINCPAC learned of the loss of Lady Lex. *Yorktown* was badly damaged, although she would reach Pearl without further attacks by planes or submarines. The destroyer *Sims* had been sunk, as had the vital oiler *Neosho*, which had wallowed for four days before ships arrived to take off her survivors.

This left Nimitz with three carriers, and *Yorktown* might require protracted repairs on the mainland. *Saratoga* was still out of commission. *Enterprise* and *Hornet* were left.

This news sent the staff in CINCPAC headquarters at Pearl Harbor into deep gloom. Lady Lex had been the navy's second carrier, and losing her was more than a tactical blow—it was a personal one. While Fletcher's force had sunk a Japanese carrier, the small *Shoho* was hardly compensation for the big *Lexington*.

The avuncular Nimitz tried to cheer up his staff by telling them, "You can bet Yamamoto is hurt too."

While Fletcher and Takagi were blundering around in the Coral Sea, Commander Joseph Rochefort in the Combat Intelligence Unit was assembling information from hundreds of decoded JN-25 intercepts. Japan was planning something big. He passed his conclusions to Captain Edwin Layton, who informed Nimitz that they were certain that an Operation MI, which concerned places coded AF and AO, seemed to be the next objective of Yamamoto's Combined Fleet.

Rochefort was certain it was Midway.

THE PRINCIPLE OF CALCULATED RISK

Nimitz, in an attempt to deceive the Japanese as to where his carriers were, told Halsey to allow his task force to be spotted before returning to Pearl. That happened when a patrol plane from Tulagi saw TF 16 four hundred miles east of the Solomons at 1015 hours on May 15, Tokyo time.

Yamamoto never expected his wild run across the Pacific to go unchallenged for long. Sooner or later the U.S. Pacific Fleet would come out and fight. But he had not reckoned on Nagumo's air fleet missing the vital carriers at Pearl Harbor. That was a serious problem. It was obvious that Nimitz, whom he understood to be a far more capable fleet commander than Kimmel, would use whatever means and ships at his disposal to hit the Imperial Navy as soon as possible.

That had already been proven in the Marshalls, at Marcus and Wake Islands, and of course Tokyo, and seemed to be happening in the Coral Sea, although that operation had not yet concluded. He was certain the big carriers *Shokaku* and *Zuikaku* would be more than enough to deal with the *Saratoga*-class carrier and *Yorktown*.

Vice Admiral Takagi, who tended, like most Japanese carrier officers, to believe his aviators' claims, reported that both American carriers had been sunk.

This was good news when *Yamato* received it, but then a second U.S. carrier task force was sighted by a land-based patrol plane in the northern Coral Sea. That, of course, was TF 16, which Nimitz had *wanted* spotted.

When Yamamoto first proposed an attack on and occupation of Midway in early April, there was some serious opposition. Even though he was far and away the most respected and revered admiral in the Imperial Navy, he had his detractors. Admiral Sadatoshi Tomioka, head of Naval Operations, was strongly opposed, stating that Midway, at 2,500 miles, was too far and remote from Japan and would be too difficult to maintain and defend. It would be under constant attack from long-range bombers from Hawaii. The atoll had no strategic value to Japan, and he even wondered if the U.S. Navy would bother to defend it.

Then Yamamoto, still testing the waters, suggested Midway would be a place from which the navy could then attack and invade Hawaii.

Again Tomioka disagreed. Even if that were so, the Imperial Navy did not have enough ships and planes to carry it out. The fleet was committed to occupying and exploiting the South Pacific and the resource-rich Far East and Dutch East Indies. Hawaii's only use was as a forward base with little strategic value. Even if Midway was taken, the area between the tiny island and the Aleutians to the north was too vast to patrol. Every ship headed to supply Midway would be sunk by U.S. submarines.

After hearing the various objections, Yamamoto, ever the gambler, played his trump card. If the Imperial General Staff did not accept his Operation MI, he would resign. It was the same play he had made before Pearl Harbor, and it had worked then, but just barely.

Now the Navy Ministry and General Staff were backed into the same corner. They had no choice. Yamamoto had led Japan to many victories. He needed free rein to move ahead, no matter how risky the plan.

But Yamamoto appeased the naysayers by outlining his follow-up campaigns for the summer of 1942. After Midway was occupied, the battleships would return to Truk and prepare for the July invasion of New Caledonia and Fiji, which would form the last link of an impenetrable barrier between the United States and Australia. Then Nagumo would launch air strikes on Sydney and other key ports in southeast Australia. Lastly, the carriers would join the battle force at Truk, and, in August, after reprovisioning, would sail east to attack Hawaii.

It is an indicator of how fully the Imperial Navy trusted Yamamoto that this immense and highly speculative plan was accepted. The only compromise Yamamoto would agree to was to mount a simultaneous attack and invasion of the Aleutians. His original plan had been to concentrate everything on Midway. But he agreed and began working with Kuroshima and Genda to lay out the revised Operations MI and AO.

His overriding objective was to destroy what remained of the Pacific Fleet. The apparent sinking of the U.S. task force in the Coral Sea left two dangerous enemy carriers in the Pacific. The commander of the Combined Fleet had to remove the Pacific Fleet's ability to interfere while his own fleet still fought. But time was running out. He had to draw out the carriers to sink them.

The overall plan involved more than 200 ships, even more than the Pearl Harbor attack force. The Combined Fleet had two heavy carrier divisions, the First and Second, along with the Fifth, although *Shokaku* would need repairs and *Zuikaku* needed a new air group. This bears some explanation.

While the surviving aircraft from *Shokaku* had landed on the undamaged *Zuikaku*, which gave her part of an air group, the policy in the IJN did not allow for the transfer of pilots to another ship. In contrast to the more flexible U.S. Navy system, which often shifted or moved air wings from ship to ship depending on need and availability, Japanese pilots and aircrews were organic to one ship.

For this reason *Zuikaku*, otherwise completely ready for combat, would not sail until her own air group was reconstituted.

Carrier Divisions Three and Four, which had smaller carriers like *Hosho*, *Ryujo*, and *Zuiho*, provided air cover for the main force of battleships and cruisers. They were not up to major fleet action, as proven by *Shoho*'s sinking at Port Moresby. Two of them would be assigned to the Aleutians operation.

Yet even with the setback at Port Moresby, Victory Disease still infected the Combined Fleet's officers. Only Yamamoto seemed immune.

As drafted, Operations MI and AO followed a schedule as rigid as everything that had come before. On M Day minus 5, June 2, a cordon of three submarine squadrons would take position between Hawaii and Midway along 21 degrees North Latitude and 152 degrees West Longitude. They were to act as a tripwire to alert Nagumo of any U.S. warships coming out of Pearl. Three submarines modified to communicate with and fuel aircraft would take station at French Frigate Shoals, 500 miles from Oahu. There they were to refuel three of the big Kawanishi flying boats, which would then fly a high-altitude reconnaissance of Lahaina Roads and Pearl Harbor. Since the Japanese consulate and intelligence operation had been eliminated after December 7, the IJN had no way to know what was happening at Pearl.

The Northern Force, under Rear Admiral Kakuji Kakuta with two light carriers, would launch air strikes on Dutch Harbor on M Day minus 1, June 3, and begin the operation, followed the next day by Rear Admiral Boshiro Hosogaya landing his 2,400 troops at Attu and Kiska.

This would force Nimitz to move, presumably sending out his last two carriers to defend the Aleutians. The sub cordon would then attack and reduce the American force.

The main thrust would begin on M Day minus 2, June 4, when Nagumo's carriers would strike Midway from a point about 250 miles to the northwest. Nagumo's carriers would launch two waves of 108 bombers and fighters. At this time there was still hope that *Zuikaku* might reconstitute its air group, giving Nagumo five flattops. Each strike was planned to destroy the airfields, hangars, fuel tanks, radio station, powerhouse, administration buildings, and the seaplane facilities. Then Admiral Raizo Tanaka's twelve transports from Saipan would begin amphibious operations, supported by Admiral Kondo's invasion force. With the four heavy cruisers of Vice Admiral Takeo Kurita shelling the island, the landing of 5,000 troops and their equipment would be accomplished on M Day, June 7.

By then the submarine cordon and Nagumo's planes would have whittled down the American carriers and their screening ships. Yamamoto and the battleships would arrive to finish off the remaining ships with the big guns. Yamamoto and Ugaki were supremely confident in the plan. Within a week of the first strike on Dutch Harbor, Midway would be in Japanese hands and the U.S. Pacific Fleet on the bottom of the ocean. This would give the IJN free rein to continue with the conquest of the Pacific. Admiral Tomioka's objections would no longer be valid.

Operations MI and AO counted on Nimitz reacting exactly as Yamamoto and his brilliant staff planned. It was also hellishly complex. In all, sixteen groups of warships had to follow a precise timetable, with little room for modification in case of bad weather or breakdown.

The preparations in the Combined Fleet did not go unnoticed in Hawaii. According to Layton, by mid-May, certain specifics concerning individual ships and divisions were adding up to an operation in the mid-Pacific. Several ships were turning up at Truk in the Carolines and Saipan in the Marianas, indicating a build-up of naval forces unconnected with the Port Moresby operations.

More intercepts came in at HYPO during the first two weeks of May, each one helping Rochefort and Layton determine the size and shape of the developing picture. On May 2, a message was picked up from Admiral Raizo Tanaka requesting anchorages at Truk for the occupation force for Operation MI. Two days later, an unidentified ship sent a message to Yamamoto that they would be undergoing repairs and be unavailable until May 21, too late to participate in the upcoming campaign. This further supported their opinion that Operation MI was scheduled for early June. The following day, Yamamoto himself requested extra fueling hoses be made ready for Cruiser Divisions Four and Seven, which were part of the MI Occupation support force. This was to be expedited. This was evidence the Imperial Navy would be conducting underway refueling for a long-term sortie.

But where exactly was Operation MI aimed? King and OP-20G in Washington were concerned it was the inevitable invasion of Hawaii, or even the West Coast. But for once, the CNO did not pester Nimitz, understanding that CINCPAC had his hands full. Instead, he continued to read the Signals Intelligence reports that came in via HYPO.

Rochefort further learned on May 6 and 11 that Imperial Navy submarines would be stationed at French Frigate Shoals between Hawaii and Midway. Several subs were to obtain new equipment, allowing them to communicate with and refuel the long-range flying boats that would fly in from the Marshalls. This almost certainly meant a high-altitude reconnaissance of Pearl Harbor, a likely precursor to operations close to Hawaii.

On May 6, Nimitz wrote, "While the operations in the South Pacific are still going on, there it is noted that they now have sufficient forces in the Central Pacific to raid in the Central and North Pacific areas."

The following day, several messages were picked up regarding tabletop war games on board *Yamato*, with all the fleet commanders attending. This was a common practice in the Imperial Navy and was intended to work out timetables for refueling, air patrols, and communications.

The five days of tabletop maneuvers were observed by impartial judges who determined the effectiveness of the attack and defense. In one scenario, the American fleet surprised Nagumo and sank two of his carriers.

Interestingly, Admiral Matome Ugaki, Yamamoto's chief of staff and a rabid supporter of the MI operation, was known to have altered the judges' scores to reflect how he thought the battle should go. He erased three hits on *Akagi*, and the flagship was raised from the dead. Yamamoto was only told of the final outcome, not how it had been reached.

Back in Hawaii, Rochefort learned of a decoded May 12 message from Yamamoto to the Second and Fourth Fleets that the necessary ordnance, bombs, torpedoes, and shells were to be sent to Truk and loaded aboard the warships.

Most revealing was another Yamamoto message the next day, stating that the Combined Fleet ships would be provided with new charts of the mid-Pacific, Hawaii, and its western approaches.

The intercepts kept coming in, revealing that the IJN was completely unaware of, or more likely contemptuous, of U.S. codebreaking abilities. One message on May 15 was only partially deciphered. It called for equipment for the AF landings to be readied for immediate use.

By this time Yamamoto knew *Zuikaku* and *Shokaku* would not go to Midway with Nagumo. It was a heavy blow to lose a third of his newest and best heavy carriers, but four carriers was still twice what Nimitz could send to sea.

On May 16, the First Air Fleet transmitted a message: "As we plan to make attacks from a generally northwest direction, from M minus 2 to M-day inclusive, please send weather [reports] three hours prior to takeoff on said day. On the day of attack we will endeavor to (unintelligible word) from a point 51 miles northwest of AF and move pilots off as soon as possible."

A more disturbing intercept on May 21 mentioned having sufficient planes sent to AF for the follow-up campaign. That could only mean Hawaii itself.

Then the pieces of the puzzle formed a clearer but more disturbing picture. The newest version of the Zero fighters were being delivered to the four carriers, which confirmed *Zuikaku* and *Shokaku* would not be included.

As for the place coded AF, Rochefort recalled a December 8 transmission from Nagumo describing Midway, which used the code AF. The famous ploy to trick the Japanese into revealing this was thought up by one of HYPO's ship plotting officers, Lieutenant Jasper Holms. He suggested they use the underwater telegraph cable to instruct Midway to transmit a message in the clear that the island had problems with its freshwater distillation plant. Station CAST in Melbourne picked this up. And at last, it was confirmed from Wake Island on May 21: AF was short of water.

It was definite. Yamamoto was sending Nagumo and the First Air Fleet to attack Midway.

Layton wrote on May 11, "All indications are that the Japanese are making very detailed plans for the occupation of Midway and also for equipment for use after the island is occupied."

Surprisingly, Admiral Richmond K. Turner, head of King's War Plans Division, in one of his few misjudgments concerning Japanese intentions, insisted that Hawaii and the West Coast were Yamamoto's target.

Rochefort was certain Operation MI would begin sometime between June 1 and 11, but that was not close enough for Nimitz to act upon. He needed an exact date. The last piece of the puzzle was fit into place on May 25, when the tired but determined team in the Dungeon finally broke the Imperial Navy's date code. They confirmed that Midway was to be attacked June 4. The key was the phase of the moon, which would be full on June 4 and 5, giving Nagumo light to conduct night operations.

In one of the only times his smiling team could remember, Rochefort took off his old smoking jacket, went into the washroom to clean up, and emerged wearing his best khakis. He gave them all a lopsided grin and announced he would brief Nimitz personally. A cheer followed him from the room.

Nimitz read over the summary of Operation MI. N Day was to be June 7, Hawaii time.

On M Day minus 4, June 3, the Second Mobile Force, centered on Carrier Division Four with the light carriers *Ryujo* and *Junyo*, would launch air raids on the western Aleutian base at Dutch Harbor, to support landings on Kiska and Attu.

While there would be some benefit for Japan to have a foothold in the far north to prevent any American moves to Japan from that area, Rochefort and Layton agreed the AO operation was largely diversionary. It was meant to distract Nimitz from the attacks on Midway the following day.

The First and Second Carrier Divisions, *Akagi*, *Kaga*, *Soryu*, and *Hiryu*, along with their cruiser and destroyer escorts and oilers, were to steam east to a point where they would turn southeast and begin launching air strikes on Midway on the morning of M Day minus 3, June 4, from the northwest. At least two waves of bombers were to put Midway's air and ground defenses out of action. Yamamoto had learned from the first aborted assault on Wake Island in December.

The air strikes and continuous air cover over Midway would then allow the Occupation Force, under Rear Admiral Raizo Tanaka with the transports and freighters, to land on and secure Midway for further operations in the Hawaiian Islands. Tanaka had an escort of battleships, cruisers, and destroyers to support the landings, more power than Goto had at Port Moresby. Midway would be in Japanese hands on M Day, June 7.

But thanks to the brilliant and tireless work of the CIU team in the Dungeon, by June 1, Admiral Chester Nimitz had a clear understanding of Yamamoto's plan. He now had more forewarning than any admiral had ever enjoyed in the history of naval warfare. The ships and forces involved, their commanders, routes, timetables, and objectives, were laid out with uncanny precision. It was so different from the bewildering haze that had persisted since December 7.

The only part of Operation MI that Nimitz was unaware of was the First Fleet's battleship participation, with Yamamoto in personal command. Seven heavy battleships, including the mighty *Yamato*, would be ready to administer the killing blow to the confused and disorganized Americans. Four older battleships of the Second Fleet under Rear Admiral Nobutake Kondo would be steaming to a point halfway between the Aleutians and Midway to be ready in case the Americans chose to defend the Aleutians instead. Whichever way Nimitz chose to go, the outcome would be the same. The last American carriers would be sunk.

What Layton and Rochefort had assembled was an accurate assessment of the Midway phase of Operation MI. Four to five carriers, three to four battleships, eight to nine cruisers, sixteen to twenty-four destroyers, twelve to fourteen transports, four seaplane tenders, a half-dozen minesweepers, and at least twenty-five submarines.

Even without the addition of the battleship force, TF 16 and 17 were heavily outnumbered. But had Nimitz known more naval strength was being sent to annihilate his fleet, he likely would not have changed his plans. After all, he had the advantage of knowing most of what Yamamoto had in mind.

Nimitz was in virtually the same position as Union General George McClellan had been in September 1862 when, by sheer chance, he was handed a copy of Confederate General Robert E. Lee's General Order No. 191, detailing the route and objectives in the Army of Northern Virginia's invasion of Maryland. It was a stroke of luck that any commander would give his right arm for.

But McClellan, cautious and unsure, threw away the opportunity and failed to destroy Lee's army at Antietam.

Nimitz was not McClellan. He was bold and decisive, moving forward to counter Yamamoto with everything he had. And that meant *everything*. Nimitz was determined that Midway not fall. He would give the small island garrison every advantage, even if it meant scraping the bottom of the navy's, army's, and Marines' barrels. Every available plane and gun would be rushed to Midway.

Captain Cyril Simard, the senior officer on Midway, coordinated the navy defense, using his patrol boats and planes, with air operations officer Captain Logan Ramsey. Ramsey had been at Pearl on the morning of December 7, and after seeing the first Japanese bombs falling, he dashed into the administration building and sent the famous telegram, "Air raid Pearl Harbor! This is no drill!" Now he was Nimitz's point man in planning how to find and attack Nagumo's force before the June 4 attack.

Colonel Harold Shannon had joined the Marine Corps in 1913 and served in Mexico with John Pershing on the expedition to find Pancho Villa and served in France during the Great War. He had been on Midway since September and was probably the one officer most familiar with the island and its vulnerability. He had lost friends at Wake and would not let the same thing happen on Midway. The three officers bent to the task of making Midway a costly target for the Japanese. Unlike Devereux and Cunningham on Wake, they knew Nimitz was sending reinforcements, aircraft, and ships to help.

The former Hawaiian air force, now redesignated the Seventh Air Force under Major General Clarence Tinker, had twenty-seven B-17 Flying Fortresses. Most were being used for long-range patrol while carrying bombs to hit any Japanese ships they found. Nimitz planned to use some of these for the defense of Midway.

Midway was under siege not from the enemy but from Pearl Harbor. Planes and ships arrived to disgorge new personnel, guns, ammunition, fuel, bombs, torpedoes, radio equipment, telephone wire, grenades, emergency and medical supplies, sandbags, barbed wire, and aircraft. Midway's famous Gooney Birds, the black-browed albatrosses, watched impassively as hundreds of men scrambled about, digging pits and trenches, filling sandbags, pouring concrete, and stringing miles of barbed wire along the beaches of Sand and Eastern Islands. AAA guns were placed in revetments while miles of telephone wire linked them to the command post. Drums of aviation fuel were buried while others were placed close to the aircraft, the number of which increased by the day. Midway was no longer a lonely outpost far out in the Pacific. It was now turning into the focus of the navy, army, and Marines, who were determined to prevent it from being another Wake Island.

The problem facing Major Vernon McCall, executive officer of Marine Air Group 22, was that Midway was large enough to support about fifty aircraft, but nothing like what Nimitz was sending. The normal consumption of fuel was about 1,500 gallons per day, enough for the fighters and bombers of MAG 22. The unit consisted of VMF-221's twenty-one Brewster F2A Buffaloes under Major Floyd "Red" Parks, and Major Lofton Henderson's seventeen flyable Vought SB2U Vindicator dive bombers of VMSB-241. There were about 150,000 gallons of fuel in the underground main and reserve storage tanks, along with two 12,000-gallon trucks and a 15,000-gallon barge. About 250 55-gallon drums were dispersed around the field. Sandbags and concrete bunkers protected the planes, but more were coming. Ammo dumps held bombs ranging from 100-pound, 500-pound, and 1,000-pound bombs and about 60,000 rounds of .30- and .50-caliber ammunition.

Midway had the radar that had been sent in mid-1941, the now-obsolete SCR-270B, which did not reveal altitude, but there were no newer sets available. So the operators practiced with the reconnaissance and patrol planes, whose course and altitudes were known.

The first aircraft to arrive on May 23 were twelve PBY Catalina flying boats of VP-44, along with forty officers and eighty enlisted men. Quarters and tents had to be found and erected for the men and new bunkers for the planes, but McCall's biggest concern was the sudden jump in fuel consumption. From a normal 1,500 gallons per day, the long-range patrols of the PBYs boosted that to 8,000 gallons, five times the normal daily use.

Then fifteen Boeing B-17s arrived, along with nineteen Douglas SBD dive bombers and seven new Grumman F4F-4 Wildcat fighters. A battery of 37mm AAA guns of the Marine Third Defense Battalion were placed at key points on both islands in such a way that they could be used for anti-aircraft and shore defense.

Then Carlson's Raiders arrived. Under Marine Major Evans S. Carlson, the Second Marine Raider Battalion had gained fame in China fighting alongside the Nationalist Chinese. Unconventional warfare was their specialty, and they began manufacturing explosives and booby traps to meet the expected Japanese troops.

Then more navy planes came in. Six brand-new Grumman TBF Avengers, the long-awaited replacement for the tired and slow Douglas TBD Devastators, came in from Ford Island. They were the second echelon of *Hornet*'s Torpedo

8, which had just taken delivery of the new planes. Only six were ready for service, and Nimitz, wanting to put them to work right away, sent them to Midway. The rest of Torpedo 8 was on *Hornet* under Lieutenant Commander John Waldron, awaiting their fateful day of combat.

No one on Midway had ever seen a TBF, and the gunners asked what to look for so they would not mistake them for enemy planes. "It looks like a pregnant F4F," they were told. When the big, ponderous blue torpedo planes arrived over the atoll, the gunners held their fire.

Not one of the pilots and aircrew of the new Avengers had ever dropped a torpedo on a ship. The approaching Japanese fleet would give them their first opportunity. Ensign Bert Ernest, one of the new pilots, was determined to do his best. Ernest loved the TBF. With close to ninety hours of flight time, he felt good about the power and speed of the new bomber. "The TBF was much, much faster than the TBD and carried the torpedo internally. We were told that the carriers were protecting the Hawaiian Islands. We shouldn't expect any help from them. We were on our own."

The newly arrived TBF crews had an idea. They affixed wide masking tape to the leading edges of the wings, at about where machine guns would be on a fighter. Then they inked black holes on the tape to appear as gun ports. They hoped the TBF might make some Zero pilot think twice about attacking it. This was borne of desperation and ingenuity. "When you are outnumbered, you will try anything," Ernest commented.

Most bizarre of all, four new Martin B-26 Marauder medium bombers of the 22nd Bomb Group arrived. The Marauder, quickly gaining a reputation as a dangerous but fast bomber, had never seen combat. But here they were, being fitted to carry, of all things, torpedoes.

While the effectiveness of medium bombers carrying torpedoes to sink warships was dramatically proven in December on *Repulse* and *Prince of Wales*, those pilots and crews were specifically trained for the mission. The B-26 crews were beginners.

For McCall, the new planes, particularly the big fuel-gulping Flying Fortresses, doubled, then quadrupled the daily fuel consumption. The island's pumping system was hardly up to the task, and soon it was necessary for the air crews to fill their thirsty tanks by hand from the 55-gallon drums. There were more pilots and aircrews than ground personnel, so they helped with the fueling and maintenance.

By June 1, just when the IJN maintained total radio silence, putting HYPO in a communications vacuum, Midway was as well manned, well defended, and ready as any Pacific base could be. But would it be enough?

Yamamoto, Genda, Kuroshima, and the rest of the officers in the Combined Fleet had drawn up their detailed plans and timetables just as they had done prior to Pearl Harbor. Nowhere in the carefully worked-out grand scheme did the Imperial Navy give any thought to what to do if the United States Navy did not follow the plan.

Nimitz had no intention of cooperating.

His first move was to order Rear Admiral Robert Theobald to form TF 8 and head north to counter the attack on Dutch Harbor. Theobald, who had been in command of the Pacific Fleet's destroyers since December, received five cruisers and ten destroyers for the task. It was all Nimitz could send. His carriers had to be ready for Nagumo at Midway.

Enterprise and Admiral Halsey's task force had been on almost continuous combat operations since early December, except for a few days now and then to let his weary crews go ashore while the ships were reprovisioning. Nimitz felt bad, but he could not let TF 16 remain idle. His biggest problem was *Yorktown*. He had only preliminary reports of her damage. The final assessment would have to wait until she reached Pearl around May 28. He needed that third flight deck, even if it was not in perfect condition.

Yorktown's captain, Elliott Buckmaster, pushed his crew and damaged ship as fast as possible. She reached a sustained speed of 20 knots, not quite enough for air operations. An iridescent slick of oil trailed for ten miles in her wake. During the eighteen days it took her to reach Pearl, her engineers and damage control parties managed to patch the gaping hole in the flight deck, doing so well that it appeared pristine.

Much more had to be done belowdecks. Buckmaster prepared a detailed report of her damage, and on May 25, a hundred miles from Pearl, a plane managed to take off and deliver it to Nimitz. Nimitz ordered the Pearl Harbor Yard superintendent, Captain Claude Gillette, and a team of specialists to fly to *Yorktown* on a PBY and determine how best to get the ship back to sea as soon as possible.

As for TF 16, Admiral Halsey would not be at Midway. During the past two months, the tough old sailor had run himself physically ragged. He had lost about twenty pounds. His uniform, usually neat, hung on his thin frame and his eyes were sunken. He had contracted a serious case of contact dermatitis, which had spread all over his body, and no one could do anything about it. *Enterprise* and *Hornet*, with the cruisers and destroyers comprising TF 16, entered Pearl Harbor at 1100 hours on May 26 and tied up at F2 and F10 on Ford Island. Barges and water hoses began loading, arming, and fueling the ships.

Since they had not expended any ordnance on their run to and from the Coral Sea, no bombs nor torpedoes would be needed. But the crews needed some time on solid ground, the freedom to get drunk and find a willing woman to be with. In twelve-hour shifts, sailors and junior officers went ashore. None knew what was coming, but they probably sensed some urgency in the air.

The two carriers received new aircraft and over 19,500 barrels of fuel oil, while the gasoline lighter YO-24 pumped 82,000 gallons of aviation fuel into their tanks.

Meanwhile, Halsey went to CINCPAC headquarters. He knew his doctor on board *Enterprise* wanted him in the hospital, but he had to report to Nimitz first. When Nimitz saw the emaciated Halsey, he ordered him to the hospital.

Then he said, "Bill, I need you to pick your replacement."

Without pausing in his scratching, the crusty and frustrated old salt said, "Ray Spruance."

At that moment, Vice Admiral Raymond Spruance, commanding Cruiser Division 6 from his flagship *Northampton*, went aboard *Enterprise* to report to his superior. When he learned Halsey was in the hospital, he chose to go to CINCPAC headquarters. There he learned that he, a "black shoe" and big-gun sailor all his professional life, was to command TF 16 in Halsey's place.

Although it appeared odd that CINCPAC would accept him, far junior to several aviation admirals, it was a shrewd move. Spruance, a graduate of Annapolis, was one of the clearest-thinking officers in the navy. His mind worked almost like a computer, analyzing and weighing options and possible outcomes before making a decision. He had followed Halsey since the fall of 1941 and was well acquainted with carrier operation. But most of all, Nimitz wanted a man who, confronted with overwhelming odds against success, would be both aggressive and prudent. Spruance would not charge into battle like Halsey, nor would he be overly cautious like Fletcher. His job was to inflict as much damage to Nagumo's force as possible while safeguarding his own ships and Hawaii.

On the morning of May 27, Japan time, Nagumo's First Carrier Striking Force headed out of the Sea of Japan and past Kyushu. It was Navy Day, the anniversary of Togo's victory at Tsushima in 1905. There were speeches and band concerts, as the cruiser *Nagaro*, followed by a semicircle of ten destroyers, then the heavy cruisers *Tone* and *Chikuma*, the ponderous battleships *Haruna* and *Kagoshima*, and at last the four majestic aircraft carriers headed for the Bungo Strait.

The First Air Fleet steamed to the anchorage at Truk Lagoon where they would refuel and continue on to Midway.

Rear Admiral Ryanosuke Kusaka, Nagumo's chief of staff, requested *Yamato* be included with the First Air Fleet. Her new radios were the best in the fleet and far better than those carried with the striking force. She would provide some warning of U.S. ships in the area. But Ugaki, who jealously guarded the battleships, refused.

At 1352 hours on May 27, a day earlier than expected, the damaged *Yorktown* limped slowly up the channel to the Navy Yard where she was tied up at Berth 16, awaiting her entry into Dry Dock No. 1. Immediately teams of engineers, officers, and surveyors streamed aboard and assessed what had been done to the ship by Japanese bombs on May 8. Captain Buckmaster oversaw the work of putting *Yorktown* back into service. He was determined to see his ship sail again. But he did not see how she could be repaired in less than two weeks.

Fletcher, after 102 days at sea without a drink, wanted only a highball but was ordered to CINCPAC headquarters. Accompanied by Rear Admiral William "Poco" Smith, his chief of staff, he met with Nimitz and Layton. The first order of business was a verbal report on what had happened in the Coral Sea. With Smith's help, Fletcher convinced Nimitz that he had not erred in his conduct and decisions in the battle. This was a relief to Nimitz, who was aware that King did not consider Fletcher aggressive enough for task force command.

"We are going to fix you up right away and send you to Midway," Nimitz told his TF 17 commander.

"Midway?" Fletcher repeated, astonished.

"Yes. Midway," said Nimitz, deadpan. He explained the details of Operation MI and how both TF 16 and 17 would be heading north to attack the Japanese carrier force before they could hit and occupy Midway.

Layton explained that there were three large naval forces headed for Midway—the strike force, the support force, and the occupation force—the first being scheduled to attack early on June 4. The other two would move in and occupy it by June 7.

"But *Yorktown* will need months to be repaired," Fletcher protested. He was stunned when he was told that *Yorktown* would be put back into service in time for the battle.

The worst damage was from the 500-pound armor-piercing bomb that had smashed through the center of the flight deck just aft of the island superstructure. It tore through the galley deck, hanger deck, and decks one and two, before hitting the bulkhead of the forward engine room and exploding. It destroyed six compartments, damaged and bent twenty-four hull frames, and put an elevator out of commission. Two more near misses on both port and starboard dented and ruptured hull plates and frames, allowing fuel oil to leak. While much of the damage was extensive, it was the twisted and torn hull frames and deck beams that were the most critical. These had to be repaired or replaced to prevent fatal weakening of the hull.

After hearing the reports from the yard engineers, Nimitz broke a cardinal rule of safety by voiding the standing rule to pump out the tanks of aviation gasoline before any work could be done on the ship. Pumping out the volatile fuel would cost a full day, time CINCPAC could not afford. At 0645 hours, *Yorktown* slid into the cavernous dry dock, coming to a stop as the huge steel doors closed. Immediately the huge pumps began draining the concrete pit. Even before it was dry, Nimitz and Rear Admiral Edward Furlong, commander of the Navy Yard, were sloshing around under the massive hull, inspecting the damage.

Nimitz, wearing hip waders, turned to Lieutenant Commander H. J. Pfingsta and said in a grave voice, "We must have this ship back in three days."

Suppressing a lump in his throat, the hull repair officer nodded and said, "Yes, sir."

So began one of the most incredible efforts in the history of any navy to repair the crippled *Yorktown* in time to steam to Midway.

As Nimitz climbed the ladder to return to his headquarters, more than 1,400 welders, technicians, electricians, shipfitters, plumbers, and draftsmen went below to begin work. It was a massive job. So much power was required for lighting, generators, pumps, ventilators, arc welding, and cutting that Nimitz made a special request to the head of the Hawaiian Electric Company to divert city power to the yard. For the next two days, Honolulu endured a series of rolling blackouts, which were explained as emergency tests.

Only the most vital spaces and frames were repaired. The ship's service store, soda fountain, and one laundry room were left to be repaired later. The starboard hull and deck frames were dealt with one by one. After cutting torches removed the worst damage, wooden templates were quickly built to match the missing metal. Then each one was taken topside to where a steel plate was cut to the same shape, brought down to the frame, and riveted or welded into place. More than twenty steel beams and bulkheads were replaced in this way.

There was no time for drawings or blueprints. Every part was custom-made and fitted with no regard for neatness. On it went, frame by frame, beam by beam, in cramped, hellishly hot, stinking spaces with only emergency lighting to penetrate the gloom. Ventilators hummed and pumped fresh air into the spaces while men worked shirtless and sweating. The foremen made sure every man drank plenty of water and grabbed one of the hundreds of sandwiches brought down by mess stewards. Injuries were unavoidable, but most men simply wrapped a bandage on the wound and returned to work. It was a heroic effort. They knew *Yorktown* had to be repaired and they would do it no matter what it took in blood, sweat, and toil.

Planes from the mainland brought new hoists for the damaged elevator and new radar and radio equipment. Through the nights, *Yorktown* was caught in a nimbus of bright yard lights as tiny blue sparks from the acetylene torches flared like fireflies. The noise of riveting guns and screeching metal never ceased. The huge ship was slowly coming back to life with the efforts of over a thousand dedicated men. Little effort was made to paint the new steel except to prevent corrosion.

As for the rupture in the hull, Pfingsta chose not to cut the damaged plating out. Instead, his crew manhandled a large steel plate over the rent and welded it tight. Hasty repairs like this could be redone later on the mainland. All they were trying to do was get *Yorktown* back into service.

Besides being able to read the JN-25 code, CINCPAC had one other advantage in communications—the undersea telephone cable connecting Oahu and Midway, which the Japanese could not tap. Nimitz could send instructions and updates to Ramsey and Shannon on the atoll by just picking up the phone.

On the early morning of May 28, Nimitz called his staff and the admirals of TF 16 and 17 for a last conference. Layton outlined what was known of the Japanese plan right down to the timetable.

Nimitz then asked him, "When and where do you estimate we will make first contact with the enemy?"

By this he was referring to the first radar contact of enemy aircraft or ships. Layton, already out on a limb, replied, "I anticipate that first contact will be by our search planes from Midway at 0600 hours, Midway time, 4 June, 325 degrees, Northwest, at a distance of 175 miles."

This was more than Nimitz, Spruance, or Fletcher could have imagined. But as things turned out, Layton was almost inhumanly precise.

It was decided that once the two task forces were clear of Hawaiian waters, they would rendezvous on June 3, about 325 miles northeast of Midway at 32 degrees North Latitude, 173 degrees West Longitude, a place euphorically called "Point Luck."

Here the carriers, under the overall command of Fletcher, could hit the First Air Fleet from the flank, hopefully before its bombers hit Midway. Timing was critical. They had to be close enough to hit Nagumo first but not so close as to invite a certain attack by the same planes that had bombed Pearl Harbor. There was no uncertainty about the skill of Nagumo's "Wild Eagles."

It was hoped that the American strikes could hit Nagumo with armed and fueled planes on the flight decks the moment when they were most vulnerable.

Then Nimitz concluded the meeting by explaining to Spruance and Fletcher that they should be governed by the principle of calculated risk, interpreted to mean the avoidance of exposure of the force to attack by superior enemy forces without good prospect of inflicting, as a result of such exposure, greater damage to the enemy.

This was exactly what Spruance intended to do, and Fletcher did as a matter of course.

The flurry of messages between Hawaii and Washington continued as King read over the dispatches from HYPO. Both King and Nimitz were keenly aware that Operation MI was not solely intended to capture Midway and the Aleutians but to lure the Pacific Fleet out to be destroyed. In this they were in total agreement. But King was still concerned that the West Coast be protected.

As if Nimitz did not have enough to worry about, Army Chief of Staff General Marshall and Secretary of War Henry Stimson were also concerned that Yamamoto might try to launch a raid like that of the Doolittle strike on Los Angeles. A single carrier might launch Betty bombers to hit the city, then fly south to land in Mexico, which still had diplomatic relations with Japan. This was ridiculous, and Nimitz ignored it. There had been absolutely no indication of a carrier being prepared for such an operation, and with *Shokaku* and *Zuikaku* out of action, Nagumo would not spare one from the First Air Fleet.

As to protection for California, Nimitz had two battleship divisions, TF 1 under Admiral William Pye at San Francisco and San Pedro, which included Pearl Harbor survivors *Maryland*, *Pennsylvania*, and *Tennessee*, along with four other battleships and eight destroyers.

Those ships would not come to Midway. Not only did they consume too much precious fuel, they were too slow to keep up with the carriers. He could not spare any planes to cover them. In any case, the battle was to be the same as at the Coral Sea, using only aircraft carriers.

During the week prior to the epic battle, Nimitz sent a minelayer and seaplane tender to French Frigate Shoals, 500 miles northwest of Oahu. This was meant to frustrate Yamamoto's Operation K, where submarines were to refuel flying boats from Kwajalein. Historians of the Battle of Midway have often overooked the significance of this move, often considering it a sideshow of the main event. But this simple precaution prevented the aerial reconnaissance of Pearl Harbor at the beginning of June, leaving Nagumo and Yamamoto in the dark as to the whereabouts of the U.S. carriers and, more importantly, their number.

Spruance's Task Force 16 moved out from Pearl at 0800 hours on May 28, starting with the destroyers and followed by the cruisers at 1015. At 1115, *Enterprise* steamed slowly out of the channel on one boiler while hundreds of men paused in their labors and lined the wharves and shore to cheer the Big E. She was followed at 1235 by *Hornet* under the command of Captain Marc "Pete" Mitscher, a name that would soon become synonymous with fast carriers. When they reached the open sea south of Oahu, they turned to a course of 155 degrees and bent on 25 knots. Steaming 2,000 yards apart and preceded by the destroyers, the only intact carrier task force headed north for Point Luck.

At 0600 on May 29 (May 28 Hawaii time), as TF 16 was leaving Pearl, bells rang on board the dark gray flagship as her moorings were cast off. A hazy plume of smoke rose from *Yamato*'s single funnel, and the hull thrummed with the power of four mighty turbine engines. All around the anchorage in Hiroshima Bay, a score of battleships, cruisers, destroyers, oilers, and minesweepers weighed anchor and turned to face the channel. *Yamato*, led by a semicircle of destroyers, steamed like a great mountain of gray steel with her nine 18.1-inch guns pointing the way into the wide Bungo Strait between Kyushu and Shikoku and turned south.

At least thirteen American subs were known to be around Japan that morning. The destroyers began hammering into the sea with high-frequency sonar to find the hidden subs. They were not so much trying to kill them as to drive them off so the Midway battleship fleet could leave without being tracked.

On board the new battleship, less than five months out of commissioning, Admiral Yamamoto went over the myriad details of his all-out plan to destroy the U.S. Pacific Fleet.

Ahead lay 2,500 miles of open ocean, but most of that was under Japanese control. From the vast anchorages at Truk Lagoon in the Carolines, Nagumo and the First Air Fleet steamed out and headed east to change the world. *Akagi*, the second-oldest carrier in the navy after *Hosho*, led *Kaga* on the starboard column while *Soryu* trailed *Hiryu*. The First Air Fleet had 250 bombers and fighters, while the cruisers carried sixteen floatplanes.

A hundred miles behind them were the ships of Tanaka's Occupation Force, with more than a dozen transports with a screen of cruisers and destroyers in a protective ring. Vice Admiral Nobutake Kondo's support force, consisting of battleships *Kongo* and *Ie*, along with the Sixth Cruiser Division, were in close support to cover the landings. Far to the north Vice Admiral Hosogaya's small carriers *Ryujo* and *Junyo* were ready to launch air strikes on the remote naval base at Dutch Harbor in the Aleutians.

Three hundred miles behind Nagumo was the main body of battleships and cruisers, with Yamamoto himself finally participating in a major fleet action. He was ready to serve his emperor and nation by fulfilling his promise to Prime Minister Konoye in 1940.

At 1100 hours on May 29 the dry dock was flooded and the patched *Yorktown* felt water under her keel again. After being towed to the ten-ten dock, more equipment was hoisted aboard and installed. The elevator and radar were back in working order a few hours later. Fuel oil was pumped into her tanks as hundreds of yard workers continued to work inside her hull.

In a remarkable forty-eight hours, twenty less than Nimitz had insisted on, *Yorktown* had risen from the dead. While she was nowhere near fully repaired, she would be at Point Luck on time, ready to fight.

What *Yorktown* needed at that moment was a new air group. Since *Saratoga* was still on the West Coast, Air Wing 3 was at NAS Kaneohe Bay on eastern Oahu. Their SBDs, TBDs, and F4Fs would be consolidated into Air Wing 5, which had been cut down at the Coral Sea. *Saratoga*'s VF-3 merged with *Yorktown*'s VF-5 under Lieutenant Commander John "Jimmy" Thach, who was already recognized as a premier fighter pilot in the Pacific. His brainchild was the innovative "Thach Weave," a cooperative maneuver between two Wildcats that proved to be deadly against the more nimble Zero.

Instead of the old F4F-3, the new air wing had the F4F-4, which had folding wings, allowing the ship to carry twenty-four of the fighters. Likewise, several of Commander Max Leslie's SBDs and pilots of Bombing 3 and Scouting 3 joined *Yorktown*, as did VT-3's TBD Devastator torpedo planes under Lieutenant Commander Lance "Lem" Massey. The American practice of shifting air wings between carriers proved to be a huge benefit for Nimitz.

Yamamoto was unable to determine what Nimitz was up to. He was certain that only two American carriers were still afloat, but since they were seen in the Coral Sea in early May, they would not have time to be ready when word of the attack on Dutch Harbor sent them racing north.

But then a blow struck the First Air Fleet. Nimitz was not the only admiral faced with a sick subordinate. As *Akagi* steamed eastward toward Midway, Admiral Nagumo learned Commander Mitsuo Fuchida, his Air Wing commander, had to undergo surgery for appendicitis.

Two days later *Akagi*'s air operations officer, the man who had helped plan both the Pearl Harbor and Midway attacks, Commander Minoru Genda, was in Sick Bay with influenza and a high fever. Nagumo, like many Japanese sailors, believed in omens. And this was a bad one. But his inborn pragmatism would not allow him to become despondent. His mission came first. Nagumo had always been a surface ship commander. While an aggressive destroyer division commander, he was often hesitant with the carriers. His failure to launch a third wave at Pearl Harbor was still a stain on his honor and courage. As is now known, Nagumo could have attacked Pearl Harbor repeatedly with impunity.

The Midway air strikes would be led by *Hiryu*'s air wing leader, Lieutenant Joichi Tomonaga, who was more aggressive than Fuchida and not as well liked in the air fleet.

The reborn aircraft carrier *Yorktown* steamed out of the channel on the morning of May 30, preceded by her cruisers and destroyers. With even more enthusiasm than they had shown to *Enterprise* and *Hornet*, thousands of men waved and cheered the carrier as she sailed serenely past the team who had worked a virtual miracle. She would be a nasty surprise for Nagumo, who had every reason to believe her on the bottom of the Coral Sea. Fletcher, Buckmaster, and her crew were bone-tired from three months of combat operations and work, but they were ready to face the enemy.

After rounding Barbers Point, Task Force 17 headed north to join TF 16.

At nearly the same moment, the submarines sent to French Frigate Shoals found two American ships already there. They dared not attack the ships, since that would alert Pearl Harbor of their presence. All they could do was wait and watch. When two PBY Catalina flying boats landed in the lagoon, the commander of submarine *I-123* radioed Kwajalein not to send the planes for the Pearl Harbor reconnaissance. Nagumo was not informed.

The next nail in Yamamoto's complex plan was already hammered in when the extensive submarine cordon arrived late. Even if they had been on time, it would have been too late. The American carriers had passed on June 1, two days earlier. The subs could not warn Nagumo that the U.S. carriers were already waiting for him.

The Aleutians strike went off as planned on June 3, with Dutch Harbor, Kiska, and Attu being bombed. Admiral Theobald's cruisers and destroyers protected themselves since the air attack was only concerned with their land targets. But it was solid proof of Rochefort's analysis of the enemy plan.

At 0530 hours on the morning of June 4, 1942, all the pieces were in place. Task Forces 16 and 17 were at Point Luck. Three hundred miles to the west, Nagumo's First Air Fleet was steaming southeast toward Midway. Kondo and Tanaka were ready to occupy Midway in three days. At 0538, Midway radar picked up the first wave of bombers and fighters. Then a PBY crew saw them heading southeast. The call went out: "Many planes headed Midway."

The Marines were vectored to the location. The fighters of VMF-211 flew at full speed to intercept the 108 Japanese fighters and bombers. In the lead Zero from *Hiryu* was Lieutenant Joichi Tomonaga.

Major Parks found them at 0555, 180 miles out on a heading of 320 degrees. Layton had been only five minutes, five miles, and five degrees off. It was at that moment that Rochefort's team at HYPO had made it possible for Nimitz to see his enemy's cards.

Although the final outcome was three days in the making, the Battle of Midway ended Yamamoto's Wild Run.

The rest, as they say, is history.

EPILOGUE

THE TERRIBLE RESOLVE

"There are only two forces in the world, the sword and the spirit.
In the long run the sword will always be conquered by the spirit."
—NAPOLEON BONAPARTE

The Battle of Midway, fought between June 4 and 7, 1942, has been picked apart and dissected by several noted naval historians, Samuel Eliot Morison, Gordon W. Prange, and Walter Lord among them. This book will not attempt to better their great works, which would require at least three more chapters. Imperial Japan's ambitions to rule the Pacific died in a five-minute cataclysm when three squadrons of SBD dive bombers from *Yorktown* and *Enterprise* screamed from the sky and slammed heavy bombs into the loaded flight decks of *Akagi*, *Kaga*, and *Soryu*. As in the long voyage to Pearl Harbor six months earlier, Nagumo's carriers had been fitted with the highly vulnerable auxiliary fuel tanks to extend their range. In addition to the fueled and armed planes on deck, and the explosive ordnance hastily laid aside, this doomed the pride of the Japanese Navy. All three foundered within hours. Later that day, *Hiryu*, after extracting revenge on the battered *Yorktown*, suffered the same fate. After colliding in the final phase of the battle, two heavy cruisers were severely damaged by U.S. Navy and Marine dive bombers. Not one Japanese soldier set foot on the beaches of Midway.

In the end, *Yorktown*, that gallant lady, was sunk by a Japanese submarine, which also sank the destroyer *Hamann*.

Admiral Spruance had two main tasks. First was to inflict as much damage on the Japanese fleet as possible, and second, to protect Midway. His decision to withdraw after sinking the fourth carrier was criticized by many in the navy and press, but was wise. Nagumo may have lost all four of his carriers, but Kondo still had an intact invasion force and Midway was still vulnerable. Spruance chose to protect Midway, thus preventing Kondo from doing an end run that might have saved the day for Japan.

The battleships Yamamoto had intended to deal the *coup de grace* to Nimitz's fleet never fired a shot. The huge *Yamato* proved a costly mistake and failed to fulfill the promise of her creators.

Yamamoto lost the battle of carriers, airplanes, and wits. Nimitz had proven to be the better tactician and commander. Against all odds, exactly three days short of six months after Pearl Harbor, the American phoenix rose from the ashes. With the sinking of four fleet carriers at Midway and the loss of more than a hundred highly trained and experienced pilots and their planes, the curtain closed on Yamamoto's plans for eradicating the U.S. carriers from the sea.

The question is, how, with all he had going for him, did Yamamoto manage to lose the initiative? Japan started the war with more modern ships, more trained airmen, and better tactics than the United States Navy. The Imperial Navy's admirals, officers, enlisted men, and aircrews were certainly better prepared, trained, equipped, and motivated in the months leading up to and after Pearl Harbor than those in the United States. But even with such an early advantage, Japan lost the Pacific War.

How, then? The word that comes to mind is adaptability. Japan's admirals carefully planned every aspect of an operation down to the day, hour, and minute, the last ton of fuel, the exact bombs to be dropped on each specific target. They were the undisputed masters of campaign tactics.

But what they lacked, in the early stages of the war and until the end, was adaptability and experience in modern warfare. As described earlier, Japan's army had no history of fighting a war with mechanized troops, armor, and massed artillery. But in most of the island campaigns, there were few situations where such tactics would help fight the sea, air, and land assault of the United States Navy, Army, Marines, and Air Force. It would take two years of war in the Pacific before the Imperial Army caught up. Only the Imperial Navy had any numerical and technical advantage in the Pacific. Also, after Midway, the air groups of all four carriers were lost—that is, all the planes and more than half the pilots. With Japan's lengthy pilot training program and its unwise policy of not swapping air groups from carrier to carrier, they were bereft of almost half of their best pilots in one day. From the end of June 1942 until the end of the war, the Imperial Navy's air arm never made up its losses, and the major burden of air support and defense fell on the army.

Any good tactician will not only plan their own moves, but will also plan for any unexpected moves by the enemy. This was not the Imperial Navy way.

The Combined Fleet commanders expected the United States to react exactly as planned. Not surprisingly, Chester Nimitz had no intention of doing so.

The United States Navy, having lost several older battleships at Pearl Harbor, adapted to the situation and changed to carriers and submarines, leaving the battleships to fulfill the new role of pre-invasion bombardment.

Conversely, Japan's senior officers proved woefully unable to react to unexpected moves by the United States Navy. Another Achilles' heel was the secure belief that Nimitz did not know what they were planning. The perfect example is Midway.

It is true that ship and division commanders could better adapt to a changing tactical situation, but they had to follow the overall battle plan. Even with the consequences of a major war in the balance, the Japanese could not break free of their set-piece tactics.

The United States Army and Navy command was far more capable of adapting and reacting to a dynamic battle situation, backed up by excellent cryptanalysis, improved radar, and a huge war industry that took the initiative away from the Japanese in late 1942.

Nimitz drew the line in the sea at a stinking, snake and bug-infested jungle pesthole in the Solomons named Guadalcanal. The Japanese had already brought in troops to build a port and airfield from which they could patrol the region between their bases at Rabaul, Bougainville, and Australia. In a remarkably short time, Nimitz and his admirals assembled a fleet of eighty-two warships and transports, manned by 44,000 men, to bring 16,000 Marines and construction engineers ashore on Guadalcanal at the beginning of August. For the next 100 days, the Navy and Marines would fight dozens of savage land and sea battles to take, fortify, and hold Guadalcanal against Yamamoto's determined efforts to drive them off.

More than 60,000 Marines would fight in that humid hellhole, killing seventy percent of the 31,000 Japanese defenders. For the U.S. Navy, the Guadalcanal campaign presented a steep learning curve. There were severe losses at Savo Island, Santa Cruz, and the Eastern Solomons, but valuable lessons were learned. It was there, by March 1943, that the Japanese finally saw the limits of their power and reach. From then on, they were on the defensive.

As things turned out, that was when Admiral Isoroku Yamamoto, the one man who most understood the Americans, the man who rarely made the mistake of underestimating them, was killed. Yamamoto died over Bougainville on April 18, 1943, exactly a year after the Doolittle Raid, when his plane was shot down by USAAF P-38 Lightnings. It was the end of a remarkable era for the Imperial Navy and a large nail in the coffin of Japan's ambitions to rule the Pacific.

Another aspect of American flexibility was in how campaigns evolved and were executed by 1943. Unlike the Japanese way, with the high command and Combined Fleet working out the objective and targeting right down to the last detail, the United States left much of the actual work to the task forces themselves. When King and the Joint Chiefs decided on an objective, such as Formosa or Okinawa, they consulted with Nimitz, whose recommendations were passed to the area and task force commanders, who turned it over to the task group and ship commanders. At that point, the objective, timing, and targets were given to the air groups and surface ships, who chose how to do the job most effectively. In other words, the U.S. Navy gave the men in the field great leeway to determine how to carry it out. While the Japanese system was fine in the first year of the war, when their enemy was unprepared to stop them, it was worse than useless when the sleeping giant was fully awake and filled with a terrible resolve.

By late 1943, the United States Navy boasted more than two million officers and men, ten times what it had in 1941. More than 21,000 pilots and 125,000 enlisted men in naval aviation served on twenty-nine fleet and light carriers. The latter number would triple by the end of the war. No one in the Imperial Army or Navy, except perhaps Yamamoto, would have believed such numbers were possible.

The American war industry Yamamoto respected had, by the end of 1944, built 30 aircraft carriers, 8 battleships, 55 cruisers, more than 500 destroyers, and 100,000 warplanes. Seabees built fully functional bases, ports, and airfields on scores of islands across the Pacific while scores of huge training camps sprouted like vast communities from coast to coast.

After the fall of Guadalcanal, the Gilberts, the Marshalls, the Carolines, New Guinea, the Philippines, and the Marianas, the outcome was inevitable. American submarines accounted for more than half the Japanese merchant ships sunk during the war, while masses of heavy bombers flew from new bases to rain aerial destruction on Kyushu, Shikoku, and Honshu. City after city was consumed by fire, the oldest primal fear of the Japanese people. Food and oil became scarce, and the rapidly dwindling navy and army could not hold back the Allied juggernaut.

By the spring of 1945, the Greater East Asia Co-prosperity Sphere that was to enrich the empire had withered to the shores of the Home Islands. But defiant as ever, the Imperial Army, whose role was now greater than the navy, chose to unleash the ultimate weapon. The old Samurai code that still infested the Japanese martial spirit reared its head to give birth to the Kamikaze planes, Kaiten human torpedoes, and the final suicide charge of their last super battleship, *Yamato,* in April 1945. Aerial Kamikazes sank about thirty ships and damaged a further 362.

Navy Minister Admiral Mitsumasa Yonai reported to Emperor Hirohito on April 8 and said *Yamato* and four of her escorts were sunk

The emperor's eyes widened in shock. "The fleet," he said hoarsely. "What of the fleet."

Yonai sighed, tears streaming down his face. "There is no fleet, Imperial Highness. The Imperial Japanese Navy no longer exists."

When the surrender was signed in Tokyo Bay on September 2, 1945, aboard the new battleship *Missouri,* the United States Navy boasted more than 5,000 ships, including 98 carriers, 23 battleships, 72 cruisers, 300 submarines, more than 700 destroyers and escorts, and 400,000 aircraft. The industrial might of the United States had done just as Yamamoto had predicted—it had overwhelmed Japan.

Knowing what we do about Yamamoto, he would never have supported such wasteful, useless schemes. Had he lived, the war might well have had a better ending. With the respect he commanded in the Combined Fleet and with Navy Minister Yonai, he might have found a way to end the war with honor.

While he would certainly have worked hard to protect Japan with the remaining fleet assets, Yamamoto's real aim had to be to end a war already lost. He would recommend Japan ask for peace terms with the Western Powers. A return to pre-war lines, a withdrawal from China, and restitutions made to the conquered territories, as distasteful as it would be, was better than the total destruction of Japan, the tens of thousands of dead young men in the Kamikaze corps and the ones who died being chewed up by the advancing Americans. Scores of ships would not have been sunk with the loss of their skilled crews.

If Yamamoto had lived, and if he had convinced the government and army to accept those terms, Hiroshima and Nagasaki might never have happened.

Yamamoto's body was located in the crashed Betty bomber deep in the Bougainville jungle. After being cremated in Papua New Guinea, his remains were divided and placed at the Tama Cemetery in Tokyo and his ancestral burial ground at Nagaoka. He was posthumously awarded the Grand Order of the Chrysanthemum First Class by Emperor Hirohito and promoted to fleet admiral. He was also awarded the Knight's Cross of the Iron Cross with Crossed Swords and Oak Leaves by Nazi Germany, the second-highest award in the Third Reich. Yamamoto would not have been impressed.

Interestingly, the most revered and influential naval commander in the history of Japan was not laid to rest in the Shinto Yasukuni Shrine in Tokyo. Ultimately more than two million of Japan's war dead were enshrined there. Most fell in service to their emperor in the Second World War.

Fleet Admiral Chester W. Nimitz died in January 1966 at Yerba Buena Island in San Francisco Bay just before his eighty-first birthday. He was buried in Golden Gate National Cemetery with full military honors. Beside him lay his wife, and his three longtime friends, Admirals Raymond Spruance, Richmond Kelly Turner, and Charles Lockwood. The plot is the most highly concentrated assemblage of naval luminaries in the world.

The victors of the Pacific War had done their duty, against all odds.

The turning point began when Yamamoto's wild six-month run ended.

GLOSSARY

AAA: Anti-aircraft gun, or anti-aircraft artillery
Air Group: The fighter, bomber, and scout squadrons assigned to an aircraft carrier
BB: Battleship
Bogie or Bogey: Slang term for unidentified radar contact
CA: Heavy cruiser
Call sign: Call name for a base or unit for use in open radio communications
CAP: Carrier Air Patrol
CINCPAC: Commander, U.S. Pacific Fleet (Nimitz)
CL: Light cruiser
COMSUBPAC: Commander, Submarines, Pacific (Lockwood)
CV: Aircraft carrier
CVE: Escort carrier
DD: Destroyer
Degree: 1/360th of a circle
Ditch: To crash-land a plane in the water
Division: The four-plance portion in a Flight
Echelon Formation: A diagonal "ladder" formation. Ex. Right echelon: all planes follow the right and behind the squadron leader
Element: The two-plane portion of a division with one leader and one wingman. Sometimes called a "section."
FMF: Fleet Marine Force
Flight: An eight-plane element of a squadron, usually under the command of a captain
Flight deck: The open deck of an aircraft carrier used for flight operations
Hangar deck: The deck below the flight deck of a carrier, used for storage, transport, maintenance, and repair of aircraft.
Kc: Kilocycles (now Kz for kilohertz)
Knot: Unit of speed used for both aircraft and ships, as well as meterology. A knot is approximately 1.15 milers per hour.

Leader: The command position of a flight, division, or element in formation
LSO: Landing Signal Officer, also known as "Paddles"
Mae West: Standard issue U.S. Navy life preserver, named for the busty Hollywood actress
MCAS: Marine Corps Air Station
Mission: Term used for a squadron's or air group's flight, route, and objective
NAB: Naval Amphibious Base
NAS: Naval Air Station
Nautical mile: Unit of distance for maritime and military use, approximately 6,070 feet or 1.15 statute miles
NCO: Noncommissioned officer, i.e. sergeant
P.A.: Public Address System
Plane captain: A flight deck crew posting on an aircraft carrier who assists the pilot as well as oversees the movement of the aircraft.
Port: Left side, or to the left
Ready Room: A room assigned to a squadron on a carrier, used for briefings.
Revetment: Area for parking an aircraft on a base, usually protected by concrete or sandbags
Section: The two-plane portion of a division with one leader and one wingman. Sometimes called an "element."
Six: Slang term for the six o'clock position behind another aircraft in combat
Sortie: A single flight by a single plane
Squadron: A full unit of pilots and aircraft, usually forty in all
Starboard: Right side, or to the right
TF: Task Force, assembled for a specific campaign
TG: Task Group, or a specialized portion of a Task Force
VF: Navy Fighter Squadron
VFB: Navy Fighter-Bomber Squadron
VFR: Visual Flight Rules
VMF: Marine Fighter Squadron
VMJ: Marine Utility Squadron
VMO: Marine Observation Squadron
VMSB: Marine Scout/Dive Bomber Squadron
VP: Navy Patrol Squadron
Wardroom: Officers' off-duty room, also used for meals and meetings
Wingman: Follows an element leader in flight (see Leader)

APPENDIX

WHAT DID ROOSEVELT KNOW BEFORE PEARL HARBOR? AN OPINION.

Americans love conspiracies. The bigger and more extensive the better, as witnessed by the Lincoln and Kennedy assassinations. Every major event has given rise to conspiracy theories like weeds growing among the truth, but like weeds they almost never enrich the facts.

But once in a while, especially with the vast information superhighway engendered by the internet, some conspiracies have gained some respectability. Among these is the growing belief that President Roosevelt not only knew of the coming attack on Pearl Harbor, but took steps to provoke it.

In September 1940, when campaigning for his fourth term as president, Roosevelt told his audience in Philadelphia, "I will not send your boys to fight in foreign wars." He reiterated this in Boston the following month. This was a brilliant example of official FDR circumlocution. Roosevelt kept his word as far as it went. But if Americans were attacked by one of the Axis Powers, it would no longer be a "foreign war."

Therein lay the key to what may have happened in the months prior to Pearl Harbor.

In recent years, especially after several secret WWII documents were declassified, a rising wave of controversy arose over whether or not Roosevelt and the War Cabinet had known of the Pearl Harbor attack prior to December 7, 1941. One telling account that promoted this view started in 1989 with the release of the BBC-TV documentary *Sacrifice at Pearl Harbor*, directed by Roy Davies.

I saw this program when it was released in the United States the following year, and to be honest, I was much intrigued by the content. It lays out a very plausible scenario that President Roosevelt, along with key members of his cabinet and the War and Navy Departments had received several early and late indications that Japan was preparing to attack Pearl Harbor. Among the compelling points made in the documentary was a letter written to Admiral Kimmel after the war, written by a man who had played poker with several high-ranking Washington officials, including J. Edgar Hoover of the FBI. In the letter, Hoover is said to have remarked that for the last few months and just prior to the attack, "we had indicators it was coming. In fact, Roosevelt also knew of it." Hoover was told not to mention this information to anyone at all and to let the president handle it his way.

Another powerful indicator was when Associated Press journalist Joseph Leib, Washington station chief, was contacted by Secretary of State Cordell Hull to meet in Lafayette Park just prior to the weekend of November 30. Hull had a good relationship with Lieb and wanted someone to know that "the Japanese are going to attack Pearl Harbor on the weekend and he had to tell someone."

Lieb put the word out on the AP wire, but the only paper that picked it up was the *Honolulu Advertiser*, which indicated the attack would come on the weekend of November 30.

Station FOX, one of the twenty-two American, British, and Dutch listening stations around the Pacific, was located on the top floor of 717 Market Street in San Francisco. It was tracking Nagumo's fleet as it moved east across the Pacific. Navy radio specialist Robert Ogg was able to track them right up to the point where the fleet turned south near Midway. This was passed up to OP-20G in Washington but nothing was done.

When Roosevelt read the decrypted fourteen-part ultimatum the night before Nomura and Kurusu were to deliver it to Hull, he said, "This means war!" But he made no effort to warn his Pacific commanders.

There are many other compelling points in the program, but must still be considered circumstantial. I recommend the reader find it on YouTube and judge for themselves.

The second wave of controversy began when the Navy Department declassified several documents in the 1990s, one of which was known as the Eight Actions Memo. First drafted on October 7, 1940, by Commander Arthur McCollum, who worked the Far East Desk at OP-20G in Washington, it was a list of political, military, and economic moves to be taken that would ensure that Japan would be forced to take overt military actions against the United States.

McCollum, having spent much of his career at the U.S. Embassy in Tokyo, was an avid observer of the Japanese people, government, and military. It was he who predicted the rise of Isoroku Yamamoto as fleet commander. He well knew the growing power of the Japanese right-wingers and that they would certainly consider the United States to be their most dangerous adversary in a Pacific War. This was while the isolationists in congress and the country were doing everything possible to keep the U.S. out of any foreign war.

APPENDIX

War was almost inevitable but it could not come at a date of Japan's choosing and convenience. This sounds both rash and even traitorous, but McCollum had a logical method to his madness. His memo, presented to his superiors in OP-20G and sent up the chain to Secretary Knox and Roosevelt, began with, "It is not believed that in the present state of political opinion the United States government is capable of declaring war against Japan without more ado; and it is barely possible that vigorous action on our part might lead the Japanese to modify their attitude."

He assembled a list of actions that would literally provoke Japan into a rash attack, which could be at a time more suited to American requirements. In addition, an attack on the United States by Japan would, in one blow, silence the isolationists. The following memo was read by FDR in November 1940:

A. Make an arrangement with Britain for the use of British bases in the Pacific, particularly Singapore.
B. Make an arrangement with the Netherlands for the use of base facilities and acquisition of supplies in the Dutch East Indies.
C. Give all possible aid to the Chinese government of Chiang Kai-shek.
D. Send a division of long-range heavy cruisers to the Orient, Philippines, or Singapore.
E. Send two divisions of submarines to the Orient.
F. Keep the main strength of the U.S. fleet now in the Pacific[,] in the vicinity of the Hawaiian Islands.
G. Insist that the Dutch refuse to grant Japanese demands for undue economic concessions, particularly oil.
H. Completely embargo all U.S. trade with Japan, in collaboration with a similar embargo.

When the government assembled the list of twelve insiders selected to be informed of the super-secret ULTRA messages generated from intercepts and foreign agencies, the list was broken up into three groups. The president and war cabinet, the Navy Department, and the War Department. Every name on this short list was that of a senior government or military official, none under the rank of admiral or general. Except one. The last name on this extremely exclusive list was Commander Arthur McCollum.

This is very intriguing, since McCollum ran the Far East Desk at the Navy Department's intelligence. He was even privy, through the ULTRA list, to intelligence dealing with Great Britain and Germany. The only reason a lowly

OP-20G commander would be on the list was so he could monitor events in Japan and the Far East imposed by the Eight Actions. He would be able to make recommendations to FDR and the war cabinet. Bear in mind that Admiral Kimmel or General Short were not on the ULTRA list. And it is well established that they, even though Hawaii was in danger, were not given any information.

While there is some dispute that FDR actually instituted these actions, there is no denying that several were carried out, and by the fall of 1941, all eight had been done. Five can be traced directly to FDR. Japan did notice and it certainly added to their paranoia of American interference with their Pacific plans, but since Yamamoto was well along on his campaign by the fall, the Eight Actions probably had little more than diplomatic and economic effects on Japan. This is powerful, if circumstantial, evidence, and author and historian Robert Stinett in his 2000 book, *Day of Deceit: The Truth About FDR and Pearl Harbor*, lays out a strong case for FDR being aware of a direct threat to Pearl Harbor as early as November 1941.

There is no doubt that navy intelligence in Washington was actively reading and decrypting Japanese diplomatic and navy codes right up to to December 7, and even today it is hard to be sure how much was read and examined. But Stinnet makes a good case for the fact that certain captured code books were withheld or altered to prevent the post-Pearl Harbor investigations from learning this fact.

But this is far from the most of it. Ambassador Joseph Grew in Tokyo picked up from a source in the Imperial Palace on November 2 that Hirohito had heard the details of Operation Hawaii and agreed to them. Drew sent one of his best navy intelligence officers, Captain Smith-Hutton, with his wife on a tour of the "beautiful Inland Sea." While on the week-long tour, the officer observed unmistakable evidence of major and advanced IJN amphibious, air, and surface forces. He reported to Grew, who immediately added the details to his next secure dispatch to Washington. Yet no word of this matter reached Hawaii.

But it gets better. Kimmel, working on information from HYPO that the IJN was definitely readying for an attack in the Pacific, on his own initiative, assembled Fleet Plan 191, to conduct war games intended to find out if the U.S. Pacific Fleet could patrol and detect an incoming "enemy" carrier force coming to attack Hawaii, which he was certain was the target regardless of what the Navy Department fed him.

It was a well-conceived plan and a good move on Kimmel's part. He had already determined that any Japanese carrier force headed for an attack on Pearl

APPENDIX

would launch from a site about 200 miles due north of Opana Point over a seamount known as Prokokiev. While his timing was off, CINCPAC had picked the exact point from which the First Air Fleet would launch.

But it came to nothing. Bad weather hampered the exercises, even though a battleship in the "White," or American force, had discovered the USS *Lexington* coming from the north.

Then CNO Stark intervened and ordered that all—that is, every single Allied merchant and naval vessel—was to steer south of the entire Northern Pacific. Kimmel protested, but he had no choice. The Pacific Fleet returned to Pearl just as Nagumo headed out of Hitokapu Bay across the North Pacific.

The seas were to be vacant to "ensure no Japanese force would be intercepted by the U.S. Navy, supposedly to prevent an international incident that might provoke a war. This critical and very obvious point was never brought up during the several investigations into the attack between December 1941 and into 1946. Never mind that a peaceful Imperial Navy had no business being in that region in the first place.

Stark told Kimmel that any attempt to hinder any IJN elements on the open Pacific would result in his court-martial.

Kimmel was trying to protect his base, ships, planes, and personnel but was thwarted by the orders of FDR and Stark.

All in all, a lot of suspicious evidence. Taken as a whole, they point to foreknowledge of the impending attack.

While I do believe FDR deliberately intended to leave Pearl Harbor a ripe target for the Japanese, I would like to point out one intriguing sentence in his famous "Day of Infamy" speech: "It will be recorded that the distance of Hawaii from Japan makes it obvious that the attack was deliberately planned many days or even weeks ago." This is an interesting point, since we know Yamamoto had begun planning as far back as January 1941. Roosevelt had to have believed the Eight Actions had precipitated the attack within the past few months.

And for that reason he may possibly have believed, and certainly hoped, that a hastily executed attack would be debilitating and driven off by normal defenses.

Even if there is no hard fact, sometimes circumstantial evidence carries weight.

I will say that while he had every reason to want the Japanese to attack and infuriate the nation, I don't think he had any conception of how bad it would be. Keeping in mind the Caucasian hubris that the Japanese were little, yellow, bucktoothed copycats, no one seriously thought them a major threat. Witness the weakening of Kimmel's fleet for the Atlantic.

This is logical and is borne out of FDR's shocked reactions to the terrible devastation and loss of life. He was probably assuming the enemy would launch an attack to disable the army air force and navy, but do little serious damage.

I believe Roosevelt took the actions in McCollum's Memo for a few basic reasons. For one thing, the closing paragraph specifically uses the words "If by these means Japan could be led to commit *an overt act of war* [author's italics]" is word for word the same as the infamous November 25 memo by General Marshall to his Pacific commanders: "If hostilities cannot, repeat, cannot be avoided, the United States desires that Japan commit the *first overt act.*"

I admit this is splitting hairs but it is worth keeping in mind.

Did FDR know the attack was coming? Did he permit it in order to inflame the American people and awaken the sleeping giant? I think he did, since there is enough evidence that leans that way.

This is my own opinion, and I will stick by it.

History as always will be the true judge.

Mark Carlson, CL, ACS
San Marcos, California January 2024

ACKNOWLEDGMENTS

I am extremely fortunate to have known many navy, air force, and Marine veterans. One of these was Commander Dean "Dizz" Laird, known for being the only navy fighter pilot to have shot down both German and Japanese planes. Dizz had no direct involvement in Pearl Harbor, or even the Pacific War, until 1944, but he could be considered one of the few Americans to have "attacked" Pearl Harbor. Dizz was employed by Twentieth Century Fox as one of the lead Japanese pilots for the epic film *Tora! Tora! Tora!* in 1969. He related some amusing and memorable moments during his time on Oahu during filming. Dizz died at the age of 101 in 2022, and I will miss him.

I also want to thank a sweet and longtime friend, Bridgette Levinsky, who enjoyed listening to my boring World War II stories. In doing so, she helped me find a better way to write and express myself in word.

The same goes for my older brother David, whose interest in history made him a good sounding board for ideas.

John Newton Powers, a navy veteran and historian, helped greatly in assuring I had the correct information on the Marines and navy personnel in Peking and Shanghai who were often overlooked by historians—the first American POWs of the Second World War. He was an excellent source of information and Marine lore. Thanks, John.

To Gene Eric Salecker, an author and historian, whom I met some years ago while researching the *Sultana* Disaster of 1865, who provided me with some important details of the B-17 flights from California. He was able to interview one of the last survivors of the flight and passed that on to me. He is the author of *Fortress Against the Sun: The B-17 Flying Fortress in the Pacific* and *Disaster on the Mississippi: The Sultana Explosion, April 27, 1865*, both books which I highly recommend.

And finally, to my veteran friends and sources, starting with John W. Finn, USN, VP-14, who was my first Pearl Harbor survivor and Medal of Honor recipient. He brought the Day of Infamy to life for me. Then there was Earl Williams, USAAF, 38th Reconnaissance Squadron, the last living member of the B-17s that arrived over Pearl that Sunday. He was a gold mine of information on that flight and the first months of the war. He was a good man to know. Also thank you to:

Stuart Hedley, USN, USS *West Virginia*
John Murphy, USN, USS *Vestal*
Woody Derby, USN, USS *Nevada*
Ray Richmond, USN, USS *Oklahoma*
Jack Evans, USN, USS *Tennessee*
Donald Stratton, USN, USS *Arizona*
Tom Foreman, USN, USS *Cushing*
Steve Pisanos, USAAF, 352nd Fighter Group
Bob Cardenas, USAF, 44th Bomb Group
Dean Laird, USN, VF-4
Edwin Davidson, USAAF, 96th Bomb Group
Ralph Kling, USAAF
Charles Hughes, USMC, VMF-221
Erwin Wendt, USN, Torpedo Squadron 8, USS *Hornet*
Patric O'Brien, USN, USS *Wasp*
Walter Boyne, USAF
Dean Caswell, USMC
Truman Cobble, USAAF, 310th Bomb Group
Wallace Griffin, USN, VB-9
James Ramage, USN, USS *Enterprise*
David Thatcher, USAAF, 17th Bomb Group, Doolittle Raider
To all these men and so many more, my eternal gratitude.

SELECTED BIBLIOGRAPHY

Ballantyne, Iain. *The Deadly Deep: The Definitive History of Submarine Warfare.* New York: Pegasus Books, 2018.
Butler, John A. *Strike Able-Peter: The Stranding and Salvage of the USS Missouri.* Annapolis: Naval Institute Press, 1995.
Chang, Iris. *The Rape of Nanking: The Forgotten Holocaust of World War II.* New York: Basic Books, Perseus Books, 1997.
Fuller, J.F.C. *A Military History of the Western World, Vol. III: From the American Civil War to the End of World War II.* New York: Plenham Publishing, 1956.
Gamble, Bruce. *Kangaroo Squadron: American Courage in the Darkest Days of World War II.* New York: De Capo Press, 2018.
Herman, Arthur. *Freedom's Forge: How American Business Produced Victory in WWII.* New York: Random House, 2012.
Hornfischer, James D. *Neptune's Inferno: The U.S. Navy at Guadalcanal.* New York: Bantam Books, 2011.
Hornfisher, James D. *The Last Stand of the Tin Can Sailors: The Extraordinary World War II Story of the U.S. Navy's Finest Hour.* New York: Bantam Books, 2004.
Hoyt, Edwin. P. *Blues Skies and Blood: The Battle of the Coral Sea.* New York: Pinnacle Books, 1975.
Hoyt, Edwin. P. *How They Won the War in the Pacific: Nimitz and His Admirals.* New York: Lyons Press, 2000.
Hoyt, Edwin. P. *The Battle of Leyte Gulf.* New York: Pinnacle Books, 1972.
Hoyt, Edwin. P. *Yamamoto: The Man Who Planned Pearl Harbor.* New York: McGraw-Hill, 1990.
Keegan, John. *Intelligence in War: Knowledge of the Enemy from Napoleon to Al-Qaeda.* New York: Vintage Books, 2003.
Layton, Edwin T. *And I Was There: Pearl Harbor and Midway—Breaking the Secrets.* New York: William Morrow, 1985.
Lewin, Ronald. *The American Magic: Codes, Cyphers, and the Defeat of Japan.* New York: Farrar, Straus & Girou, 1982.

Lord, Walter. *Day of Infamy*. New York: Henry Holt and Company, 1957.
Manchester, William. *The Glory and the Dream: A Narrative History of America, 1932–1972*. New York: Bantam, 1973.
Maas, Peter. *The Terrible Hours: The Greatest Submarine Rescue in History*. New York: HarperCollins, 1999.
Mahan, Alfred T. *The Influence of Sea Power Upon History*. New York: Little, Brown and Company, 1890.
Massie, Robert K. *Castles of Steel: Britain, Germany, and the Winning of the Great War at Sea*. New York: Ballantine Books, 2003.
Miller, Donald L. *D-Days in the Pacific*. New York: Simon & Schuster, 2005.
Mrazak, Robert J. *A Dawn Like Thunder: The True Story of Torpedo Squadron Eight*. New York: Back Bay Books, 2008.
Offley, Ed. *The Burning Shore: How Hitler's U-boats Brought War to America*. New York: Basic Books, 2014.
Parkin, Robert Sinclair. *Blood on the Sea: American Destroyers Lost in World War II*. Cambridge: Da Capo Press, 1995.
Phister, Jeff, Thomas Hone, and Paul Goodyear. *Battleship Oklahoma (BB-37)*. Norman: University of Oklahoma Press, 2008.
Potter, E.B. *Nimitz*. Annapolis: Naval Institute Press, 1976.
Prange, Gordon W. *At Dawn We Slept: The Untold Story of Pearl Harbor*. New York: Penguin Books, 1982.
Prange, Gordon W. *December 7, 1941: The Day the Japanese Attacked Pearl Harbor*. New York: Warner Books, 1988.
Prange, Gordon W. *Miracle at Midway*. New York: Penguin Books, 1982.
Sloan, Bill. *Given Up for Dead: America's Heroic Stand at Wake Island*. New York: Bantam Books, 2003.
Sloan, Bill. *The Ultimate Battle: Okinawa 1945—The Last Epic Struggle of World War II*. New York: Simon & Schuster, 2007.
Specter, Ronald H. *Eagle Against the Sun: The American War with Japan*. New York: Free Press, 1985.
Spur, Russell. *A Glorious Way to Die: The Kamikaze Mission of the Battleship Yamato*.
New York: New Market Press, 1981.
Stinnett, Robert B. *Day of Deceit: The Truth about FDR and Pearl Harbor*. New York: Touchstone, 2000.
Stratton, Donald. *All the Gallant Men: The Battleship Arizona at Pearl Harbor*. New York: William Morrow, 2016.

Toland, John. *But Not in Shame: The Six Months After Pearl Harbor*. New York: Ballantine Books, 1961.

Toll, Ian W. *Pacific Crucible: War at Sea in the Pacific, 1941–1942*. New York: W.W. Norton & Company, 2012.

Zullo, Matt. *War in the Pacific: The U.S. Navy's On-the-Roof Gang*. ZooHaus Books, 2021.

INDEX

NOTE: due to the complexity of the narrative, many entries are inclusive or approximate, rather than specific.

IJN denotes Imperial Japanese Navy
IJA denotes Imperial Japanese Army
RAN denotes Royal Australian Navy
RDN denotes Royal Dutch Navy
RN denotes Royal Navy

First Destroyer Squadron (IJN), 95
Eleventh Air Group, 181–82
14th Army (IJA), 237
14th Bomb Squadron, 183
Fourteenth Naval District, 95, 100–101, 110–11, 184, 212, 266–67
Fifteenth Pursuit Group, 93, 132
Sixteenth Naval District, 182
17th Medium Bomb Group, 261
19th Bomb Group, 125, 128–33, 183
2nd Combined Air Corps (IJN/A) 42
20th Fighter Group, 181–83
22nd Army (IJA) 35
22nd Air Flotilla, 189–91
24th Air Flotilla, 216
24th Infantry Division, 93
25th Infantry Division, 93
38th Reconnaissance Squadron, 89, 125, 128–32
396th Medium Bomb Squadron, 232
IV Corps, 237–39
4th Air Force, 234
4th Army, 223–24
4th Army (IJA), 13
4th Fleet (IJN), 228, 287
453 Squadron, RAAF, 189–92
46th Pursuit Squadron, 132, 134
47th Pursuit Squadron, 93, 132–34
5th Bombardment Group, 62, 91
6th Bombardment Group, 236
6th Defense Battalion, 175
6th Submarine Fleet (IJN) 65, 76
7th Air Force, 290
78th Pursuit Squadron, 105
Destroyer division, 80, 94
88th Reconnaissance Squadron, 89, 125, 128–32

ABDACOM, 222–25-228, 272
ABCD Nations, 37–38, 228
Abe, General Nobuyuki, 30
Abukuma (IJN)
    (cruiser), 95
    (destroyer), 268, 287–88, 299, 301, 303
Admiralty Island, 228
Aeda, Lieutenant, 123
Akagi (IJN carrier), 21, 26, 48, 54, 64, 67, 69, 70, 75, 77, 80-81, 96, 99, 112, 115, 122, 226, 263–64, 287, 299, 303
Aichi D3A dive bomber (Val) 26, 28–29, 79–80, 98, 114, 121, 133–34, 275, 277–78
Air Wins, 284-285
    Consisting of Bombing, Fighting, Scouting, Torpedo:
    Air Wing 2, 86
    Air Wing 3, 300
    Air Wing 5, 277, 300
    Air Wing 6, 83, 120, 185-186, 216–19, 259–60
Alameda Naval Air Station, 261
Aleutian Island, 68, 284–86, 301
    Attu, 285, 301
    Dutch Harbor, 285–86, 293, 300–301
    Kiska, 285, 301
Allen, Lieutenant Bruce, 127
Ambrose, Stephen, 266
America First Movement, 30, 50, 61, 87
American Volunteer Group AVG, (Flying Tigers), 53, 221–22, 262
Anders, Lieutenant Arthur, 29
Anders, General William, 29
Angelini, Sergeant Joe, 126–29, 132
Annapolis (Naval Academy), 28, 94, 200, 273
Antares (supply ship), 100
Araki, General Sadao, 25
Arizona (battleship), 19, 87–88, 92, 106, 110, 112–17, 136, 184–85, 206
Army Signal Corps, 69
Arnold, General Henry, 63, 77, 88, 126, 182, 209–210, 261

INDEX

Astoria (cruiser), 196, 209
Atlanta (cruiser), 250
Atlantic Ocean, 50–52
Augusta (cruiser), 202
Austin, Major Gordon, 134
Australia, 15, 182–83, 210, 224, 229, 238, 242–43, 266, 284, 305
   Darwin, 226–28
   Fremantle, 228
   Melbourne, 288
   Sydney, 284
Axis Powers, 52, 54, 61, 20

B-17 Flying Fortress, 52, 63, 89, 105, 110, 125–33, 180-183, 237, 290–92
Baltimore (cruiser), 200
Barber's Point, 120
Barthelmess, Lieutenant Carl, 129–30
Bastogne, 237
Battleship Division 1, 98
Battleship Division, 2, 98
Battleship Division 3, 98
Bellinger, Admiral Patrick, 62, 207, 212
Bellows Field, 53, 93, 125, 206
Bennion, Captain Mervyn, 119
Bergdoll, Lieutenant Charles, 129–30
Best, Lieutenant Commander Richard "Dick," 217–18
Big E. *See Enterprise*
Bismarck (German battleship), 188, 191–92
Bismarck Archipelago, 228, 242
Bismarck Sea, 228
Bogart, Humphery, 91, 253
Bostrom, Lieutenant Frank, 132
Blake, Major Gordon, 126–27, 130
Bletchley Park, 78
Bomb Plot messages, 53, 64, 78, 86
Bombs and Bombsights
   German Boyko, 56
   Norden, 56, 126
Bloch, Admiral Claude, 212
Brandon, Lieutenant Harry, 131
Bratton, Colonel Rufus, 97
Brereton, General Lewis, 89, 125, 179–82, 243
Brewster F2A Buffalo, 189–92, 196
Bristol Blenheim, 18, 291
British Far East Command, 188
Brown, Admiral Wilson, 26, 196, 209, 211, 214, 258, 269
Buckmaster, Captain Elliott, 293

Bureau of Navigation, 202–203, 205
Burma, 52, 88, 176, 188, 197, 210, 222

Cagney, Jimmy, 88
California, 89, 125, 230
   Civilian concerns and preparations, 222–23, 230–31
California (battleship), 92, 113–14, 185, 206
Camp Pendleton, 231
Cannon, Lieutenant George, 175
Cape Hatteras, 236
Carlson, Major Evans, 291–92
Carlson's Raiders, 291–92
Carmichael, Captain Richard, 126, 130–31
Caroline Islands, 10, 176, 228, 270, 272, 286, 306
   Truk Lagoon, 176, 228, 270, 272, 284, 286–87, 294
Carrier Divisions
   First Carrier Division, 48, 67, 227, 284, 288, 299
   Second Carrier Division, 48, 67, 69–70, 73, 196, 227, 264, 284, 288, 299
   Third Carrier Division, 67, 77, 285
   Fourth Carrier Division, 67, 77, 285, 288
   Fifth Carrier Division, 65, 67, 74, 270, 272, 284
Casablanca (film), 91
Cassin (destroyer), 93, 123
Chavez, Seaman 1/C Ray, 95
Chester (cruiser), 211, 213, 217
Chief of Naval Operations, CNO, 51, 54, 205, 211
Chiang Kai-shek, 14–15, 25, 27, 52, 82
Chicago (cruiser), 202, 272
Chicago Daily News, 213
Chicago Tribune, 50
Chinese Air Force, 53
Chinese Nationalist Army, 26–27, 229
Chikuma (IJN cruiser), 95, 97, 197, 294
China, 5–17, 58–59, 70
Churchill, Winston, 52, 192, 251
Cimmaron (oiler), 262, 277, 279
Clapper, Raymond, 59
Clark, Charlie, 124
Kliewer, Lieutenant David, 196
Climb Mount Niitaka, 59, 85–86
Colorado (battleship), 87
Combat Intelligence Unit (CIU), 68, 77, 266–70, 274, 279, 282–83

Cryptanalysis (Signals Intelligence), 266–68, 305
  JN-25, 267–69, 282–83
  Magic (Purple code), 53, 69, 77–78, 86, 267
  Pacific Code Stations, 266
    CAST, 266
    FOX, 26, 312
    HYPO, 68, 266–69, 272, 282, 286–87, 298
    ITEM, 266
    SAIL, 266
Chesapeake (training ship), 200
Cooper, Gary, 88
Construction Battalion (Seabees), 211, 214
Coral Sea, 241, 270, 298
  Battle of, 269–81, 283
CINCPAC, 44, 47, 90, 196, 204, 211, 268–72, 282
Combined Fleet (IJN), 17, 48, 62, 75, 77, 85, 136, 173, 284–87, 292–94
Combined Fleet Order Number 14, 176
Condor (minesweeper), 95, 135
Consolidated PBY Catalina flying boat, 77, 93, 124–25, 174–75, 205–206, 272, 291
Crace, Admiral John, 274–79
Crossbill (minesweeper), 95, 135
Cunningham, Captain Winfield S., 194–97, 290
Curtiss (seaplane tender), 93, 135
Curtiss aircraft
  P-36 Hawk, 93
  P-40 Tomahawk/Warhawk, 51, 93, 123, 130, 132–33, 180–82, 228, 272
  NC-1, 94, 221–22

Derby, Woodrow, 110, 117, 122–23
Detroit (cruiser), 93, 109, 114, 206
Devereux, Major James, 194–97, 290
Dewey, Admiral George, 11–12, 201
DeWit, General John, 223–24, 230–32
Dillinger, John, 109
Dixon, Commander Robert, 276
Doolittle, Colonel James, 261–65
Doolittle Raid, 261–66, 270–71, 298, 305
  Casualties, 265
  Letter to Tojo, 265–66
Doorman, Admiral Karel Willem, 226–27
Douglas Aircraft
  B-18 Bolo Medium Bomber, 232–33

SBD Dauntless, 121, 186, 215–18, 259–60, 275–79, 291–92, 300, 305
TBD Devastator, 215–18, 259–60, 262, 276, 278, 291, 300
Douhet, General Julio, 41
Dougherty, Ensign Jack, 218
Downes (destroyer), 93, 123
Dreadnought (RN battleship), 8
Dutch East India Company, 223
Dutch East Indies, 15, 35, 37, 67, 76, 222, 224–28, 242, 283
  Bali, 224–25, 228
  Batavia, 227
  Borneo, 15, 83, 224, 229
  Java, 227–28
  Java Sea, 76, 222, 224, 227, 260
    Battle of, 227–28
  Makassar Strait, 225
  Molucca Sea, 225
  Sumatra, 224
  Sunda Strait, 227–28
  Surabaya, 225
  Timor, 224–26

Earhart, Amelia, 228
Eaton, Ensign John, 175
Edgars, Dorothy, 86
Eglin Field, 261
Electra (RN destroyer), 227
Elliot, Private George, 103, 126
Elrod, Captain Henry, 195
Elwood Oil Refinery, 231–32
Enterprise (carrier), 83, 86, 88, 106, 120, 135, 185–87, 196, 205, 211–20, 247–59, 262–63, 280–82, 293, 299, 303
Ernest, Ensign Bert, 292
Eta Jima Military Academy, 19, 20–21, 64, 199, 252
Evans, Jack, 116–23
Exeter (RN cruiser), 226–28
Ewa Mooring Mast Field, 9, 108, 120, 133, 206

Far East Air Force (FEAF), 89, 180–82, 183, 228, 237
Farthing, Colonel William, 62
Fickel, General Jacob, 234
Fiji, 211, 213, 241, 284
Filmore, President Millard, 5
Finn, John, 123–25

INDEX

Fisk, Corporal Richard, 115
Fitch, Admiral Aubrey, 269, 271, 274, 279
Fletcher, Admiral Frank, 196–99, 200,
    211–20, 269, 271–82, 295
  Force Z, 189–92
Foreign Ministry, 137
Formosa (Taiwan), 77, 88, 176, 179–82, 243, 306
Forrestal, James, 203–204
Fort, Cornelia, 107
Fort Kamehameha, 220
Fort MacArthur, 234
Fort Shafter, 45, 89, 102–103, 105, 139
French, Colonel Edward, 97
French Indochina (Vietnam), 15–16, 35, 37,
    57–59, 70, 82, 88, 176, 223–24
  Cam Rahm Bay, 237
  Saigon, 59, 176, 188–89
Fuchida, Commander Mitsuo, 64-68, 227, 300
  Appointment to First Air Fleet, 64
  Leading air attack, 67, 75, 78, 80, 99–101,
    105–106, 117, 121, 133, 227
  Special weapons, 64, 74
  Training air crews, 64–65, 67, 74–75
  First Wave, 98–99
  Second Wave, 100–101
Fuki (IJN cruiser), 20
Fukudome, Admiral Shigeru, 39, 41, 49
Furlong, Admiral Edward, 108–109, 296

Genda, Commander Minoru, 41–58, 64–65,
    68–69, 98, 176, 284–85, 301
  Airpower advocate, 41–45, 55
  Battle of Britain witness, 42
  Early career, 41–45
  Midway plan, 284–86, 292–93
  Pearl Harbor plan, 68–69, 75, 80–81,
    82–89, 98
  Theories on warfare, 41–45
Gentlemen's Agreement, 9–10
Genzan Air Group, 189–92
Gepner, Lieutenant O. W., 100
Germany/Third Reich, 14–15, 24, 30, 33–35,
    205, 229, 307
  Occupation of Czechoslovakia and Austria, 30
  Invasion of Poland, France, and Russia,
    33–35, 37
Giichi, Baron Tanaka, 14

Gilbert Islands, 182, 210, 215–19, 306
Gillette, Captain Claude, 293
Glassford, Admiral William, 177
Gustavus, Adolf I, 199
Guido, Bruno Peter, 219–20
Goto, Aritomo, 112–13, 273–78
Graf Spee (German battleship), 226
Grannis, Commander Lawrence, 100
Gray, Lieutenant Commander Jim, 216–18
Great Depression, 12, 22–23, 30
Great Circle Route, 78
Greater East Asia Co-prosperity Sphere, 37,
    228, 306
Great War, 10–12, 17, 22, 27, 94, 109, 202, 215
Great White Fleet, 10, 18
Grew, Joseph, 15, 29, 36, 76, 314
Grumman aircraft,
  F4F Wildcat, 194–97, 206, 218, 259–60,
    269, 272, 276–79, 291, 300
  TBF Avenger, 262, 291–92
Guangdong Army, 14, 22–23, 26–27, 177

Hachimaki (scarf), 99
Haguro (IJN cruiser), 227
Haleiwa Field, 130, 132–34
Halsey, Admiral William F., 20, 84, 89, 121,
    184–85-186–200, 208–209, 211–13,
    214–20, 228, 259–63, 271, 280, 293
  Quotes: 84, 185–86, 215–16, 263
Hamilton Army Air Field, 88, 125
Hamma, General Masaharu, 237
Hamman (destroyer), 303
Hanabusa, Lieutenant Commander Hiroshi, 94
Hara, Admiral Chuichi, 65, 68–69, 95, 278
Hart, Admiral Thomas, 179, 182, 190, 222,
    225, 227, 237
Haruna (IJN battleship), 95, 183, 190, 294
Hashimoto, Lieutenant Mochitsura, 89
Hawaiian Air Force, 62, 212, 290
Hawaiian Department, 44–45, 93
Hawaiian Electric Company, 296
Hayate (IJN destroyer), 195
Hazelwood, Corporal Harold, 175
Hedley, Stuart, 110–30, 139
Henderson, Major Lofton, 290
Helena (cruiser), 93, 109
Hepburn, Admiral Arthur, 30
Here Comes the Navy (film), 88

Hermes (RN carrier), 238
Hickam Army Air Base, 46, 53, 89, 93, 107–108, 112, 114, 117, 126, 131–32, 206, 220
Hinomaru (Meatball), 98
Hirohito, 17, 21–23, 25, 34, 36, 65, 70, 75–76, 307
Hiroshima, 5, 41, 76, 280, 299, 307
Hitler, Adolf, 14–15, 33, 50, 52, 82, 228
Hirota, Koki, 25
Hiryu (IJN carrier), 48, 69, 70, 73, 77, 80–81, 96, 109, 115, 117, 122, 196, 264, 288, 299, 303
Hitokapu Bay, 75, 77–78, 81, 103
Holmes, Commander Jasper, 288
Hong Kong, 28, 37, 176, 188–90, 210
Hood (RN battle cruiser), 188, 192
Hoover, J. Edgar, 312
Hopkins, Harry, 17
Honolulu, 91, 93
Honolulu (cruiser), 114
Honolulu Advertiser, 312
Hornet (carrier), 261–63, 271, 280–82, 293, 299
Hosho (IJN carrier), 13, 21, 285
Hosogaya, Admiral Boshiro, 285, 300
Houston (cruiser), 182, 223–27, 260
Howard, Captain James, 18, 263
Hughes, Commander James, 28–29
Hull, Cordell, 30, 35–36, 50, 57–59, 76, 82, 87, 97, 136, 312

IBM 405, 267
Idaho (battleship), 52–53
Ie (IJN battleship), 95, 3000
Illustrious (RN carrier), 40
Imamura, General Hitoshi, 227–28
Imaizumi, Captain Kaijiro, 96
Imperial Japanese Army, 5, 12, 15, 25–26, 30, 34, 88, 178–79, 210, 306
  Shortcomings, 12–13, 34
Imperial Japanese Navy
  Air Arm, 23–24, 39–41, 43, 304
  Carrier doctrine, 31–35, 39–43, 254–55, 284–85, 304
  Fleets
    First Air Fleet, 43, 48, 55–56, 64–67, 69–70, 75, 77–78, 81, 83, 86, 99, 136, 175, 213, 294, 297, 299–301
    Second Fleet, 48

Third Fleet, 27
Eleventh Fleet, 41, 69, 70, 189–90
Modernization,12, 15, 23, 26, 252–53
Naval Affairs Committee 24, 74–75
Organization, 39, 41, 252–56
Origin and expansion, 7–8, 12, 252–53
Training and culture, 252–57
Imperial Naval General Staff, 8, 10, 21, 27–28, 34, 40–41, 48–49, 52–53, 65, 67, 72–73, 75, 193, 223–24, 228
India, 22, 224
Indianapolis (cruiser), 89
Indomitable (RN carrier), 188
Inoue, Admiral Shigeyoshi, 26, 216–19, 228, 270–81
Internment camps, 232, 235
Isolationists, 30–31, 50, 87
Ishiwara, General Kanji, 13–14
Itaya, Commander Shigeru, 64, 75, 99–101, 127
Ito, Admiral Seiichi, 49
Iwasa, Lieutenant Naoji, 135

Japan, 5–16, 58
  Hokkaido, 77, 265
  Honshu, 264
  Kyushu, 64–65, 75–76, 299
  Shikoku, 64, 76, 265, 299
  Culture, geography and history, 5–16, 58
  Economy, 22–23
  Militaristic and racial beliefs, 6–8, 58
  Politics, 7–11, 23–25, 68–70
  Resources, 7, 9–11, 14, 24–25, 37, 57, 223
Japanese Consulate, Honolulu, 53, 69, 86, 89, 285
Japanese Embassy, 20, 87, 97, 106, 204
Java (RDN destroyer), 227
Joint Chiefs of Staff (JCS), 209, 222, 241–43, 306
Johnston (destroyer), 247
Junyo (IJN carrier), 288, 300
Jutland, Battle of, 210, 226

KGMB, radio station, 89, 102, 130, 233
Kaga (IJN carrier), 41, 48, 68–75, 77, 80–81, 96, 113, 115, 122, 288, 299, 303
Kagoshima Bay, 55, 74
Kagoshima (IJN battleship), 29, 74
Kanoya Air Group, 189–92
Kahuku Golf Course, 132

INDEX

Kahuku Point, 95, 107
Kaiten, 307
Kajioka, Admiral Sadamichi, 194–97
Kakuta, Admiral Kakuji, 285
Kamikaze, 137, 306–307
Kane, Lieutenant Harry, 232–37
Kaneohe Bay, 93, 101, 110, 121, 123–25, 206, 300
Kasumigaura Air Academy, 20, 55
Katori (IJN cruiser), 216
Kawanishi flying boat, 272, 279, 285, 299
Keegan, John, 47
Kelly, Captain Colin P., 183
Keosanqua (Tug), 100
Kenpeitai, 25
Kidd, Admiral Isaac, 87, 112, 118
Kimmel, Admiral Husband, 44–45, 53–54, 71, 76–78, 91–92, 96–97, 137, 202, 206–207
  Appointment to CINCPAC, 43–44, 311
  Concerns about Pearl Harbor, 44–45, 52–54, 62, 77, 86, 89, 91, 97, 314–15
  Conversations with Layton, 77, 85, 137
  During Pearl Harbor attack, 108–109, 118–19, 137
  Post attack actions, 139, 185–86, 195–97, 204–205
  Relief from command, 203–10
  Working with General Short, 44–46, 62–63, 83
King, Admiral Ernest J., 54, 200, 204, 208–11, 222, 243, 228, 261, 269–71, 273, 286, 295, 298, 306
Kahlefent, Sergeant Nicholas, 130
King George V, 25
Kisaragi (IJN destroyer), 195
Kita, Nagao, 53, 89
Kitt, Captain Willard, 137
Knox, Frank, 44, 50, 71, 97, 203–205, 211–13, 224, 235
Koga, Admiral Mineichi, 48
Kondo, Admiral Nobutake, 70, 285, 300
Kongo (IJN battleship), 183, 190, 300
Konishi, Captain, 174–76
Konoye, Prince Fumimaro, 25, 27, 34–37, 65, 70, 173, 300
Korat, 189
Korea, 5, 7, 57, 62
Kortenaer (RN destroyer), 227
Kramer, Commander Alwin, 84, 86–87, 96

Kure Naval Base, 76
Kuril Islands, 75
Kahuku Point, 103
Kurita, Admiral Takeo, 285
Kuroshima, Captain Tomiko, 47, 48, 72–73, 284, 292–93
Kurusu, Saburo, 15, 34, 58, 62, 87, 97, 136, 312
Kusaka, Admiral Ryanosuke 49, 50, 68–69, 72, 74–75, 295
Kusumi, Lieutenant Tadashi, 117
Kyokujitsu (battle flag), 98

Lady Lex. *See Lexington*
Lahaina Roads, 98, 106, 285
Landon, Major Truman H., 125–26, 129, 133
Langley (carrier/nee *Jupiter*), 21, 121, 228, 249, 276
Larkin, Colonel Claude, 108
Layton, Captain Edwin, 85, 90, 208, 228, 267–69, 271, 286, 288, 295–96
Leach, Captain John, 192
League of Nations, 10–11, 192, 214
Leahy, Admiral Wiliam, 209–210
Leib, Joseph, 312
Leslie, Commander Maxwell, 237, 298, 300
Lexington (carrier) 21, 52, 86, 135, 186, 205, 209, 211, 214, 247, 269, 271–72, 275, 278–82
Lindbergh, Charles, 30, 50, 60–61, 87
Lindsey, Commander Gene, 216–18
Link Trainer, 24
Lockard, Private Joseph, 103, 126
Lockheed, 233
  Lockheed A-29 Hudson, 236
Lockwood, Admiral Charles, 251, 308
Louisville (cruiser), 218–19
Los Angeles, 232–33, 298
Los Angeles, Battle of, 233–35
Los Angeles Times, 232
Low, Captain Francis, 261
Luftwaffe, 10

MacArthur, General Douglas, 54, 57, 72, 83, 89, 179–82, 190, 224, 237, 242, 271–72
MacNulty, Colonel Bill, 179
Mahan, Captain Alfred Thayer, 199
Malaya, 15, 52, 70, 88, 173, 176, 188–92, 197, 210
Mao Tse-tung, 14

Manchuria, 7–8, 14–15, 23–24
  Manchukuo, 23–24
  Marco Polo Bridge Incident, 25–26
Mare Island Navy Yard, 94
Marianas Islands, 10, 88, 177–79, 306
  Guam, 13, 76, 88, 173, 176–79, 221, 230
  Saipan, 176, 178, 285–86
  Tinian, 178
Marblehead (cruiser), 182, 225–27
Marcus Island (Minami Torishima), 260–61, 283
March Army Air Base, 233–34
Marine Air Group (MAG) 21–22, 108, 291
Marine Corps, 27, 17, 193–97
Marshall, General George C., 33, 45, 52, 83, 87, 97, 204–205, 209–10, 222, 316
  Concerns in the Pacific, 33, 45, 52, 83, 97, 139, 298
  War warning, 83, 97, 139, 316
Marshall Islands, 10, 88, 176, 210–12, 219, 271, 283, 306
  Jaluit, 212, 214, 218–19, 271, 273
  Kwajalein, 88, 194–97, 212–18, 299, 301
  Makin, 212, 214, 218–19
  Maloelap, 214
  Mele, 214, 218
  Roi, 212–17
  Taroa, 214, 217–18
  Wotje, 214, 217
Martin B-26 Marauder, 292
Martin-Bellinger Report, 62–63
Martin, General Frederick, 62
Martin, Commander Hal, 124
Maryland (battleship), 19, 72, 92, 110, 123, 210, 298
Marus (Japanese merchant vessels), 69
Massey, Commander Lance "Lem," 216–18, 300
Matsonia (liner), 44
Matsui, General Iwane, 15, 29
Maumee (oiler), 202
McCain, Admiral John, 201
McCall, Major Vernon, 291–292
McCann, Commander Alan, 182
McClellan, General George, 289–90
McCloy, Ensign R. C., 95
McCluskey, Commander Wade, 217
McCollum, Commander Arthur, 19, 57, 312–13
  Eight Actions Memo, 312–16
McCormick, Robert, 50

McDonald, Private Joseph, 105
McMillin, Captain George, 179
Medal of Honor, 114, 125, 175, 227, 275
Mediterranean Theater, 228
Meiji, Emperor, 6–7
Midget Submarine Ko Hyoteki, 65, 76, 89, 100, 135
Midway Island, 30, 71, 76, 86, 173, 176, 281, 284–86
  Battle of, 271, 281–305
  Midway Neutralization Force, 86, 173–76
Mihoro Air Group, 188
Miller, Doris, 119
Mitscher, Admiral Marc, 94, 299
Minneapolis (cruiser), 196
Mississippi (battleship), 52–53
Missouri (battleship), 307
Mitchell, General William, 19–20, 41–42, 52
Mitsubishi aircraft
  A5M Claude, 26, 42, 217, 221
  A6M Zero, 26, 42, 64–65, 79–80, 98, 114–15, 123–25, 133, 135, 176, 181–83, 194–97, 216–18, 225–26, 275, 278, 287
  A6M Zero Floatplanes, 97–98, 278, 299
  G3M Nell, 176, 181–82, 189, 194–97, 225, 276
  G4M Betty, 26, 176, 181–82, 217, 225, 228, 259, 261, 275–76, 307
Momsen, Commander Charles B. "Swede," 182
Monahan (destroyer), 93, 132, 135
Morgenthau, Henry, 50
Morison, Samuel Eliot, 271
Morrison-Knudsen, 194–97
Munitions building, 203–205
Murata, Commander Shigeharu, 74–75, 98, 102, 108, 112
Murphy, Radioman John, 112–22
Murray, Captain George, 84, 217–19
Musashi (IJN battleship), 26, 42
Mutsu (IJN battleship), 47

Nachi (IJN cruiser), 226
Nagasaki, 1, 307
Nagano, Admiral Osami, 24, 48–49, 62, 65, 67, 73, 83–84
Nagaro (IJN cruiser), 294
Nagato (IJN battleship), 19, 21, 31, 33, 47, 56, 70, 73, 76, 84–85, 138

INDEX 329

Nagumo, Admiral Chuichi, 20, 26–27, 49–50, 65, 67–70, 75, 81, 84, 86, 95, 99, 136, 175–76, 186, 215, 227, 238, 263, 281, 283, 285, 294, 299–301, 303
Nanking, 26–29, 30
Nakajima B5N Kate, 26, 55, 79–80, 98, 108, 113–14, 117, 122–23, 275, 277–79
Nakamura, General Aketo, 35
Nashville (cruiser), 262–63
Naval Expansion Act, 30, 35
Naval Reserve Officer Corps (NROTC), 202
Naval War College, 202
Natori (IJN cruiser) 183
Navy Department, 30, 71, 178
Naval Intelligence (ONI), 53, 68, 214, 232, 235, 312–14
  OP-20G, 57, 68, 266, 268, 286, 312–14
  Fourteen-Part Ultimatum, 83, 87, 96, 106, 136–37, 312
Navy Ministry, IJN, 22–23, 41, 48–49, 73, 284
Neches (oiler), 196
Neosho (oiler), 92, 114, 116, 258, 274–76, 279, 282
Nevada (battleship), 19, 92, 113–16, 122, 137, 206
New Britain, 71, 215, 228, 242, 258
  Rabaul, 71, 215, 228, 269, 258–59, 269–71, 273, 275–79, 305
New Caledonia, 211, 241, 259, 272, 284
Numea, 272
New Guinea, 222, 228, 242, 269–71, 306
  Lae, 228, 269
  Owen Stanley Mountains, 269, 273
  Port Moresby, 269–71, 273–74, 276–77, 285
New Hebrides, 211
New Mexico (battleship), 52–53
New Zealand, 259, 272
Newton, Admiral John, 86
Nimitz, Admiral Chester W., 33–35, 125, 162, 199–220, 228, 242–43, 282–306, 308
  Appointment as CINCPAC, 202–208
  Comparisons to Yamamoto, 201, 208–209
  Dealing with press, 213
  Early life and career, 199–205
  Innovations, 201–202, 214–15
  Moves to counter Yamamoto, 209–20, 228, 241, 258–60, 268–70, 274, 282–305
  Preparations for Midway, 289–300
  Opinion of Pearl Harbor attack, 207–208
  Working with HYPO, 210, 267–69, 291–99
Nishino, Captain Kozo, IJN, 231–32
Nisshin (IJN cruiser), 18
Nitto Maru (IJN boat), 263
Nomura, Admiral Kichisaburo, 36–37, 51–52, 61, 83, 96–97, 106, 136–37, 312
North American Aircraft, 233
  B-25 Mitchell, 261–65
Northampton (cruiser), 89, 213, 185, 211, 213, 217, 259, 293
North Carolina (battleship), 54

O'Brian, Pat, 88
O'Brien (destroyer), 137–38
Ogg, Radioman Robert, 312
Oglala (minelayer), 93, 108–109
Ohio (battleship), 200
Oikawa, Admiral Koshiro, 41
Oklahoma (battleship), 92, 111–13, 123, 184, 206
Okinawa, 306
Okiyama, Lieutenant Masaki, 28–29
Omori, Admiral Sentaro, 95
Onishi, Admiral Takijiro, 40–41, 43, 67–68, 70
Opana Point, 102–106, 315
Operation(s)
  AF Midway, 272, 282–88
  AK Hawaii, 282–83
  AL/AO Aleutians, 282–87
  K, French Frigate Shoals, 285–86, 298–99, 301
  MI Midway, 272, 282–87
  MO Port Moresby, 268–72, 280
  RY, Nauru, 280
  Operation Drumbeat, 236
Oregon (battleship), 9
Osaka, 31
Ostfriesland (German dreadnought), 19
Outerbridge, Lieutenant Commander William W., 94–95, 100, 138
Ozawa, Admiral Jisaburo, 39–40, 190–92

Pacific Mandate, 10–11, 18, 52, 72, 178
Pacific Ocean commands, 242
  Description of, 10–11
Palau, 10
Palmer, Sergeant Bob, 131

Palmyra Island, 30, 100, 210–11
Pan American Airways (PAA), 173, 178, 193, 195
Panama, 68, 78, 97
Panama Canal, 9–10, 200, 261
Panay (gunboat), 28–31, 177, 203
Parks, Major Floyd "Red", 291
Peacetime draft, 35, 58
Pearl City, 92
Pearl Harbor, 30, 44–45, 77–78, 268
  Administration building, 68
  Attack on, 91–136
  Channel, 91–92, 95
  Ford Island, 67, 87, 91, 114, 118, 121, 135, 185, 206, 220
  Anchorages, 91–93
  Battleship Row, 91–93, 107–108, 112, 185, 206, 258
  Casualties, 136, 204–205
  Geography, 91–94
  Navy Hospital / Hospital Point, 122, 184, 220
  Navy Yard, 91–92, 121, 206, 295–96
  Drydocks, 92, 295–96
  Security Zone, 92, 94–95
  Submarine Base, 91, 93, 112, 202
Peking, 177
Pennsylvania (battleship), 43, 87, 93, 109, 122, 210, 298
Percival, General Arthur, 188
Perry, Commodore Matthew, 26, 252
Pershing, General John, 290
Perth (RAN cruiser), 227
Peterson, Chief Oscar, 275
Pfingsta, Commander, H. J., 296
Phelps (destroyer), 279
Phillips, Admiral Thomas A., 188–92
Philippines, 5, 8–9, 11–12, 15, 30, 36, 45, 52, 56–57, 63, 67, 70, 72, 76, 83, 88, 97, 173, 177, 180–97, 200, 213, 219, 222–24, 226, 229–30, 237
  Attacks on, 67, 72, 88, 176, 180–83, 197
  Bataan, 183, 230, 237–38, 262
  Cavite Naval Base, 11–12, 37, 182, 210, 223
  Clark Field, 89, 125, 180–82, 183
  Corregidor, 221, 230, 238–41
  Eba Field, 180–82
  Leyte Island, 137
  Lingayen Gulf, 183, 237
  Luzon, 180–82, 237
  Malinta Tunnel, 238–40
  Manila, 11–12, 78, 170, 199
  Mindanao, 180–82, 237–38
    Del Monte Field, 178, 183
  Nichols Fields, 178
  Olongapo Naval Base, 11–12, 182
Platte (oiler), 213–14
Poindexter, Governor Joseph, 184
Point Acorn, 272
Point Luck, 296, 299–300
Port Arthur, 8–9
Portsmouth Naval Base, 182
Pouncey, Sergeant Leroy, 127
Pound, Admiral Dudley, 192
Prange, Gordon W., 1, 38, 48, 58, 62, 136
Prince of Wales (RN battleship), 183, 188–92, 227, 276, 292
Prinz Eugen (German cruiser), 188
Patrol Torpedo (PT) boat, 238
Putnam, Colonel Paul, 84, 194–97
Pye, Admiral William, 196, 200, 204, 207, 212, 298

Radar, 45, 102, 173, 219, 243, 260, 269, 277
  Aircraft Warning System (AWS), 102–106
  Mark 37 Fire Control System, 215
  SD High-Frequency Radar, 215
  SQR-270B, 45, 102–106, 174, 232, 291
  Type 284, 227
Radio Direction Finding (RDF), 68, 230, 266, 268
Raleigh (cruiser), 93, 109, 114, 206
Ramsey, Captain Logan, 290
Rawls, Lieutenant David, 131
Rayburn, Senator Sam, 187
Reed, Lieutenant Ernest, 128–29
Republic P-35 Lancer, 180
Richards, Lieutenant Robert, 127
Richardson, Admiral James O., 54
Richmond, Raymond, 110–23
Ricketts, Lieutenant C. V., 119
Roarke's Drift, 197
Rochefort, Commander Joseph J., 68, 77, 267–74, 282–83, 286–88, 301
Rook, Captain Albert, 227
Roosevelt, Franklin D., 15, 17, 27, 30, 32–33, 44, 50, 53–54, 56–57, 61, 71, 87, 96, 106, 184, 192, 204–205, 223–224, 230, 311–15

INDEX 331

Day of Infamy speech, 187, 312, 316
Embargoes on Japan, 27, 36–37, 57–58, 62
Fireside Chats, 221, 230
Knowledge of Pearl Harbor, 311–16
War cabinet, 50, 87, 96, 311–16
Roosevelt, James, 187
Roosevelt, Theodore, 8–9, 10, 199–201
Royal Air Force (RAF), 37, 103, 183
Royal Australian Air Force (RAAF), 188–92, 227, 259
Royal Australian Army, 228, 259, 273
Royal Australian Navy (RAN), 226–28, 259
Royal Dutch Armed Forces, 222–228
Royal Hawaiian Hotel, 90
Royal Navy (RN), 7–14, 37, 40, 50, 189–90, 211, 226–28
Repulse (RN battle cruiser), 183, 188–92, 292
Ruyter (RDN destroyer), 227, 276
Russo-Japanese War, 5–13, 200–201
Ryujo (IJN carrier), 285, 288, 300

Sabine (oiler), 262
Saburo, Tomo, 13
Sacramento, 232
Sakamaki, Lieutenant Kazuo, 136
"Sacrifice at Pearl Harbor," (BBC documentary), 311
Sakai, Saburo, 183
Samoa, 210–12, 214, 241, 272
Sanders, Lieutenant Lewis, 134–35
Salt Lake City (cruiser), 211, 213, 217
Samar, Battle of, 247
Samuel B. Roberts (destroyer), 247
San Diego, 68, 211, 222, 230–31, 233
San Francisco, 68, 200, 223, 230, 232–33, 271, 298
San Francisco Chronicle, 232
San Francisco (cruiser), 196
San Luis Obispo, 232
San Pedro, 230, 298
Santa Barbara, 231, 233
Santa Fe Super Chief, 205
Santa Monica, 233
Saratoga (carrier), 21, 196–99, 205, 211, 213, 247, 269, 282, 300
Sasaki, Captain Hanku, 65
Sazanami (IJN destroyer), 174
Schick, Lieutenant William, 128–29, 132
Schofield Barracks, 93, 102, 114, 117
Security Intelligence Communications, 86

Seattle, 68, 222, 230
Sergeant York (film), 88
Shanghai, 23, 25–28, 177
Shannon, Lieutenant Colonel Harold, 173–75, 290–92
Shaw (destroyer), 93, 136
Sherman, Captain Forrest, 279
Shiriya (IJN oiler), 174–75
Shimada, Commander Koichi, 173
Shimazaki, Commander Shigekazu, 78, 121, 279
Shimizu, Admiral Mitsumi, 65
Shoho (IJN carrier), 272–76, 282, 285
Shokaku (IJN carrier), 65, 69–70, 74, 77, 80–81, 96, 114, 121, 270, 272–73, 275, 277–79, 284, 287
Short, General Walter, 44–46, 89, 93, 97, 139, 209, 313
  Appointment to Hawaii, 44
  Concerns about sabotage, 44–46, 62, 93, 103, 132, 135
  Duties to defend U S. Fleet, 44, 46, 52, 62, 83, 97
  Post-Pearl Harbor actions, 139
Siam (Thailand), 88, 189, 221
Simard, Captain Cyril, 173–175, 195, 290–92
Sims (destroyer), 274–76, 282
Singapore, 37, 67, 70, 76–78, 176, 188–90, 197, 210, 224, 266
Signal Corp, 239–40
Sino-Japanese War(s), 7–8, 14–15, 23–28, 188
Skipper (Dog), 126–29, 132
Smith, General Holland, 208
Smith, Admiral William "Poco," 295
Solomon Islands, 209, 224, 228, 242, 259, 272, 283
  Bougainville, 273, 305, 307
  Guadalcanal, 273–74, 305–306
  Tulagi, 273–74, 283
  Savo Island, 209, 305
Soryu (IJN carrier), 48, 69–70, 73, 77, 80–81, 96, 99, 109, 117, 119, 122, 196, 226, 264, 288, 299, 303
Southern Operation(s), 47, 57, 70, 73, 77, 88, 173
South Carolina (battleship), 202
South China Sea, 188, 223–24
Soviet Union, 12–16, 22–23, 27, 30, 33, 58–59, 62, 229

Invasion by Germany, 54, 62
Non-aggression Pact with Germany, 33, 54
Neutrality Agreement with Japan, 14–15, 62
Siberia, 229
Spanish-American War, 8–10, 178, 192, 199
Special weapons (IJN)
  Type 99 20mm cannon, 65, 79
  Type 99 No. 80-3 Aerial Bomb, 65, 115
Spruance, Admiral Raymond, A., 89, 200, 213, 259, 293–94, 296–99, 303–304, 308
Squadrons (USN USMC)
  Bombing 3, 300
  Bombing 6, 217
  Fighting 3, 300
  Fighting 5, 300
  Fighting 6, 271
  Marine Fighting 211, 84, 194–97
  Marine Fighting 221, 108, 196, 291
  Marine Fighting 241, 291
  Scouting 3, 300
  Scouting 5, 300
  Torpedo 3, 300
  Torpedo 8, 291
  VP-14, 100, 112, 124
  VP-21, 173–74
  VP-44, 291
St. Louis (cruiser), 114
Stalin, Josef, 33, 229
Stark, Admiral Harold C., 51, 53–54, 71, 77–78, 83, 87, 96, 200, 203–205, 313–15
Sterling, Lieutenant Jim, 135
Stimson, Henry, 45, 50, 187, 235, 298
  Post-attack measures, 187–88
Stinnet, Robert, 313
Stratton, Donald, 110–23
Strobing, Corporal Irving, 239–40
Submarines, Japanese
  Submarine Doctrine, 255–57
  Special Submarine Force, 65, 76
  Submarine Cordon, 285–90, 301
  I-16, 135
  I-17, 231–32
  I-20, 137
  I-24, 89, 94, 136
  I-58, 89
  I-65, 190
  I-123, 301

Submarines, United States
  Submarine Doctrine, 248–52, 306
  Cachalot, 93
  Dolphin 93, 214
  Grayling, 208
  Holland, 201
  Narwhal, 93, 201
  Plunger, 201
  S-47, 280
  Sargo, 237
  Sculpin, 182
  Snapper, 201
  Squalus/Sailfish, 182
  Tautog, 93
Supermarine Spitfire, 64
Sugiyama, Admiral Rokuzō, 27, 65
Sutherland, General Richard, 179–82, 243
Suzuki, Admiral, 76
Swensen, Captain Raymond, 12

Takahashi, Commander Kakuichi, 101, 112, 114, 275, 278–79
Taniguchi, General Kureo, 238–41
Tangier (seaplane tender), 92, 196, 272
Tanner, Ensign William, 100–101
Task Force(s)
  TF 1, 258
  TF 8, 89, 196, 211–13, 219, 258, 293
  TF 11, 211, 214, 274
  TF 12, 8, 196, 209
  TF 14, 196–99, 211, 258–59
  TF 16, 259, 280–81, 283, 293, 296, 299, 301
  TF 17, 211-214, 269, 274, 276, 282, 295–96, 301
  TF 17.3, 275, 277, 279
  TF 18, 261–62
  TF 44, 274–78
Takhli, 189
Takagi, Admiral Takeo, 225–28, 273–78, 280, 283
Tainan Air Group (IJA), 183
Tanaka, Admiral Raizo, 285, 299
Taniguchi, General Kureo,
Taranto, 39–40
Taylor, Lieutenant Kenneth, 110, 130, 132–34
Tennant, Captain William, 191
Tennessee (battleship), 19, 92, 115–16, 122, 210, 298
Tetley, Colonel William, 102–103

INDEX

Texas (battleship), 194
Thach, Commander John, 300
Thach Weave, 300
Thacker, Lieutenant Bob, 131
Thermopylae, 197, 237
Theobald, Admiral Robert, 293, 301
Thirty Years' War, 199
Thompson, Private Merle, 108
Time Magazine, 58–59, 61
Tinker, General Clarence, 290
Togo, Admiral Heihachiro, 8, 18, 99, 175, 200, 294
Togo, Captain Minoru, 175
Togo, Foreign Minister Shigenori, 96
Tojo, General Hideki, 25–27, 36, 70, 83–84
Tokyo, 5, 27, 54–58, 283
Tomioka, Admiral Sadatoshi, 283–86
Tomonaga, Commander Joichi, 301
Tone (IJN cruiser), 95, 97, 197, 294
Tonga, 272
Tora! Tora! Tora! (film), 97, 107, 138–39
Torpedo, 46–47, 55, 65, 74–75
   Mark 10 aerial, 216
   Mark 14, 225, 227, 237, 244
   Type 91, 47, 68, 74, 98, 109, 115
   Type 93, 65, 227
   Type 97, 76
Towers, Admiral John H., 203
Travis Army Air Base, 232
Treaties
   1902 Anglo-Japanese Treaty, 10–11
   1905 Treaty of Portsmouth, 8–9
   1919 Treaty of Versailles, 10
   1922 Washington Naval Treaty, 12–13, 19–20, 22–23, 178
   1930 London Naval Treaty, 22–23
   Atlantic Charter, 192
   Tripartite Pact, 15, 32, 34, 52, 229
Tsingtao, 10
Tsushima, Battle of, 8–9, 18, 39, 99
Turner, Admiral Richmond K., 208–209, 243, 288, 308
Tyler, Lieutenant Kermit, 105, 126

Ubari (IJN cruiser), 195–97
U-boat, 23, 50–51
U-701, 236–37
Ugaki, Admiral Matome, 62, 70, 78, 85, 176, 285, 287, 295
ULTRA, 312–13

Underway replenishment, 46, 50, 74–75, 202–203, 214–15, 260, 273–74
Unit 731, 25
Ushio (IJN destroyer), 174–75, 227
U.S. Embassy, 177
Utah (AAA training ship), 93, 98, 109, 114, 206
United States Armed Forces, Far East (USAFFE), 237–38
United States Army Air Corps (USAAC), 17, 27, 51, 63, 88, 89, 102, 223, 237
United States Forces in the Philippines (USFIP), 238–40
United States Navy, 25–27, 37, 39–40, 51, 199–200, 210, 306
   Budget, 25–27, 51, 243–44
   Carrier doctrine, 41–42, 204, 210–11, 248–52
   Fleets
      Asiatic Fleet, 182, 190, 200, 204, 208, 210, 222–24, 237
      Atlantic Fleet, 50–51, 243
      Pacific Fleet, 43–44, 51, 62–63, 71, 120–26, 204, 208, 210, 284–86, 298–99, 314
   Organization, 44, 199–200, 210, 243–45, 306
   Ships, 44–45, 199–200, 210–11, 243–46, 306–307
   Training and culture, 243–52
Vampire (RAN cruiser), 238

Van Valkenburgh, Captain Franklin, 118
Vietnam Memorial, 203
Vestal (repair ship), 92, 112–18
Vincennes (cruiser), 262–63
Vinson Naval Act, 17
Vought SB2U Vindicator, 291
Vought OS2U Kingfisher, 119

Waikiki, 90, 94
Wainwright, General Johnathan, 183, 221, 228, 237–41
Wake Island, 31, 71, 76, 84, 88, 173, 176, 186, 192–97, 209, 214, 230, 259–60, 290
   Wake Island Defense Zone, 194
   Battle of, 176, 183, 192–97, 205
Waldron, Commander John, 292
Wallace, Vice President Henry, 187
Walters, Ensign Buck, 218

War Department, 312–13
War Plan(s), 71,
 Orange, 71–72
 Rainbow, 71
Ward (destroyer), 94–95, 102, 105, 110, 137, 212
Washington (battleship), 54
Watanabe, Commander Yasuki, 47–48
Wee Vee. *See West Virginia*
Welch, Lieutenant George, 110, 130, 132–34
West Virginia (battleship), 19, 92, 113–14, 139, 206
Wheeler Army Air Base, 46, 53, 63, 79, 93, 103, 114, 117, 130, 132–33, 185, 206
Wiliams, Sergeant Earl, 127–29
Woman's Air Service Pilots (WASP), 107
Wood, General Leonard, 11–12
World War I. *See* Great War

Yamaguchi, Admiral Tamon, 48, 65 , 68–70, 95, 99, 197
Yamamoto, Admiral Isoroku, 8, 10, 15, 17–23, 34–36, 58, 80–112, 138–39, 173, 199, 202, 214, 228, 241, 243, 299–300, 303–305
 Air Power advocate, 19–21, 39–40, 42
 Appointment as Commander Combined Fleet,17, 25, 31
 Death, 305, 307–308
 Opinion of United States, 16, 19–20, 35–36, 38, 138

 Meeting with Konoye, 34–35
 Origin of name, 18
 Planning of Midway, 280, 283–86, 299–300
 Planning of Pearl Harbor attack, 38–48, 62–90, 98
 Political issues, 24–25, 29, 34–35, 38, 228
 Problems with Army and Navy commanders, 25, 35–38
 Time in America, 19–20
Yamato (IJN battleship), 19, 26, 42, 49, 273, 280, 283, 287, 295, 299, 303, 307
Yamashita, General Tomoyuki, 189
Yangtze River, 26, 28–29, 201
Yellow Sea, 8
Yokohama, 263
Yokosuka Naval Base, 18, 55–56, 74, 76, 231
Yonai, Admiral Mitsumasa, 25–26, 29, 31, 307
Yorktown (carrier), 52–53, 205, 211–20, 271–79, 281–82, 293–301, 303
Yoshikawa, Lieutenant Tateo (Tadashi Morimura), 53, 63–64, 76, 78, 86, 98
Young, Commander Howard "Brigham", 121, 216–18, 259–60
Young, Commander Cassin, 120

"Z" Flag, 99
Zuiho (IJN carrier), 285
Zuikaku (IJN carrier), 65, 69–70, 74, 77, 80–81, 96, 114, 226, 270, 272–73, 275, 277–81, 284, 287, 298

ABOUT THE AUTHOR

Mark Carlson, a resident of San Diego, has been a lifelong student of military history. Legally blind, he works with advanced software on his computer and travels with a guide dog. He has never considered his blindness to be an obstacle, only a challenge.

For the past twenty years, Carlson has been a regular contributor to more than a dozen military history publications. In that time, he has written over two hundred articles and interviewed hundreds of veterans, actors, historians, and authors. A former Civil War and Roman re-enactor, Carlson has gained an insight into the world of the fighting man to bring depth and realism into his writing. He is passionate about history, considering it an obligation to remember the past with respect.

His magazine articles run the gamut of topics from aviation, naval, and military history, classic film and television, dogs, humor, and essays. He started by writing stories about his first guide dog, Musket, and later about his work at the San Diego Air & Space Museum. A former president of a San Diego Toastmasters Club, he tours the country doing lectures on history for colleges and adult education programs. A popular speaker for several national military museums and groups, he is a member of several veteran and historical organizations.

OTHER BOOKS BY MARK CARLSON

The Marines Lost Squadron: The Odyssey of VMF-422
(Sunbury Press, 2017)

Wart at Sea: Essays on Naval Warfare 1776–1945
(Sunbury Press, 2023)

VENGEANCE OF THE LAST ROMAN LEGION SERIES

Book I – Out of the Darkness
Book II – Legionary
Book III – Hunters & Hunted
Book IV – Vindicta
(Sunbury Press, 2022)

Confessions of a Guide Dog: The Blonde Leading the Blind
(iUniverse, 2011)

Confessions of a Labradiva: Another Blonde Leading the Blind
(iUniverse, 2020)

Flying on Film: A Century of Aviation in the Movies 1912–2012
(Bear Manor Media, 2012)

www.ingramcontent.com/pod-product-compliance
Lightning Source LLC
Chambersburg PA
CBHW031755220426
43662CB00007B/415